T0303495

The Origin of

The Buddha Image

& Elements of Buddhist Iconography

Ananda Kentish Coomaraswamy

Fons Vitae
The Matheson Trust

First published in 2006 by
Fons Vitae
49 Mockingbird Valley Drive
Louisville, KY 40207
http://www.fonsvitae.com

Library of Congress Control Number: 2005939152

ISBN 1-887752-80-3

Printed in Canada by Friesens through
Four Colour Imports, Ltd., Louisville, Kentucky

The Matheson Trust is a charity whose principal aim
is to further the study of comparative religion and
the great metaphysical and religious traditions.

Contents

Introduced by Coomaraswamy's "The Nature of Buddhist Art" (1938), "The Origin of the Buddha Image" (1927) is crowned by a supremely important metaphysical and spiritually transformative text, "Elements of Buddhist Iconography" (1935). Although this essay is about sacred art, it actually is sacred art itself in that it is able to transport the reader to the very threshold of an awakening. This is achieved through the etymological and artistic explication of the archetypal nature and profoundest meaning intended by the Cosmic Tree of Life (symbolizing the Buddha) and the Lotus Throne which are not actually situated in "art" but may be beheld within the human heart and found in each one of us.

We are truly fortunate to be able to provide a facsimile reproduction of the author's personal copies of these formative works with his own annotations and corrections.

The Publisher

The Nature of Buddhist Art

"He is not himself brought into being in images presented through our senses, but He presents all things to us in such images," Hermes Trismegistus, Scott, *Hermetica, I.159.*

IN order to understand the nature of the Buddha image and its meaning for a Buddhist we must, to begin with, reconstruct its environment, trace its ancestry, and remodel our own personality. We must forget that we are looking at "art" in a museum, and see the image in its place in a Buddhist church or as part of a sculptured rock wall; and having seen it, receive it as an image of what we are ourselves potentially. Remember that we are pilgrims come from some great distance to see God; that what we see will depend upon ourselves. We are to see, not the likeness made by hands, but its transcendental archetype; we are to take part in a communion. We have heard the spoken Word, and remember that "He who sees the Word, sees Me"; we are to see this Word, not now in an audible but in a visible and tangible form. In the words of a Chinese inscription, "When we behold the precious characteristics, it is as though the whole and very person of the Buddha were present in majesty. . . . The Vulture Peak is before our eyes; Nāgarahāra is present. There is a rain of precious flowers that robs the very clouds of colour; a celestial music is heard, enough to silence the sound of ten thousand flutes. When we consider the perfection of the Body of the Word, the eight perils are avoided; when we hear the teaching of the Mighty Intellect, the seventh heaven is reached" (Chavannes, *Mission Archéologique*, I.ii.340). The image is of one Awakened: and for our awakening, who are still asleep. The objective methods of "science" will not suffice; there can be no understanding without assimilation; to understand is to have been born again.

The epithet "Awakened" (Buddha) evokes in our minds today the concept of an historical figure, the personal discoverer of an ethical, psychological, contemplative, and monastic Way of salvation from the infection of death: which Way extends hence toward a last and beatific End, which is variously referred to as a Reversion, Despiration, or Release, indescribable in terms of being or non-being considered as incompatible alternatives, but certainly not an empirical existence nor an annihilation. The Buddha "is"; but he "cannot be taken hold of."

In the developed Buddhist art with which the present volume is mainly concerned we take for granted the predominance of the central figure of a "Founder" in a form that can only be described, although with important reservations, as anthropomorphic. If we take account of the manner in which this usually monastic but sometimes royal figure is sharply distinguished from its human environment, for example, by the nimbus, or by the lotus support, or similarly take account of the "mythical" character of the life itself as described in the early texts, we generally say that the man who is spoken of as "Thus-come" (Tathâgata) or as the "Wake" (Buddha) has been "deified," and presume that miraculous elements have been combined with the historical nucleus and introduced into the representations for edifying purposes. We hardly realize that "Buddhism" has roots that can be traced backwards for millennia; and that though the Buddha's doctrines are in the proper sense of the word original, they are scarcely in any sense novel; nor that this applies with equal force to the problems of Buddhist art, which are not in reality those of Buddhist art in particular, but rather those of Indian art in a Buddhist application, and in the last analysis the problems of art universally. It would be possible, for example, to discuss the whole problem of iconoclasm in purely Indian terms; and we shall in fact have something to say about it, in making the nature and genesis of the anthropomorphic image the main theme of this "Introduction."

If "Buddhism" (we use quotations because the connotation is so vast) is a heterodox or Protestant doctrine in the sense that it rejects the impersonal authority of the Vedas and substitutes or seems to substitute for this the authority of an historically spoken Word, it is nevertheless becoming more and more apparent every day that the content of Buddhism and Buddhist art are far more orthodox than was at first imagined; and even orthodox not only in a Vedic sense, but universally. For example, the famous formula, *anicca, anattā, dukkha,* "Impermanence, Non-spirit, Suffering," does not, as was once believed, involve a denial of the Spirit (*ātman*), but asserts that the soul-and-body or individuality (*nāma-rūpa, saviññāna-kāya*) of man are passible, mutable, and above all to be sharply distinguished from the Spirit. *Anattā* does not assert that "There is no Spirit," or "Spiritual-essence," but that "*This* (empirical self, *Leibseele*) is not my Spirit," *na me so attā*, a formula constantly repeated in the Pali texts. It is in almost the same words that the Upaniṣads assert that "What is other than the Spirit is a misery" (*ato anyad ārtam*) and that "This (its station) is not the Spirit, no indeed: the Spirit is naught that can be taken hold of, naught perishable, etc." (*sa eṣa neti nety ātmā agrāhyo ... aśīryaḥ*, etc., BU. III.4.1 and 9.26). This is the greatest of all distinctions, apart from which there can be no intelligence of man's last end; and we find it insisted upon, accordingly, in all orthodox traditions, for example, by St. Paul when he says, "The word of God is quick and powerful, and sharper than any two-edged sword, piercing even to the dividing asunder of soul and spirit" (Heb. IV.12).

We have traced elsewhere[1] the Vedic sources and universal values of Buddhist symbolism, and shall presently discuss the nature of symbolism itself. Here it will suffice to add that the Vedic and Buddhist, or equally Vedic and Vaiṣṇava or Vedic and Jaina scriptures, taken together in continuity, enunciate the dual doctrine, which is also a Christian doctrine, of an eternal and a temporal birth; if the former alone is expounded in the Rigveda, the Buddha's historical nativity is in reality the story of

[1] *Elements of Buddhist Iconography,* Cambridge, 1935.

the aeonic manifestation of Agni—*Noster Deus ignis consumens est*—compressed "as if" into the span of a single existence. The "Going forth" from the household to the homeless life is the ritual transference of Agni from the household to the sacrificial altar: if the Vedic prophets are forever tracking the Hidden Light by the traces of its footsteps, it is literally and iconographically true that the Buddhist also makes the *vestigium pedis* his guide; and if Agni in the Vedic texts, as also in the Old Testament, is a "Pillar of Fire," the Buddha is repeatedly represented as such at Amarāvatī. We need hardly say that from our point of view to speak of the "lives" of the Buddha or Christ as "mythical" is but to enhance their significance.[1]

We very naturally overlook that the central problem of Buddhist art, of which a solution is essential to any real understanding, is not a problem of styles, but of how it came about that the Buddha has been represented at all in an anthropomorphic form: which is almost the same thing as to ask why indeed the Great King of Glory should have veiled his person in mendicant robes—*Cur Deus homo?* The Buddhist answer is, of course, that the assumption of a human nature is motivated by a divine compassion, and is in itself a manifestation of the Buddha's perfect virtuosity (*kosalla, kauśalya*) in the use of convenient means (*upāya*): it is expressly stated of the Buddha that it belongs to his skill to reveal himself in accordance with the nature of those who perceive him. It had indeed already been realized in the Vedas and Brāhmaṇas that "His names are in agreement with his aspect" and that "As He is approached, such He becomes" (*yathôpāsate tad eva bhavati*, ŚB. X.5.2.20); as St. Augustine, cited with approval by St. Thomas, expresses it, *Factus est Deus homo ut homo fieret Deus.*

The notion of a Creator working *per artem*, common to the Christian and

[1] To speak of an event as *essentially* mythical is by no means to deny the possibility, but rather to assert the necessity of an *accidental,* i.e., historical eventuation; it is in this way that the eternal and temporal nativities are related. To say "that it might be fulfilled which was said by the prophets" is not to render a narrative suspect, but only to refer the fact to its principle. Our intention is to point out that the more eminent truth of the myth does not stand or fall by the truth or error of the historical narrative in which the principle is exemplified.

all other orthodox ontologies, already implies an artist in possession of his art, the fore-measure (*pramāṇa*) and providence (*prajñā*) according to which all things are to be measured out; there is, in fact, the closest possible analogy between the "factitious body" (*nirmāṇa-kāya*[1]) or "measure" (*nimitta*) of the living Buddha, and the image of the Great Person which the artist literally "measures out" (*nirmāti*) to be a substitute for the actual presence. The Buddha is in fact born of a Mother (*mātṛ*) whose name is Māyā (Nature, Art, or "Magic" in Behmen's sense of "Creatrix"), with a derivation in each case from *mā*, to "measure," cf. *prati-mā* "image," *pra-māṇa*, "criterion," and *tāla-māna*, "iconometry."[2] There is, in other words, a virtual identification of a natural with an intellectual, metrical, and evocative generation.[3] The birth is literally an evocation; the Child is begotten, in accordance with a constantly repeated Brāhmaṇa formula, "by Intellect upon the Voice," which intercourse is symbolized in the rite; the artist works, as St. Thomas expresses it, "by a word *conceived* in intellect." We must not overlook, then, that there is also a third and verbal image, that of the doctrine, coequal in significance with the images in flesh or stone: "He who sees the Word sees Me" (*Saṁ-*

[1] The expression *nirmāṇa-kāya* is evidently derived from *Jaiminīya Br.* III.261–3. Here the Devas have undertaken a sacrificial session, but before doing so propose to discard "whatever is crude in our Spirit (*tad yad eṣāṁ krūram ātmana āsit,* i.e., whatever are its possibilities of physical manifestation), and to measure it out" (*tan nirmāmahai,* i.e., fashion it). Accordingly "they measured it out (*nirmāya*) and put what had thus been wiped off (*sammārjam*) in two bowls (*śarāvayoḥ,* i.e., heaven and earth) . . . Thence was born the mild Deva . . . it was verily Agni that was born . . . He said, 'Why have ye brought me to birth?' They answered, 'To keep watch'" (*aupadraṣṭyāya*). Here, then, Agni's embodiment in the worlds is already a *nirmāṇa-kāya.* That Agni is to keep watch corresponds on the one hand to the Vedic conception of the Sun as the "Eye of the Devas," and on the other to that of the Buddha as the "Eye in the World" (*cakkhuṁ loke*) in the Pali texts. Cf. my article "Nirmāṇa-kāya" in JRAS, Oct. 1937.

[2] The origin of the name of the Buddha's mother, Māyā, can be followed backward from the *Lalita Vistara,* XXVII.12 through AV. VIII.9.5 to RV. III.29.11. "This, O Agni, is thy cosmic womb, whence thou hast shone forth . . . Metered in the mother (*yad amimīta mātari*)—Mātariśvān," cf. X.5.3, "Having measured out the Babe" (*mitvā śiśum*).

[3] Observe, in this connection, that in John I.3–4, the Latin *quod factum est* represents the Greek ὅ γέγονεν (Skr. *jātam*). "The teaching of our school is that anything known or born is an image. They say that in begetting his only-begotten Son the Father is producing his own image" (Eckhart, Evans ed. I.258).

It is from the same point of view, that of the doctrine of ideas, that for St. Thomas, "Art imitates nature (i.e., *Natura naturans, Creatrix universalis, Deus*) in her manner of operation" (*Sum. Theol.* I.117.1 c): and that Augustin "appuie plus nettement (i.e., que même Plotin) sur la même origine de la nature (i.e., *Natura naturata*) et des oeuvres d'art, *l'origine en Dieu*" (Svoboda, K., *L'Esthétique de Saint Augustin et ses sources,* Brno, 1933, p. 115).

yutta Nikāya, III.120). These visible and audible images are alike in their information, and differ only in their accidents. Each depicts the same essence in a likeness: neither is an imitation of another, the image in stone, for example, not an imitation of the image in flesh, but each directly an "imitation" (*anukṛti,* mimesis) of the unspoken Word, an image of the "Body of the Word" or "Brahma-body" or "Principle," which cannot be represented as it *is* because of its perfect simplicity.

It was not, however, until the beginning of the Christian era, five centuries after the Great Total-Despiration (*mahā parinibbāna*), that the Buddha was actually represented in a human form. In more general terms it was not until then (with certain exceptions, some of which date back as far as the third millennium B.C., and despite the fact that the Rigveda freely makes use of a verbal imagery in anthropomorphic terms) that any widespread development of an anthropomorphic iconography can be recognized at all. The older Indian art is essentially "aniconic," that is, it makes use only of geometrical, vegetable, or theriomorphic symbols as supports of contemplation, just as in early Christian art. An artistic inability to represent the human figure cannot be invoked by way of explanation in either case; not only had human figures already been represented very skilfully in the third millennium B.C., but as we know, the type of the human figure had been employed with great effect from the third century B.C. onwards (and no doubt much earlier in impermanent material), *except* to represent the Buddha in his last incarnation, where even at birth and before the Great Awakening he is represented only by footprints, or generally by such symbols as the Tree or Wheel.

In order to approach the problem at all we must relegate to an altogether subordinate place our predilection for the human figure, inherited from late classical cultures, and must, to the extent that we are able, identify ourselves with the unanimous mentality of the Indian artist and patron both as it had been before, and as it had come to be when, a necessity was actually felt for the representation of what we think of as the "deified" Buddha (although in fact that he cannot be regarded as a man amongst others, but rather as "the form of humanity that has nothing to do with time," is plainly enough set forth in the Pali texts). Above all must we refrain from assuming that what was an inevitable step, and one already foreshadowed by the "historicity" of the life, must be interpreted in terms of spiritual progress. We must realize that this step, of which an unforeseen result was the provision for us of such aesthetic pleasures as everyone who considers even the accompanying reproductions must derive from Buddhist art, may have been itself much rather a concession to intellectually lower levels of reference than any evidence of an increased profundity of vision. We must remember that an abstract art is adapted to contemplative uses and implies a gnosis; an anthropomorphic art evokes a religious emotion, and corresponds rather to prayer than contemplation. If the development of an art can be justified as answering to new needs, it must not be overlooked that to speak of a want is to speak of a deficiency in him who wants: the more one is, the less one wants. We ought not, then, to think so much of a deficiency of plastic art in aniconic rituals as of the adequacy of the purely abstract formulae and the proficiency of those who could make use of purely symbolic representations.

The aniconic character of Vedic ritual and early Buddhist art was, then, a matter of choice. Not only is the position iconoclastic in fact, but we can hardly fail to recognize a far-reaching iconoclastic tendency in such words as those of the *Jaiminīya Upaniṣad Brāhmaṇa*, IV.18.6: "The Brahman is not what one thinks with the mind (*yaṁ manasā na manute*), but, as they say, is that whereby there is a mentation, or concept (*yenâhur manomatam*): know that That alone is Brahman, not what men worship here" (*nêdaṁ yad idam upâsate*). At the same time the Upaniṣads distinguish clearly between the Brahman in a likeness and the Brahman not in any likeness, mortal and immortal (*mūrtaṃ câmūrtaṃ ca martyaṁ câmṛtaṁ ca*, BU. II.3.1, where it may be noted that one of the regular designations of an image is precisely *mūrti*); and between the concept by which one distinctly remembers and the lightning-flash at which one can only exclaim (*Kena Up.* IV.4-5). The distinction is that of Eckhart and Ruysbroeck between the knowledge of God *creaturlicher wise, creatuerlikerwijs* and *âne mittel, âne wise, sonder middel, sonder wise*, and involves the universal doctrine of the single essence and two natures. It is clear that these texts and their implied doctrine are tantamount to a justification both of an iconography and of iconoclasm. It is the immediate value of an image to serve as the support of a contemplation leading to an understanding of the exterior operation and proximate Brahman, the Buddhist Sambhogakāya: it is only of the interior operation and ultimate Brahman, Buddhist Dharmakāya, Tattva, Tathatā, or Nirvāṇa, that it can be said that "*This* Brahman is silence."[1]

No one whose life is still an active one, no one still spiritually under the Sun and still perfectible, no one who still proposes to understand in terms of subject and object, no one who still is anyone, can pretend to have outgrown all need of means. It is not a question of the virtually "infinite possibilities of the simple soul" (Bouquet, *The Real Presence*, p. 85), which it would be absurd to deny, but one of *how* these potentialities can be reduced to act. One is astounded at the multitude of those who advocate the "direct" approach to God, as if the end of the road could be reached without a wayfaring; and forget that an immediate vision can be only theirs in

1 A traditional saying quoted by Śaṅkara on *Brahma Sūtra,* III.2.17. Cf. the Hermetic "Then only will you see it, when you cannot speak of it; for the knowledge of it is deep silence, and suppression of all the senses" (Hermes, *Lib.* X.5, Scott, *Hermetica,* I.191). Just as for the Upaniṣads the ultimate Brahman is a Principle "about which further questions cannot be asked" (BU. III.6), so the Buddha consistently refuses to discuss the quiddity of Nibbāna. In the words of Erivgena, "God does not know what He himself is, because He is not any what," and of Maimonides, "By affirming anything of God, you are removed from Him." The Upaniṣads and Buddhism offer no exception to the universal rule of the employment side by side of the *via affirmativa* and *via remotionis.* There is nothing peculiarly Indian, and still less peculiarly Buddhist, in the view that we cannot know what we may become, which "Eye hath not seen, nor ear heard" (I Cor. II.9). In the meantime, the function of the image bodily, verbal, or plastic, or in any other way symbolic, is mediatory. See also my "Vedic Doctrine of Silence," *Indian Culture,* 1937, III.559 f.

whom "the mind has been de-mented," to employ a significant expression common to Eckhart, the Upaniṣads, and Buddhism.

The *present* problem is not, then, one of the propriety or impropriety of the use of supports of contemplation, but of what sort the most appropriate and efficacious supports of contemplation must be, and of the art of making use of them. For *us*, the work of art both exists and operates on an altogether human, visible, and tangible level of reference; we do not, as Dante requires that we should, "marvel at the doctrine that hides itself behind (*s'asconde sotto*) the veil of the strange verses" (*Inferno*, IX.61); the verses are enough for us. It is otherwise in a traditional art, where the object is merely a point of departure and a signpost inviting the spectator to the performance of an act directed toward that form for the sake of which the picture exists at all. The spectator is not so much to be "pleased" as to be "transported": to see as the artist is required to have seen before he took up brush or chisel; to see the Buddha in the image rather than an image of the Buddha. It is a matter of *penetration*, in the most technical senses of the term (cf. *Muṇḍaka Up.* II.2.3): the variegated presentation in colours is merely a conceptual exteriorization of what in itself is a perfectly simple brilliance—"Just as it is an effect of the presence or absence of dust in a garment that the colour is either clear or motley, so it is the effect of the presence or absence of a penetration into Release (*āvedha-vaśān muktau*) that the Gnosis is either clear or motley. That one alludes to the profundity of the Buddhas on the Unsullied Plane in terms of iconographic-characteristics, stances, and acts (*lakṣaṇa-sthāna-karmeṣu*) is a mere painting on colours in space."[1] Or again, and with

[1] *Mahāyāna Sūtrâlaṁkāra* of Asaṅga, IX.35, 36. Lévi, Sylvain, Paris, 1907 and 1911, I.39, 40 and II.77, 78. M. Sylvain Lévi has not quite understood *lakṣaṇa-sthāna;* the reference is to the descriptive iconography of narrative and visual art. Dr. Kramrisch (*A Survey of Painting in the Deccan*, pp. 27 and 203, note 31) has mistaken the bearing of the passage: "to paint with colours on space" is a proverbial expression implying "to attempt the impossible" or "effort made in vain," as for example in *Majjhima Nikāya*, I.127, where it is pointed out that a man cannot paint in colours on space, because "space is without form or indication." What Asaṅga is saying is that to think of any representation of the transcendant Principle as it is in itself is no more than an idle dream; the representation has a merely temporary value, comparable to that of the ethical raft in the well-known parable (*Majjhima Nikāya*, I.135).

reference equally to verbal and visual imagery, the Buddha is made to say that the metaphorical expression "is adduced by way of illustration... because of the great infirmity of babes... I teach as does the master-painter or his pupil who disposes his colours for the sake of a picture, which picture is not to be found in the colours, nor in the ground nor in the environment. It is only to make it attractive to[1] creatures that the picture is contrived in colour: what is actually taught is irrelevant; the Principle eludes the letter.[2] In taking up a stand amongst things,[3] what I really teach is the Principle as understood by the Contemplatives:[4] a spiritual reversion evading every form of thought. What I teach is not a doctrine for babes, but for the Sons of the Conqueror. And just as whatever I may see in a diversified manner has no real being, so is the pictorial doctrine communicated in a manner irrelevant. Whatever is not adapted to such and such persons as are to be taught cannot be called a 'teaching.'... The Buddhas indoctrinate beings according to their mental capacity."[5] That is as much as to say with St. Paul, "I have fed you with milk and not with meat: for hitherto ye were not able to bear it, neither yet now are ye able" (I Cor. III.2): "Strong meat belongeth to them that are of full age" (Heb. V.14).

It is only one who *has* attained to an immediate Gnosis that can afford to dispense with theology, ritual, and imagery: the Comprehensor has

It is, nevertheless, as the *sādhanas* express it, against a background of "space in the heart" that the picture that is "not in the colours" must be imagined; just as also Śaṅkarâcārya's "world-picture" (the intelligible cosmos seen in the *speculum aeternum*) is "painted by the Spirit on the canvas of the Spirit." And because the picture has been thus imagined as an appearance manifested over against an *infinite* ground, the picture (of Amida, for example) painted in actual colours and on canvas stands out against an analogous background of *indefinite* extent.

1 *Karṣaṇârthāya:* the notion coincides with the Platonic and Scholastic concept of the *summoning* quality of beauty.

2 "Eludes" is precisely Dante's *s'asconde sotto*. "Speech does not attain to truth; but mind (*νοῦς = manas*) has mighty power, and when it been has led some distance on its way by speech, it attains to truth" (Scott, *Hermetica,* I.185).

3 I.e., in being born, and consequently in using material figures, speaking parabolically, etc.

4 *Tattvaṁ yogīnām:* cf. RV. X.85.4, "Of whom the Brahmans understand as Soma, none ever tastes, none tastes who dwells on earth" and AB. VII.31, "It is metaphysically (*parôkṣeṇa*) that he obtains the drinking of Soma, it is not literally (*pratyakṣam*) partaken of by him."

5 *Laṅkâvatāra Sūtra,* II.112–114.

found what the Wayfarer is still in search of. This has too often been misinterpreted to mean that something is deliberately withheld from those who are to depend on means, or even that means are dispensed to them as if with intent to keep them in ignorance; there are those who ask for a sort of universal compulsory education in the mysteries, supposing that a mystery is nothing but a communicable, although hitherto uncommunicated, secret and nothing different in kind from the themes of profane instruction. So far from this, it is of the essence of a mystery, and above all of the Mysterium Magnum, that it cannot be communicated, but only realized:[1] all that can be communicated are its external supports or symbolic expressions; the Great Work must be done by everyone for himself. The words attributed to the Buddha above are in no way contradictory of the principle of the open hand (*varadā mudrā*) or expository hand (*vyākhyānā mudrā*). The Buddha is never ineloquent: the solar gates are not there to exclude, but to admit; no one can be excluded by anyone but himself. The Way has been charted in detail by every Forerunner, who *is* the Way; what lies at the end of the road is not revealed, even by those who have reached it, because it cannot be told and does not appear: the Principle is not in any likeness.

Of what sort are, then, the most appropriate and efficacious supports of contemplation? It would scarcely be possible to cite an authoritative Indian text condemning explicitly the use of anthropomorphic as distinguished from aniconic images. There is, however, one Buddhist source, that of the *Kālinga-bodhi Jātaka*, in which what must have been the early position is still clearly reflected. The Buddha is asked by what kind of hallow, shrine, or symbol (*cetiya*)[2] he can properly be represented in his absence. The answer is that

[1] "This sort of thing cannot be taught, my son; but God, when he so wills, recalls it to our memory" (Hermes, *Lib.* XIII.2, Scott, *Hermetica,* I.241).

[2] *Cetiya, caitya,* are generally derived from *ci,* to pile up, originally used in particular connection with the edification of a fire-altar or funeral pile, and this is not without its significance in connection with the fact to be discussed

he can properly be represented by a Bodhi-tree[1] whether during his lifetime or after the Despiration, or by bodily relics after this Decease; the "indicative" (*uddesika*)[2] iconography of an anthropomorphic image is condemned as "groundless and conceptual, or conventional" (*avatthukam manamattakam*). It will be seen that the wording corresponds to that of the Brāhmaṇa as cited above: *manamattakam* = *manomatam*.

Before we proceed to ask how it could have been that an anthropomorphic image was accepted after all, we must eliminate certain considerations extraneous to the problem. It must be realized, in the first place, that although an iconoclastic problem is present, it was as a matter of convenience, and without reference to any supposed possibility of a real localization[3] or fetishism that the advent of the image can be said to have been

below, that the Buddha image really inherits the values of the Vedic altar. But as the Jātaka itself makes clear, a *cetiya* is by no means necessarily a stūpa, nor anything constructed, but a symbolic substitute of any sort, to be *regarded as* the Buddha in his absence: and there must be assumed at least a hermeneutic connection of *ci*, to edify, with the closely related roots *ci* and *cit*, to regard, consider, know and think of or contemplate; it is, for example, in this sense that *cetyaḥ* is used in RV. VI.1.5, "Thou, O Agni, our means-of-crossing-over, *art-to-be-known-as* man's eternal refuge and father and mother," all of which epithets have, moreover, been applied also to the Buddha.

[1] This is not, of course, an exclusively Buddhist position. The Vedas already speak of a Great Yakṣa (Brahman) moving on the waters in a fiery glowing at the centre of the universe in the likeness of a Tree (AV. X.7.32) and this Burning Bush, the Single Fig, is called in the Upaniṣads the "one Awakener" (*eka sambodhayitṛ*), and everlasting support of the contemplation of Brahman (*dhiyâlamba, Maitri Up.* VII.11). In *Śāṅkhāyana Āraṇyaka,* XI.2 the spirant Brahman is "As it were a great green tree, standing with its roots moistened."

[2] Cf. my *Elements of Buddhist Iconography,* pp. 4–6. I now render *uddesika* by "indicative" in view of the discussion by Professor De La Vallée Poussin in JHAS. II.281–282: from the passage which he cites from the *Yogaśāstra* of Asaṅga it is clear that the *uddiśya* means "indicative of the Buddha"; the examples given of such indicative symbols are "stūpa, building, and ancient or modern shrine." If it was only later that *uddesika cetiya* came also to mean "Buddha-image" (*tathâgata paṭimā*), this would mean that the Jātaka takes no account at all of Buddha-images: alternatively, Buddha images must be held to have been deprecated with other indicative symbols, as "arbitrary." The net result, that Buddha images were either ignored, or condemned, suffices for our purpose, the demonstration of the trace of an originally aniconic attitude.

[3] The question is one at the same time of localization and temporality. In modern Indian personal devotions it is typical to make use of an image of clay temporarily consecrated, and discarded after use when the Presence has been dismissed; in the same way the Christian church becomes the house of God specifically only after consecration, and if formally desecrated can be used for any secular purpose without offence. The rite, like the temporal Nativity, is necessarily eventful; the temporal event can take place *anywhere,* just because its reference is to an intemporal omnipresence. In any case, it is not a question of contradiction as between a "God extended in space" (Bouquet, *loc. cit.,* p. 52) and a special presence at a given point in space: extension in space is already a localization in the same sense that procession is an apparent motion. All Scripture employs a language in terms of time and space; it is not only

"postponed," and also as a matter of convenience that the image was realized when a need had been felt for it; and in the second place, that the resort to an anthropomorphic imagery by no means reports any such humanistic or naturalistic interests as those which led to the subordination of form to figure in European art after the Middle Ages or in Greek art after the sixth century B.C. The question of localization has been fundamentally misunderstood. If it is practically true that "the omnipresent Spirit *is* where it acts or where we are *attending* to it" (Bouquet, *The Real Presence*, p. 84), it is equally true that this "where" is *wherever* there is posited a centre or duly set up an image or other symbol: the symbol can even be carried about from place to place. Not that the Spirit is therefore in one place more than another or can be carried about, but that we and our supports of contemplation (*dhiyâlamba*) are necessarily in some one place or another. If the use of the symbol is to function mediately as a bridge between the world of local position and a "world" that cannot be traversed or described in terms of size, it is sufficiently evident that the hither end of such a bridge must be somewhere, and in fact wherever our edification begins: procedure is from the known to the unknown; it is the other end of the bridge that has no position.

By fetishism we understand an attribution to the physically tangible symbol of values that really belong to its reference; or in other words a confusion of actual with essential form. It is a fetishism of this sort that the Buddhist texts deprecate when they employ the metaphor of the finger pointing to the moon, and ridicule the man who either will not or cannot see anything but the finger. The modern aesthetic approach makes fetishes of traditional works of art precisely in this sense. Our own attitude is indeed so naturally and obstinately fetishistic that we are shocked to find and unwilling to believe that it is taken for granted in Buddhism that "those who

visual images that must be shattered if this is to be avoided. The iconoclast does not always realize all the implications of his ideal: that it cannot be said of anyone who still knows who he is, that all his idols have been broken.

consider the earthen images, do not honour the clay as such, but without regard to them in this respect, honour the Immortals designated" (*amara-saṁjñā*, *Divyâvadāna*, Ch. XXVI), and in Christian practice that "honour is paid, not to the colours or the art, but to the prototype" (St. Basil, cited in the *Hermeneia* of Athos).

As regards the second point it will suffice to say that "anthropomorphic" in the sense in which this word is appropriate to Indian images does not import "naturalistic"; the Buddha image is not in any sense a portrait, but a symbol; nor indeed are there any Indian images of any deity that do not proclaim by their very constitution that "This is not the likeness of a man"; the image is devoid of any semblance of organic structure; it is not a reflection of anything that has been physically seen, but an intelligible form or formula.[1]

Even at the present day there survives in India a widespread use of geometrical devices (*yantra*) or other aniconic symbols as the chosen supports of contemplation. If in the last analysis the intellectual has always preferred the use of abstract and algebraical or vegetable or theriomorphic or even natural symbols, one cannot but be reminded of the position of Dionysius, to whom it likewise appeared more fitting that divine truths should be expounded by means of images of a less rather than a more noble type in themselves (the noblest type in itself being that of humanity): "For then," as St. Thomas follows, "it is clear that these things are not literal descriptions of divine truths, which might have been open to doubt had they been expressed under the figure of nobler bodies, especially for those who could think of nothing nobler than bodies" (*Sum. Th.* I.1.9). What the Buddha anticipated was not that the figure in stone could ever have been worshipped literally as such, but that he might come to be thought of as a man, who denied of himself that he was "either a man, or a god, or a daimon" as one amongst others and had not in

[1] The image in pigment or stone, "indicative" of the Buddha, is as much an image of (and as little in the nature of) the God "whose image it is" as is the image in flesh or in words: each is "a sensible God in the likeness of the intelligible God" (εἰκὼν τοῦ νοητοῦ [θεοῦ] θεὸς αἰσθητός, Plato, *Timaeus*, 92: we do not shrink from the implied identification of the *aparinibbuto* Tathâgata with ὅ κοσμος οὗτος).

fact "become anyone." He prognosticated precisely such a humanistic interpretation of the "life" as that which leads the modern scholar to attempt to disengage an "historical nucleus" by the elimination of all "mythical elements," and to repudiate any attribution of omniscience to him to whom the designation "Eye in the World" was appropriate. It is just those "who can think of nothing nobler than bodies"[1] who in modern times have discovered in the incarnate Deity, Christian or Buddhist, nothing but the man; and to these we can only say that this "his manhood is a hindrance so long as they cling to it with mortal pleasure" (Eckhart).

The iconolatrous position developed in India from the beginning of the Christian era onward is apparently in contradiction of that which has been inferred in the *Kālingabodhi Jātaka.* It is, however, the iconoclastic position, that of Strzygowski's "Mazdaean" and "Northern" art, that still determines the abstract and symbolic nature of the anthropomorphic image and can be said to account for the fact that a naturalistic development had never taken place in India until the idea of representation was borrowed from Europe in the seventeenth century. The fact that the *Śukranītisāra* condemns portraiture at the same time that it extols the making of divine images very well illustrates how the Indian consciousness has been aware of what has been called "the ignominy implicit in representational art"—an ignominy closely related to that of an obsession with the historical point of view, to which in India the mythical has always been preferred. The parallels between the Indian and Christian artistic development are so close that both can be described in the same words. If, as Dr. Rowland[2] justly remarks, "With the sculptures of Hadda and the contemporary decoration of the monasteries at Jaulian (Taxila), the Gandhara school properly so-called is at an end. Counter currents of influence from the workshops of Central and Eastern India have almost transformed

1 A remarkable anticipation of the Renaissance point of view. "Coming events cast their *shadows* before."

2 *Art Bulletin*, XVIII.400.

the Indo-Greek Buddha image into the ideal norm for the representation of Sakyamuni that prevailed at Mathura and Sarnath and Ajanta," it can only have been because a sense of the unsuitability of any would-be humanistic style had been felt; an idea of the "Buddha type" had already been formed, "but the Hellenistic ideal of representation, the engrained, debased, and commonplace naturalism of a millennium, was incapable of achieving it. Hence the excessive rarity [in India proper] of the Greek type of Christ [Buddha], and the prompt substitution of the Semitic [Indian]."[1] A further parallel can be pointed out in the effects of the European iconoclasm on the nature of Byzantine art—"The chief outcome of the controversy was the formulation of a rigid iconography, which sufficed to prevent, once and for all, any backsliding towards meaningless naturalism. The picture, the human representation, was designed henceforth as an illustration of Reality, and as a vehicle of the deepest human emotions. . . . In this elevation of art to its highest function, though at the price of the artist's freedom, the iconodule defence, raised by the controversy to a high philosophical level, also played a part. . . . This was the chief iconodule contention: that pictures, like statues to Plotinus, were an effective means of communication with the extra-terrestrial universe.[2] . . . The concern of the artist was to evoke, through his pictures, not this world, but the other . . . that he [the beholder] might attain, through the reminder of these events, actual communion during life on earth with that firmament of divine arbitration of which the Latin Church taught only the post-human expectation."[3] These distinctions of the Byzantine from the Roman point of view are analogous to the differences between the Mahā-

[1] Adapted from Byron and Rice, *The Birth of Western Painting*, p. 56, by the addition of words in brackets.

[2] "In these outlines, my son, I have drawn a likeness (εἰκών) of God for you, as far as that is possible; and if you gaze upon this likeness with the eyes of your heart (καρδίας ὀφθαλμοῖς, Islamic *'ayn-i-qalbī*), then, my son, believe me, you will find the upward path; or rather, the sight itself will guide you on your way" (Hermes, *Lib.* IV.11b, Scott, *Hermetica*, I.157).

[3] Byron and Rice, *loc. cit.*, pp. 67, 78. It was, however, in both cases rather a matter of the recognition and endorsement of an older and originally neither Christian nor Buddhist, but universally solar, iconography and symbolism than one of the invention of an iconography *ad hoc*.

yāna and Hīnāyana points of view, and between the more or less didactic art of Sāñcī and the epiphanies of Bāmiyān, Ajaṇṭā, and Lung-men.

We do not know whether or not the deprecation of an "indicative" (*uddesika*) likeness which we have cited from the Jātaka is intended to refer to the old lists of *lakkhaṇas*, or thirty-two major and eighty minor iconographic peculiarities of the "Great Person." It must certainly have been in accordance with these prescriptions that a mental image of the Buddha had been entertained before any other image had been made; and equally certain that the validity of the images themselves has always been held to rest upon an accurate rendering of these peculiarities, or such of them as could be realized in any wrought material. For the Buddhist, iconography is art; that art by which he works. The iconography is at once the truth and the beauty of the work: truth, because this is the imitable form of the ideas to be expressed, and beauty because of the coincidence of beauty with accuracy, the Scholastic *integratio sive perfectio*, and in the sense in which a mathematical equation can be "elegant." As a Chinese inscription puts it, "I have sculptured a marvellous beauty . . . all of the iconographic peculiarities have been sublimely displayed" (Chavannes, *loc. cit.*, I.i.448). In the traditional view of art there is no beauty that can be divided from intelligibility; no splendor but the *splendor veritatis.*

The authenticity and legitimate heredity of Buddha images are established by reference to what are supposed to have been originals created in the Buddha's own lifetime, and either actually or virtually by the Buddha himself, in accordance with what has been said above with respect to an iconometric manifestation. The capacities of the artist exercised at empirical levels of reference have not sufficed for the dual operation of imagination and execution; the Buddha "cannot be apprehended"; what has been required is not an observation, but a vision. One is reminded of the fact that certain Christian images have been regarded in much the same way as "not made by hands" (ἀχειροποίητοί). It is of no importance from the present point of view that the legends of the first images cannot be interpreted as records of historical fact: what is important for us is that the authentication of the images themselves is not historical but ideal. Either the artist is transported to a heaven to take note there of the Buddha's appearance, and afterwards uses this model (Hsüan-tsang, *Buddhist Records of the Western World*, Beal, I.235), or the Buddha himself projects the "shadow" or outline of his likeness (*nimitta*), which the painters cannot grasp, but must fill in with colours, and animate[1] by the addition of a written "word," so that all is done "as prescribed" (*yathā saṁdiṣṭam*, *Divyâvadāna*, Ch. XXVII); or finally, the image is made by an artist who, after the work has been done, reveals himself to have been in fact the future Buddha Maitreya (Hsüan-tsang, *loc. cit.*, II.121).

Interpreted thus, the iconography can no longer be thought of as a groundless product of conventional realization or idealization, but becomes an ascertainment; the form is not of human invention, but revealed and "seen" in the same sense that the Vedic incantations are thought of as having been revealed and "heard." There can be no distinction in principle of vision from audition. And as nothing can be said to have been intelligibly uttered unless in certain terms, so nothing can be said to have been revealed unless in some form.[2] All that can be thought of as prior to formulation is without form and not in any likeness; the meaning and its vehicle can only be thought of as having been concreated. And this implies that

[1] We say deliberately "animate" because the inscription of an essential text (usually the formula *Ye dharmā*, etc.), or the enclosure of a written text within the body of a metal or wooden image, implies an eloquence; and it is far more literally than might be supposed that the words of a Chinese inscription, "The artist painted a *speaking* likeness" (Chavannes, *loc. cit.*, p. 497), are to be understood. We have to alter only very slightly the Buddha's words, "He who sees the Word, sees Me" to make them read "He who sees my Image, hears my Word."

[2] We must avoid an artificial distinction of "terms" from "forms." The symbol may be verbal, visual, dramatic, or even alimentary; the use of material is inevitable; it is not the kind of material that matters. It is with perfect logic that the Buddhist treats the verbal and the visual imagery alike: "How could the Luminous Personality be demonstrated otherwise than by a representation of colours and iconographic-peculiarities? How could the mystery be communicated without a resort to speech and dogma?" The sculptured figures of Buddhas and Bodhisattvas "furnish knowledgeable men with a means of raising themselves to the perfection of truth" (Chinese inscriptions, Chavannes, *loc. cit.*, pp. 501, 393).

whatever validity attaches to the meaning attaches also to the symbols in which it is expressed; if the latter are in any way less inevitable than the former, the intended meaning will not have been conveyed, but betrayed.

We need hardly add that all that is said in the preceding paragraph has to do with the art in the artist, which is already an expression in terms, or idea in an imitable form, and holds good irrespective of whether or not any mimetic word has actually been spoken aloud or any image actually made in stone or pigment; if it is not historically true that any tangible image of the Buddha had been made before the beginning of the Christian era, it is equally certain that an essential image not made by hands had been conceived, and even verbally stated, in terms of the thirty-two major and eighty minor peculiarities of the "Great Person"; when the first image was to be made, there already existed the "ascertained means of operation." If at last the artist made a corresponding figure in stone or pigment, he was only doing what the Indian imager has always done, and in accordance with such familiar instructions as that of the *Abhilaśitârthacintāmaṇi*, where the painter is told to "Put down on the wall what has been seen in contemplation" (*tad dhyātam bhittau niveśayet*). Even for Monsieur Foucher, who holds that the earliest Buddha images are those of the school of Gandhāra[1] and the product of a collaboration between the Hellenistic artist and the Indian Buddhist patron, the prescription or concept of the work to be done was Indian; the Hellenistic artist performing only the servile operation, the Indian patron remaining responsible for the free act of imagination. The sculptors of Mathurā, on the other hand, had at their command not only the visual image of the "Great Person" as defined in the Pali texts, but also the tradition of the standing types of the colossal Yakṣas of the latter centuries B.C., and for the seated figure also a tradition of which the beginning

[1] We are more inclined to agree with Dr. Rowland that "the Gandhāra school came into existence only shortly before the accession of Kanishka in the second century of the Christian era" (*Art Bulletin,* XVIII.399); thus either making the earliest Gandhāran images and those of Mathurā almost contemporary or giving some priority to the latter.

must have antedated the Śiva types of the Indus Valley culture of the third millennium B.C. The Buddha image came into being because a need had been felt for it, and not because a need had been felt for "art."

The practice of an art is not traditionally, as it is for us, a secular activity, or even a matter of affective "inspiration," but a metaphysical rite; it is not only the first images that are formally of superhuman origin. No distinction can be drawn between art and contemplation. The artist is first of all required to remove himself from human to celestial levels of apperception; at this level and in a state of unification, no longer having in view anything external to himself, he sees and realizes, that is to say becomes, what he is afterwards to represent in wrought material. This identification of the artist with the imitable form of the idea to be expressed is repeatedly insisted upon in the Indian books, and answers to the Scholastic assumption as stated in the words of Dante, "No painter can paint a figure if he have not first of all made himself such as the figure ought to be."

The later artist is not, then, imitating the visual aspect or style of the first images, which he may never have seen, but their form; the authenticity of the later images does not depend upon an accidental knowledge (such as that by which our "modern Gothic" is built) but upon a return to the source in another sense. It is just this that is so clearly expressed in the legend of Udāyana's Buddha image, which is said to have flown through the air to Khotān[1] and thus established the legitimacy of the lineage of Central Asian and Chinese iconography.[2] "Flight through the air" is always a technicality implying an independence of local position and ability to attain to whatever desired plane of apperception: a form or idea is "winged" in precisely this sense that like the Spirit it is wherever it operates or is entertained, and cannot be a private property. What the legend tells is not that an image of

1 Hsüan-tsang, *Buddhist Records*, Beal, II.322.

2 For an image called "Udāyana's" at Lung-men, see Chavannes, *loc. cit.*, p. 392, and Mus, "Le bouddha paré," *BÉFEO*, 1928, p. 249.

stone or wood flew through the air; it tells us, nevertheless, that the Khotanese artist saw what Udāyana's artist had seen, the essential form of the first image: that same form which Udāyana's artist had similarly seen before he returned to earth and took up the chisel or brush.

A distinction must then be very clearly drawn as between an archaistic procedure, which involves no more than the servile operation of copying, and the repeated entertainment of one and the same form or idea in a manner determined by the mode or constitution of the knower, which is the free operation of the artist whose style is his own. The distinction is that of an academic from a traditional school of art, the former systematic, the latter consistent. That "Art has fixed ends and ascertained means of operation" asserts an immutability of the idea in its imitable form—that the sun, for example, is *always* an adequate symbol of the Light of lights, but is not in any way a contradiction of another Scholastic dictum, that "To be properly expressed, a thing must proceed from within, moved by its form." It is because there is an endless *renewal* of the imaginative act that the artist's interior operation is properly spoken of as "free"; and the evidence of this freedom exists in the fact of a stylistic sequence always observable in a traditional art, followed from generation to generation; it is the academician that repeats the forms of "classic" orders like a parrot. The traditional artist is always expressing, not indeed his superficial "personality," but himself, having made himself that which he is to express, and literally *devoting* himself to the good of the work to be done. What he has to say remains the same. But he speaks in the stylistic language of his own time; and were it otherwise would remain ineloquent, for, to repeat the words of the *Laṅkâvatāra Sūtra* already cited, "Whatever is not adapted to the such and such persons as are to be taught, cannot be called a 'teaching.'"

It is not only the artist, but also the patron who *devotes* himself, not merely by the gift of his "substance" to defray the cost of operation, but also in a ritual, symbolical, and spiritual sense, just as the Christian who is not merely a spectator of the Mass, but participates in what is enacted, sacrifices himself. It is the merit of Monsieur Mus to have recognized for the first time that the essential values of the Vedic sacrifice are inherited and survive in the later iconolatry; the royal patron, for example, donates precisely his own weight of gold to be made into an image, which image is also made at the same time in accordance with an ascertained canon or proportion and employs as modulus a measure taken from his own person; and when the image has been made, offers to it himself and his family, afterwards to be redeemed at a great price. It is in just the same way that the stature of the patron is literally built into the Vedic altar, and that the sacrificer himself is offered up upon the altar—"That sacrificial Fire knows that 'He has come to give himself to Me'" (*paridām me*, ŚB. II.4.1.11). As Monsieur Mus expresses it, "It is, in fact, well known that the construction of the fire-altar is a veiled personal sacrifice. The sacrificer *dies*, and it is only upon this condition that he reaches heaven: at the same time, this is only a temporary death, and the altar, identified with the sacrificer, is his substitute. We freely recognize an analogous significance in the identification of the king with the Buddha, and in particular in the manufacture of statues in which the fusion of the personalities is materially effected. It is less a question of apotheosis than of *devotio*. The king gives himself to the Buddha, projects his person into him, at the same time that his mortal body becomes the earthly 'trace' of its divine model. . . . The artistic activity of India, as we have indicated, has always exhibited the trace of the fact that the first Brahmanical work of art was an altar in which the patron, or in other words the sacrificer, was united with his deity" (Mus, *loc. cit.*, *92, *94). If the deity assumes a human form it is in order that the man for his part may put on the likeness of divinity, which he does metaphysically and as if to anticipate his future glorification. The inadequacy of the worship of any principle as other than oneself or proper spiritual essence is strongly emphasized in the Upaniṣads; and it may be called an established principle of Indian thought that "Only by becoming God can one worship Him" (*devo bhūtvā devaṁ yajet*): it is only to one who can say "I am the Light, Thyself" that the answer is given, "Enter thou, for what thou art I am, and what I am thou art" (*Jaiminīya Up. Brāhmaṇa*, III.14).[1] The work of art is a devotional rite.

If the original artist and patron are thus devoted to and literally absorbed in the idea of the work to be done, which the artist executes and for which the patron pays, we have also to consider the nature of the act to be performed by those others for whose sake the work has also been done, amongst whom may be reckoned ourselves: the donor's inscriptions almost always indicating that the work has been undertaken not only for the donor's benefit or that of his ancestors, but also for that of "all beings." This will be more than a matter of mere "aesthetic appreciation": our judgment, if it is to be the "perfection of art," that is, a consummation in use, must involve a reproduction. Or to put it in other words, if it is by their ideas that we judge of what things ought to be like, this holds good as much *post factum* as *a priori*. In order to understand the work we must stand where the patron and artist stood and have done as they did; we cannot depend upon the mere reactions of "our own unintelligent nerve-ends." The judgment of an image is a contemplation, and as such can only be consummated in an assimilation. A transformation of our nature is required. It is in the same sense that Mencius says that to grasp the true meanings of words requires not so much a dictionary or a knowledge of epistemology as a rectification of personality. The *Amitāyur-Dhyāna Sūtra* is explicit: if you ask *how* is one to behold the Buddha, the answer is that you have done so only when the thirty-two major and eighty minor characteristics (i.e., of the iconography) have been assumed in your own heart: it is your own heart that becomes the Buddha and is the Buddha (SBE. XLIX.ii.178). It is in the same sense that the words of an inscription at Lung-men are to be understood: "It is as if the

1 "If then you do not make yourself equal to God, you cannot apprehend God; for like is known by like" (Hermes, *Lib.* XI.ii.20b, Scott, *Hermetica*, I.221). "He that is joined unto the Lord is one spirit" (I Cor. VI.17).

summit of the mountain has been reached and the river traced to its source: the fruition is accomplished, and one rests upon the Principle" (Chavannes, *loc. cit.*, p. 514). The aesthetic surfaces are by no means terminal values, but an invitation to a picture of which the visible traces are only a projection and to a mystery that evades the letter of the spoken word.

The reader may be inclined to protest that we have been speaking of religion rather than of art: we say, on the contrary, of a religious art. One can speak of a "reduction of art to theology" (Bonaventura) just because in the traditional synthesis plastic art is as much as any literary form a part of the art of knowing God. The aesthetic experience empathetically realized and cognitive experience intuitively realized can be logically distinguished, but are simultaneous in the whole or holy man who does not merely feel but also understands. It is not at all that the value of beauty is minimized, but that the occasional beauty of the artefact is referred to a formal cause in which it exists more eminently; there is a transubstantiation of the image, in which there is nothing taken away from the participant, but something added.

All that has been said above applies as much to the literary narrative of the Buddha's "life" as to the iconographic representation of his "appearance"; just as the latter is not a portrait but a symbol, so the former is not a record of facts but a myth. The supernatural iconography is an integral part of the image, as are the miracles of the life; both are essential elements rather than accidental or adventitious accretions introduced for the sake of "effect."

We have no intention to explain away the miracles by a psychological analysis, any more than we propose to consider the art in its merely affective aspects. As regards the historicity of miracles, there is, of course, a fundamental divergence between the rationalist and traditional positions. The actual demonstration of a magical effect would upset the rationalist's entire philosophy: his "faith" would be destroyed if the sun should stand still at noon or a man walk on the water. For the traditionalist on the other hand, magic is a science, but an inferior science about which he feels no curiosity; the possibility of magical procedure is taken for granted, but regarded only as illustrating, and by no means as proving, the principles on which the exercise of powers depends.

It matters very little from the present point of view which of these positions we assume. Rationalist and Fundamentalist fall together into the pit of an exclusively literal interpretation. Actually to discuss the historicity or possibility of a given miracle is far beside the main point, that of significance. We can, however, illustrate by a glaring example how the rationalistic, far more than the credulous point of view, can inhibit an understanding of the true intention of the work. The *Sukhāvatī-Vyūha* speaks of Buddhas as "covering with their tongue the world in which they teach." What Burnouf has to say in this connection is almost unbelievable: "This is an example of the incredible stupidities that can result from an addiction to the supernatural.... To speak of a sticking out of the tongue, and as the climax of the ridiculous also to speak of the vast number of assistant teachers who do the like in the Buddha's presence, is a flight of the imagination scarcely to be paralleled in European superstition. It would seem as though Northern Buddhists had been punished for their taste for the marvellous by the absurdity of their own inventions."[1] *Voilà le crétinisme scientifique dans toute sa béatitude!*[2] Contrast, however, what St. Thomas Aquinas has to say in a similar connection: "The tongue of an angel is called metaphorically the angel's power, whereby he manifests his mental concept.... The intellectual operation of an angel abstracts from *here and now*.... Hence in the angelic speech, local distance is no impediment" (*Sum. Th.* I.107.1 and 4).

[1] *Le Lotus de la Bonne Loi,* ed. 1925, p. 417.

[2] Ziegler, *Überlieferung,* 1936, p. 183. One cannot wonder that some Indians have referred to European scholarship as a "crime." At the same time the modern Indian scholar is capable of similar banalities. We have in mind Professor Chaṭṭopādhyāya who considers RV. X.71.4, where it is a question both of the audition and the vision of the Voice (*vāc*), proof of a knowledge of writing in the Vedic period—an example of intellectual myopia at least as dense as Professor Burnouf's own.

We alluded above to a "flight through the air" of Udāyana's Buddha image from India to Khotān, which image became in fact, as Chavannes observes, the prototype of many others fashioned in Central Asia. We repeat, in the first place, that the very existence of an "Udāyana's image" made in the Buddha's lifetime is of the highest improbability. In the second place, what is really meant by "aerial flight" and "disappearance"? The ordinary Sanskrit expression for "to vanish" is *antar-dhānaṁ gam*, literally to "go-interior-position." In the *Kālingabodhi Jātaka*, flight through the air depends upon an "investiture of the body in the garment of contemplation" (*jhāna veṭhanena*). As Monsieur Mus has very aptly remarked in another connection, "Toute le miracle résulte donc d'une disposition intime" (*BÉFEO*, 1929, p. 435). It is not then a matter of physical translocation that is involved, but literally one of concentration; the attainment of a centre that is omnipresent, and not a local motion. It is altogether a matter of "being in the Spirit" as this expression is used by St. Paul: that Spirit (*ātman*) of whom it is said that "Seated, he fares afar, recumbent he goes everywhere" (KU. II.21).[1] Of what importance in such a context can be a discussion of the possibility or impossibility of an actual levitation or translocation? What is implied by the designation "mover at will" (*kāmcārin*) is the condition of one who being in the Spirit no longer needs to move at all in order to be anywhere. Nor can any distinction be made between the possible intellect and the ideas it entertains *in adaequatione rei et intellectus:* to speak of an intellectual omnipresence is to speak of an omnipresence of the forms or ideas which have no objective existence apart from the universal intellect that entertains them. The legend does not refer to the physical transference of a material image, but to the

[1] Hermes, *Lib.* XI.ii.19 (Scott, *Hermetica*, I.221) "All bodies are subject to movement; but that which is incorporeal is motionless, and the things situated in it have no movement. . . . Bid your soul travel to any land you choose, and sooner than you can bid it go, it will be there . . . it has not moved as one moves from place to place, but it *is* there. Bid it fly up to heaven, and it will have no need of wings." RV. VI.9.5 "Mind (*manas*, νοῦς) is the swiftest of birds"; PB. XIV.1.13 "The Comprehensor is winged" (*yo vai vidvāṇsas te pakṣiṇaḥ*).

universality of an immutable form that can be seen as well by the Khotanese as by the Indian contemplative; where the historian of art would see what is called the "influence" of Indian on Central Asian art, the legend asserts an independent imagination of the same form. It will be seen that we have not had in view to explain away the miracle; but to point out that the marvel is one of interior disposition and that the power of aerial flight is nothing like an aeroplane's but has to do with the extension of consciousness to other than physical levels of reference and, in fact, to the "summit of contingent being."[1]

Consider another case, that of "Walking on the Water,"[2] a power attributed to some, alike in the Hindu, Buddhist, Christian, and Taoist, and very likely many other traditions. We do infer that such a thing can be done, but are not at all curious as to whether it was or was not done upon a given occasion; that we leave to those who suppose that the Vedic Bhujyu was actually picked up from the physical ocean by a passing "tramp." The matter of interest is one of significance. What does it mean that this power has been universally attributed to the deity or others in his likeness? To speak of a motion at will on the face of the waters is to speak of a being all in act, that is, to speak of the operation of a principle wherein all potentiality of manifestation has been reduced to act. In all traditions "the waters" stand for universal possibility.

The direct connection between the symbolic myth and mythical symbol can nowhere be illustrated better than in this context. For if the Buddha is invariably represented iconographically as supported by a lotus, his feet never

[1] "For man is a being of divine nature . . . and what is more than all beside, he mounts to heaven without quitting the earth; to so vast a distance can he put forth his power" (Hermes, *Lib.* X.24b, Scott, *Hermetica,* I.205).

[2] For the history of the symbol see Brown, W. N., *Walking on the Water,* Chicago, 1928; and also Waley, A., *The Way and its Power,* London, 1934, p. 118. The form of the Hermetic statements, "But from the Light there came forth a holy Word (λόγος = *uktha*) which took its stand upon the watery substance . . . motion, by reason of the spiritual (πνευματικὸς = *ātmanvat*) Word which moved upon the face of the water" (Hermes, *Lib.* I.8b, Scott, *Hermetica,* I.117, 119), although perhaps dependent on Genesis, is especially significant in its use of the expression "took its stand"; cf. *adhitiṣṭhati,* as predicated of the *ātman* in the Upaniṣads, *passim.*

touching any physical or local earth, it is because it is the idiosyncrasy of the lotus flower or leaf to be at rest upon the waters: the flower or leaf is universally, and not in any local sense, a ground on which the Buddha's feet are firmly planted. In other words, all cosmic, and not merely some or all terrestrial, possibilities are at his command. The ultimate support of the lotus can also be represented as a stem identical with the axis of the universe, rooted in a universal ground, and inflorescent at all levels of reference: and if in Brahmanical art this stem springs from the naval of Nārâyāṇa, the central ground of the Godhead recumbent on the face of the waters, and bears in its flower the figure of Brahmā (with whom the Buddha is virtually identified), the universality of this symbolism is sufficiently evident in the Stem of Jesse and in the symbolic representation of the Christian Theotokos by the rose. The expression "*rose des vents*," a compass-card, and Dante's *quant' è la larghezza di questa rosa nell' estreme foglie* (*Paradiso*, XXX.116-117) illustrate the correspondence of rose and lotus in their spatial aspects, cf. *Maitri Up.* VI.2, where the petals of the lotus are the points of the compass: directions, that is, of indefinite extension. We need hardly say that the universality and consistent precision of an adequate symbolism do not preclude an adaptability to local conditions and do not depend on the identification of botanical species.[1]

Now this significance of the lotus to which we have referred is inseparably bound up with the problem of Buddhist representation in plastic art. If we take the mythical symbol literally, as the modern Indian artist has sometimes done, we get a picture of what is no longer formally but figuratively a man supported by what is no longer a ground in principle but by what Monsieur Foucher calls "the frail cup of a flower" (*Mem. ASI.* 46.13); the picture is reduced to absurdity, and we expect the "man" to fall into the "water" at any moment. The correspondence of the aesthetic surfaces to the picture not in the colours has been destroyed; the picture is no longer beau-

[1] For a fuller discussion of the lotus see my *Elements of Buddhist Iconography*, Cambridge, 1935.

tiful, however skilfully executed, precisely because it has been robbed of meaning. It is a case in point of the principle that beauty cannot be divided from truth, but is an aspect of truth.

It has been a fundamental error of modern interpretation to have thought of Buddhist symbolism both as *sui generis* and as conventional, in the sense that Esperanto can be called a conventional language. That is what symbols seem to *us* to be, who are accustomed to the "symbolism," or rather "expressionism," of poets and artists who speak individually in terms of their own choice, which terms are often obscure but are nevertheless sometimes taken over into current usage. It is from these points of view that Monsieur Foucher can think that he is "able to observe retrospectively the old image-maker's increasingly bold attempts" and opines that elephants "naturally came to take their stand on lotuses... a kind of specific detail subsequently added... the superstition of precedent alone prevented them from going further" (*loc. cit.*). Had he remembered that the Vedic Agni is born in and supported by a lotus, he would surely have asked, "How could man have imagined that a fire could have been kindled on the frail cup of a flower in the midst of the waters?" He does protest, in fact, that "Had not the lotus filled from the beginning all the available space, no one would ever have dreamt of using the frail cup of a flower as a support for an adult human being" (*loc. cit.*).[1]

This is to remove the symbols altogether from their traditional context and values and to see in an art of ideas merely an idealizing art. The modern view of symbols is in fact bound up with the modern theory of a "natural religion," invoked by some in explanation of the "evolution" of all religions and by others in explanation of all but the Christian religion.

1 That "the lotus filled from the beginning all the available space" is for Monsieur Foucher merely a fact of iconography and in this sense a "superstitious precedent." The words are true, however, in this far deeper and more original sense that *in the beginning there was no other space*, and as it was in the beginning is now and ever shall be: because the lotus is the symbol and image of all spatial extension, as stated explicitly in *Maitri Up.* VI.2, "What is the lotus and of what sort? What this lotus is is Space, forsooth; the four quarters and four inter-quarters are its constituent petals." The "precedent" is primarily metaphysical and cosmic, and *therefore also* iconographic.

But from the point of view of the tradition itself, Brahmanism is a revealed religion, that is to say, a doctrine of supernatural origin; a revelation, then, in terms of an adequate symbolism, whether verbal or visual, in the same sense that Plato speaks of the first Denominator as a "more than human Power" and of the names given in the beginning as necessarily "true names." Whatever we think of this,[1] the fact remains that symbolism is of an immemorial antiquity, an antiquity as great as that of "folk-lore" itself; many of the Vedic symbols, that of the tracking of the Hidden Light by its footprints, for example, imply a hunting culture antecedent to the beginnings of agriculture. The commonest word for "Way," Skr. *mārga*, Pali Buddhist *magga*, derives from a root *mṛg*, "to hunt," and implies a "following in the tracks of." In any case, the Indus Valley peoples, three thousand years B.C., already made use of "symbols, such as the *svastika*, that India has never relinquished. Dare we think that the spirituality of Indian art is as ancient as the Indus civilization? If so, we may never hope to penetrate the secret of its origin" (Brown, W. N., in *Asia*, May, 1937, p. 385).

Symbolism is a language and a precise form of thought; a hieratic and a metaphysical language and not a language determined by somatic or psychological categories. Its foundation is in the analogical correspondence of all orders of reality and states of being or levels of reference; it is because "This world is in the image of that, and vice versa" (*Aitareya Brāhmaṇa*, VIII.2, and KU. IV.10) that it can be said *Coeli enarrant gloriam Dei.*

The nature of an adequate symbolism could hardly be better stated than in the words "The parabolical (Skr. *parôkṣa*) sense is contained in the lit-

[1] The notions of a "revelation" and "philosophia perennis" (Augustine's "Wisdom uncreate, the same now as it ever was, and the same to be for evermore," *Conf.* IX.10) are, of course, anathema to the modern scholar. He prefers to say that the Vedic hymns "contain the rudiments of a far higher species of thought than these early poets could have dreamt of... thought which has become final for all time in India, and even outside of India" (Bloomfield, *Religion of the Veda*, 1908, p. 63). It is true that the writer has here in mind an evolution of thought, but just how *does* the Vedic poet formulate "a far higher species of thought than he could have dreamt of"? It is as much as to say that man accomplished what man cannot do.

eral (Skr. *pratyakṣa*)." On the other hand, "The sensible forms, in which there was at first a polar balance of physical and metaphysical, have been more and more voided of content on their way down to us: so we say, This is an 'ornament'" (Andrae, *Die ionische Säule*, p. 65). It becomes, then, a question of the restoration of significance to forms that we have come to think of as merely ornamental. We cannot take up here the problems of symbolic methodology, except to say that what we have most to avoid is a subjective interpretation, and most to desire is a subjective realization. For the meanings of symbols we must rely on the explicit statements of authoritative texts, on comparative usage, and on that of those who still employ the traditional symbols as the customary form of their thought and daily conversation.[1]

Our present concern is not, however, so much with the methodology of symbolic exegesis as with the general nature of a typically symbolic art. We have spoken above of a transubstantiation, and the word has also been properly used by Dr. Kramrisch in speaking of art of the Gupta period and that of Ajaṇṭā in particular, with reference to the coincidence in it of sensuous and spiritual values. Our primary error when we consider the Eucharist is to suppose that the notion of a transubstantiation represents any but a normally human point of view. To say that this is not merely bread but also and more eminently the body of God is the same as to say that a word is not merely a sound but also and more eminently a meaning: it is with perfect consistency that a sentimental and materialistic[2] generation not only ridicules the Eucharistic transubstantiation, but also insists that the whole of any work of art subsists in its aesthetic surfaces, poetry consisting, for example, in a conjunction of pleasurable or interesting sounds rather than in a logically ordered sequence of sounds with meanings. It is from

[1] See my "The Rape of a Nāgī: an Indian Gupta Seal," Pt. II, in MFA. Bulletin, August, 1937.

[2] Sentimentality and materialism, if not in every respect synonymous, coincide in the subject. Man in search of spirit has become ~~Freud's~~ "modern man in search of a soul," who discovers . . . spiritualism and psychology.

Jung's

the same point of view that man is interpreted only as a psychophysical being, and not as a divine image, and for the same reason that we laugh at the "divinity of kings." That we no longer admit an argument by analogy does not represent an intellectual progress; we have merely lost the art of analogical procedure or, in other words, ritual procedure. Symbolism[1] is a calculus in the same sense that an adequate analogy is proof.

In the Eucharistic sacrament, whether Christian, Mexican, or Hindu, bread and wine are "charged with meaning" (Bouquet, *loc. cit.*, p. 77): God is a meaning. The Vedic incantation (*brahman*) is physically a sound but super-audibly *the* Brahman. To the "primitive" man, first and foremost a metaphysician and only later on a philosopher and psychologist, to this man who, like the angels, had fewer ideas and used less means than we, it had been inconceivable that anything, whether natural or artificial, could have a use or value only and not also a meaning: this man literally could not have understood our distinction of sacred from profane or of spiritual from material values; he did not live by bread alone. It had not occurred to him that there could be such a thing as an industry without art, or the practise of any art that was not at the same time a rite, a going on with what had been done by God in the beginning. *Per contra*, the modern man is a disintegrated personality, no longer the child of heaven and earth, but altogether of the earth. It is this that makes it so difficult for us to enter into the spirit of Christian, Hindu, or Buddhist art in which the values taken for granted are spiritual and only the means are physical and psychological. The whole purpose of the ritual is to effect a translation, not only of the object, but of the man himself to another, and no longer peripheral but central level of reference. Let us consider a very simple case; in which, however, our fictitious distinctions of barbarism from civilization must be discarded. That neolithic man already called his celts and arrow-heads "thunderbolts" is preserved in the memory of the folk throughout the world. When Śaṅkarâcārya exclaimed "I

1 Webster, "any process of reasoning by means of symbols."

cf. on Bu. III. 9.28.7

have learnt concentration from the maker of arrows" he may well have meant more than to say "I have learnt from the sight of this man, so completely forgetful of himself in his concern for the good of the work to be done, what it means to 'make the mind one-pointed.'" He may also have had in mind what the initiated artisan and initiated archer[1] had been made aware of in the Lesser Mysteries, that an arrow made by hands is transubstantially the point of that bolt with which the Solar Hero and Sun of Men first smote the Dragon and pillared-apart heaven and earth, creating an environment and dispelling the darkness literally with a *shaft* of light. Not that anybody could have thought that the man-made object had actually "fallen from heaven," but that the "arrow feathered with the solar-eagle's feathers and sharpened by incantations" had been made to be now not merely a thing of wood and iron, but at the same time metaphysically of another sort.[2] It is in the same way that the warrior, also an initiate, conceived himself to be, not merely a man, but also in the image of the wielder of the bolt, the Thundersmiter himself. In the same way the Crusader's sword was not merely a piece of iron or steel, but also a shard detached from the Cross of Light; and for him, *in hoc signo vinces* had neither exclusively a practical nor only a "magical" value; actually to strike the heathen foeman and to bring light into darkness were of the essence of a single act. It belonged to the secret of Chivalry, Asiatic and European, to realize oneself as, that is, metaphysically, to *be*, a kinsman of the Sun, a rider on a winged stallion or in a chariot of fire, and girded with very lightning. This was an imitation of God in the likeness of a "mighty man of war."

We could have illustrated the same principles in connection with any of the other arts than that of war; those, for example, of carpentry or weaving, agriculture, hunting, or medicine, or even in connection with such games as

[1] It is said that the last company of French archers was dissolved by Clemençeau, who objected to their possession of a "secret."

[2] For the cult and transubstantiation of weapons, cf. RV. VI.47 and 75 and ŚB. I.2.4.

checkers—where the pawn that reaches the "farther shore" becomes a crowned king and is significantly called to this day in the Indian vernacular a "mover at will" (*kāmâcārin*, already in the Upaniṣads the technical designation of the liberated man in whom the spiritual rebirth has been accomplished). The same holds good for all the activities of life, interpreted as a ritual performed in imitation of what was done in the beginning. This point of view in connection with sexual acts, sacrificially interpreted in the Brāhmaṇas and Upaniṣads, is, for example, essential to any understanding of the Tantric and Lamaistic Buddhist iconographies, or equally of the Krishna myths and their representation in art; the point of view survives in our own expression, "the sacrament of marriage." The bivalence of an image that has been ritually quickened by the in-vocation of Deity and by the "Gift of Eyes" is of the same kind. In the same way relics are deposited in a stūpa and called its "life" (*jīvita*); the stūpa being, like the Christian altar and church, at once an embodiment and the tomb of the dying God. A formal presence of the altogether despirated Buddha, *Deus absconditus*, is thus provided for on earth: the veritable tomb in which the Buddha, himself a Nāga,[1] really lives, is *ab intra*, and guarded by Nāgas; the cult establishes a link between the outward facts and inward reality for the sake of those who are not yet "dead and buried in the Godhead." We indeed speak, although only rhetorically, of the "life" of a work of art; but this is only a "folk-memory" and literally a "superstition" of what was once a deliberate animation metaphysically realized.

From the traditional point of view the world itself, together with all things done or made in a manner conformable to the cosmic pattern, is a theophany: a valid source of information because itself in-formed. Only

[1] The Buddha is sometimes referred to as a Nāga. In *Majjhima Nikāya,* I.32, the *arhats* Mogallāna and Sāriputra are called "a pair of Great Serpents" (*mahānāgā*); *ib.* I.144–145, the Nāga found at the bottom of an ant hill (considered as if a stūpa) is called a "signification of the monk in whom the foul issues have been eradicated"; and in *Sutta Nipāta,* 522, "Nāga" is defined as one "who does not cling to anything and is released" (*sabatta na sajjati vimutto*). Parallels abound on Greek soil, where the dead and deified hero is constantly represented as a snake within a conical tomb, and the chthonic aspect of Zeus Meilichios is similarly ophidian.

those things are ugly and ineloquent which are informal or deformed. Transubstantiation is the rule: symbols, images, myths, relics, and masks are all alike perceptible to sense, but also intelligible when "taken out of their sense." In the dogmatic language of revelation and of ritual procedure this general language is reduced to a formulated science for purposes of communication and transmission. It is more necessary that the doctrine should be transmitted forever, for the sake of those that have ears to hear,—"such souls as are of strength to see,"—than possible that everyone who plays a part in the transmission should also be a Comprehensor; and hence there is an adaptation in terms of folklore and fairy-tale for popular transmission as well as a formulation in hieratic languages for sacerdotal transmission and finally also an initiatory transmission in the Mysteries. It is equally true with respect to all of these transmissions that "Whereas in every other science things are signified by words, this science has the property, that the things signified by words have themselves also a signification. . . . The parabolical sense is contained in the literal" (St. Thomas, *Sum.Th.* I.1.10); that "Scripture, in one and the same sentence, while it describes a fact, reveals a mystery" (Gregory, *Moral,* XX.1).

It is in this way only that the formality of the whole of traditional art and ritual, Christian, Buddhist, or other, can and must be understood; all of this art has been an applied art, never an art for art's sake; the values of use and meaning are prior to those of ornament. Aesthetic virtues, adequate relations of masses and so forth, survive in the "art forms" even when their meaning has been forgotten; the "literary" values of Scripture and the "musical" values of the liturgy hold, for example, even for the "nothing-morist" (Skr. *nâstika*).[1] No doubt, our "feelings" about works of art can be psychologi-

[1] *Nâstika,* one "who thinks 'There is naught beyond this world'" (*ayaṁ loko nâsti para iti mānī, Kaṭha Up.* II.6), not realizing that "There is not only this much, but another than this" (*naîtāvad enā anyad asti,* RV.X.31.8). If Buddhists themselves have sometimes been regarded as *nâstikas,* this has been because *anattā* has been misunderstood to mean "There is no Spirit"; the true Buddhist position is that it is only of "what is not the Spirit" (*anattā; na me so attā*), only of "life under these conditions" that it can be said that "there is nothing else" (*nâparam, Saṁyutta Nikāya,* III.118).

cally or even chemically explained, and those who wish may rest content with knowing what they like and how they like it. But the serious student of the history of art, whose business it is to explain the genesis of forms and to judge of achievements without respect to preferences of his own, must also know what the artist was trying to do, or in other words what the patron required.

We may have to admit that it is beyond the competence of the rationalist, as such, to understand Buddhist art. On the other hand, we are far from maintaining that in order to understand one must be a Buddhist in any specific sense; there are plenty of professing Buddhists and professing Christians who have not the least idea what Buddhist or Christian art is all about. What we mean is that in order to understand one must be not merely a sensitive man, but also a spiritual man; and not merely a spiritual, but also a sensitive man. One must have learnt that an access to reality cannot be had by making a choice between matter and spirit considered as things unlike in all respects, but rather by seeing in things material and sensible a formal likeness to spiritual prototypes of which the senses can give no direct report. It is not a question of religion versus science, but of a reality on different levels of reference, or better, perhaps, of different orders of reality, not mutually exclusive.

Ananda K. Coomaraswamy

The Origin of the Buddha Image

By

ANANDA K. COOMARASWAMY

Reprinted from

THE ART BULLETIN

Vol. IX, No. 4

The College Art Association of America

New York University: Washington Square, New York

1927

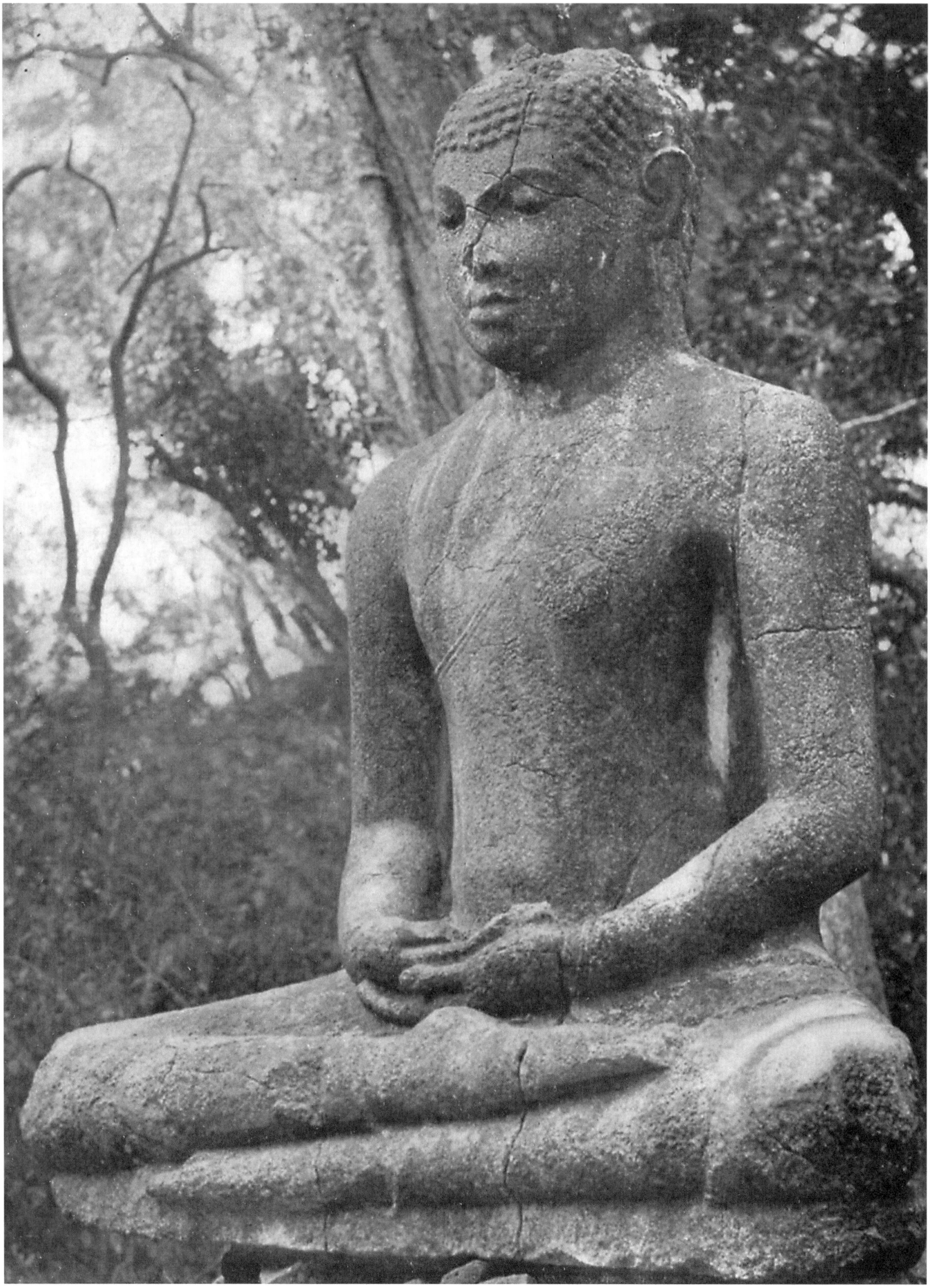

1—Typical Buddha Figure. Anurādhapura. C. IV Cent. A. D.

THE ORIGIN OF THE BUDDHA IMAGE*

BY ANANDA K. COOMARASWAMY

"*Nothing beyond what is self-developed in the brain of a race is permanently gained, or will survive the changes of time.*"

—Flinders Petrie, in *Social Life in Ancient Egypt*

INTRODUCTION

THE question of the origin of the Buddha image is, of course, but a part of the general problem of the origin of Indian iconography and plastic types. In view of the thoroughly Indian character of mediaeval works it was natural in the first place to suppose that these types had been created and developed on Indian soil, and by Indian sculptors. This might well have seemed most obvious in the case of the Buddha figure, representing as it does, a conception of spiritual attainment altogether foreign to European psychology, and a formula quite un-European in its indifference to natural fact.

But it was soon realized, on the one hand, that the Buddha (Gautama, Śākya-Muni), in early Indian art, say before the first century A. D., is never represented in human form but only by symbols; and, on the other hand, that the Graeco-Buddhist or Indo-Hellenistic art of Gandhāra in the period immediately following presents us with an innumerable series of anthropomorphic images, certainly with some peculiarities of their own, but resembling in a general way the later Gupta and mediaeval images of India proper, not to speak of those of Farther India and the Far East. At once it was taken for granted that the idea of making such images had been suggested to the Indian mind from this outside source, and that Greek or at any rate Eurasian craftsmen had created the first images of the Buddha for Indian patrons on the foundation of a Hellenistic Apollo; and that the later images were not so much Indian as Indianized versions of the Hellenistic or, as it was more loosely expressed, Greek prototypes. This view was put forward, as M. Foucher himself admits, in a manner best calculated to flatter the prejudices of European students and to offend the susceptibilities of Indians: the creative genius of Greece had provided a model which had later been barbarized and degraded by races devoid of true artistic instincts, to whom nothing deserving the name of fine art could be credited.

From the standpoint of orthodox European scholarship the question was regarded as settled, and all that remained was to work out the details, a study which was undertaken by the founder of the theory in his already classic *L'art gréco-bouddhique du Gandhara*, and continued by Grünwedel and others, with this result at least, that the art of Gandhāra is now very thoroughly known. When, a little later, doubts were expressed from various quarters external to the circle of orthodox scholarship, doubts suggested rather by stylistic and *a priori* psychological considerations, than by purely archaeological evidence, M. Foucher, the author most committed to the Greek theory, did not hesitate to suggest in

*In order to get a large amount of comparative material together on the plates, short and incomplete captions have been printed there. A fuller record of the illustrations will be found in the list appended to the article.

his genial way that in the case of European students, these doubts were only the result of aesthetic prejudice, in the case of Indian students, of nationalist rancour ("*engouement d'aestheticien ou rancune de nationaliste*").[1]

Times have changed. I cannot better indicate the nature of this change than by a quotation from Mr. Dalton's recent work on *East Christian Art:* "The principles governing this Christian art have received their due; that which the eighteenth and nineteenth centuries refused to consider has been regarded with favouring eyes. Thus aid has come from another side to those who have striven to combat the erroneous view that Early Christian art was nothing more than classical art in decadence. The very features for which Hellenistic art was once praised are now condemned as its worst. . . . In no other field of research have archaeology and criticism better helped each other to overcome ungenerous tradition." If the echoes of the battle on this front, "*Orient oder Rom,*" are still to be heard, at any rate we no longer confuse the qualities of Hellenistic and Hellenic art; the deserved prestige of the latter no longer protects the former from destructive criticism.

In view of these facts, which it would be almost superflous to recapitulate, were it not for the peculiar attitude assumed by the author of the Greek theory and his followers, it should now be possible to discuss the subject calmly and to substitute argument for rhetoric. However this may be, I propose to outline here the evidences that exist to support the more obvious, but not therefore necessarily erroneous, theory of the Indian origin of the Buddha image in particular and of Indian iconography generally. Need I protect myself by saying that I do not mean by this to deny the existence of foreign elements and influences traceable in Indian art? I do mean, however, to imply that the proper time and place for their study and analysis is after, and not before, we have achieved a general understanding of the internal development of the art. The matter is of importance, not because the existence of foreign elements in any art (they exist in all arts) is not of great aesthetic significance, but just because when too much stress is laid upon this significance, the way to a clear apprehension of the general development of the art is obscured.[2] The subject has bulked already far too largely in the literature of Indian

1. To this, and numerous other remarks by M. Foucher in the same vein, sometimes more suggestive of propaganda than of sober science, I might well reply in the recent words of Dr. Salmony (*Die Rassenfrage in der Indienforschung*, in *Socialistischen Monatsheft, Heft* 8, 1926) "*Man darf ruhig sagen: Das europaische Urteil wurde bisher durch den Drang nach Selbstbehauptung verfälscht.*" In scientific writings, references to the nationality of those who do not or may not agree with us are not always in the best of taste; not all of M. Foucher's eloquence can make them gracious, and in any case they are no good substitute for reasoned argument.

As a matter of fact, Indian (and Japanese) scholars have shown a singular humility, and perhaps some timidity, in their ready acceptance of all the results of European scholarship; see, for example, Gauranganath Banerjee, *The Art of Gandhara*, and *Hellenism in Ancient India.* Most of those who have expressed doubts regarding the Foucher theory have been European (Havell, Cohn, Laufer, Goloubew, Sirén, Kramrisch, etc.).

2. As remarked by Laufer, *Das Citralakṣaṇa*, p. viii, note 1.

With some authors, Indo-Greek art has become a veritable obsession. The extent to which the dependence of Asiatic on Greek art has been pressed may be illustrated by the following examples: M. Blochet (*Gaz. des Beaux-Arts*, V, p. 114) recognizes Greek elements in Pahārī Rājput drawings, "*dans laquelle on retrouve toutes* [!] *les caractéristiques de l'art indo-grec du Gandhara,*" and remarks that in the twelfth and thirteenth centuries "*les temples brahmaniques sont des répliques du Mausolée qu'Artémise avait fait construire et decorer par des praticiens grecs.*" G. de Lorenzo (*India e Buddhismo Antico*, p. 45) suggests that Greek art, transformed and transported by Buddhism, may have animated the ancient art of the Aztecs and Incas of America. Jouveau-Dubreuil, *The Pallavas*, p. 7, calls the sculptures of Amarāvātī "almost entirely Roman in workmanship."

art; my object in discussing it here is not so much to continue the controversy as to dismiss it.[3]

The subject can best be expounded under a series of heads, as follows: (1) What is the Buddha image? (2) The early representation of deities by means of symbols. (3) The necessity for a Buddha image. (4) Elements of the later anthropomorphic iconography already present in early Indian art. (5) Style and content: differentiation of Indian and Hellenistic types. (6) Dating of Gandhāra and Mathurā Buddhas.

1. WHAT IS THE BUDDHA IMAGE?

By the Buddha image, the ultimate origin of which is in question, I understand to be meant both the earliest Indian examples and the fully developed type as we meet with it in Gupta and mediaeval India, and in Farther India and the Far East. There can be no doubt that this fully developed type is the subject of M. Foucher's thesis, for he is careful to extend his filiation throughout the area and periods referred to. As he has also pointed out, the question of the origin of Jaina and Brahmanical types and iconography is equally involved; the Jaina figures, on account of their close resemblance to those of the Buddha, and because of the parallelism of the Jaina and Buddhist development, are here considered together with the Buddha type, while the Brahmanical figures, in order to avoid too great an extension of the field to be examined, are only incidentally referred to. The question of the origin of Bodhisattva types is inseparable from that of the origin of the Buddha figure.

It will suffice to illustrate a few examples of the fully developed type of which the beginnings are to be discussed. In plastic and ethnic character these figures are products of the age and place in which they are found, at the same time that their descent from some common ancestor is evident. Iconographically the types of Buddhas and even of Bodhisattvas (we are not here concerned with the later differentiation of innumerable many-armed forms) are few. For seated Buddhas there are five positions, one in which both hands held at the breast form the *dharmacakra mudrā*, one in which both hands rest palms upward on the lap in *dhyāna mudrā*, and three in which the left hand rests in the same way on the lap, the right hand either hanging over the right knee (*bhūmisparśa mudrā*) or resting on the knee palm upwards in *varada mudrā*, or raised in *abhaya mudrā*. Sometimes the left hand grasps the folds of the robe. In standing images the right hand is generally raised in *abhaya mudrā*, while the left holds the folds of the robe. Finally, there are reclining images. The robe in some cases covers one, in others both, shoulders. The drapery clings closely to the figure, and is felt to be almost transparent ("wet drapery"). The palms of the hands and soles of the feet are sometimes marked by symbols. Of physical peculiarities, the *uṣṇīṣa* or protuberance on the crown of the head is very evident, the *ūrṇā* or tuft of fine hair between the brows is commonly found, and the fingers are sometimes webbed. The hair is represented by short curls, turned to the right, and

3. I have quite recently (*The Indian Origin of the Buddha Image*, in *Journ. Am. Or. Soc.*, XLVI, 1926) assembled a series of quotations, mainly from authors committed to the Greek theory, sufficient to suggest the outlines of the true history of the Buddha image. That the reader will have consulted these references is here taken for granted. I may also refer to a review of the last published part of *L'art gréco-bouddhique du Gandhara*, published in the *Ostasiatische Zeitschrift*, N. F., 1, 1924, pp. 51-53, and to the essay on Buddhist primitives in my *Dance of Siva;* in the latter I would now present certain points in a different way.

forming little protuberances which cover the whole of the head and the *uṣṇīṣa.* The ears are elongated by the weight of earrings worn before the adoption of the monastic robes. Some kind of confusion between the Buddha and Bodhisattva type is indicated by the existence of a Buddha type with crown and jewels; strictly and normally, the Buddha should be represented in monastic robes, the Bodhisattva, whether Siddhārtha or any other, in secular royal costume. The Bodhisattvas are represented in less rigid positions, never, for example, with hands in *dhyāna mudrā;* they are commonly distinguished by attributes held in the right or left hand, Vajrapāṇi by the *vajra*, Padmapāṇi by the rose lotus, Avalokiteśvara by the blue lotus, Maitreya by the *amṛta* flask; these attributes may be held in either hand, but the right hand is often raised in the pose of exposition (*vyyākhyāna mudrā* or *cin mudrā*, sometimes called *vitarka*). Bodhisattvas are further distinguished by symbols indicated in the headdress, for example the Dhyāni Buddhas in the crowns of Avalokiteśvara and Mañjuśrī, the stupa in that of Maitreya; and in some cases by their "vehicles," Mañjuśrī, for example, often riding on a lion. Each and all of these deities are almost invariably represented as seated or standing on an expanded rose lotus flower, with or without a lion throne or "vehicle" in addition. Jinas or Tīrthaṁkaras are represented like Buddhas seated in *dhyāna mudrā*, but generally nude, and otherwise only to be distinguished by special signs, such as the *śrīvatsa* symbol on Mahāvīra's breast, or by their attendants.

Fundamentally then, there are two Buddha-Jina types to be considered, that of the seated Buddha or Jina with hands resting in the lap or in one of a few other positions and that of the standing figure with the right hand raised in *abhaya mudrā*, both types being represented in monastic robes, and neither carrying attributes; and one Bodhisattva type, seated or standing, in secular costume and usually carrying attributes.

The fully evolved types described above are illustrated in Figs. 1, 5, 31, 40, 62-64, 66-73.

2. THE EARLY REPRESENTATION OF DEITIES BY MEANS OF SYMBOLS

It is extremely doubtful whether any of the Vedic deities were anthropomorphically represented in the Vedic period, that is to say, before the time of Buddha. References to images, however, become common in the later additions to the Brāhmaṇas and Sūtras and in the Epics; while a well-known passage of Patañjali, commenting on Pāṇini (V., 3, 99) refers to the exhibition of images of Śiva, Skanda, and Viśākha. Very probably, we may regard the symbolic method as, broadly speaking, Aryan, the anthropomorphic as aboriginal (Dravidian), or as respectively "Northern" and "Southern" in Strzygowski's sense. Images may have been characteristic of aboriginal religious cults from a remote time, only making their appearance in Brahmanical literature at the time when popular belief was actively affecting Brahmanical culture, that is to say in the early theistic period, when *pūjā* begins to replace *yajña*. We find traces of this aboriginal iconolatry not only in the early figures of Yakṣas, but also in such passages of the Gṛhya Sūtras as refer to the moving about of the images of bucolic deities, and the making of images of Nāgas for the Nāga Bali. In the early votive terra cottas, all apparently non-Buddhist, and usually representing goddesses, and as a subordinate element in early Buddhist and Jaina art, we find a well-developed and quite explicit popular iconography.

Here, however, we are concerned with the symbolic or aniconic method, which was at one time so universal, at least in orthodox and official circles, as to constitute by itself a

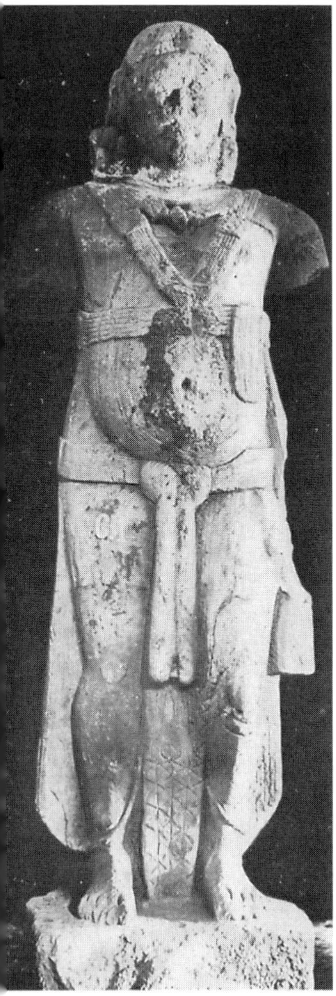

2—*Yakṣa (Besnagar)*
III Cent. B. C.

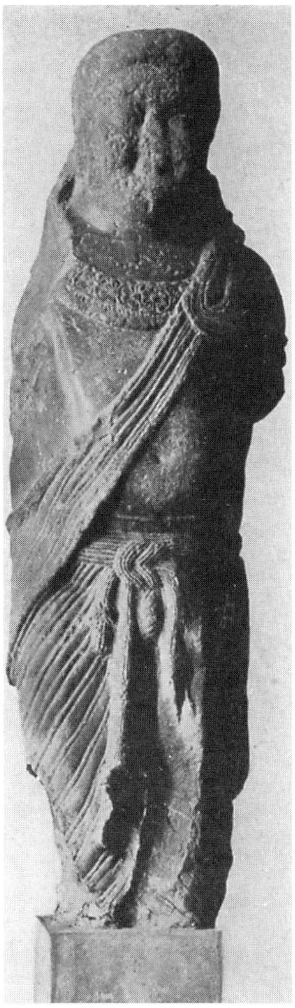

3—*Yakṣa (Patna)*
II Cent. B. C.

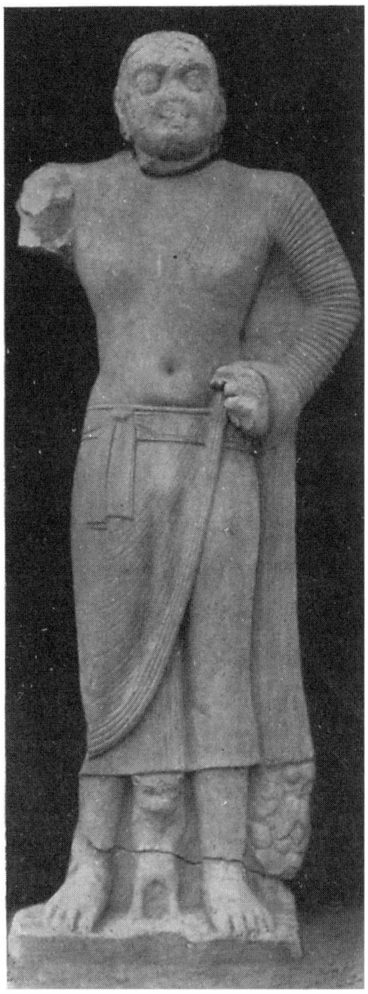

4—"*Bodhisattva*" *(Buddha)*
(Mathurā). 123 A. D.

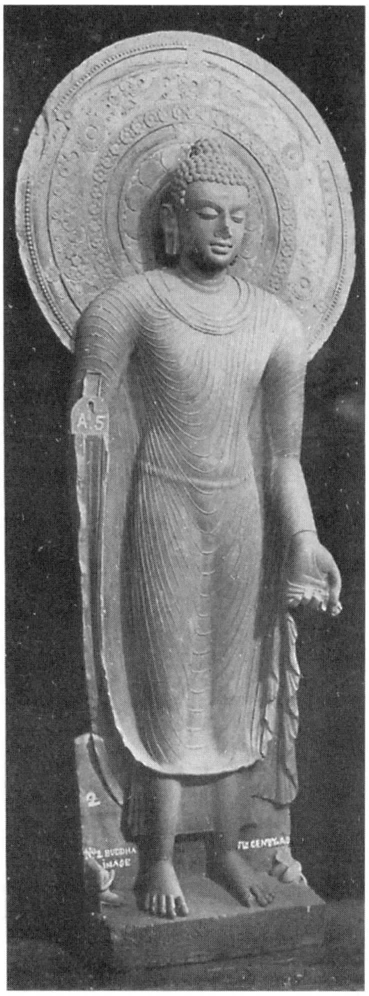

5—*Buddha (Sārnāth)*
V Cent. A. D.

Stylistic Sequence of Yakṣa and Buddha Figures

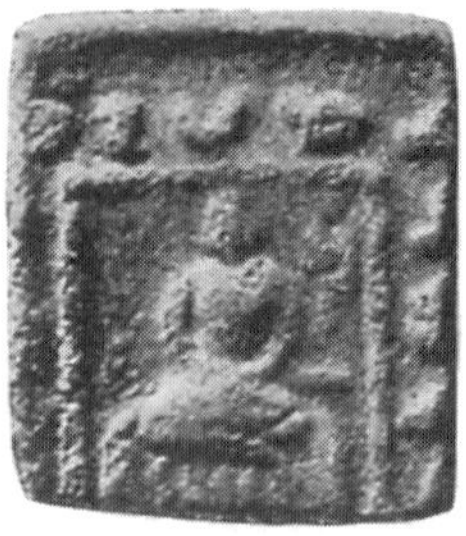

6—*Maues*

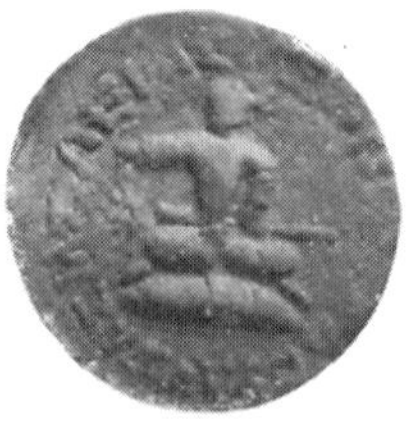

7—*Azes*

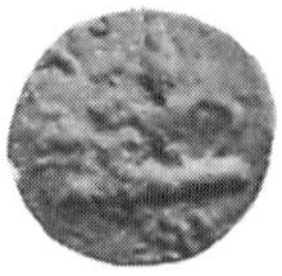

8—*Kadapha*

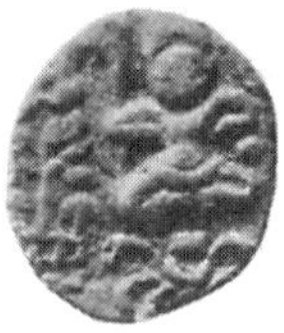

9—*Ujjain*

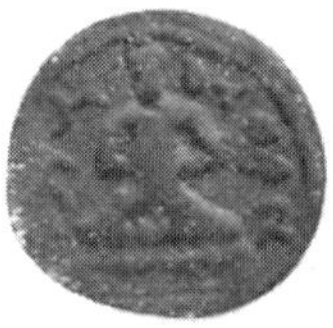

10—*Kaniṣka*

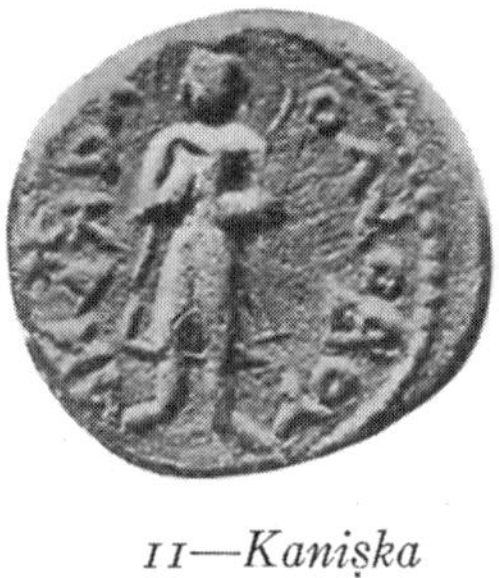

11—*Kaniṣka*

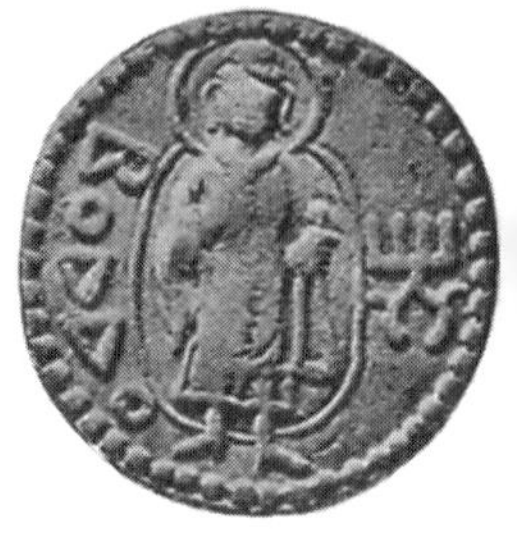

12—*Kaniṣka*

6–8, Supposed (by some) and 9-12, Actual Buddha Figures on Coins

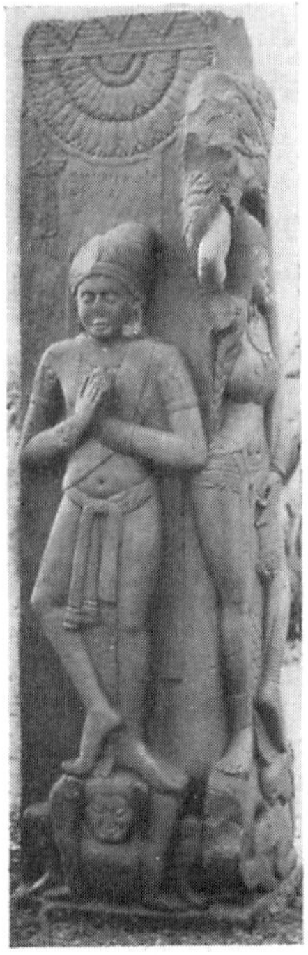

13—*Yakṣa* (*Bharhut*)

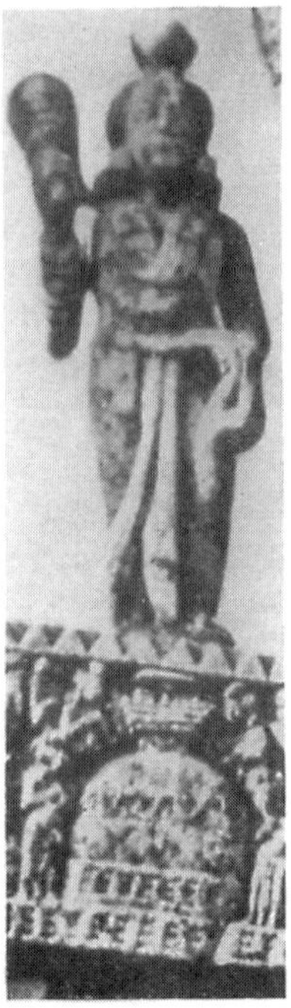

14—*Yakṣa* (*Sāñcī*)

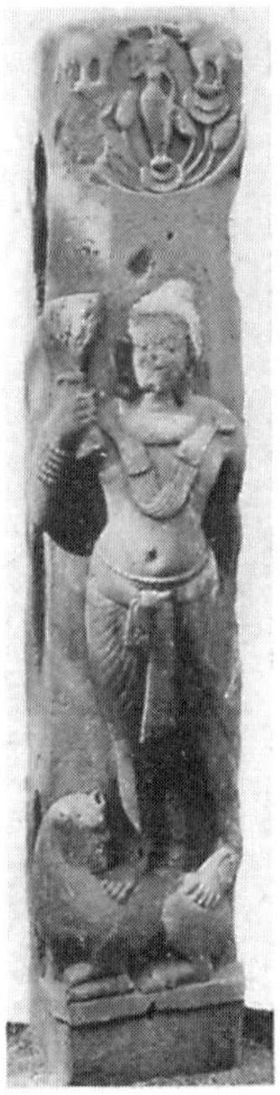

15—*Indra as Śānti* (*Bodhgayā*)

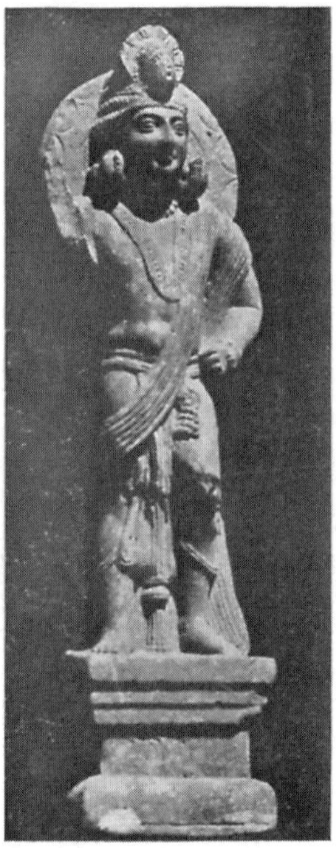

16—*Bodhisattva* (*Mathurā*)

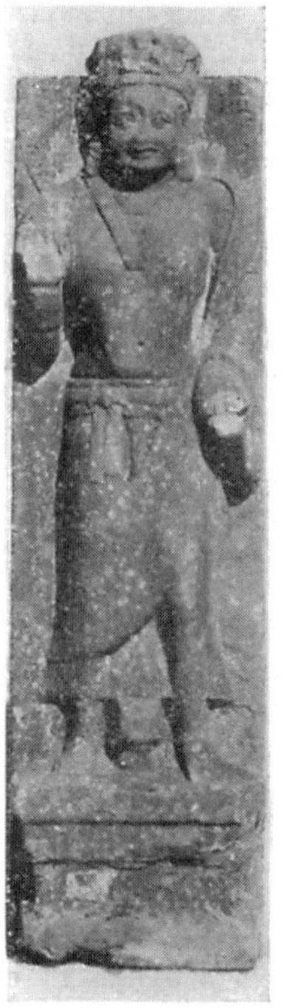

17—*Bodhisattva* (*Mathurā*)

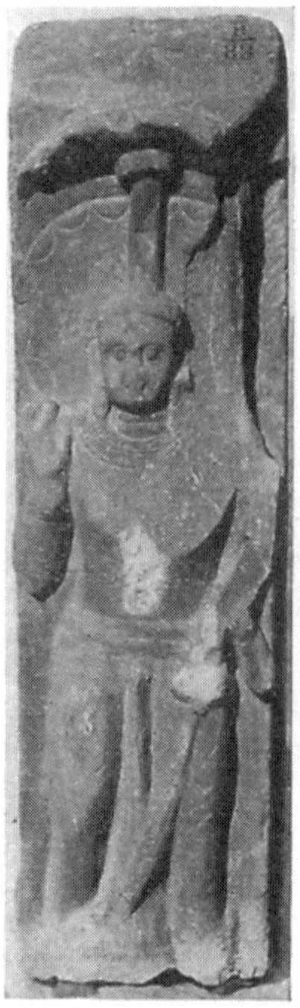

18—*Buddha* (*Mathurā*)

13-18, Yakṣas, Bodhisattvas, Buddha, etc.

complete artistic vocabulary and an iconography without icons. Of the symbols in use, those found on the punch-marked coins and early cast and struck coins include several hundred varieties; but some are much commoner than others.

Amongst these symbols, some of the commonest are the bull, *caitya-vṛkṣa* (railed sacred tree), mountain with one or several peaks (so-called *caitya* of numismatists), river, solar symbols (several varieties, all wheel-like), "*nandi-pada*" (circle surmounted by stemless trident), *triśūla* (trident part of the last without the circle), svastika, lotus, bow and arrow. I cannot here go into the evidence proving that neither the mountain nor the bow and arrow represent a stupa;[4] taking this for granted, it will be observed that none of these symbols, though most of them are used by Buddhists and Jainas in the early art, is in itself any more Buddhist or Jaina than it is Brahmanical, or simply Indian. The whole series constituted an assemblage of forms so explicit that, as the *Visuddhi Magga* informs us, an expert banker could tell from the marks at what place and mint the coin had been stamped. Each sign had a definite meaning, sometimes secular, sometimes sectarian.

M. Foucher has rightly observed that the beginnings of Buddhist art are characterized by the use of some of these symbols and one or two others; and that they were used to designate the presence of the Buddha in the story-telling reliefs of Bhārhut and Sāñcī, where no anthropomorphic representation of the Master can be found, that is to say, so far as the last incarnation is concerned. Thus in the long *Abhiniṣkramaṇa* scene (Fig. 19) Siddhārtha's presence on Kanthaka is indicated only by the royal umbrella borne beside

4. A much rarer symbol found on certain coins (e. g., Amoghabhūti, 100–150 B. C.) is commonly called a square stupa. Actually all that it represents is a railed umbrella (*chatra*) like those represented in relief at Gayā (Cunningham, *Mahābodhi*, pl. IX, fig. 14), and like the *harmikā* of the great stupa at Sārnāth, thus conceivably designating, though not representing, a stupa. A stupa would naturally be represented as a dome within and rising above a railing. Something of this kind is to be seen on certain Āndhra coins (Rapson, *Coins of the Andhra Dynasty*, pl. VIII, nos. 235, 236, etc.); but these suggest not the ordinary Buddhist stupa but the unusual type with a square railing and ovoid body seen in one relief at Amarāvatī (Fergusson, *Tree and Serpent Worship*, pl. LXXXVI) and one at Sāñcī, *ibid.*, pl. XXXII), both associated with bearded, apparently not Buddhist, ascetics. Regular stupas are first unmistakably represented on Gupta seals (Spooner, *Excavations at Basāṛh*, *A. S. I.*, *A. R.*, 1913–14, pl. XLVI, no. 159).

As regards the many-arched mountain, it may be remarked that this type is found on certain coins in unmistakably Hindu associations, e. g., on the coins of Svāmi Brahmaṇya Yaudheya, accompanying a six-headed Kārttikkeya, where a stupa would be meaningless. Apparently the interpretation of this type as a *caitya* (in the sense of stupa) has resulted from an *a priori* conviction that the coin symbols must be Buddhist, and secondly, from the necessity that was felt to find a prototype for the *parinirvāṇa* symbols of the reliefs. A comparative study of the abstract formulae used in Indian landscape compositions (e. g., the Maṇḍor stele, Govardhana-dhara composition, Bhandarkar, *Two Sculptures at Mandor*, *A. S. I.*, *A. R.*, 1905-06; or my *Rajput Painting*, pl. 2, or Petrucci's comment on this, *Burlington Maga ine*, V, 29, 1916), and likewise in early Western Asiatic and Eastern Mediterranean art would have indicated the true significance. It is quite probable that the "caitya" of three arches surmounted by a crescent represented Siva, "the three-peaked mountain being originally the god" (Hopkins, *Epic Mythology*, p. 220). Śiva is said to have been the tutelary deity of the Śākyas (*Ep. Ind.*, V, p. 3).

One further point: the word *caitya* (Pali, *cetiya*) ought not to be used as though it were synonymous with stupa, nor as a purely Buddhist term. In the Epics, *caitya* usually means a *caitya-vṛkṣa:* in the (mediaeval) *Prabandhacintāmaṇi*, always a temple. In Buddhist literature the reference is sometimes to sacred trees, sometimes to stupas; two sacred trees with their altars represented at Bharhut are described in the contemporary inscriptions as *cetiyas* (Cunningham, *Bharhut*, Pls. XLIII, 4 and XLVIII, 6). The *Yakkha cetiya* so often mentioned in Buddhist and Jaina literature are in some cases *caityavṛksas* with an altar, in others, temples with images. Any holystead is a *caitya*, notwithstanding that the word is said to be derived from a root *ci*, to build or pile up; cannot the word, perhaps, be connected with *cit*, and understood to mean an object to be meditated upon?

The proper designation of the "nandipada", also often miscalled *vardhamāna*, is unknown. These and other coin symbols will be discussed at greater length in a forthcoming number of the *Ostasiatische Zeitschrift.*

him; his sojourn in the wilderness is indicated by foot-prints (*pāduka*); and the First Meditation by the central railed *caitya-vṛkṣa*. Some of these symbols taken alone came to be used to designate the Four Great Events (afterwards eight) of the Buddha's life: I am rather doubtful of the nativity symbols, but certainly the Bodhi-tree (a similar *caitya-vṛkṣa*) designated the Enlightenment, the *Dharma-cakra* (Wheel), the First Sermon, and the stupa, the Parinirvāṇa. Further detail is immaterial for present purposes. It need only be remarked that M. Foucher assumes that the symbols were thus used by Buddhists in the first place upon *signacula*, little documents carried away by pilgrims visiting the sacred sites of the Four Great Events.[5] Presumably these would have been of terra cotta or metal; but no trace of such objects has ever been found, and such early terra cottas as are known in some abundance are, as indicated above, of a quite different sort. The point, however, is unnecessary to M. Foucher's argument, as in any case an abundance of symbols was available to be made use of by every sect according to its own needs; and that each actually did so is only another illustration of the general rule that styles of art, in India, are not sectarian. M. Foucher's statement of the theory is only misleading to the extent that he implies that there was anything especially Buddhist about the process. When however he goes on to say[6] that the sculptors of Bhārhut, Bodhgayā, and Sāñcī "*devaient se sentir terriblement gênés par cette incapacité ou cette interdiction d'introduire dans leurs compositions les plus compliquées l'image du héros principal*" he is only preparing the way for the later revelation from Gandhāra; as he has admitted elsewhere, there existed neither an incapacity (the same sculptors represented the Buddha freely as a human being in previous incarnations) nor an interdiction (for nothing of the kind can be found in Buddhist literature), and, as is readily apparent, the sculptor was by no means embarrassed, but in fact perfectly successful in telling his story.[7] It is hardly to be supposed that the meaning of these reliefs needed to be explained to contemporary Buddhists.

At this point an earlier than Gandhāra indebtedness of Indian art to that of Greece has been inferred in more than one connection. Della Setta, endorsed by Foucher, has pointed

5. *Beginnings of Buddhist Art*, p. 11.

6. *L'art gréco-bouddhique du Gandhara*, I, p. 612.

7. It may as well be observed here that the later representation of the Buddha figure in Indian art is not the same thing as the introduction of a naturalistic *style;* a new object, the human figure, is introduced where it had been absent, but this figure is treated in the traditional abstract manner. The only naturalistic *style* in question is that of Gandhāra. No phase of Indian art can be described as naturalistic in this sense; if we sometimes call the early style realistic, this only means that its theme is corporeal rather than spiritual.

The tendency to represent the human figure need not involve a naturalistic style: in Greek art the use of the figure and a naturalistic style are associated; in Indian art it is not the appearance, but the significance of objects, human or otherwise, that is sought for. In Greek art the emphasis is laid upon the object; in an abstract art it is not the object, but a concept that stands before us.

Every work of art is of course to some extent a compromise between the two points of view, naturalistic and abstract (or expressionistic); but what it is important to observe here is that the two extremes are contrasted, not in Indian Buddhist art before and after the introduction of the cult image (the Indian style remaining abstract throughout, whether it represents a sacred tree or a Buddha figure), but in Indian and Hellenistic art, respectively abstract and naturalistic. We are not here discussing questions of merit; as remarked by H. Frankfort in a clear definition of terms (*Studies in Early Pottery of the Near East*, I, London, 1924, p. 18): "The sense of beauty or aesthetic activity may equally well find expression in both ways." The only possibility of embarrassment is found when the artist for arbitrary reasons adopts one of these styles opposed to his innate idiosyncracy; Asiatic art under European influence in the nineteenth century affords many examples of such embarrassment. It is ridiculous to speak of embarrassment at Sāñcī, or to suppose that a decadent naturalistic art could have inspired a young and vigorous abstract art.

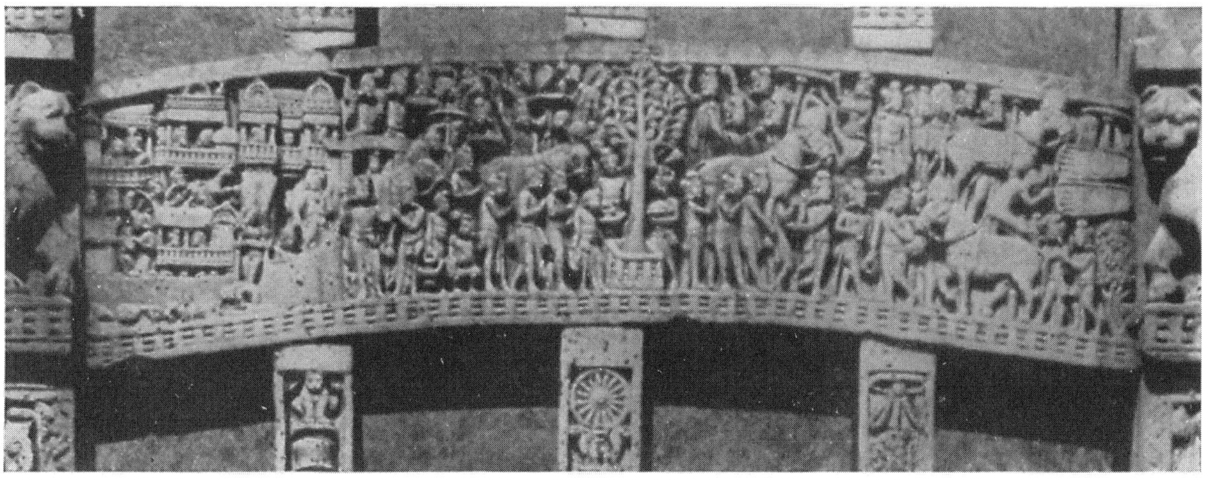

19—Abhiniṣkramaṇa (Great Renunciation) (Sāñcī)

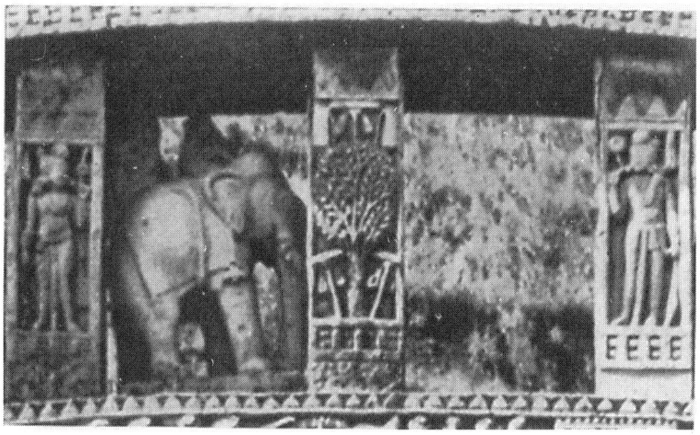

20—Buddha Triad (Sāñcī)

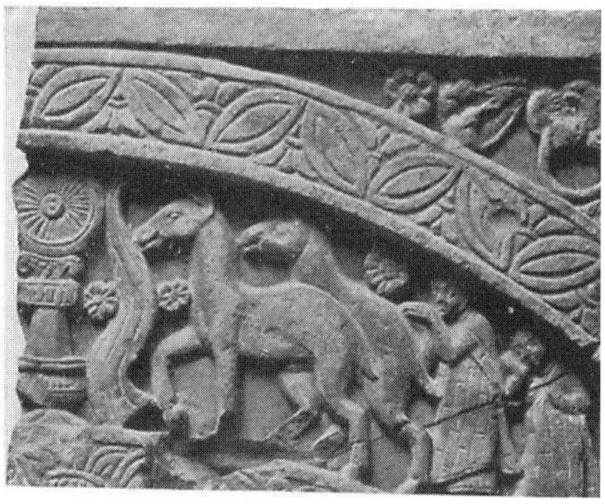

21—First Sermon (Mathurā)

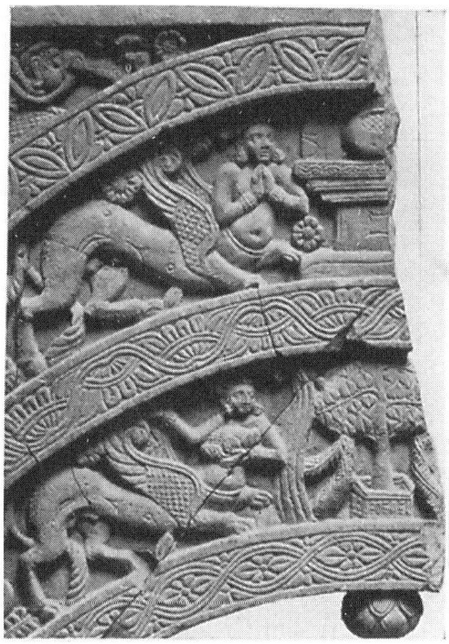

22—Bowl Relic and Great Enlightenment (Mathurā)

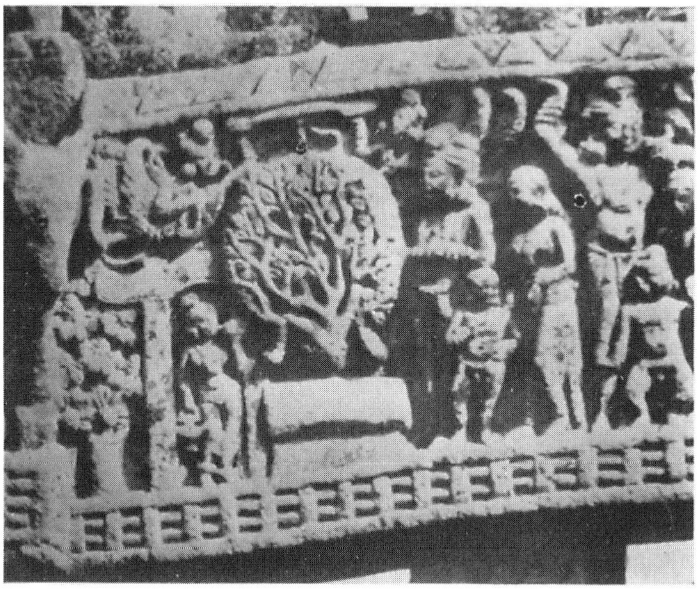

23—Sujātā's Offering (Sāñcī)

Aniconic Reprcsentations of the Buddha. Sāñcī and Mathurā

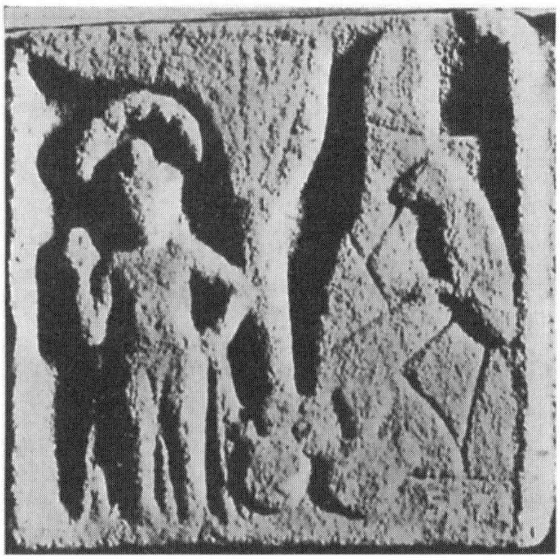

24—Nāga (Pāṭaliputra)

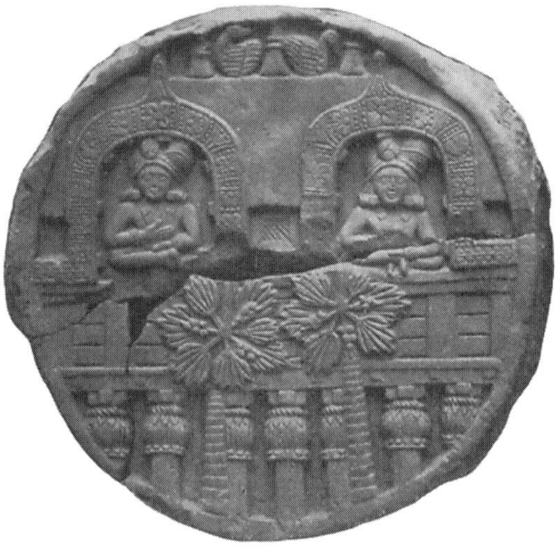

25—Seated Figures (Bharhut)

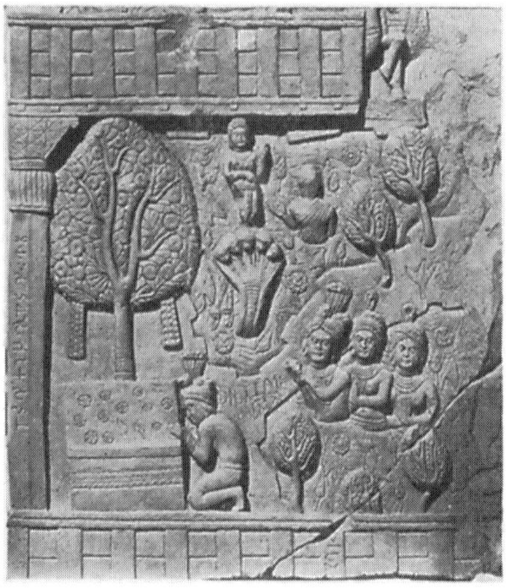

26—Nāga Erāpata Worshipping Buddha (Bharhut)

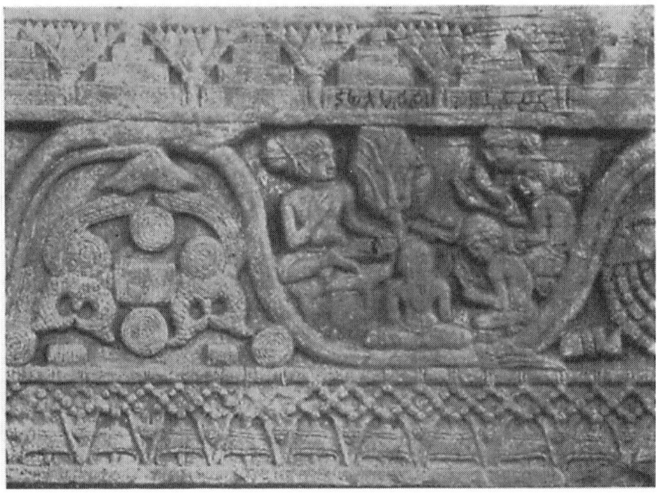

27—Teacher and Disciples (Bharhut)

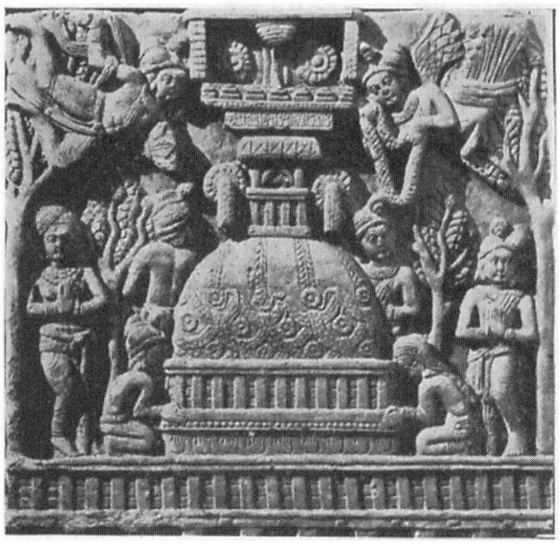

28—The Parinirvāṇa (Bharhut)

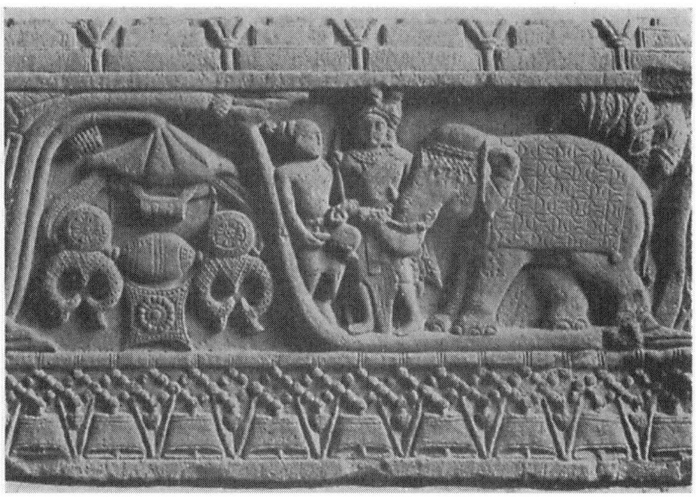

29—Vessantara Jātaka (Bharhut)

Aniconic Representations of Buddha; Early Nāga, Bodhisattva, etc.

out that the representation of three-quarters profile, and the use of continuous narration are illustrated somewhat earlier in Greece than in India. Strzygowski holds that the method of continuous narration was developed in the Hellenistic Near East. Marshall believes Western influences felt through Bactria may account for the artistic progress recognizable at Sāñcī; but, as recently observed by Rostovtzeff, "we know so little of Bactrian art that it is a mistake in method to explain '*ignotum per ignotius*'." It has not yet been suggested that inverted perspective and vertical projection are of Hellenistic origin (see Dalton, *East Christian Art*, p. 166). But a discussion of these points lies outside the scope of the present essay, as in any case these technical methods antedate Gandhāra.

Nor need anything further be said upon the subject of the symbolic language, except to remark that it remained in use, particularly at Amarāvatī, but also in Mathurā, for some time subsequent to the introduction of the anthropomorphic image.

For aniconic representations of Buddha referred to in this section see Figs. 19-23, 26, 28.

3. THE NECESSITY FOR A BUDDHA IMAGE

Inasmuch as neither the Upaniṣads nor Buddhism nor Jainism, considered in their original character as systems of thought, contemplated the worship (*pūjā*) of any personal deity, it may well be asked how it came to pass that Hinduism, Buddhism, and Jainism alike became "idolatrous" religions. The answer to this question was admirably expressed by Jacobi over forty years ago:[8] "I believe that this worship had nothing to do with original Buddhism or Jainism, that it did not originate with the monks, but with the lay community, when the people in general felt the want of a higher cult than that of their rude deities and demons, when the religious development of India found in Bhakti the supreme means of salvation. Therefore instead of seeing in the Buddhists the originals and in the Jainas the imitators, with regard to the erection of temples and worship of statues, we assume that both sects were, independently of each other, brought to adopt this practice by the perpetual and irresistible influence of the religious development of the people in India."

Bhakti, as is well known, means loving devotion, loyalty, attachment, service to one who is *Bhagavata*, worshipful, adorable, Lord, and he who feels such devotion and is devoted to any such being, is called *Bhāgavata* or *Bhaktā*. The conception comes into prominence together with, and is inseparably bound up with, the development of theistic cults in India, as these are with the making of images and the building of temples. Theistic elements are recognizable in the Upaniṣads; the development, as proved by the inscription of Heliodora, who calls himself a Bhāgavata, with reference to Viṣṇu, was already advanced in the second century B. C. Vaiṣṇava inscriptions, indeed, of the third or fourth century B. C. have been found at Nagarī (Madhyamikā) near Chitor. The most famous Bhakti scripture is the *Bhagavad Gītā* referred to above, a work that must have been composed before the beginning of the Christian era, and perhaps about the fourth century B. C. "Be assured, O son of Kunti," says Kṛṣṇa, "that none who is devoted to Me is lost." In the same way the Buddhist *Majjhima Nikāya* assures us that even those who have not yet entered the Paths "are sure of heaven if they have love and faith toward Me."

8. Jacobi, *Gaina Sūtras*, in *S. B. E.*, XXII, 1884, p. xxi.

Much discussion has been devoted to the question of the origin of Bhakti cults. Let us examine the usage of the word. Outside the field of religion revealed in Vedic literature there lay a world of popular beliefs including the worship of Yakṣas and Nāgas as tutelary divinities or *genii loci*, and of feminine divinities, powers of fertility.[9] Buddhist and Jaina texts contain many references to the cult or shrines of Yakṣas or Nāgas.[10] To what extent the *Yakkha-cetiya* (*Yakṣa caityas*) of Buddhist texts may have been actual temples, or merely "haunts" (*bhavana*) marked by the establishment of a throne, or rather altar, beneath a sacred tree or beside a lake need not concern us here. What does concern us here is the importance of these divinities, and the relation that existed between them and their worshippers. There is no reason to doubt the tradition preserved in the Tibetan *Dulva* that the Śākyas were accustomed to present all newborn children before the image of the Yakṣa Śākya-vardhana, evidently the tutelary deity of the clan.[11] Another Tibetan source relates that a gatekeeper of Vaiśāli, in the Buddha's lifetime, was reborn among the spirits, and requested the inhabitants of Vaiśāli to confer on him the status of a Yakṣa, in return for which he would warn them of any danger threatening them, "So they caused a Yakṣa statue to be prepared and hung a bell round its neck. Then they set it up in the gatehouse, and provided it with oblations and garlands along with dance and song to the sound of musical instruments."[12] In the *Mahābhārata*, a Yakṣiṇī is referred to as receiving a daily service and cult at Rājagṛha, and another Yakṣiṇī shrine was "world-renowned." The city of Nandivardhana in Magadha seems to have been called after the tutelary Yakṣas Nandi and Vardha.[13] Jaina and Buddhist traditions are in agreement as to the names of some of the Yakṣa *caityas*. The *Mahāvaṁsa*, Chapter X, describes the cult of Yakṣas in Ceylon. Yakṣas are usually gentle; sometimes they act as familiars or guardian angels of individuals.[14]

The Yakṣa Kuvera (Vaiśravaṇa, Vaiśramaṇa), who is closely associated with Śiva, and Regent of the North, thus one of the Four Great Kings, the Lokapālas, is a very powerful genius. But the term "Yakṣa" seems once to have implied something more than Kuvera or one of his attendants. *Yakṣattva* in the *Rāmāyaṇa* is spoken of as a valued boon; like immortality, it is bestowed by the gods when rightly propitiated.[15] This older and wider significance, as remarked by Kern,[16] is sometimes met with in Buddhist references to

9. Both Yakṣas and Nāgas are aboriginal, non-Aryan types. Macdonell's surmise (*Vedic Mythology*, p. 153) that the Aryans "doubtless found the cult (of Nāgas) extensively diffused among the natives when they spread over India, the land of serpents," has been curiously justified by the discovery of Nāga types on Indo-Sumerian seals (*A. S. I.*, *A. R.*, 1924-5, p. 61). See also Vogel, *Indian Serpent Lore*, and my article on Yakṣas to appear as a Smithsonian publication in 1928.

10. *Yakkha-Saṁyutta* of the *Saṁyutta Nikāya*, X, 4, Other references in Chanda, *Four Ancient Yakṣa Statues*. in *University of Calcutta, Journ. Dep. Letters*, IV, 1921 (pp. 5, 34-36 of the reprint).

11. Rockhill, *Life of the Buddha*, p. 17. The episode is twice represented at Amarāvatī (Fergusson, *Tree and Serpent Worship*, pls. LXIX and XCI, 4).

12. Schiefner, *Tibetan Tales from the Kah-gyur*, trans. Ralston, p. 81.

13. O. C. Gangoly, in *Modern Review*, Oct., 1919; and Chanda, *op. cit.*, with reference to a statement in the *Mahāmayurī*.

14. Hopkins, *Epic mythology*, p. 57; Foucher, *L'art gréco-bouddhique du Gandhara*, II, p. 40 ff. It is precisely the rôle of guardian angel that some Yakṣas play in relation to Buddhas and Jinas, in relation to Buddha, particularly the Yakṣa Vajrapāṇi.

15. *Rāmāyaṇa*, III, 11, 94; Hopkins, *op. cit.*, p. 67.

16. *Manual of Indian Buddhism*, p. 59. Foucher, *op. cit.*, insists on the cruel nature of Yakṣas as referred to in Buddhist texts; but this is usually where some story of miraculous conversion is related, and may well be designed to emphasize the marvel. That *ugra* Yakṣa types also existed need not be denied; but the familiar example of Kālī or of Śiva himself would show how little this need have interfered with their existence as objects of a Bhakti cult.

The subject of Yakṣas will be treated at some length in a Smithsonian publication in 1928. See also the admirable summary under *Yakkha* in Rhys Davids and Stede, *Pali Dictionary*.

Yakṣas; Indra, for example, may be called a Yakṣa, and even the Buddha is glorified by Upāla in the *Majjhima Nikāya* as an *āhuneyyo yakkho utamapuggalo atulo.*

Many references to Nāga cults are scattered through the Buddhist texts. The Chinese pilgrims constantly refer to monasteries and stupas occupying sites originally haunted by Nāgas. Hsüan Tsang informs us that Nālandā was originally the name of a Nāga "and the monastery built by the side of a pool is therefore called after his name."[17]

The significance for us of these cults so widely diffused and so popular in ancient India will be apparent when, in the first place, we observe that the nature of the worship offered was in many respects similar to that offered in a Buddhist temple, including particularly the erection of statues and the offering of flowers, garlands, incense, and music; in the second place that Buddhism, like other religions in similar circumstances, constantly inherited the prestige of sites already sacred, as at Bodhgayā and Nālandā; and finally, and most important, that the designation *Bhagavata* is applied not alone to Vāsudeva (Viṣṇu),[18] to Śiva[19] and to Buddha,[20] but also to the Four Great Kings, the Mahārājas, Regents of the Quarters,[21] of whom some are Yakṣas and some Nāgas, and also to various Yakṣas and Nāgas specifically.[22]

Buddhism exhibited no hostility to these popular cults: the Buddha indeed expressly exhorts the Licchavi-Vajjis to continue "to honour and esteem and revere and support the Vajjian cetiyas in the city or outside it, and allow not proper offerings and rites as formerly given and performed to fall into desuetude," and so long as this were done, "so long may the Licchavi-Vajjis be expected not to decline but to prosper."[23]

Historically, the Bhāgavata cults of Yakṣas and Nāgas must have yielded only gradually and peacefully to the Bhāgavata cults of Viṣṇu and Buddha; the cult of Nāgas and Yakṣas, indeed, is still widely prevalent, and though I do not know that the term Bhagavata is still employed, the lower classes throughout India still worship innumerable local godlings of this character, and it is significant that the priesthood of the temples of such godlings is always non-Brāhman.[24] Officially, these cults were replaced by the "higher"

17. Beal, *Life of Hiuen Tsang*, p. 110; *Buddhist Records of the Western World*, pp. 63ff., 123, 149ff., 200.

18. Pāṇini, IV, 3, 98; inscription of Heliodora at Besnagar, proclaiming himself a Bhāgavata (D. R. Bhandarkar, *Excavations at Besnagar*, in *A. S. I., A. R.*, 1913-14 and 1914-15; R. G. Bhandarkar, *Vaiṣṇavism, Śaivism, and Minor Religious Systems*, p. 5; R. P. Chanda, *Archæology and Vaishnava Tradition*, in *Mem. A. S. I.*, 1920).

19. Patañjali mentions Śiva bhāgavatas (*in re* Pāṇini, V, 2, 76): Śiva is called Bhagavat in the *Atharvaśiras Upaniṣad*. Cf. *Mahābhārata*, XII, 18, 65: "Even after committing all crimes, men by mental worship of Śiva are freed from all sin" with *Bhagavad Gītā*, ix, 30.

20. E. g., *Bhagavato Saka Munino* at Bhārhut, also the Piprahwā vase inscription.

21. Pāṇini, IV, 3, 97, speaks of Bhakti directed to Mahārājas (not in a political sense as interpreted by Jayaswal, but with reference to the Four Great Kings, see Bhusari in *Ann. Bhandarkar Inst.*, VIII, 1926, p. 199); also in *Mahābhārata*, VIII, 45, 31, but here the Regent of the North is Soma (Hopkins, *Vedic Mythology*, p. 149).

22. Kubera, in *Mahābhārata*, V, 192, 42 ff. (Hopkins, *Epic Mythology*, p. 145); Māṇibhadra, image and inscription from Pawāyā where his worshippers, the *goṣṭha* or corporation (guild) who installed the image, describe themselves as Māṇibhadra-bhaktā (M. B. Garde, *The Site of Padumāvatī*, in *A. S. I., A. R.*, 1914-15, pt. I; Chanda, *op. cit.*); the Nāga Dadhikarṇa, Mathurā inscription, Lüders list, no. 85; Nāgas in the Mathurā Museum, Vogel, *Catalogue*, Nos. C 13 and C 21.

23. *Anguttara Nikāya*. It need hardly be pointed out again that *caitya, cetiya*, signifies any kind of holystead such as a sacred tree, grove, or temple, not necessarily a stupa.

24. For these cults at the present day see Hutchinson and Vogel, *History of Basohli State*, in *Journ. Panjab Hist. Soc.*, IV, 2, 1916, p. 118; S. C. Mitra, *On the Worship of the Pipal Tree in North Bihar*, in *J. B. O. R. S.*, VI, 1920, p. 572, and *The Village Deities of North Bengal*, in *Hindustan Review*, Feb., 1922; Callaway, *Yakkun Nattanawā . . . Ceylon System of Demonology . . .*, London, 1829; R. B. Whitehead, *The Village Gods of Southern India*, London and Calcutta, 1916; Fergusson, *Tree and Serpent Worship*, p. 258; Longhurst, *Tree and Serpent Worship in Southern India*, in *A. S. I., A. R., Southern Circle*, 1914-15; R. E. Enthoven, *Bombay Folklore*, 1924; E. Upham, *History and Doctrine of Buddhism*, 1829.

faiths, Vaiṣṇava, Śaiva, Bauddha, and Jaina; but even officially the Nāgas and Yakṣas were not dismissed, as the gods of ancient Ireland were dismissed by the Christian monks, but represented as worshippers or guardians of the Buddha or Jina. Nor could the "higher religions," when from systems of pure thought and of monastic discipline they developed into popular faiths, have succeeded in securing the adhesion of the mass of the people had they not both tolerated and reflected popular beliefs. Iconolatry, ritual,[25] devotion, profound preoccupations of the popular Indian non-Aryan consciousness, made of Buddhism, Jainism, and Hinduism what they are, and that is something other than they were in their intellectual inception. The sculptures themselves (Figs. 26, 28) bear witness to the power of the spirit of devotion.

If we are to believe the *Nidānakathā*, Sujātā mistook the Bodhisattva for the sylvan deity for whom her offering of milk-rice had been originally intended (Fig. 23); the story proves at least that Buddhists conceived that such a mistake might very naturally have been made. Later on, to simple folk, statues of Yakṣas and Buddhas, both associated with trees, both legitimately spoken of as Bhagavata, "The Lord," both worshipped with flowers, garlands, and incense, must have looked very much alike.[26] Nor can we altogether ignore the fact that figures of a Buddha or Jina protected by a many-headed Nāga, whose hoods form a canopy above their heads, bear, no less than certain Vaiṣṇava types (Balarāma, and Viṣṇu Anantaśayana), a striking resemblance to an actual Nāga, as represented in the early sculptures—having a human body, but with serpent hoods rising from a point on the back behind the shoulders. We shall presently recognize a sculptural type which represents equally well a *padmapāṇi* Yakṣa and a Bodhisattva Padmapāṇi.

We have traced above, in popular Indian religion, sources of theism, image worship, and devotion, as we find them appearing in orthodox Brāhmanism and Buddhism toward the beginning of the Christian era, in Buddhism as tendencies that point toward the Mahāyāna. When we realize in this way how naturally the demand for a Buddha image must have arisen, and how readily available were suitable types,[27] we may be less inclined to jump to the conclusion that the cult image of the Tathāgata was of extra-Indian origin. That such had really been the case we could only believe, against all *a priori* probabilities, if in fact the earliest Indian Buddha figures, instead of perpetuating the plastic tradition and repeating the iconographic formulae of the old Indian school, had really resembled Hellenistic prototypes. Even the most ardent advocates of the Greek theory cannot claim so

25. It is interesting to recall in passing the close parallels that exist between Buddhist (and Hindu) and Christian ritual, such as the use of lights, incense, bells, rosaries, tonsure, formal gestures, and music. These cult elements probably found their way into the Christian office through Alexandria and Coptic monasticism during the first few centuries of the Christian era (cf. Garbe, *Indien und Christentum;* and H. Berstl, *Indo-koptische Kunst*, pp. 180, 188, in *Jahrb. as. Kunst*, 1924). Thus the pagan elements surviving in Christian practice may be traced back to a remote pre-Buddhist and non-Aryan Indian antiquity; and the problems here discussed are found to possess an interest not exclusively Indian, but bound up with the general history of religion and art. On *bhakti* and *pūjā* see de La Vallée Poussin, *Indo-Européens et Indo-Iraniens: l'Inde jusque vers 300 av. J. C.*, 1924, pp. 314 ff., and Charpentier, *Über den Begriff und die Etymologie von pūjā* in *Festgabe Hermann Jacobi*, 1926.

26. Apparently one of the *caityas* of Vaiśālī was a banyan tree which was the abode of a Yakṣa by name Gotama. Remembering that in early Buddhism the Bodhi-tree is generally spoken of as a banyan (though always represented in art as *Ficus religiosa*) it will be seen that in this particular case a transference of significance from a Bhagavata Yakṣa Gotama to the Bhagavata Gautama Śākya-muni would have been especially easy. See Chanda, *Mediaeval Sculpture in Eastern India*, in *Calcutta Univ. Journal, Dept. Letters*, III, 1920, pp. 232 f.

27. See the next section.

much as this; nor would it be possible to put forward such a claim with Friar Bala's Bodhisattva and the Kaṭrā and Aṇyor Mathurā Buddhas before our eyes.

4. ELEMENTS OF THE LATER ANTHROPOMORPHIC ICONOGRAPHY ALREADY PRESENT IN EARLY INDIAN ART

Actual remains and literary evidences abundantly prove that images of divinities and of human beings, both in relief and in the round, existed already in the third and second centuries B. C., and it is very possible that similar figures in precious metal or impermanent materials had been made at a still earlier date. Even in specifically Buddhist art we find the Bodhisattva freely represented in human form in Jātaka illustrations, side by side with the purely symbolic indications of Gautama as Bodhisattva (Siddhārtha) or as Buddha (Tathāgata).[28] Craftsmen capable of producing the Pārkham and Patna images, and the reliefs at Bhārhut and Sāñcī would have had no difficulty in representing Gautama in human form had they been required to do so.

India had long associated the attainment of higher stations of consciousness and the perception of ultimate truths with the practice of disciplined meditation, and had long been familiar with ascetic teachers. When a Buddha image was required, he would naturally be represented either as an adept or as a teacher; conceptions that immediately connote, in the one case the cross-legged seance,[29] hands at rest in the lap, and abstracted gaze directed toward the tip of the nose, in the other, the same seance, but with the right hand raised, the left resting on the hip, and a more active demeanor. The practice of yoga is older, of course, than Buddhism or Jainism and neither of these religions did more than adopt and adapt the existing technique of contemplation. A beautiful description of the seated yogī will be found in the *Bhagavad Gītā*, VI, 10-21; condensed as follows:

"Abiding alone in a secret place, without craving and without possessions, with thought and self controlled, he shall take his seat upon a firm seat, neither over-high nor over-low making the mind single-pointed, with the working of the intellect and senses held in check, with body, head and neck maintained in perfect equipoise, looking not round about him, so let him meditate, and thereby reach the peace of the Uttermost Abyss; and the likeness of one such, who knows the boundless joy that lies beyond the senses and is grasped by intuition, and who is free from longing for all desirable things, is that of a lamp in a windless place, that does not flicker."

A briefer description will be found in the canonical Buddhist *Dīgha Nikāya*, sutta 22:

"And how, O monks, does a monk live, observant of the body?

"Whereas, O monks, a monk, retiring to the forest, or to the foot of a tree, or to some other uninhabited spot, sits him down cross-legged, with body erect and contemplative faculty intent . . . training himself to be conscious of all his expirations and inspirations."

28. The figure of the Bodhisattva, Siddhārtha, is *not* represented in certain reliefs which have been regarded as illustrating the Approach to the Bodhi-tree, at Bodhgayā and Sāñcī (Cunningham, *Mahābodhi*, pl. VIII, fig. 4, as interpreted by Bloch, *Notes on Bodh-Gayā*, in *A. S. I., A. R.*, 1908-09; Maisey, *Sanchi*, pl. XVI; and Fergusson, *Tree and Serpent Worship*, pl. XXXIII).

29. Cf. *Bhagavad Gītā*, VI, 10-21, describing the firm and easy (*sthira-sukha*) seance of the yogi. I use the word *seance* to translate *āsana* in the sense of a mode of sitting, as I use *stance* to translate *sthānam*.

No new effort on the part of the sculptor was needed for the realization of these types, which appear already at Bhārhut, once in a relief of uncertain significance (Fig. 25) and once in a composition representing Digha instructing his disciples (Fig. 27).[30] Seated figures which have in fact been identified as Buddha are also found on coins of Maues (c. 100 B. C.) and Kadapha (Kadphises I, c. 40-78 A. D.).[31] In both coins we find the cross-legged seance. In the case of the Maues coin (Fig. 6) the two hands are folded in the lap; but there is a horizontal bar extended to the right which may be a sword or scepter, or possibly the back edge of a throne or seat. In the case of the Kadapha coins (Fig. 8), of which there are two closely related varieties, the right hand is raised, holding some hammer-like object, perhaps a scepter, the left hand rests on the thigh, and the elbow is extended, while the breadth of the shoulders and slenderness of the waist are conspicuous. It seems to me that these personages represent a king, and not a Buddha. The Kadapha type, however, apart from the object held in the hand, is exactly that of the early Mathurā Buddhas (Figs. 34-39) and of figures of kings or perhaps Bodhisattvas, and of Buddha, at Amarāvatī. The characteristic and vigorous gesture of the palm or clenched fist resting on the thigh is rarely met with in later art, but survives, for example, in certain mediaeval Bodhisattva types (Fig. 65) and is often used by Javanese actors at the present day.

More convincing than any of the types above referred to are the seated figures found on early Ujjain coins. One of these (Fig. 9) can hardly be anything but a Buddha, as it represents, to quote Cunningham's words, a "figure squatting in the native fashion beside a holy tree surrounded by a railing," and, moreover, squatting on a lotus seat. This is perhaps the earliest male figure so represented as seated upon an expanded lotus. However we cannot exactly date these coins; they can hardly be earlier than the first century A. D.[32] The type, however, is precisely that which appears on Kaniṣka's seated Buddha coins (Fig. 10), with the identifying designation.

As regards the physical peculiarities of the Buddha type, we find the *uṣṇīṣa* represented in the Indian fashion as a rounded cranial protuberance already in the case of the relief representing Indra as Śānti on one of the Bodhgayā railing pillars, dateable about 100 B. C.[33] Buddha-like heads with an *uṣṇīṣa*-like protuberance, and many short curls, are

30. Also in the unpublished relief from Bharhut, a scene from the *Vessantara Jātaka*, in which the Brahman Jujaka is seen seated cross-legged in his leaf hut. Berstl, *Indo-koptische Kunst*, in *Jahrb. as. Kunst*, I, 1924, has traced the westward migration of the "yogi-*motif*" about and somewhat before the beginning of the Christian era. He inferred its early occurrence in Indian sculpture but does not seem to have known the Bharhut examples above referred to. As a matter of fact, the *motif* has since been found on Indo-Sumerian seals probably to be dated well before 2000 B. C. (*A. S. I.*, *A. R.*, 1924-5, p. 61).

31. Maues: Longworth Dames, in *J. R. A. S.*, 1914, p. 793, calls it Buddha; Whitehead, *Cat. Coins in the Panjab Museum, Lahore*, p. 102 and pl. X, 31, calls it a king; Vincent Smith, *Cat. Coins in the Indian Museum, Calcutta*, p. 40 and pl. VIII, 4, calls it a deity or king; Gardner, *Cat. Coins in the British Museum, Greek and Scythian Kings of Bactria and India*, p. 71 and pl. XVII, 5, calls it a king with a sword on his knees. The similar but better preserved type on a coin of Azes, Gardner, *op. cit.*, pl. XVII, and *A. S. I.*, *A. R.*, 1912-13, pl. XL, 18, shows that the latter description should be correct.

Kadapha: Whitehead, *op. cit.*, pp. 181, 182 and references there cited; Marshall, *Excavations at Taxila*, in *A. S. I.*, *A. R.*, 1913-14, p. 44 and pl. XL, 53, 1914-15, p. 33 and pl. XXIX, 38, and 1915-16, p. 34 and pl. XXV, 18, 19. Both call it a seated Buddha, but cf. the coin of Huviṣka, seated king, crossed legs, with attributes in both hands, Vincent Smith, *Numismatic Notes, I*, in *J. B. A. S.*, 1897, fig. iv, also the Gandhāra sculpture in *A. S. I.*, *A. R.*, 1914-15, pl. X, 18.

32. Cunningham, *Coins of Ancient India*, p. 97 and pl. X, 7, 8, 10.

33. L. Bachofer, *Ein Pfeiler-Figur aus Bodh-Gaya*, *Jahrb. as. Kunst*, II, 1925; Sir J. H. Marshall, *J. R. A. S.*, 1908, p. 1096 and pl. IV. Stella Kramrisch describes this figure as psychologically a Buddha prototype (*Grundzüge der indischen Kunst*, p. 83). In general appearance it is nearer to the standing Bodhisattva types.

* (but these belong to the Gupta series)

represented on several of the Bodhgayā railing medallions.* There is, indeed, a prominence very suggestive of an *uṣṇīṣa* to be seen on the head of the Nāga figure on the Pāṭaliputra railing (Fig. 24). I cannot recall any pre-Kuṣāna sculpture in which an *ūrṇā* is represented, nor any earlier example of even a Buddha with webbed fingers than the Māṅkuwāṛ image (448/9 A. D., Fig. 61). In the representation of the hair in many curls, which does not appear until after the middle of the second century A. D., it is evident that literary tradition has been followed. It has been suggested, and is quite possible, that the webbed fingers represent what was at first a technical device, intended to avoid breakage.

Turning now to the standing figure in early Indian art, we find its chief iconographic peculiarities are the symmetrical stance, with well-separated feet, the raising of the right hand usually in the *abhaya* position,[34] and the placing of the left hand upon the thigh either clenched, or holding the folds of the robe. Later the left hand is generally somewhat raised, but still grasps the drapery. Unfortunately, the arms of the oldest Indian figures, the Pārkham (Fig. 2) and Patna (Fig. 3) Yakṣas[35] are missing. But the characteristic attitude of the early standing Buddhas is well seen in the case of a panel relief on one of the railing crossbars found by Waddell[36] at Pāṭaliputra (Fig. 24), representing a Nāga beside a tree; see also Fig. 47. In later, that is to say pre-Kuṣāna and early Kuṣāna sculpture the pose is so usual that we may fairly regard it as typical; Yakṣas, Nāgas, and goddesses are alike represented in this way. Sometimes the left hand rests simply on the hip (*kaṭyavalambita hasta*), sometimes it seems to grasp the drapery, sometimes, particularly in the case of the Bacchanalian Yakṣa and Nāga types (Fig. 49), it holds a flask suggesting the *amṛta* flask of Maitreya.

34. Regarding this *mudrā*, or *hasta*, which is the only one except the *añjali* common in early Indian art, it should be observed (1) that the hand is sometimes *vyāvṛtta*, sometimes *parivṛtta*, the latter position being usual in the later art, and (2) this hand serves apparently to indicate several meanings which are later more carefully differentiated. The various meanings of the *patāka* hand in dancing include removing fear, graciousness, benediction, taking an oath, addressing an audience, closing a dispute, and any of these are appropriate to the early usage; other meanings, such as "wave" require a *movement* of the hand (cf. *Mirror of Gesture*, p. 27). The treatment of gesture in Bharata's *Nāṭya Śāstra*, which may date back to the second century B. C., implies a long established tradition; for gesture language (which is one of the sixty-four *kalās*, accomplishments) in everyday life, see *Jātaka*, No. 546 (Cowell's translation, p. 182), where the "hands" employed seem to have been *śikhara* and *patāka*.

As regards the clenched fist (*muṣṭi*) of Mathurā types, I have not observed this in earlier Indian, or in Gandhāra types; the most suitable meaning given in *abhinaya* books is that of "steadiness." The energy of the gesture is enhanced by the holding of the elbows away from the waist; the arm thus held akimbo is characteristic of early Indian types, is found sparingly in mediaeval works (Fig. 65), and survives in the Javanese theater, while it is not seen in Gandhāra.

35. The equally ancient archaic Yakṣa at Deoriyā, Allahābād (Fig. 47) has the left hand on the hip; and this was almost certainly the same in the case of the ~~Besnagar~~ Pārkham figure (Fig. 2).

For present purposes it is unnecessary to enter upon the controversy as to whether these figures represent pre-Mauryan kings, or represent Yakṣas, of Maurya and Śuṅga date. I now agree with Chanda (*Four Ancient Yakṣa Statues*, Calcutta, 1921) and others in taking the latter view. It is not disputed that these are the oldest known examples of Indian stone sculpture in the round (recent Indo-Sumerian discoveries aside), and represent the true "primitives" of an original and indigenous style.

36. L. A. Waddell, *Report on the Excavations at Pataliputra*, Calcutta, 1903, pl. 1. Other early examples are found on coins, e. g., Dhara Ghoṣa, Audumbara, Cunningham, *Coins of Ancient India*, pl. IV, 1; early Taxila, *ibid.*, pl. II, 14; early Kosāmbi, *ibid.*, pl. V, 15. Credit is due to Waddell, who, although a subscriber to the Greek theory and ardent admirer of Gandhāra art, remarked that "Buddhism . . . manifestly took the preëxisting images of the Brahmanist gods such as we see on the Bhārhut stupa as their models" (*Evolution of the Buddhist Cult, its Gods, Images and Art*, in *Imp. and As. Qtly. Review*, Jan., 1912); and equally to Laufer (*Das Citralakṣaṇa*, p. 18): "*Wenn die Buddhisten das ganze brahmanische Göttersystem adoptiert haben, dann ist auch die grösste Wahrscheinlichkeit vorhanden, dass sie die Ikonographie dieser empfangen haben; es ist undenkbar, dass sie die künstlerische Gestaltung selbst erfunden haben sollten.*"

The phylogeny of the standing Bodhisattva types is even clearer, because here the secular costume is retained, whereas in the Buddha figures we expect, and generally find, a monastic costume without jewelry. Starting with Yakṣa prototypes, the Bodhisattvas seem to have been developed in two directions, that of the independent figures, and that of the figures associated with the Buddha in a triad. Yakṣas as guardians, attendants, and worshippers in early Buddhist art are represented with a flower, or as *caurī*-bearers, or with folded hands; and these types appear as members of a triad long before the central figure is anthropomorphically represented. Thus, if we look at the Sāñcī north *toraṇa*, outer face, we find on the topmost architrave in the center a *Dharma-cakra* (Wheel), that is to say, the Buddha turning the Wheel of the Law, in other words preaching the first sermon at Benares; and on either side, though one is now missing, a *caurī*-bearing Yakṣa (Fig. 14). It may be noted the left hand grasps the folds of the drapery—a feature very characteristic of Buddha figures. Again, between the lowest and second architraves we see three uprights (Fig. 20), in the center a Bodhi-tree, representing the Buddha on the occasion of the Great Enlightenment, and on either side a Yakṣa holding a rose lotus. The *caurī*-bearing type persists long after the anthropomorphic image appears (Figs. 34, 35, 60) but is later on replaced by differentiated Bodhisattva types holding attributes. If however we consider the lotus-bearing type just referred to and illustrated in Figure 20, we are immediately struck by the fact that there is only one way in which they can be described, from an iconographic point of view, namely as *padmapāṇi*, that is to say, "having a rose lotus in the hand." I do not mean to assert that these figures already represent the Bodhisattva Padmapāṇi, though that may be possible; I do mean to say that when it became necessary to present this Bodhisattva to the eye, the type lay ready to hand. It may well be that the very conception of a Bodhisattva Padmapāṇi was suggested by the existence of *padmapāṇi* Yakṣas. A parallel case is that of the Yakṣa Vajrapāṇi (Figs. 35, 40), originally the Buddha's faithful attendant, later the Bodhisattva Vajrapāṇi (Fig. 65). Incidentally, this Yakṣa and Bodhisattva Vajrapāṇi should not be confused with Indra, to whom the epithet *vajrapāṇi* also applies, but who never became a Bodhisattva. Regarding the generally similar aspect of Bodhisattvas and Yakṣas little more need be said, except to remark that the resemblance of type is such that in more than one instance modern students have mistaken ancient Yakṣa figures for Bodhisattvas.[37] As regards a resemblance in function, it need scarcely be pointed out that Bodhisattvas, like Yakṣas, are frequently worshipped, not for the sake of enlightenment, but as guardians and protectors from earthly ills.[38]

In the case of Jaina iconography, the sequence is even clearer; only here there are no Bodhisattvas, and the *caurī*-bearing attendants remain to the last as attendants, well known to be Yakṣas. It is noteworthy that some of these Jaina Yakṣas, attendant on Jinas, bear the names of Hindu deities, such as Brahmā, who are not, from the usual Hindu point of view, Yakṣas at all.[39] We are reminded here of the iconographic descent of the Hindu deities, which like the Buddhist divinities are derived from a limited early

37. Cf. Diez, *Die Kunst Indiens*, fig. 131; H. P. Sastri, in *J. B. O. R. S.*, 1919, p. 552.

38. References to Yakṣas as guardian or familiar spirits will be found in Foucher, *L'art gréco-bouddhique du Gandhara*, II, 47; in the *Prabandhacintāmaṇi* of Merutunga, Tawney's translation, p. 203 (there is a corresponding passage in the *Kathākośa*; and *Mahāvaṁsa*, ch. X).

39. Glasenapp, *Der Jainismus*, pp. 361, 362. J. Burgess, *Digambara Jaina Iconography*, in *Indian Antiquary*, *XXXII*, 1903.

stock of types in which the Yakṣa, or king formula predominates; the two types are essentially similar—Yakṣas are by no means always represented as pot-bellied. It may indeed have been objected that some of the worshipping figures associated with symbols of Buddha in early Buddhist art are not really Yakṣas, but kings; this may be true, but only illustrates the fact that the early conception of a divine personage is based upon that of an ideal ruler (Cakravartin). This being the case, indeed, it is the less surprising that the similarity of Bodhisattva and royal types should have persisted throughout the later development; this only accords with the view, moreover, that on the one hand, kings are earthly divinities, while on the other hand divinities by their very nature are persons who exercise dominion (*aiśvarya*) over a more or less extended domain in accordance with their special functions. The phylogeny of Hindu iconography, however, lies outside the scope of the present article; I may point out merely in passing the close relation existing between such early Śiva types as that of the Guḍimallam *liṅgam* and such early Yakṣa types as those of Bhārhut and Sāñcī.

The origin of the Buddhist and Hindu feminine divinities, can be only briefly referred to. If we do not meet with them very early under their Buddhist and Hindu names, that is not to say that they were not known in the same forms but under other names at an earlier date. Forms like those of Tārā or Devī in their simplest *sāttvik* aspect, representing beautiful deep-bosomed women whose only attribute is a lotus flower held in the hand are iconographically indistinguishable from the proto-Lakṣmī so often represented in reliefs of Sāñcī and Bhārhut, on coins, for example those of Amoghabhūti and of Azes, and by early terra cottas. India forms no exception to the general rule that in all religious development it is the natural human tendency to continue the worship of the ancient forms, and even in the ancient manner, accepting at first tacitly and then as a matter of course the newer interpretations and terminology. It may well be, indeed, that the image of Tārā, as Dr. Barnett has suggested,[40] goes back to the time when Anahita, whether known by that or by some other name, was worshipped alike in Western Asia and Indo-Sumerian India.[41]

The Buddhas of Mathurā and Gandhāra are both nimbate; in the former the nimbus is simply scalloped at the edge, in the latter it is plain. That the Mathurā Buddhas are nimbate is regarded by Foucher and others as a distinctive mark of Greek influence, inasmuch as both a nimbus and rays are found in Greek art of the Alexandrian period.[42] In the first place it may be remarked that the nimbus or rays must have originated in some classic area of sun-worship, and may be older than the known Greek examples.[43] In India it

40. *J. R. A. S.*, 1926, p. 765.

41. It is true that another goddess of prosperity, Ardochṣo, to use her name as it appears on early coins, enters into the body of Indian iconography; this is probably a Hellenistic form, a western Fortune, and with her characteristic cornucopia, she can be followed far into the mediaeval imagery. But how small a part this form, to be identified by the un-Indian cornucopia, plays beside the innumerable feminine divinities, Buddhist or Hindu, who hold in their hand a lotus flower, the *līlā-kamala* of Indian poetry! As we have already remarked, it is far from our object to deny the existence of any foreign element whatever in Indian iconography; we wish only that the matter should be apprehended with a due sense of proportion.

For the early Indian terra cottas see Museum of Fine Arts *Bulletin*, No. 152, and a fuller account to appear in *Ipek*, 1928, also *A. S. I.*, *A. R.*, 1924-5, pls. XXII, XXVII.

42. Foucher, *L'art gréco-bouddhique du Gandhara*, I, p. 42.

43. So also the thunderbolt of Zeus is older than the earliest known Greek representations (Jacobsthal, *Der Blitz in der orientalischen und griechischen Kunst*, Berlin, 1906). In such cases it is simpler to regard the Indian occurrences as belonging to the common Indo-Western-Asiatic inheritance than as late borrowings; more especially

cf. Sundisk behind altar, Assyrian relief of King Natu-apla-iddina (King, Boundary stones in the B.M. Pl. XCVIII) ✓

occurs on coins of Maues, c. 100 B. C., and so even if of western origin need not have any specific bearing on the Gandhāra question. But it would have been a most natural development within the Indian tradition. In Vedic ritual a golden disc was placed on the fire altar to represent the sun; it may well be that in other cases such a disk was placed behind the altar, at any rate this would naturally tend to be so in the case of smaller altars bearing cult objects. Radiance is a quality associated with all the Devas, and we might expect that when an anthropomorphic image took its place upon the altar, once empty or occupied by a symbol, the disc would remain—just as the Bodhi-tree remains behind the Vajrāsana when the visible Buddha takes his place upon it. At any rate we do in fact find representations of altars bearing symbols (the bowl relic, Fig. 22), having behind them just such a hemisphere as we might expect, with the usual scallop edge of the Kuṣāna nimbus; a similar half-disc appears (with rays) behind a seated Sūrya type (D 46 in the Mathurā Museum) of the Kuṣāna period (Fig. 44). It seems to me very likely that we have before us a direct traditional continuity. In any case, the nimbus cannot be regarded as an argument of much weight in the Gandhāra question. As I have constantly repeated and as cannot be too often repeated, the only real argument would consist in showing that the earliest Indian Buddha figures, whatever their date, resemble Gandhāra types and are not in the iconographic or stylistic tradition of the older indigenous works.

A rather constant distinction of Gandhāra from Mathurā Buddha figures appears in the form of the throne, which in Gandhāra is usually a lotus, in Mathurā, a *siṁhāsana*, that is to say, a rectangular pedestal supported by lions. The exact significance of this difference is hard to explain. It may be remarked that the Gandhāra lotus is somewhat un-Indian in that it is represented not as a broad expanded surface, but rather suggesting a prickly artichoke, as if the Indian conception of a firm and easy seance, had been somewhat misunderstood. If the Gandhāra sculptors depended wholly or partly on a literary tradition, perhaps the distinction arose in connection with the double meaning of the word *padmāsana*, which signifies both the lotus seance and the lotus seat. In India proper the sculptor would have been better aware that the Buddha could be represented in *padmāsana* (lotus seance) without necessarily being seated upon a lotus. That the Indian sculptors followed a tradition in which the lion had importance, no doubt in connection with the conception of the Tathāgata as Śākyasiṁha, the Lion of the Śākyas, is also shown by the fact that in some standing figures, for example Friar Bala's Bodhisattva, a lion is represented seated between the rather widely separated feet of the Master.

In Gandhāra Bodhisattvas, the turban, when represented, is usually of a typically Indian, Kuṣāna, form. When, as in Figures 17 and 32 we find in this headdress a Dhyāni

when we have also early literary references to the form (*Atharva Veda*, XI, 10, 3) where the *trisaṁdhi*, the three-pointed bolt of Indra, is deified (Bloomfield, *Artharva Veda* . . . p. 75). For the earliest Indian representation of a *vajra* (Maurya or Śuṅga) see *A. S. I.*, *A. R.*, 1911-12, p. 93 and pl. XXXII, 5. As regards the innumerable *motifs* such as winged lions common to Indian and Western Asiatic art, it is not only (as Fergusson long ago perceived, *Tree and Serpent Worship*, p. 132) "not clear that the Indian form may not be of an original stock as old or older than the Assyrian," but very probable that this is so, the *motifs* being cognates rather than late borrowings.

The oldest nimbus with which I am acquainted appears as a circle with flaming rays surrounding the flying deity Asur on an enameled faience from Assur now in the British Museum and dating from the ninth century B. C. (W. Andrae, *Farbige Keramik aus Assur*, Berlin, 1923, p. 13 and pl. 8). It is interesting to observe on the same plaque a representation of clouds and raindrops according to a formula later traceable in Central Asia and in India (see my *Catalogue of Indian Collections*, Boston, part V, nos. CLVIII and CCCXCIVb, pp. 120, 201).

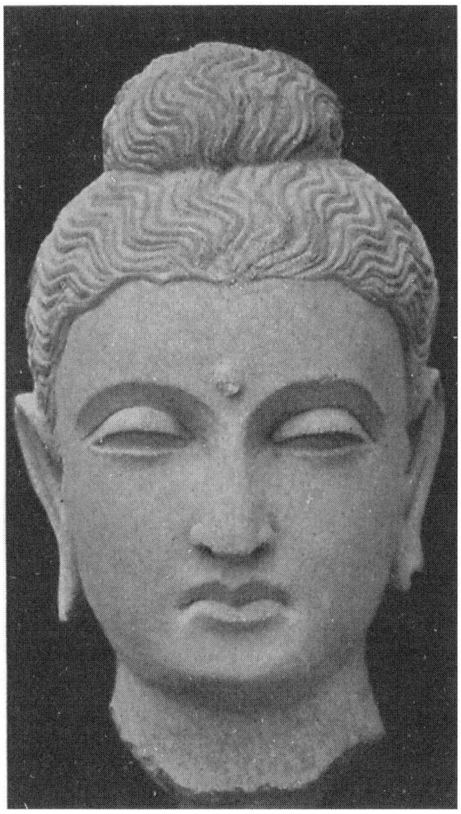

30—Buddha

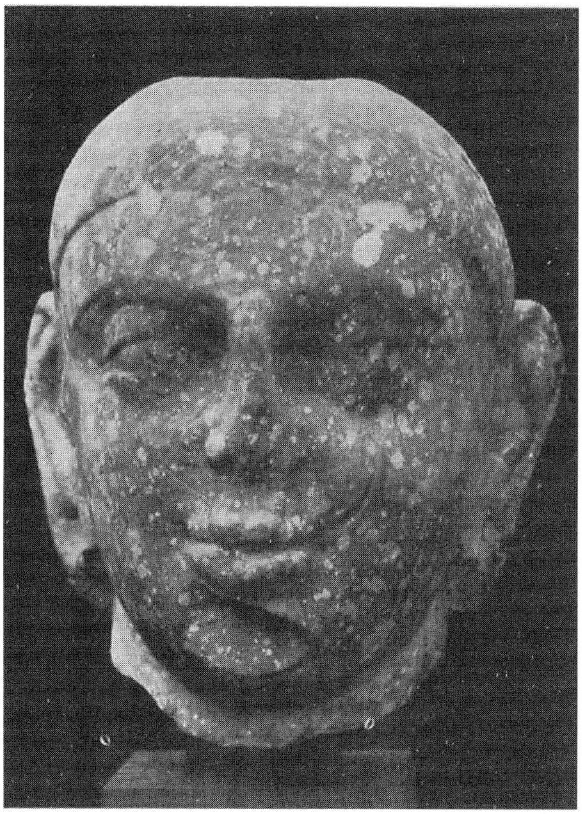

31—Buddha

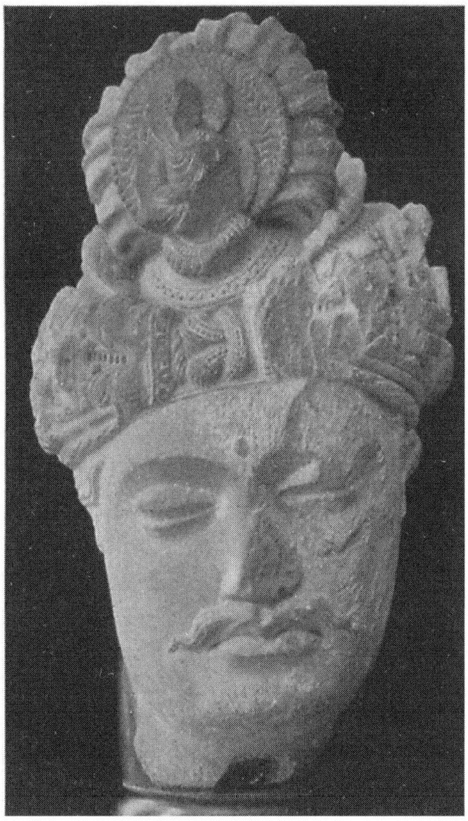

32—Bodhisattva

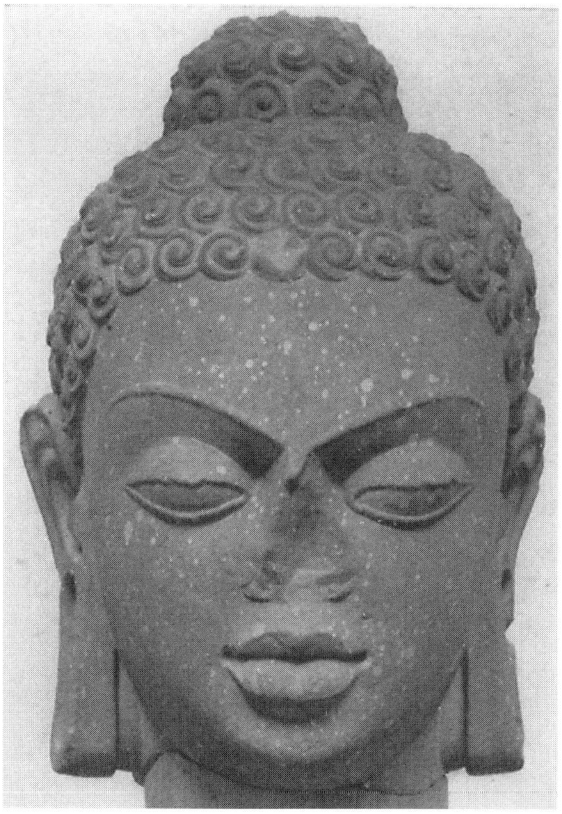

33—Buddha

30, 32, Buddha and Bodhisattva Types, Gandhāra; 31, 33, Mathurā

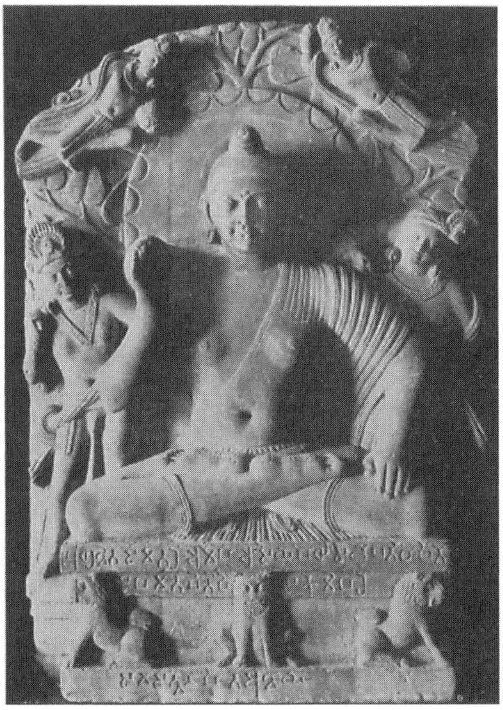

34—"Bodhisattva" (Buddha) with two Attendants; Lion Throne

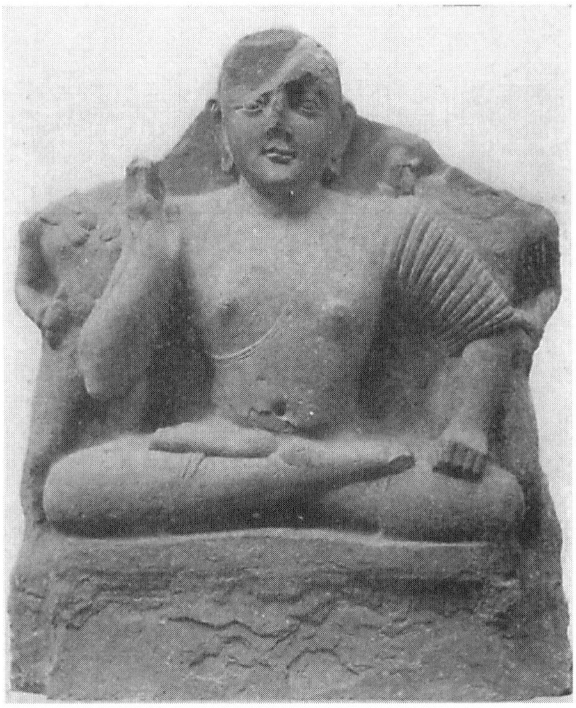

35—Buddha with two Attendants (Yakṣa Vajrapāṇi on Proper Right)

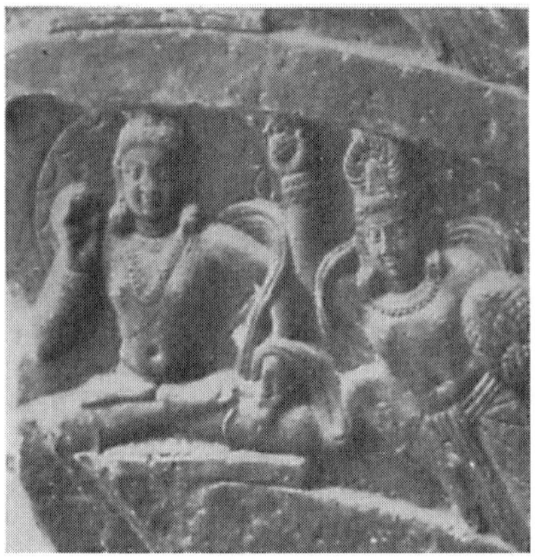

36—Bodhisattva Maitreya

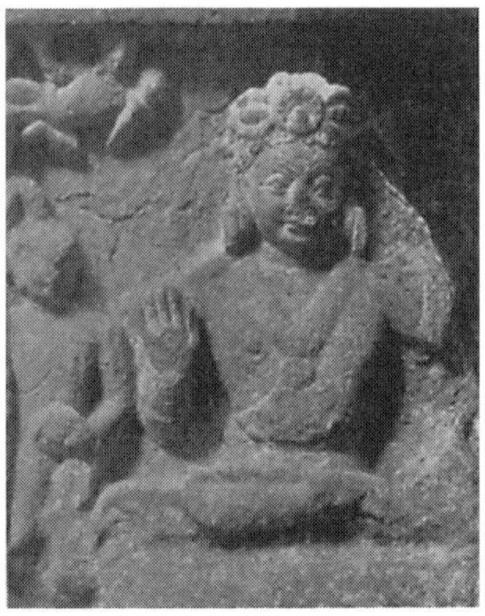

37—Buddha (?) with Turban

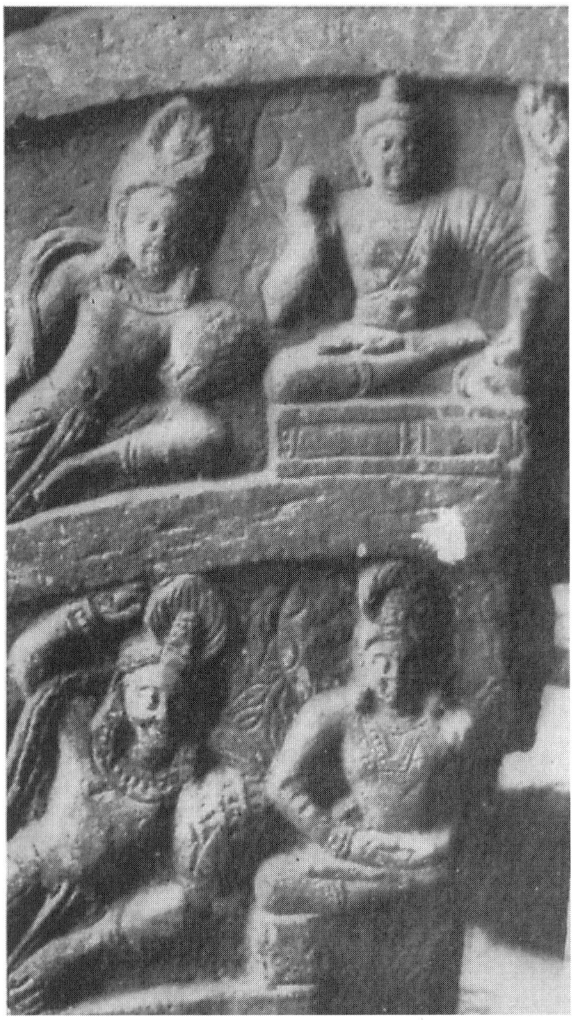

38—Buddha Teaching, and Great Enlightenment

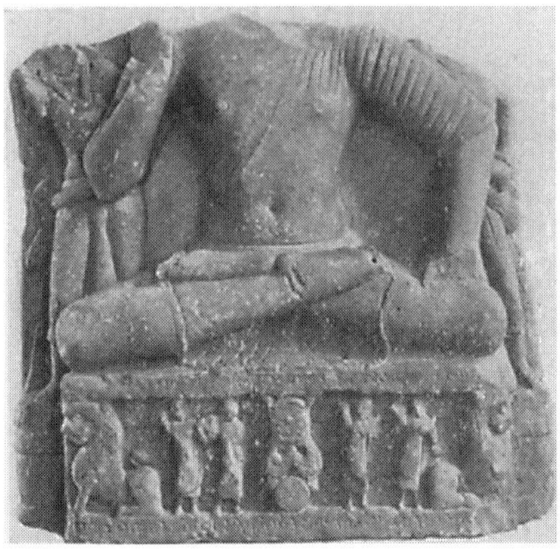

39—Buddha with two Attendants

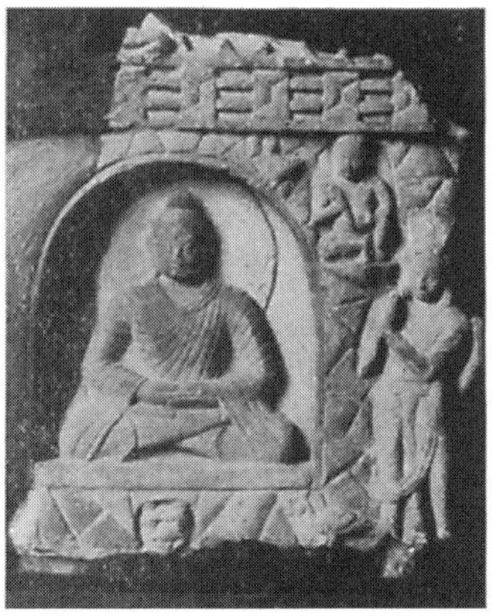

40—Visit of Indra; Yakṣa Vajrapāṇi above

Early Mathurā Seated Buddha Type

Buddha represented, in Mathurā works in an Indian manner and in Gandhāra works in the Hellenistic tradition, it seems most natural to assume that the Indian type is original. Incidentally it may be remarked that the occurrence of this formula in the Kuṣāna period is one of the earliest plastic evidences available of an already advanced stage in the development of Mahāyāna theology. Be it observed that it is not inconceivable that such a small Buddha figure had been actually worn by Indian Buddhist kings, who might have wished to be regarded as Bodhisattvas, just as Kadphises II using the title of Maheśvara suggests that he is an incarnation of Śiva; at a much later period such a Buddha figure was certainly worn in the headdress by the Sinhalese king Vimala Dharma Sūrya.[44]

Another cycle of the same kind is represented by the *līlā kamala* or *līlābja*, lotus of dalliance, held in the hand by divinities and by kings and queens from the time of the earliest reliefs up to the present day; whether this lotus had originally a precise symbolic significance, or, as the *Mahāpadāna Sutta* expresses it, was simply "dear to and beloved of all," we can hardly say.[45]

Great differences are found too in the treatment of the hair. In Gandhāra the hair is generally thick and undulating (Fig. 30) and the *uṣṇīṣa* is either covered by the hair or replaced by a kind of chignon. In Mathurā, however, both Buddha and Jina images are represented at first with a spiral protuberance (Fig. 34) which is a lock of hair and not an *uṣṇīṣa*; later the whole head and hair are covered with small short curls, and this type after the second century becomes the almost universal rule, the only example (Fig. 61)

44. Reproduced in Rouffaer and Juynboll, *Indische Batikkunst*, and in my *Mediaeval Sinhalese Art*, pl. xxii.

45. In early Indian art the lotus is held in the hand, is used as a seat or pedestal, is represented in medallions, and in the full-vase (*puṇṇa-ghaṭa, bhadda-ghaṭa*) *motif*, and constantly employed in the decorative borders. Foucher is undoubtedly right in regarding the lotus when treated *per se* as of symbolic significance, and as designating the feminine divinity who holds the lotus in her hand and is sometimes accompanied by elephants who pour down waters upon her from jars held in their trunks. This type, exactly corresponding to the later Lakṣmī and Gaja-Lakṣmī, when met with in Buddhist art, Foucher describes as Māyā-Devī; and this goddess, or the lotus alone, he regards as designating the nativity of the Buddha. The type, however, is equally a favorite one in early Jaina art; it appears on early votive terra cottas, and on coins which we have no special reason to regard as Buddhist. Perhaps the most fully realized type is that of the pillar from the Jamālpur mound, Mathurā, now B 89 in the Lucknow Museum (Cunningham, *A. S. W. I., Reports*, I, or my *History of Indian and Indonesian Art*, fig. 74); here we have the full-vase *motif*, with masses of lotus flowers rising from it, and the goddess standing on one of the flowers amongst the others. This proto-Lakṣmī *may* have designated the nativity in some special instances, but we have no evidence that such was the case: Māyā-Devī when unmistakably represented in the later nativities belongs to the dryad (*vṛkṣakā*) type. What we may well be sure of is that fundamentally the goddess of the lotus is a figure of Abundance, drawn from the warm and living imagery of popular cults. Like the dryads and many of the railing figures, the aspect of fertility is emphasized. When the elephants are present, these are surely the life-giving monsoon clouds. And the rose lotus, which Foucher recognized as her particular symbol, is at once an emblem of the waters and of abundance.

In old Jaina texts the Gaja-Lakṣmī composition is always described as the lustration (*abhiṣekha*) of Fortune (Śrī).

The significance of the lotus seat and pedestal must be another than this. It will not be overlooked that Brahmā in the Epics is called *abjaja*, lotus-born, and *kamalāsana*, seated on a lotus. In the *Śatapatha Brāhmaṇa* (VII, 4, 1, 8 and X, 5, 2, 6) the lotus plant is said to represent the (cosmic) waters, and the earth is a lotus leaf floating on the waters. Here the idea of divine and miraculous birth is present. In later works the mysterious purity of the lotus, which springs from the mud and is yet so fair, and whose leaves though they rest on the water are not wetted by it, is often referred to. Also, it is characteristic of the gods that they do not touch the earth; the lotus flowers that rise beneath their feet and which, even in seated images, are, as it were, their footstool designate this peculiarity.

In the later cosmologies both macrocosm and microcosm are in various ways compared to a lotus, and it is possible that some conception of this kind is present when a lotus is seen in the hand of a deity; the *līlā-kamala*, lotus of dalliance, a toy as it were in human hands, is likewise the cosmic scene of the divine *līlā*.

Finally, it can hardly be doubted that at the time we are speaking of the history of decorative art was already so ancient that the lotus may well have been extensively used simply as a familiar design, without special or conscious significance.

of the smooth head dating from the Gupta period being the Māṅkuwāṛ image, 448/9 A. D. In Gandhāra, as the process of Indianization of the type proceeds, the flowing locks are restricted and by gradual transitions come to conform to the Indian curly formula. Both types, the early single spiral (Fig. 34) and the later multiplicity of short curls seem to reflect, though in different ways, the tradition of the *Nidānakathā* that when the Bodhisattva shore his locks, his hair "was reduced to two inches in length, and curling from the right, lay close to his head, and so remained as long as he lived."

The occurrence of Jaina types, practically identical with the Buddha types, except for the absence of the robe, is noteworthy. It is generally assumed, and must be assumed, when the Hellenistic theory is adopted, that the Jaina types are derived from Buddhist ones. But such little (palaeographic) evidence as is available tends to show that the Jaina type as found on *āyāgapaṭas* (votive slabs) (Figs. 41, 42) are somewhat older than any dated Buddha figures. Laufer[46] has suggested with some plausibility that Jainas preceded the Buddhists in the adoption of an iconolatrous cult.

It is a rather mysterious fact that though the Jainas, like the Buddhists, were well established in Taxila in the Scytho-Parthian period, as architectural remains prove, not a single example of Graeco-Jain sculpture appears either then or at any subsequent period.

A few sculptures that may be called Graeco-Hindu are known, but these belong to the later period (third century) when Gandhāra art is much Indianized. The most interesting of these figures is a three-headed Maheśa (so-called Trimūrti) from Chārsada,[47] comparable to the three-headed Śiva with the bull on one of the coin types of Vāsudeva.[48] This Maheśa type can be traced across Central Asia (possibly in the sense of a Lokeśvara) and to China and Japan.[49] In the same way a Buddha type of Mathurā origin can be followed through Turkestan to China.[50]

The Buddha and Jina (Fig. 43) type of a seated or standing figure, sheltered by the expanded hoods of a polycephalous Nāga, and the similar Hindu type (Viṣṇu-Anantaśayin—but not always reclining, there being a fine seated example in the Vaiṣṇava Cave at Bādāmī) present a common interest. Here in the same way it would be usual to derive the Hindu from the Buddhist type; but the converse is more probable. At any rate the *Mahābhārata* story of Rāja Adi in which the sleeping Droṇa is found sheltered by a serpent's hoods is older than any possible Buddha figure. From this story is derived the place name Ahichatra, "serpent-umbrella," and, as Cunningham suggests, the Buddhists probably took over the idea from the Hindus.[51] There is a close resemblance between

46. Laufer, *Das Citralakṣaṇa*, p. 18.

47. Natesa Aiyar, *Trimurti Image in the Peshawar Museum*, in *A. S. I.*, *A. R.*, 1913-14.

48. R. B. Whitehead, *Catalogue of the Coins in the Panjab Museum*, pl. XX, 11; Gardner, *Coins of the Greek and Scythic Kings . . .*, pl. XXIX, 10; another good specimen is in Boston.

49. Stein, *Ancient Khotan*, pl. LX; Chavannes, *Mission archéologique dans la Chine septentrionale*, pl. 224; and appearing in Japan as Dai Itoku.

50. Foucher, *L'art gréco-bouddhique du Gandhara*, fig. 563; Stein, *Ancient Khotan*, pl. LXXXII; Sirén, *Chinese Sculpture*, pp. xxxvii f. (the affinity of style of a great number of Chinese sculptures from the end of the fifth to the beginning of the following century "is so evident and uniform that it hardly needs to be pointed out in detail," and if this is ignored by Foucher, it is because he "made it his task to trace the influence of Gandhāra in as many places as possible"), xli, lxvi, and pls. 116, 117, also *Documents d'art chinois*, pls. XLIX, LIV, LVI (Indian treatment of the hair).

51. *A. S. W. I.*, *Reports*, I, pp. 255, 256. Ahichatra is one of the places where a stupa, traditionally of Aśoka, was erected by the side of a Nāga tank (Beal, *Buddhist Records of the Western World*, p. 200).

It may be added that, as is well known, modern standing figures consisting of a human figure with serpent hoods rising from the back between the shoulders, are known as Baldeo (Balarāma); but Balarāma in the *Mahābhārata* is identified with Śeṣa Nāga, and is described as having his head wreathed with snakes (Hopkins, *Epic Mythology*, p. 212). It is possible therefore that the iconography is ancient, and not the result of a modern confusion of types.

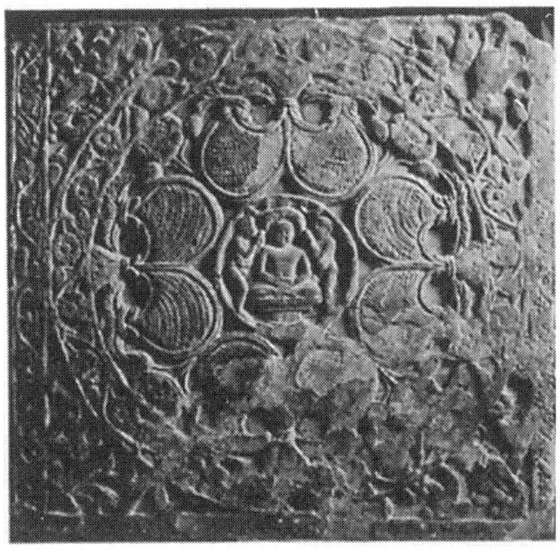

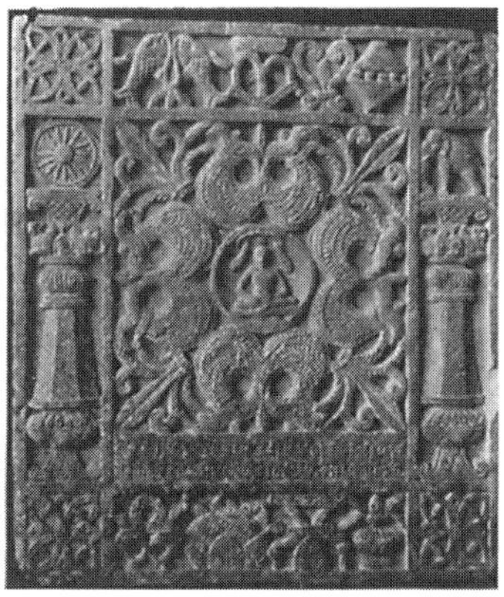

41 42

Two Ayāgapaṭas with Seated Jinas in the Centers (Mathurā)

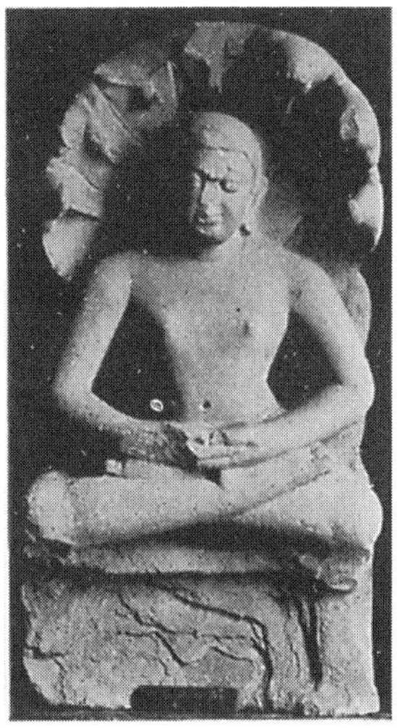

43—*Pārśvanātha (Mathurā)*

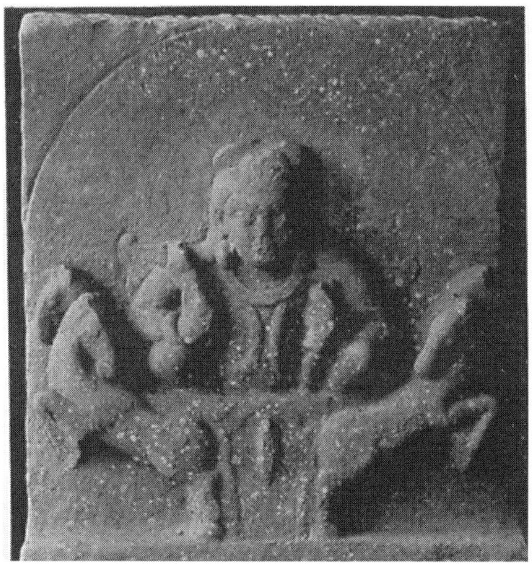

44—*Sūrya (Mathurā)*

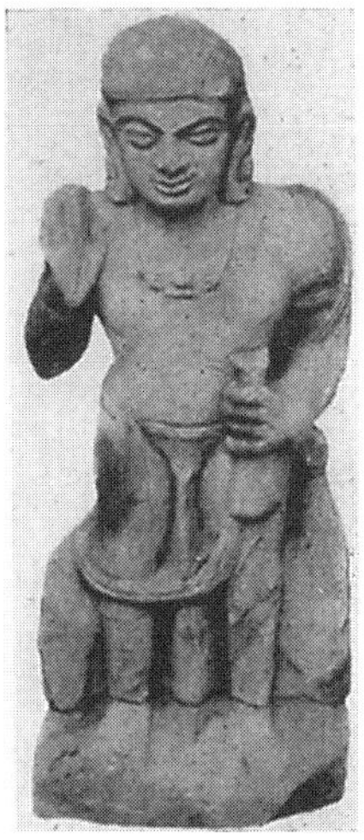

45—*Yakṣa with Purse (Mathurā)*

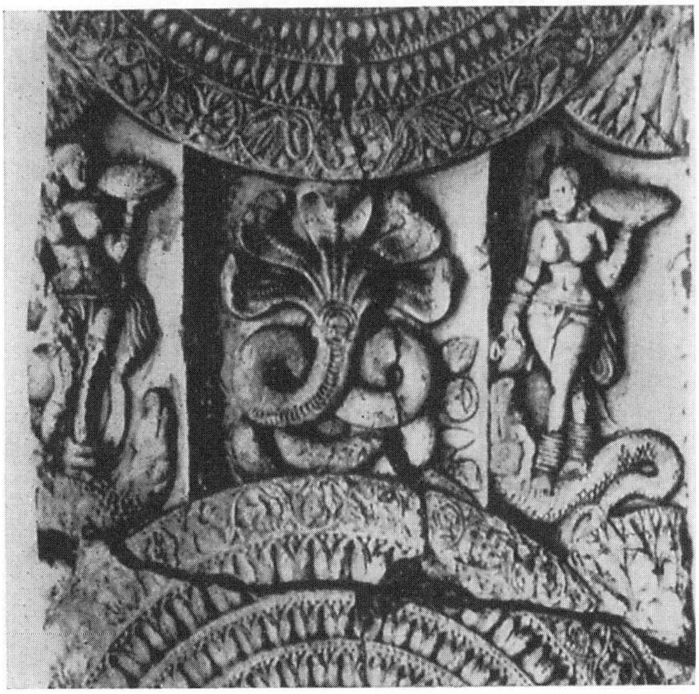

46—*Nāga with Attendants (Amarāvatī)*

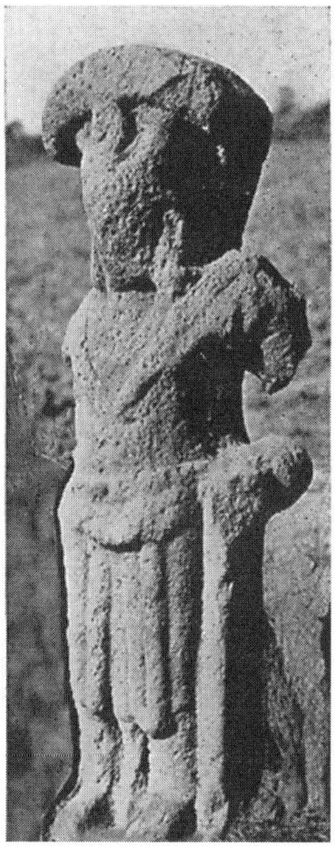

47—*Yakṣa (Deoriyā)*

Early Jina Types, Yakṣas, etc.

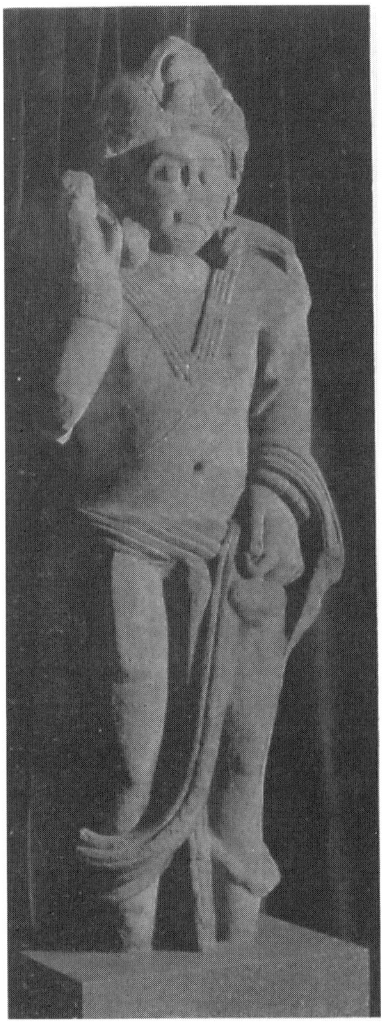

48—Bodhisattva Maitreya (Mathurā)

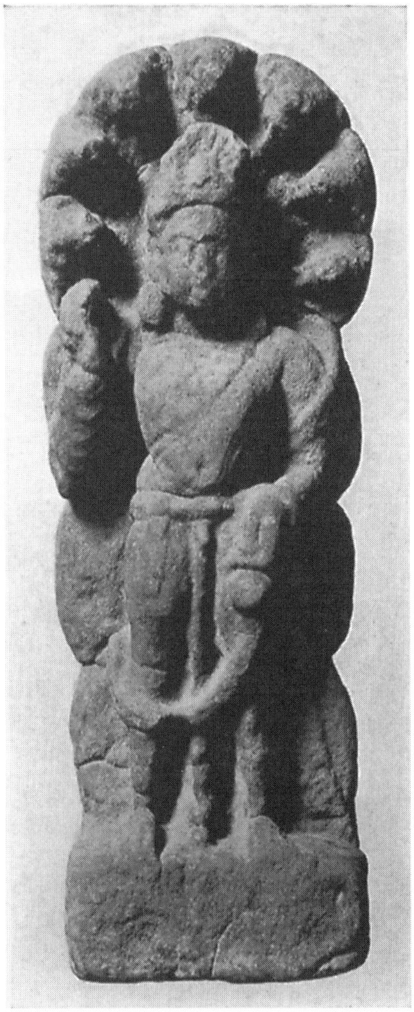

49—Nāga with Flask (Mathurā)

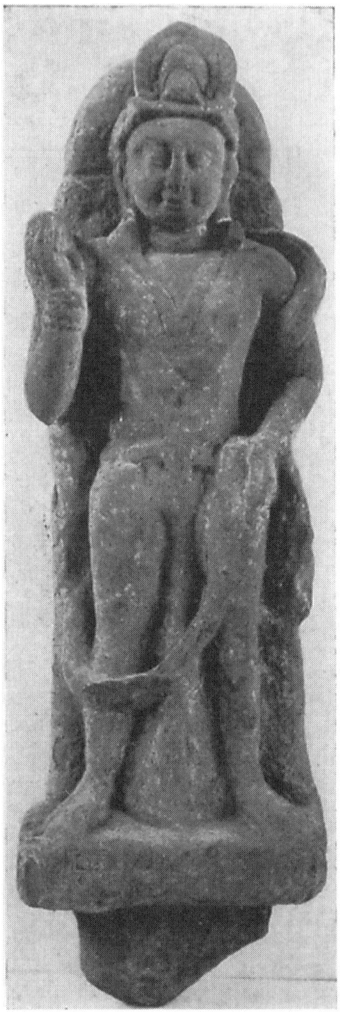

50—Bodhisattva (Mathurā)

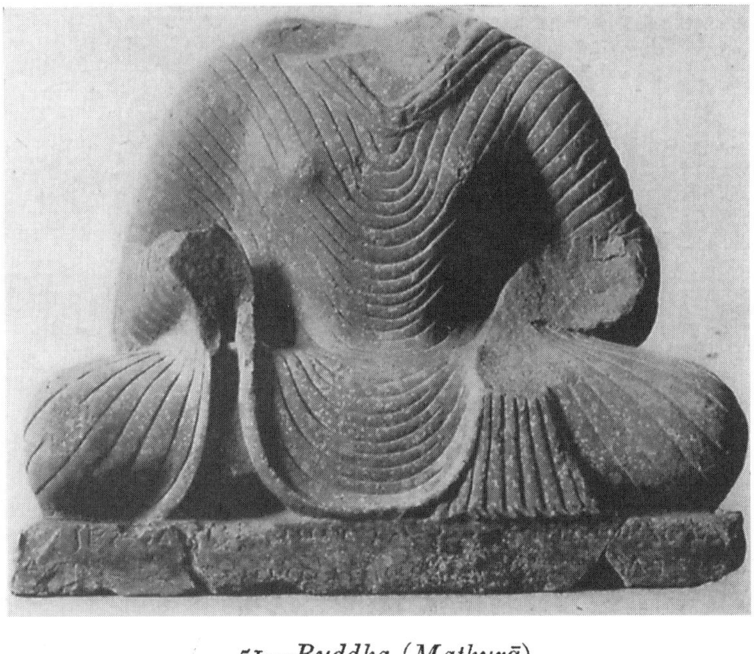

51—Buddha (Mathurā)

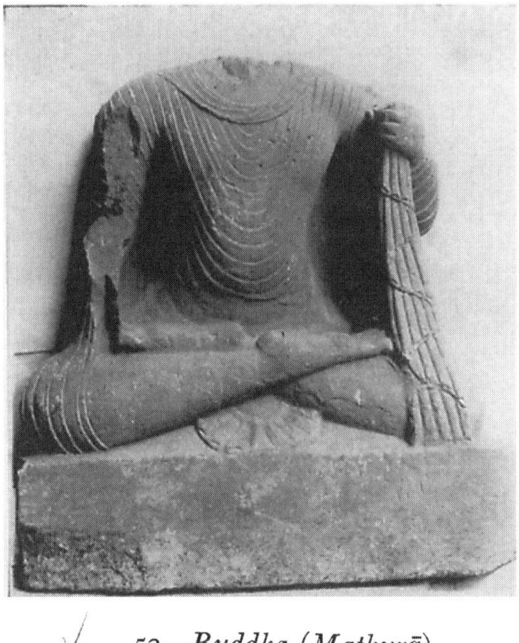

52—Buddha (Mathurā)

Budda, Bodhisattva, and Nāga Types (Mathurā)

the appearance which would be presented by a seated polycephalous Nāga of the Mathurā or Sāñcī[52] type, and a seated Buddha or Jina sheltered by a Nāga, the only difference being that in the one case the hoods rise from the back between the shoulders, in the other the coiled tail of the Nāga forms a seat, and its whole body is really quite distinct from that of the principal figure. There *may* be a genetic connection here. The polycephalous Nāga is very rarely met with in Gandhāra.

If the Indian Buddha figure, Mathurā type, is not derived from Gandhāra, what is the relation between the two schools, that is to say, in the beginning and during the period preceding the stylistic Indianization of the Gandhāra school? Exactly to what extent Gandhāra iconography is derived from preëxisting Indian forms, either through Mathurā or otherwise, is still a matter for further research. Certainly some Gandhāra sculptures are replicas, or very closely related developments, of preëxisting Indian ones. When Spooner remarks[53] of a Bodhisattva fragment found at Takht-i-Bāhī, "The resemblance of this figure to some of the Bhārhut sculpture is remarkable, but of course this can only be accidental," the "of course" seems to be dictated by a preconceived view. The resemblance is not accidental in the case of the *Vessantara Jātaka*[54] compositions (Fig. 57), or in that of the Gandhāra Vṛkṣakā types (woman-and-tree). M. Foucher, indeed, has himself shown to what an extent Gandhāra made use of older Indian formulae.[55] How far this was also true in the case of the Buddha figure needs further investigation. I by no means positively assert that Buddha figures were first made in Mathurā and afterwards copied in Gandhāra, though as Goloubew says, that is possible. The Gandhāra school may have been based, like the Northern Wei school in China, mainly on literary traditions. Stylistically, of course, Gandhāra is independent; but hardly more definitely so than China or even Java, and Chinese or Javanese style are no proof of Chinese or Javanese origins. All we can say definitely is that practically every element essential to the iconography of Buddha and Bodhisattva figures appears in early Indian art before the Buddha figure of Gandhāra or Mathurā is known.

5. STYLE AND CONTENT: DIFFERENTIATION OF INDIAN AND HELLENISTIC TYPES

In the previous chapter only the iconographic elements (theme and shape) have been referred to; it remains to point out that the Indian stylistic sequence presents a similar continuity, and to define the distinction of the Indian from the Hellenistic types in respect of content and form.

In the Pārkham and Deoriyā images (Figs. 2, 3) we have works of archaic aspect, characterized by frontality and an abrupt transition from the plane of the chest to that of the sides; in the Patna image (Fig. 3) the same features are equally evident. These archaic features, of course, are gradually refined upon as time passes. More significant and permanent is the great plastic voluminousness; everything is felt in mass, and nothing

52. As at Sāñcī, Fergusson, *Tree and Serpent Worship*, pl. XXIV, 1 and 2.

53. Spooner, *Excavations at Takht-i-Bahi*, in *A. S. I., A. R.*, 1907-08, with reference to fig. 6, *ibid.*

54. Cf. also another Gandhāra example, *A. S. I., A. R.*, 1909-10, pl. XVIII. If the Bhārhut relief had been lost, it would surely have been claimed that this composition originated in Gandhāra; and, in fact, Sir Aurel Stein takes this for granted (*Desert Cathay*, I, p. 489). The same composition occurs in a Miran fresco of the second or third century A. D. (Stein, *op. cit.*), and survives in modern Buddhist art (see my *Mediaeval Sinhalese Art*, frontispiece).

55. *L'art gréco-bouddhique du Gandhara*, I, pp. 206 ff.

in outline; this quality is maintained in Indian sculpture until after the Gupta period, while it is the very opposite of what we find in Gandhāra, where sculpture represents the decadence of a tradition, and is, as we should naturally expect, attenuated and linear. The early Indian figures stand symmetrically, with the feet somewhat apart, and this is also the case with later images of the type of Friar Bala's Bodhisattva (Fig. 4). In the early figures the sculptor has at his command an adequate scheme for the representation of the folds of drapery; and this drapery clings closely to the figure. In many Śuṅga and early Andhra works the body is revealed almost as though it were nude. Here again is a feature that is highly characteristic of the early Mathurā Buddhist figures, and of Gupta art generally. In Gandhāra the drapery is treated realistically, the folds rising well above the level of those parts of the material that are actually in contact with the flesh; at Mathurā the treatment is schematic and clinging.

Nothing is more characteristic of the early Indian art than its affirmative force; the Gandhāra style by comparison is listless. This radiation of force is scarcely at all reduced in the Mathurā standing and seated figures, which in this respect, indeed, are somewhat at variance with the dispassionate serenity which we are apt to regard as characteristic of Buddha types. In the early Indian works and up to the end of the second century A. D. there is hardly ever to be found deliberate grace; it is not without reason, though the language may sound strange in the ears of students of art, that some archaeologists have described the Gandhāra figures as graceful, the Mathurā types as clumsy and unwieldy. This only expresses the common and unsophisticated view that regards all early art as "awkward," and all late art as "better;" but in the present connection it serves to exhibit very well the stylistic gulf that separates Gandhāra from Mathurā. In fact the Gandhāra types, like other Hellenistic works, are soft and woolly; those of Mathurā, tense, and even strained. Whatever we may think about the iconography, it would be impossible to imagine a genetic connection of either school with the other in point of style.

Again, the earlier Indian types are products, not of observation, but of cerebration; they are mental abstractions. As Indian culture became more conscious, racial taste was more and more a determining factor in such abstractions. That the model upon which the artist worked was regarded from the standpoint of knowledge, and not of observation, is reflected in the use of *sādhanās* or *dhyāna mantrams*, which constitute the main part of the *śilpa śāstras* so far as they are concerned with the making of cult images. No natural form is imitated merely because it is present in nature; on the contrary, all the formulae of art are as much *saṁskṛtam* as Sanskrit itself, and every phrase was intended to have a definite significance. Of course, the art as it develops, comes to have an appearance of greater "truth to nature;" the actuality and spontaneity of the Ajaṇṭā paintings, for example, have been remarked upon. But it would be an error to suppose that even here we have an unsophisticated art, like that of those who take nature for their model. The Indian theory of knowledge, as M. Masson-Oursel has pointed out[56] amounts to this, that objects are created by thought, not that preëxisting objects are perceived. Hence the importance of correct thought; and this in relation to art is theoretically a matter of revelation, and secondarily, one of tradition. The forms created by correct thought need

56. *Notes sur l'esthetique indienne* in *Revue des arts asiatique*, III, 1926. Cf. also Zimmer, *Kunstform und Yoga*, 1926—"*Kultbild ist Yantra.*"

not by any necessity conform to those perceived in nature by untrained perception; all that is necessary is that they should be consistent and significant.

Where we think we recognize an increasing "truth to nature" and assume a closer observation, as in the Ajaṇṭā paintings referred to, what we have in reality is greater consciousness;[57] the artist, *mehr einfühlende*, is more aware of the tensions that he represents, and consequently represents them more convincingly. But the corresponding gestures had already been codified in dictionaries of gesture (Bharata's *Nāṭya Śāstra*); and the painter is really using a highly artificial and conventional language of glances, inclinations, and gestures, all with definite significance. When we come to examine his supposed realism more closely, we find that it has no foundation in the observation of anatomy or modeling, and that it depends entirely on an understanding of the psychology of gesture. When later on the same formulae have become rigid habits, this only means that the race has fallen from the high level of consciousness and subtlety that marked the zenith of its culture, not that observation of nature has been abandoned; the suggestion of realism is immediately lost, which is by no means the case in decadent Greek art.

Śilpa śāstras were certainly current in the Gupta period; Hsüan Tsang refers to such works as forming a section of the *Śāstras* studied by laymen.[58] But the use of formulae goes back to a much earlier time. Indians from the beginning were deeply interested in physiognomy, and it is with this preoccupation that a fundamental type like that of the Mahāpuruṣa-Cakravartin was conceived. This theoretical type, with its thirty-two principal marks (*lakṣaṇas*) and other minor marks, is older than the Buddha image, older presumably than the Buddha himself. At least, the Buddha is described as a Mahāpuruṣa in canonical books, and as possessing these marks, of which some are represented in the sculptures. Thus the Buddhist had taken over at an early period from non-Buddhist sources a conception of the Buddha as Mahāpuruṣa or Cakravartin; the *lakṣaṇas* were certainly not the invention of Buddhists, but were taken over by them and applied to the person of the Master. In other words, a definite idea of the Buddha's appearance existed before the time of actual representations; nor did this idea differ from that which a Hindu would have had of the appearance of such a god as Viṣṇu, likewise a Mahāpuruṣa.[59] That the Buddha could not be regarded as a man in the ordinary sense of the word may be gathered from the words attributed to himself, in reply to the questions of Droṇa, a Brāhman who found him seated at the foot of a tree; was he a Deva, Gandharva, Yakṣa, or man? The Master replies that he is none of these, but a Buddha.[60] Like the gods, he is anthropomorphic, but not a man; and as a deity he stands with them as a fit and natural subject for iconographic representation.

57. The case of painting is not quite the same as that of the religious sculpture. Painting was to some extent cultivated as a fine art and as an accomplishment. Portraits must certainly have been likenesses. In sculpture, even the effigies of donors are types, rather than likenesses. The sculptor should represent the gods, as Śukrācārya says, not men—though the latter may be pleasing, it is not the way to heaven (*Śukranītisāra*, IV, iv, 154-157). It is significant that a knowledge of the science of dancing was considered essential to the understanding of painting (*Viṣṇudharmottaram*, III, II, 3).

58. As stated in the *Si yu ki*, Beal, *Buddhist Records of the Western World*, I, p. 78.

59. On the subject of the Mahāpuruṣa, see Laufer, *Das Citralakṣaṇa*, pp. 14 ff.; Grünwedel, *Buddhist Art in India*, pp. 80, 120 ff., 133; Kern, *Manual of Indian Buddhism*, pp. 62, 95; other references, Beal, *Buddhist Records of the Western World*, I, p. 1; R. O. Francke, *Der dogmatische Buddha nach dem Dighanikáya*, *W. Z. K. M.*, 28, 1924.

60. *Anguttara Nikāya*, II, 37. Cf. *Lalita Vistara*, ch. xvi, "Is this Brahmā, Indra, or Vaiśravaṇa, or some mountain deity?"

All this mentality and formulation are foreign to the Hellenistic tradition, which represents the last term of a long development that had been determined by a profound interest in human form studied for its own sake. Greek idealism regarded even ideal forms as objective realities, not as fashioned by thought; hence, or in other words, Greek instinct was perceptive and outwardly directed. Even though the story be a myth, it is still significant that a Greek sculptor should have been supposed to have created a perfect type by combining the beauties of five different individuals. An Indian, connoisseur of the beauty of women as he was, would never have resorted to models, because he knew *a priori* in what the beauty of women consisted, or if we can imagine him in doubt, would have consulted a *śāstra*; it would never have occurred to him to find out what it was by turning to nature. The Greeks, like Wordsworth, though not perhaps in quite the same way, were "fond of nature;" and this kind of art they brought to perfection. But while the Indian kind of art in its decadence becomes a repetition of stereotyped formulae no longer felt, the Greek kind in its decadence becomes rhetorical and facile.

We are dealing, in fact, not merely with two different kinds of art, but with two arts in entirely different stages of their development; the Greek already decadent, the Indian still primitive. A serious stylistic influence of a realistic or decadent art upon a formal or primitive art (and we have seen that both distinctions held) could only have been destructive; we have seen too much of the influence of European art on Asiatic art within the last hundred years not to be aware of this; nothing inwardly resembling Gandhāra art had been produced in India before the nineteenth century. The fact that art of the Indian school pursued a normal course (i. e., it "develops") from first to last is not a proof that the refinement of the primitive types was due to external influences, but a proof of continuity in the indigenous tradition.

Apparently only one example of Mathurā sculpture in the round representing a Buddha or Bodhisattva has been regarded as an actual imitation of a Gandhāra prototype:[61] and only one piece of actual Gandhāra sculpture has been found in Mathurā.[62] It is admitted by all students and will be obvious from the most cursory examination of the accompanying illustrations that the sculptures of Kaniṣka's reign differ so much from Gandhāra types that a genetic connection seems inconceivable.[63] It is only in certain reliefs mostly of the middle period (Vāsudeva and later), as justly noted by Codrington,[64] that Gandhāra influence can be definitely recognized (Figs. 58, 59). The Dhruv Tīlā stupa drum[65] described by Foucher as a "*caricature lamentablement indianisée*"[66] must be reckoned amongst these.

Why did not the Mathurā craftsman adopt more freely Hellenistic mannerisms? I think it was mainly because the required types lay ready to hand in the local tradition. The transition from a Buddha type like that of the Ujjain coin (Fig. 9) to a designated Go(tama) Boydo (the legend of Kaniṣka's seated Buddha coin), and from a *padmapāṇi*

61. A 47 in the Mathurā Museum, Vogel, in *A. S. I., A. R.*, 1906-07, p. 151.

62. F 42 in the Mathurā Museum, Burgess, *Ancient Monuments*, pls. 56, 57.

63. See my *Indian Origin of the Buddha Image, J. A. O. S.*, XLVI, p. 169.

64. *Ancient India*, p. 47.

65. V. A. Smith, *The Jain Stupa of Mathurā*, pls. CV-CVII.

66. In *J. A.*, X, 11, 1903, p. 323.

attendant to an attendant Padmapāṇi took place almost unnoticed. That which seems to us a kind of artistic revolution really implied no new iconographic invention; it involved a new terminology much more than a new art. India had long been familiar with images of gods; Patañjali, presumably in the second century B. C., speaks of images of Śiva, Skandha, and Viśākha, not to mention other and earlier indications and the known Yakṣa figures. The whole process belongs to the theistic development which had been taking place, and is naturally reflected in the substitution of anthropomorphic figures for the older abstract symbolism. Buddhism cannot be considered alone; that Buddha had come to be regarded as Devatideva, God of gods, shows that, as usual, each religion is affected by the current tendency. There is no canonical proscription of images in Buddhist literature, early or late; and very soon the Buddhist authors take it for granted that images had been made even in the Buddha's own lifetime.

Mathurā sculptors, then, had no more occasion to adopt the Hellenistic iconography or style than they had to replace their own Brāhmī by Kharoṣṭhī, which must have been the official script of Kaniṣka's capitals at Peshāwar and Kapiśa. I do not believe that the slightest prejudice against Gandhāra art, as such, existed; or if so, only as an instinctive taste, the nature of which is indicated in Le Coq's just remark: "*Allen Asiaten erscheinen Europaergesichter* (*also auch die der Hellenen*) *sehr unschön.*"[67] I once showed to a Kandyan craftsman, a descendant of *śilpins* and *ācāryas*, and proficient in his art, a good example of European design, rather thinking he would admire it; in fact, however, he seemed neither attracted nor repelled, and merely remarked, "*Ek eka raṭa, ek eka veḍa,*" that is, "every country has its own style." I believe that a Mathurā craftsman would have regarded a Gandhāra work in the same way.

It must be remembered too that Buddhist and Hindu images were not regarded and never have been regarded in India as works of art; they were made as means of edification. Prestige attached to sanctity, not to style; the same situation may be observed in modern times in connection with such relatively uncouth types as those of the Śrī Nātha-jī[68] of Nāthadvār and Jagannātha of Purī, of which painted replicas are constantly made, adhering rigidly to type, regardless of the availability of much more attractive (humanly speaking) Kṛṣṇa and Viṣṇu types. The modern imager is totally unaware of stylistic degeneration; in the same way he must in early times have been unaware of the virtue of his art. He did not think at all in terms of our connoisseurship; the plastic style of his day came to him as naturally as the spoken language, and both as a matter of course. Particular images would only be copied on account of their special sanctity, not because of their artistic merits.[69] Particular places would only become centers of distribution, as Mathurā was, or as Jaipur still is, because the religious importance and prosperity of such places during an extended period had necessitated the existence there of ateliers, able to

67. *Bilderatlas zur Kunst und Kunstgeschichte Mittelasiens*, p. 28. Cf. Lafcadio Hearn, *About Faces in Japanese Art*, in *Gleanings in Buddha Fields*.

68. It is perhaps worth while to remark here that the image of Śrī Nātha-jī which was found underground near Mathurā, and subsequently removed to Nāthadvāra near Udaipur, still the main sanctuary of the Vallabhācāryas, may well be in fact a Kuṣāna Buddha. The image, so far as I know, has never been photographed or published, but the painted replicas show a standing figure, with the left hand on the hip, and the right raised in *abhaya mudrā*, with a certain angularity suggestive of early Mathurā types. This would not be by any means an isolated instance of the later worship of an old Mathurā Buddhist figure under the name of a Hindu deity.

69. In this fact there is nothing peculiar to Indian psychology: the same has held good from first to last in the history of Christian iconographic art.

supply the needs of the devout inhabitants or pilgrims. Now we know that in the time of Kaniṣka Mathurā was a most important Buddhist center, probably the most important in India; as remarked by Przyluski[70] in quite another connection, "*Mathurā eût parmi les communautés bouddhiques une situation privilegée;*" and it played a very great part in the dissemination of the faith. This being so, it is not in the least surprising that the Mathurā school should have played such an important part as it did in the history of Buddhist art.[71]

We are able, moreover, to trace the influence of the Mathurā types, not only at Amarāvatī, but as the formative basis of Gupta art, by means of archaeological data, and not only by stylistic evidence. In the time of Kaniṣka Mathurā had already such a reputation that Buddha and Bodhisattva images were exported thence to Sāñcī, Prayāg, Amīn (near Thanesar), Kasiā, Śrāvastī, Pāṭaliputra, Sārnāth, Bodhgayā, Rājagṛha, and to many parts of the Panjāb, including even Taxila. At Sārnāth, copies of Mathurā types have been definitely recognized. In the Gupta period, while local ateliers had developed at places like Sārnāth and Sāñcī, Mathurā sculptures were still exported to these and other sites. These facts sufficiently explain the close relation of the Kuṣāna and Gupta forms.

Gupta art bears within itself the proof of its Indian origins. As Dr. Laufer has remarked, one has no need of the panoply of anthropology to recognize that the Buddha types of Ajaṇṭā are representations of true Indians, and have no connection with the sculpture of Gandhāra; they are "*echt indisch und haben keinen Gandhara-geruch.*"[72] This is only what has been remarked by Vincent Smith, Goloubew, and Foucher himself, in connection with the sculpture.[73] The Gupta type is a normal and direct development of the Mathurā type; and this Gupta type is the dominating model underlying all those of Farther India and Indonesia. We have only to look at a sequence of examples beginning with the Pārkham image (Fig. 2) and culminating in the Mathurā types of the Gupta period (Fig. 5) to realize that there is no room at any point in the development for the intercalation of any model based on Hellenistic tradition. If such an influence was exerted, and to some extent it can be recognized in the middle Kuṣāna period, it was so slight and ephemeral as to have become unrecognizable within a century, or at the most within two centuries.

70. J. Przyluski, *Aśokāvadāna*, 1923, p. 9.

71. A fact more than once emphasized by Vogel (in *A. S. I., A. R.*, 1909-10, p. 78, and *Catalogue Mathurā Museum*, p. 28), who can only have regarded it as "not a little curious" because of his preconviction that it should have been not Mathurā, but Gandhāra, that exercised a great influence on Buddhist art in other parts of India.

72. Laufer, *Das Citralakṣaṇa*, p. 16.

73. References to the statements made in this and the preceding paragraph will be found in my *Indian Origin of the Buddha Image*, in *J. A. O. S.*, XLVI, 1926. In addition, Foucher, *L'art gréco-bouddhique du Gandhara*, p. 611: "*ce sont les répliques de Mathurâ qui ont servi de modèle à Bénarès, et ce sont les répliques de Bénarès que le Magadha a copiées a son tour . . . Son évolution . . . se traduit encore et toujours par l'élimination progressive de l'élément étranger sous la pression du goût indigène*"; and Sahni, *Guide to Sārnāth*, 1926 ed., p. 11: "The arrival of this (Friar Bala's) statue at Sārnāth must have been so welcome that local artists at once set to work and the Sārnāth Museum contains two statues (Ba 2 and 3) which are almost exact copies of the one from Mathurā. Vincent Smith goes so far as to say that "The style of the Sārnāth works (of Kusāna date) is so closely related to that of Mathurā that illustrations may be dispensed with." The Sārnāth types of Buddha and Bodhisattva images which followed are rightly regarded as the finest creations of the Gupta period. It was no wonder therefore, that this new art so rapidly spread not only to the rest of India, but also to the neighboring countries of Siam, Cambodia, and Ceylon." It will be seen that *all* that is required to establish a Hellenistic origin of the Buddha image as it appears in the Gupta period, fully evolved, is to show that Friar Bala's Bodhisattva type (Fig. 4) is a "*réplique*" of the Gandhāra type (e. g., Fig. 53). When this has been done, I shall be ready to accept the Greek theory, bag and baggage.

6. DATING OF GANDHĀRA AND MATHURĀ BUDDHAS

Here we know nothing for certain; and what we do not know cannot be used with much cogency in support of any argument. Nor can the question of dates, whatever discoveries may be in store for us, ever by itself provide us with a final solution of our problem. For, if the Gandhāra Buddhas could be proved older than any Mathurā ones, this would not alter the admitted fact that the conception of the figure is Indian, nor the equally obvious fact that the earliest Indian Buddha figures are in stylistic and iconographic continuity with the older indigenous art. Nor, on the other hand, if priority could be proved for the Mathurā types would it alter the fact that the Gandhāra types are Hellenistic in style; the iconography in Gandhāra might still have been derived from elements already present in early Indian art, or constructed from literary sources, and a Mathurā origin of the Buddha image *in Gandhāra* would not be proven. Nor would it alter the fact that a considerable element of Hellenistic style can be followed across Central Asia into China, Korea, and Japan, nor the fact that even in India definite traces of the Gandhāran influence can be detected. Nevertheless, it will be worth while to recapitulate the few available facts, and refer to some of the conclusions that have been or may be drawn from them.

Advocates of the Hellenistic theory assume, and probably rightly, that the best works are the earliest, and, further, opine that the Gandhāra school, so far as the earliest Buddha figures are concerned, developed in the first century B. C. The Bīmarān reliquary excavated by Masson in Afghanistan before 1840 has been assigned to the first century B. C. on account of coins of Azes associated with it;[74] but methods of excavation nearly ninety years ago were not by any means as critical as they are now, coins in any case merely provide a *terminus post quem*, and Wilson himself was of the opinion that the stupas of Afghanistan "are undoubtedly all subsequent to the Christian era."[75] Marshall dates the reliquary about the beginning of the Christian era; of Gandhāra sculptures in general he remarks more cautiously that "it may be safely asserted that a number of them . . . are anterior to the reign of Kaniṣka."[76] From the inferior workmanship and *deja stéreotypée* character of the Buddha figures on the Kaniṣka reliquary (Fig. 56), made by Agesila subsequent to 120 A. D. (the date of Kaniṣka's accession here assumed, *vide infra*), Foucher and others have concluded that the period of the finest work must be pushed back to the first century B. C.[77] This is a rather bold inference to draw from the inferior workmanship of a single object, even though it would seem that it must have been one of importance. Marshall holds that "considerations of style do not permit us to determine the chronological sequence with any approach to accuracy."[78]

Three dated Gandhāra figures have been found; but it is not known to what era the dates refer. On the assumptions that have been made, the date of a standing figure from Loriyān Tangai is 6 A. D.[79] and that of a standing figure, and of a pedestal with a seated

74. Bachofer, *Zur Datierung der Gandhara Plastik*, p. 14 ("*keine zweifel zu, das es in die Zeit des Azes I gehört*").

75. *Ariana Antiqua*, p. 322.

76. *Cambridge History of India*, I, p. 648; *Guide to Taxila*, p. 60.

77. *L'art gréco-bouddhique du Gandhara*, II, p. 443; Spooner, in *A. S. I., A. R.*, 1908-09, p. 50.

78. *Guide to Taxila*, p. 31; *Cambridge History of India*, I, p. 648.

79. Bachofer, *op. cit.;* Vogel, *Inscribed Gandhara Sculptures*, in *A. S. I., A. R.*, 1903-04. Foucher assigns the date 4 B. C. If we assume the Vikrama era which is used on the Dharmarājikā silver scroll (Marshall, *Guide to Taxila*, p. 52), the date Samvat 318 becomes equivalent to c. 262 A. D. Fleet, in *J. R. A. S.*, 1913, p. 999, points out that a use of the Śaka era would make the date 396 A. D. It will be realized that the selection of eras in the various interpretations of Gandhāra Buddha image dates is often *tendenziös*.

figure, both from Haṣṭnagar, 72 A. D.[80] The Bodhisattva illustrated in Fig. 55 is not dated, but is assigned by Bachofer to the third quarter of the first century A. D. More reliable than any of these doubtful cases is the very definite negative evidence provided by scientific excavations at Taxila. Here the Scytho-Parthian and early Kuṣāna strata at the Dharmarājikā site have not yielded a single fragment of Graeco-Buddhist sculpture.[81] At Sirkap, the city in occupation at Taxila from the second century B. C. to the time of Wima Kadphises, c. 75-80 A. D., not a single piece of Graeco-Buddhist sculpture appears in the long list of finds;[82] the only sculpture of any kind in Gandhāra stone is a small figure in the round of a semi-nude goddess holding a lotus flower, quite an old Indian type, and in style intermediate between Indian and Hellenistic. The terra cotta and stucco heads from the apsidal Buddhist temple include no Buddhas or Bodhisattvas. This is very significant negative evidence, and seems to indicate that Gandhāra Buddha figures can hardly have been made until a little before the time of Kaniṣka. All that we can be quite sure of is that the Gandhāra school of Buddhist sculpture was most productive in the time of Kaniṣka, a point on which almost all authorities are agreed.[83]

The date of Kaniṣka is not yet a fact established beyond dispute; datings have ranged from 58 B. C. to the third century A. D., the substantial controversy being between those who support the date 78 A. D. and those who support the date 120 or 125 A. D. The date c. 120 A. D. adopted here is regarded by Marshall as proved by the results of excavation, and has been accepted by Vincent Smith and Sten Konow. The point is not essential to our study, where the relative dating alone is of significance.

Friar Bala's Bodhisattva at Sārnāth is dated in the third year of Kaniṣka, thus c. 123 A. D. The Kaṭrā Bodhisattva and Aṇyor Buddha from Mathurā have inscriptions palaeographically similar, and must be of the same period. A large number of other Buddha figures from Mathurā, some in the round, others in relief, are identical in style and must be dated near the same time; some are probably a little earlier than Kaniṣka, most of the others of this type assignable to his reign or that of Huviṣka. We are certainly not entitled to assume that Friar Bala's figure or any of the other figures in our possession was the first of its kind ever made. Nor is it conceivable that an image exported to Sārnāth, not to mention those of Mathurā origin found at other sites, should have been one of the

80. Bachofer; Vogel, *loc. cit.* It should be noted that the former takes Kaniṣka's date as 78 A. D., and using the 1904 edition of Vincent Smith's *Early History of India* fails to observe that Smith since returned to the date 120 A. D., in agreement with Marshall and Konow. Smith (in *J. A. S. B.*, 1889) assigned the Haṣṭnagar pedestal to the fourth century A. D., and this dating would in fact hold good if we assume the era of Azes, the numeral of the actual inscription being 384. Fleet, in *J. R. A. S.*, 1913, p. 999, uses the Vikrama era, making the date 343 A. D.

81. Marshall, in *A. S. I.*, *A. R.*, 1912-13, pt. I, p. 12.

82. For lists of Sirkap finds, see Marshall, *Guide to Taxila*, ch. VI, and *Excavations at Taxila*, in *A. S. I.*, *A. R.*, 1912-13, 1914-15, 1919-20.

For the Sirkap statuette see *A. S. I.*, *A. R.*, 1919-20, p. 20 and pl. IX; and cf. the same type in Egypt, a terra cotta of about the beginning of the Christian era, Berstl, *op. cit.*, p. 173 and pl. 103, 2. The type recurs on the Limarowka vase and in other places cited by E. Herzfeld, *Die Malereien von Samarra* (*abb.* 5, etc.).

The absence of Buddhist and Jaina sculpture at Sirkap is the more striking as the architectural remains prove Buddhism and Jainism to have been flourishing.

83. Foucher, *L'art gréco-bouddhique du Gandhara*, I, p. 42; ~~Vogel,~~ Fergusso *op. cit.*, p. 258; Smith, *History of Fine Art in India and Ceylon*, p. 132; Grünwedel, *Buddhistische Kunst in Indien*, 2nd ed., 1920, p. xiv. During the third and fourth centuries A. D. the Gandhāra school continued to flourish abundantly, but the stone is largely replaced by terra cotta and stucco, and the type becomes thoroughly Indianized (see Marshall, *Stūpa and Monastery of Jauliāñ*, in *Mem. A. S. I.*, VII, 1921). The monasteries seem to have been destroyed and the activity of the school brought to an end by the Hūṇa invasions at the end of the fifth century.

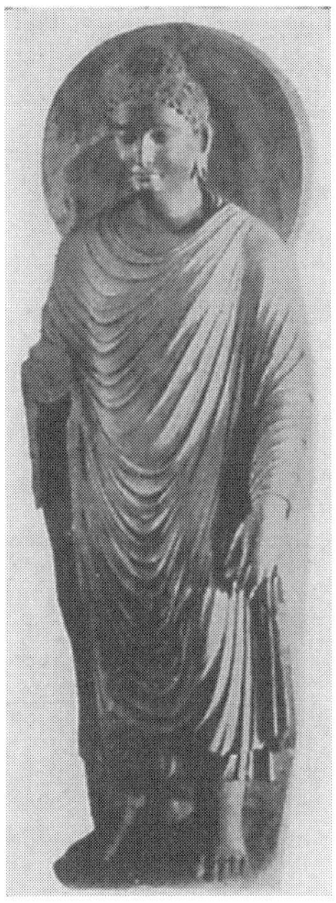

53—*Buddha*

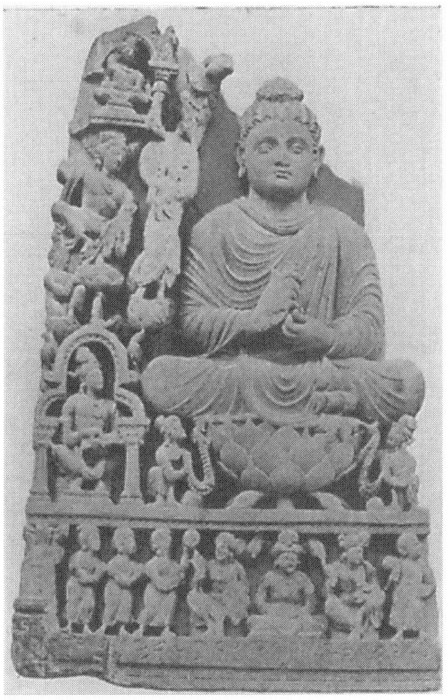

54—*Buddha Teaching*

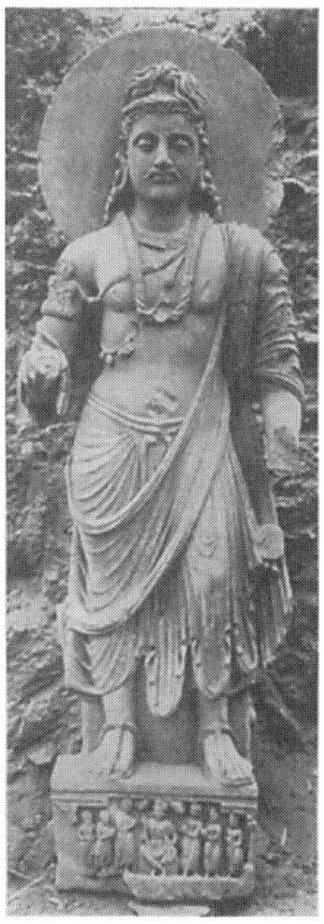

55—*Bodhisattva*

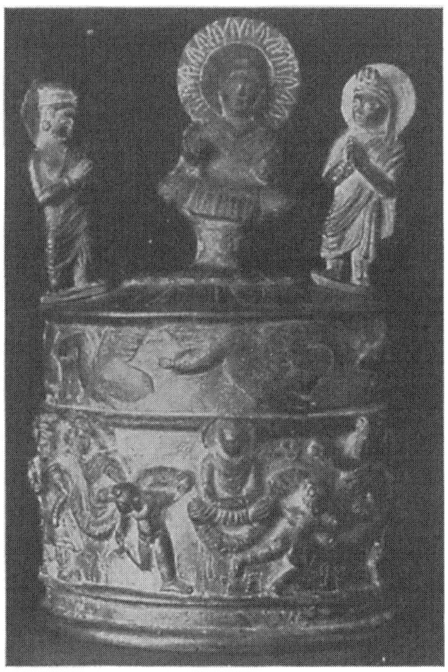

56—*Kaniṣka's Reliquary (Peshāwar)*

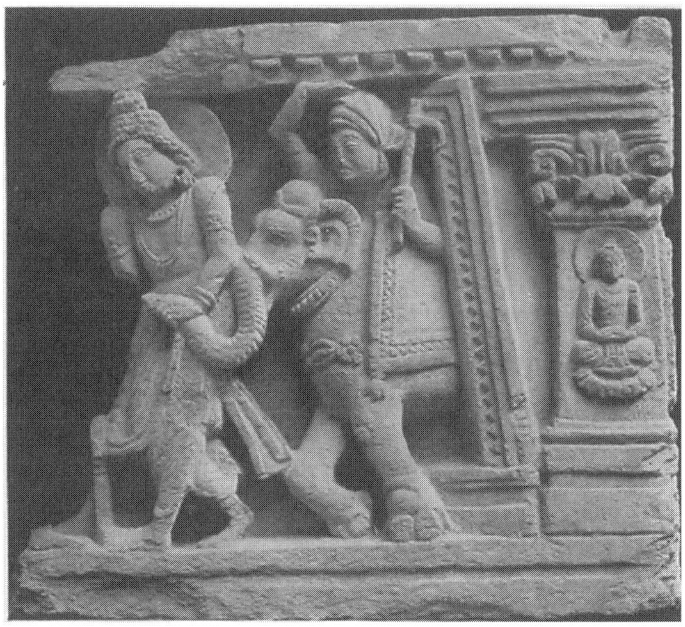

57—*Vessantara Jātaka*

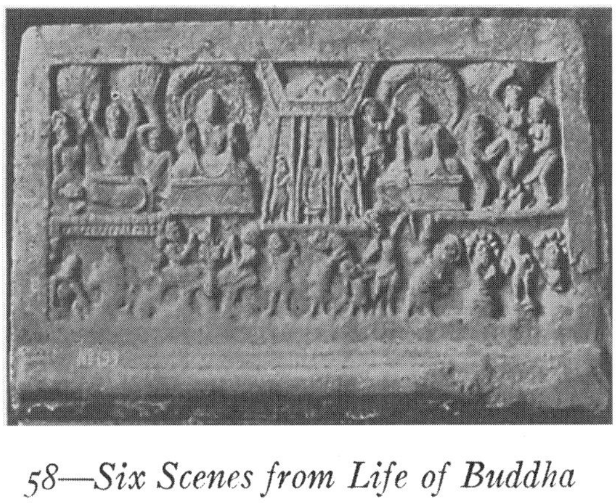

58—*Six Scenes from Life of Buddha*

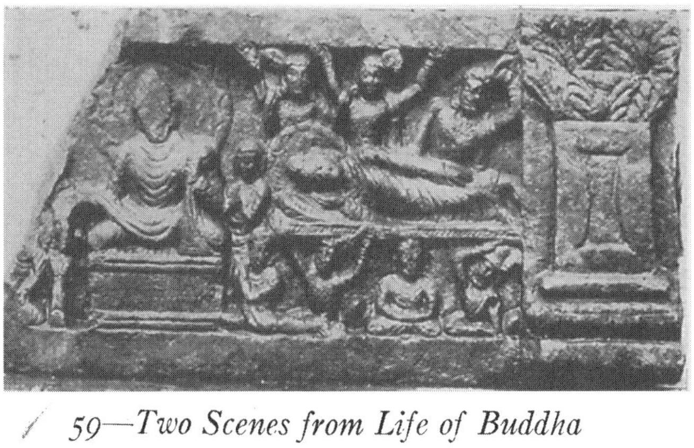

59—*Two Scenes from Life of Buddha*

53-57—*Gandhāra Types;* 58, 59—*Reliefs from Mathurā Showing Some Gandhāra Features*

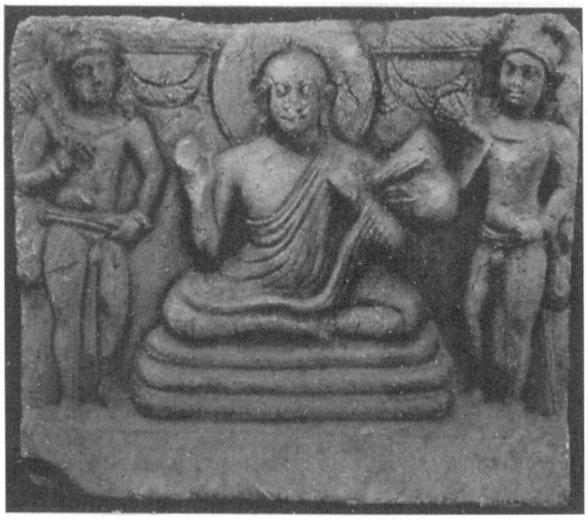

60—Buddha with two Attendants (Yakṣas), Amarāvatī School

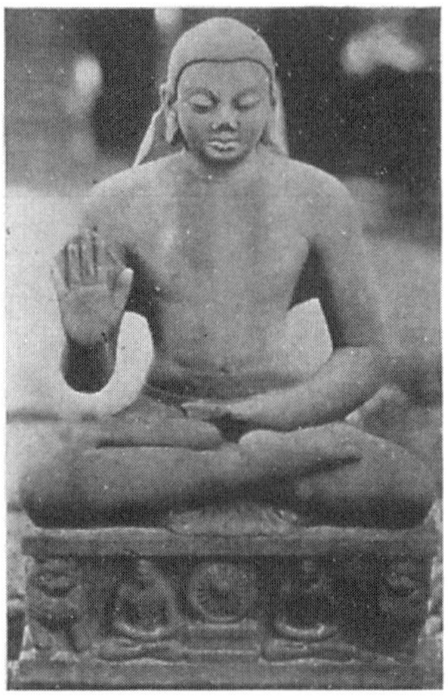

61—Buddha (Māṅkuwāṛ)

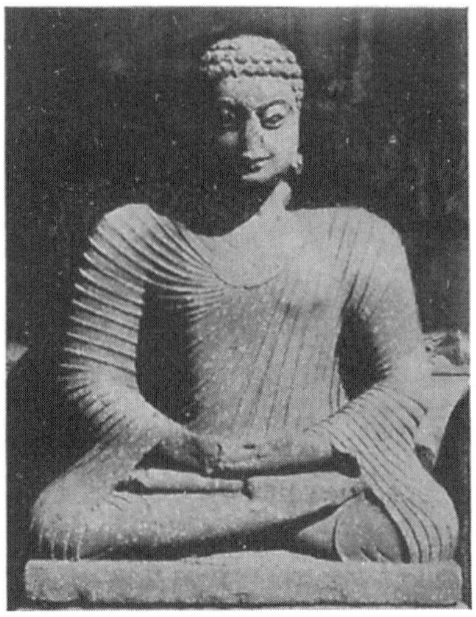

62—Buddha (Sāñcī)

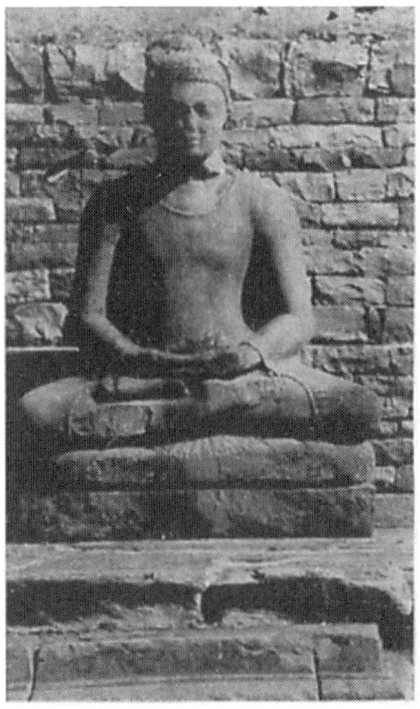

63—Buddha (Sāñcī)

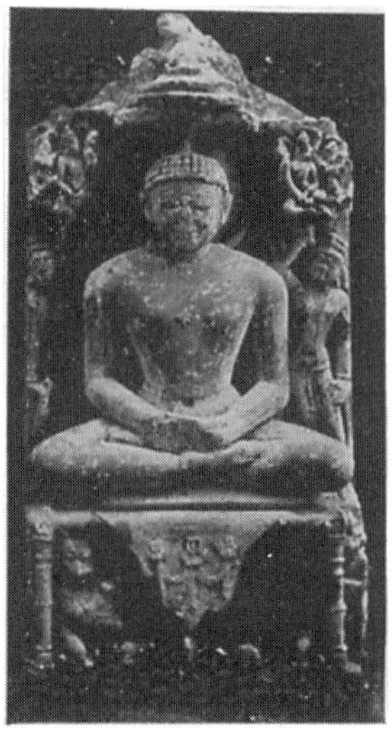

64—Jina (Mathurā)

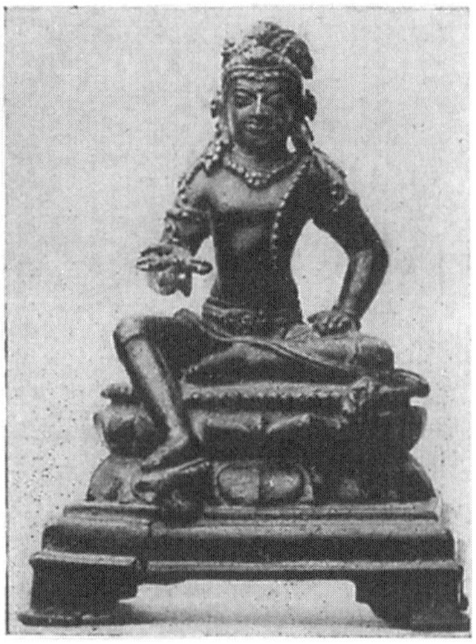

65—Bodhisattva Vajrapāṇi (Ceylon)

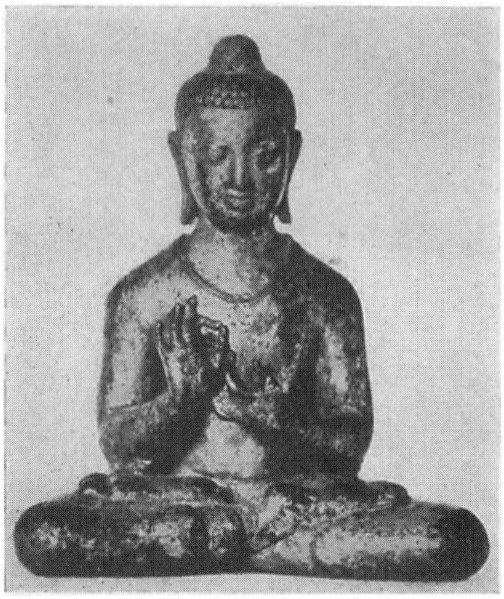

66—Buddha (Nepal)

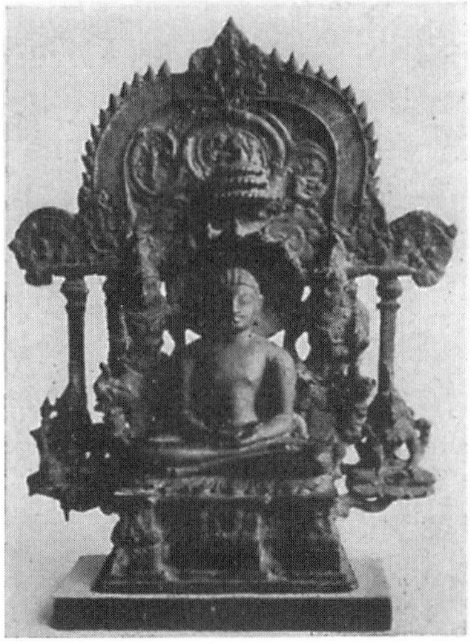

67—Pārśvanātha (Kannaḍa)

Buddha, Jina, and Bodhisattva Types

first Buddha images ever made; however quickly the fashion developed, however great the prestige of the Mathurā ateliers may already have been, some time must have elapsed between the first acceptance of the type in Mathurā and the development of a general demand for Mathurā Buddha images at other and distant sites throughout the Ganges valley. These considerations compel us to suppose that Buddha images must have been made in Mathurā soon after the middle of the first century A. D., at least before the end of the century.

It should be observed that the Jaina *āyāgapaṭas* from Mathurā bearing Jina figures of the same type as that of the seated Buddha figures have Brāhmī inscriptions which seem to be pre-Kuṣāna; that they were dated by Bühler in the first century B. C. depended, however, on an earlier dating of Kaniṣka than that now adopted. A reëxamination of the inscriptions is needed; all that we can say is that these slabs may well be assigned provisionally to the middle of the first century A. D.[84]

As regards the Buddha figure on an Ujjain coin (Fig. 9) I see no reason at present to date this before the first century A. D.; the fact that a coin of the same class and character bears a figure of a three-headed Maheśa, notwithstanding that it has been assigned to the second century B. C.,[85] is in itself evidence that the general type should be assigned to the first or even the second century A. D.

The so-called Buddha figures on the coins of Maues and Kadapha (Kadphises I) are indeed dateable, and the former would take us back to the beginning of the first century B. C. As stated above, however, I do not think that these can be accepted as Buddha figures; all that they certainly show is a type closely related to that of the seated Buddha figure when it finally appears and can be recognized without possibility of error.

It will be seen from what has been said above that the whole evidence for the dating of Gandhāra Buddha types in the first century B. C. or early first century A. D. rests upon five objects, of which three are dated in unknown eras, one excavated nearly a hundred years ago is dated on the evidence of coins alone, and one is of the Kaniṣka period. This is a very slender foundation upon which to base an argument flatly at variance with the evidence of the excavations at Taxila. The balance of real evidence tends to show that the Buddha figure came into general use somewhat before the beginning of the reign of Kaniṣka, and not more than fifty years at most, if so much, before his accession. The evidence is not sufficiently precise to warrant us in forming a theory as to the priority of either school. I am inclined to presume on general grounds a priority for Mathurā; but that is not evidence. All that we can assert is that the earliest Buddha types in each area are in the local style; and that later on, though some mutual influence was felt, the outstanding character of the development is one of stylistic Indianization in Gandhāra, and one of adherence to the Mathurā type in the Ganges valley, subject to the normal stylistic

84. See p. 304 above. Many of these *āyāgapaṭas* are illustrated by Vincent Smith, *The Jain Stūpa of Mathurā.*

One of the slabs from the Kaṅkālī Tīlā is dated in the reign of Śoḍāsa and is thus pre-Kuṣāna, but it is hardly safe to assume that the slabs with Jina figures are of the same age.

85. The Maheśa is illustrated by Cunningham, *Coins of Ancient India*, pl. X, 6. Rapson, *Indian Coins*, p. 14, justly remarks that there does not exist sufficient evidence to arrange the early Ujjain coins in chronological order. The ascription of the Maheśa type to the second century B. C. will be found in the *Cambridge History of India*, p. 532, the coin being again illustrated in pl. V, 19. But no polycephalous type is certainly older than the reign of Vāsudeva, and it is impossible to date the Ujjain coin before the second century A. D.

evolution which marks the transition from Kuṣāna to Gupta types. Great scorn has been poured upon the view that Gupta art would have been just what it is had the Graeco-Buddhist school of Gandhāra never existed, and of course such a statement could not be literally defended; yet I am prepared to assert that the Hellenistic element actually traceable in Gupta art is really insignificant. In view of the considerations and facts brought forward above, it becomes impossible to treat the phrase "Greek origin of the Buddha image" as representing anything more than a rhetorical misuse of language; if art of the Gandhāra school, as its students admit, is half Indian, art of the Kuṣāna and Gupta periods in the Ganges valley is altogether Indian, for it deals with the same ideas, and uses a plastic language that is in direct continuity with that of the preceding centuries.

FIG. 1—Typical Buddha figure, seated in *dhyāna;* curly hair, but the *uṣṇīṣa* is not preserved. Over life-size. C. third-fourth century A. D. Anurādhapura, Ceylon, *in situ.*

FIG. 2—Yakṣa. From Besnagar. Over life-size. (Cf. Fig. 47.) Usually assigned to the third century B. C. Indian Museum, Calcutta.

FIG. 3—Yakṣa. From Patna. Second century B. C. Indian Museum, Calcutta.

FIG. 4—Friar Bala's Bodhisattva (Buddha), made in Mathurā and set up at Sārnāth. Over life-size. (Cf. Figs. 18, 31.) Dated in the third year of Kaniṣka, i. e., 123 A. D. Sārnāth Museum.

FIG. 5—Buddha. From Mathurā. Typical Gupta example. Over life-size. (Cf. Fig. 33.) Mathurā Museum.

FIG. 6—Coin of Maues. Enlarged. (Gardner, *Coins of the Greek and Scythic Kings . . . ,* XVII, 5.) C. 100 or 80 B. C.

FIG. 7—Coin of Azes. (Whitehead, *Cat. Coins Panjab Museum,* XI, 195.) C. 58 B. C.

FIG. 8—Coin of Kadapha (Kadphises I, c. 40-78 A. D.).

FIG. 9—Ujjain coin, with seated Buddha on lotus, beside railed tree with *chatra.* Enlarged. (Cunningham, *Coins of Ancient India,* X, 10.) Probably first century, A. D.

FIG. 10—Coin of Kaniṣka, with seated Buddha. (Whitehead, *loc. cit.,* pl. XX, viii.) 120-165 A. D.

FIG. 11—Coin of Kaniṣka, with standing Buddha. (Gardner, *loc. cit.,* pl. XVII, 2.)

FIG. 12—Coin of Kaniṣka, with standing Buddha. British Museum.

FIG. 13—Kupiro Yakho (Kubera Yakṣa). From Bharhut. Early second century B. C. Indian Museum, Calcutta.

FIG. 14—Yakṣa with *caurī,* summit of north *toraṇa.* Sāñcī, *in situ.* C. 100 B. C.

FIG. 15—Indra as the Brahman Śānti. Bodhgayā, *in situ.* C. 100 B. C.

FIG. 16—Bodhisattva. From Mathurā. C. 100 A. D. Mathurā Museum.

FIG. 17—Bodhisattva Maitreya, Dhyāni Buddha in headdress, *amṛta* flask in left hand. From Mathurā. C. 100 A. D. Lucknow Museum.

FIG. 18—Buddha. From Mathurā. (Cf. Fig. 4.) C. 100 A. D. Lucknow Museum.

FIG. 19—The *Abhiniṣkramaṇa* of Buddha. 100-50 B. C. East *toraṇa,* front, middle architrave, Sāñcī, *in situ.*

FIG. 20—Buddha triad. C. 100 B. C. Three uprights between architraves of the north *toraṇa,* Sāñcī, *in situ.*

FIG. 21—The First Sermon in the Deer Park, Benares. Detail of a pediment from Mathurā. C. 100 A. D. Museum of Fine Arts, Boston.

FIG. 22—Detail from the same pediment; above, the Bowl-Relic on an altar with nimbus; below, the Bodhi-tree (Great Enlightenment of the Buddha).

FIG. 23—Sujātā approaching the Bodhi-tree, beneath which the Buddha is understood to be seated immediately prior to the Enlightenment. C. 100 B. C. Detail of middle architrave, north *toraṇa,* Sāñcī, *in situ.*

FIG. 24—Nāga standing under a tree. From railing, Pāṭaliputra. Third or early second century B. C. Indian Museum, Calcutta.

FIG. 25—Men seated in yoga pose, cross-legged, in the windows of an upper story. Early second century B. C. Railing medallion, from Bharhut. Indian Museum, Calcutta.

FIG. 26—The Nāga Erāpata worshipping the Buddha (represented by the Bodhi-tree and altar). Early second century B. C. Bharhut.

FIG. 27—Digha instructing his disciples. From the rail coping, Bharhut. Early second century B. C. Indian Museum, Calcutta.

FIG. 28—Stupa with worshippers; representing the *Parinirvāṇa* of the Buddha. Early second century B. C. Bharhut.

FIG. 29—*Vessantara Jātaka:* Gift of the Elephant. From the rail coping, Bharhut. Early second century B. C. Indian Museum, Calcutta.

FIG. 30—Head of Buddha. From Gandhāra. Early second century A. D. (?) Museum of Fine Arts, Boston.

FIG. 31—Head of Buddha. From Mathurā. Early second century A. D. Museum of Fine Arts, Boston.

FIG. 32—Head of Bodhisattva, probably Maitreya, with Dhyāni Buddha in headdress. From Gandhāra. Early second century A. D. Field Museum, Chicago.

FIG. 33—Head of Buddha, typical Gupta type. From Mathurā. Fifth century A. D. Museum of Fine Arts, Boston.

FIG. 34—Bodhisattva (so called in inscription). From Kaṭrā mound, Mathurā. Early second century A. D. Mathurā Museum.

FIG. 35—Buddha, similar to the last. Museum of Fine Arts, Boston.

FIG. 36—Bodhisattva Maitreya, with *amṛta* flask in left hand. Detail of pediment, Mathurā. C. 100 A. D. (?) Mathurā Museum.

FIG. 37—Seated Buddha or Bodhisattva with turban. From Mathurā. Second century A. D. Property of Messrs. Yamanaka.

FIG. 38—Above, the Buddha teaching; below, the ~~Great Enlightenment~~. Detail of same pediment as Fig. 36.

FIG. 39—Seated Buddha or Bodhisattva, similar to Figs. 34, 35, and 38 above. From Mathurā. Early second century A. D. Mathurā Museum.

FIG. 40—The visit of Indra to the Buddha in the Indra-sāla guhā; on the upper right, the Yakṣa Vajrapāṇi, below, with mitre-like crown, Indra. From Mathurā. Second century A. D. Present location unknown; formerly the property of L. Rosenberg, Paris.

FIG. 41—*Āyāgapaṭa*, with seated Jina in center, attended by two Yakṣas. From Mathurā. Late first century A. D. (?) Lucknow Museum.

FIG. 42—Another *āyāgapaṭa*, in the center a seated Jina without attendants. Same source and present location.

FIG. 43—The Jina Pārśvanātha. From Mathurā. C. 100 A. D. (?) Mathurā Museum.

FIG. 44—Sūrya, the Sun-god, winged, with nimbus, in a chariot drawn by four horses. From Mathurā. First century A. D. (?) Mathurā Museum.

FIG. 45—Yakṣa with a purse, probably Kuvera. From Achnagar, near Mathurā. Second or third century A. D. Present location unknown.

FIG. 46—Nāga with two attendants supported by *makaras*. From railing pillar, Amarāvatī. Late second century A. D. Madras Museum.

FIG. 47—Yakṣa, Deoriyā, Allahābād. The deity wears a turban, and has a chatra over his head. (Cf. Fig. 18.) Third century B. C.

FIG. 48—Bodhisattva Maitreya, with the *amṛta* flask in the left hand. (Cf. Fig. 49.) First century A. D. (?) Timken (Burnet) Collection, New York.

FIG. 49—Nāga, with a flask in the left hand. (Cf. Fig. 48, and also *A. S. I.*, *A. R.*, 1919-20, pl. XXI, b, the same type seated, mediaeval, called Nāgārjuna, but in Vogel, *Indian Serpent Lore*, pl. XIV, designated a Nāga. Cf. also the Nāga Dadhikarṇa with a flask, *A. S. I.*, *A. R.*, 1924-5, pl. XL, a.) First century A. D. (?) Author's collection.

FIG. 50—Bodhisattva. From Mathurā. Early second century A. D. (?) University Museum, Philadelphia.

FIG. 51—Buddha. From Mathurā. Second century A. D. Present location unknown.

FIG. 52—Buddha. From Mathurā. Third century A. D. Present location unknown.

FIG. 53—Buddha. From Gandhāra. C. 100 A. D. (?)

FIG. 54—Buddha. From Gandhāra. C. 100 A. D.

FIG. 55—Bodhisattva. From Gandhāra (Sahr-i-Bahlol). C. 100 A. D. (?)

FIG. 56—Reliquary of Kaniṣka. From Peshāwar. Second quarter of second century A. D. Calcutta Museum.

FIG. 57—*Vessantara Jātaka*. From Gandhāra. (Cf. Fig. 29.) Second or third century A. D. Museum of Fine Arts, Boston.

FIG. 58—Six scenes from the life of the Buddha. From Mathurā. (This and the next show some Gandhāra features.) Second century A. D. Mathurā Museum.

FIG. 59—Two scenes from the life of the Buddha. From Mathurā. Second century A. D. Mathurā Museum.

FIG. 60—Seated Buddha, with two attendant caurī-bearers (Yakṣas). School of Amarāvatī. About 200 A. D. Field Museum, Chicago.

FIG. 61—Buddha. From Māṅkuwāṛ. Inscription dated equivalent to 448/9 A. D.

FIG. 62—Buddha. From Mathurā. Late second century A. D. (?) Sāñcī, *in situ.*

FIG. 63—Buddha. Fifth century A. D. Sāñcī, *in situ.*

FIG. 64—Jina with two Yakṣa attendants. Mediaeval. Mathurā Museum.

FIG. 65—The Bodhisattva Vajrapāṇi, copper. From Ceylon. Ninth century. Museum of Fine Arts, Boston.

FIG. 66—Buddha, copper, Nepal. C. tenth century. Museum of Fine Arts, Boston.

FIG. 67—The Jina Pārśvanātha, bronze, Kannaḍa. Mediaeval. Kay collection, Madras.

FIG. 68—Buddha. From Dong Duong, Annam, possibly of Indian or Sinhalese manufacture. C. third century A. D. Hanoi Museum.

FIG. 69—Buddha. From Mathurā. Third century A. D. Mathurā Museum.

FIG. 70—Buddha. From Anurādhapura, Ceylon. Third or fourth century A. D. Colombo Museum.

FIG. 71—Buddha. Said to have been found in Burma, but probably of Indian manufacture. C. sixth century A. D. Museum of Fine Arts, Boston.

FIG. 72—Buddha. From Sārnāth. C. fifth century A. D. Sārnāth Museum.

FIG. 73—Bodhisattva Padmapāṇi. From Sārnāth. C. fifth century A. D. Sārnāth Museum.

APPENDIX

As remarked by Kern (*Manual of Indian Buddhism*, p. 94), "There is no lack of legends anent the origin of Buddha images, but it would be difficult to discover in those tales, which are wholly discordant, something like a historical nucleus. Nothing definite results from the legends, except the fact that images of the Tathāgata were venerated by the faithful at the time of the tales being invented." The stories are well known. Most of the references will be found in Kern, *loc. cit.*, p. 94; see also J. Hackin, *Illustrations tibétaines d'une légende du Divyāvadāna*, in *Ann. du Musée Guimet, Bib. de Vulg.*, XL, 1914. I have not thought it worth while to cite any of these stories above. But there are some which are of considerable interest in connection with what has been said about the lay origin of the cult, the analogy with images of other deities in current use, and the hesitation with which a Buddha image was at first accepted as orthodox. The citations below are of interest as illustrating the psychology of those whose devotional feelings led to the use of Buddha images.

The *Mahāvaṁsa*, V, 90 ff., written no doubt when images were already well known, very naturally ascribes to Aśoka a desire to behold the likeness of Buddha. " 'Let us behold,' he is made to say, 'the form of the omiscient Great Sage, of him who hath boundless knowledge, who hath set rolling the Wheel of the True Doctrine.' " Then a Nāga king in response to this expressed desire "created a beauteous figure of the Buddha, endowed with the thirty-two greater signs and brilliant with the eighty lesser signs, surrounded by the fathom-long rays of glory and adorned with the crown of flames."

In the *Divyāvadāna*, ch. ~~LXXXVII~~, Upagupta compels Māra to exhibit himself in the shape of Buddha. Upagupta bows down to the form thus produced, and Māra is shocked at this apparent worship of himself and protests. Upagupta explains that he is adoring not Māra, but the person represented, "just as people venerating earthen images of gods do not revere the clay but the immortal ones represented by them. . . ."

"Indeed, I am well aware of this, that the foremost of teachers has passed away into Nirvāṇa, yet beholding his lovely likeness (*nayanakāntāṁ ākṛtiṁ*), I have bowed to that Rsi; it is not you whom I worship."

Analogous to the coming into use of a Buddha icon is the first use of the Buddha legend as material for a drama. In this connection the Kah-gyur (Schiefner, *Tibetan Tales*, no. XIII) has a story about an actor, who went first to the Nāga Nanda, a faithful worshipper of the Buddha (in whose lifetime the events are supposed to have taken place), to obtain from him the necessary data for the drama. Nanda, on hearing the purpose for which the information was required, refused contemptuously: "Wretched man," he said, "do you wish us to portray the Teacher for you? begone, for I will tell you nothing." The actor, however, obtained the required information from a learned nun and composed his drama. "He pitched a booth in Rājagṛha on the day when the festival of the Nāgarājas Girika and Sundara was celebrated and sounded a drum. And when a great crowd had collected, he exhibited in a drama . . . events in the life of Bhagavant, in harmony with the Abhiniṣkramaṇa Sūtra. Thereby the performers and the assembled crowds were confirmed in the faith. And they uttered sounds of approval, and he made a large profit."

All this must have been very like what took place when Buddha images first came into use. Incidentally it has some value for the history of the Indian drama.

Art Bulletin Vol. IX, No. 4

Origin of the Buddha Image: Corrigenda

Captions:

Figure 2—For *Besnagar* read *Pārkham*
Figure 4—For *Mathurā* read *Sārnāth*
Figure 5—For *Sārnāth* read *Mathurā*
Figure 38—For *Great Enlightenment* read *First Meditation*

Description of Plates:

Figure 2—For *Besnagar* read *Pārkham* and for *Indian Museum, Calcutta*, read *Mathurā Museum*
Figure 8—Add *Lahore Museum*
Figure 38—For *Great Enlightenment* read *First Meditation*

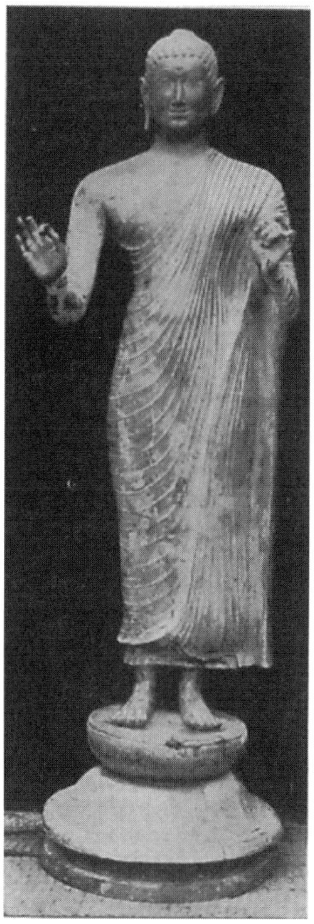

68—Buddha (Annam)

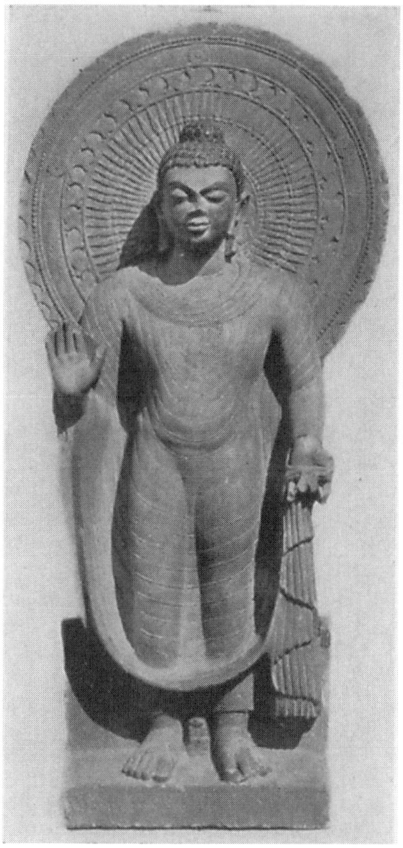

69—Buddha (Mathurā)

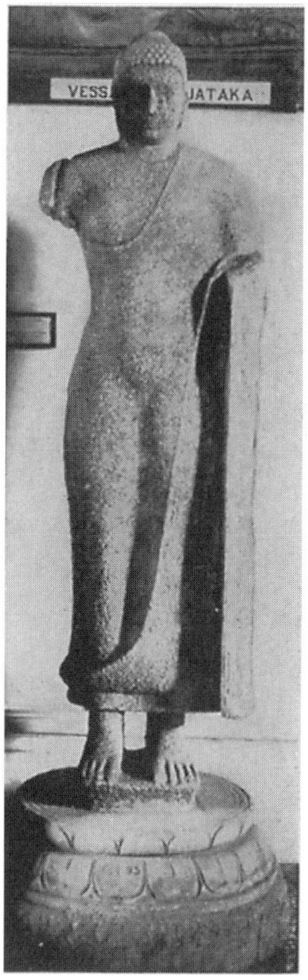

70—Buddha (Ceylon)

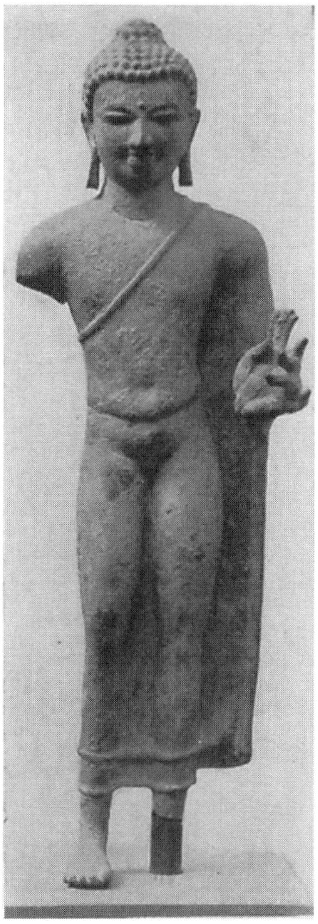

71—Buddha "Burma"

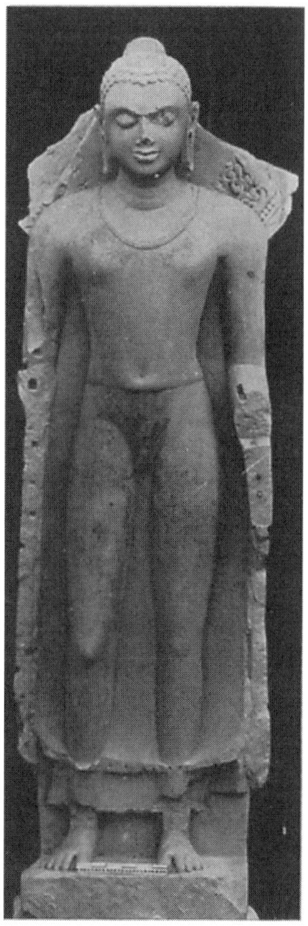

72—Buddha (Sārnāth)

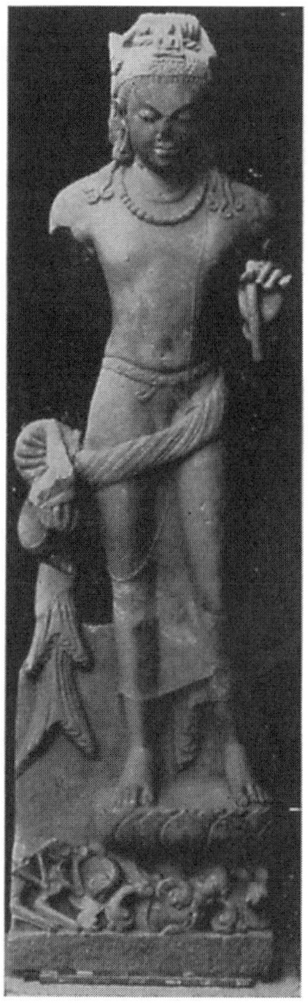

73—Bodhisattva Padmapāṇi (Sārnāth)

Late Kuṣāna and Gupta Buddhas and Bodhisattvas

ELEMENTS OF BUDDHIST ICONOGRAPHY

BY

ANANDA K. COOMARASWAMY

CAMBRIDGE, MASSACHUSETTS
HARVARD UNIVERSITY PRESS
1935

FOREWORD

Coomaraswamy's *A New Approach to the Vedas,* Luzac and Company, 1933, *The Transformation of Nature in Art,* Harvard University Press, 1934, and the present volume, which is published under the auspices of the Harvard-Yenching Institute, are based on the following convictions, which have gradually been developing in his mind.

In the first place, Buddhist art in India — and that is practically equivalent to saying art in India — begins about the second century before Christ with a well-developed set of symbols in its iconography. It does not seem possible to completely separate Buddhism as religion and as art from the main current of Indian religion and art, or to think that these symbols suddenly developed as a new creation. Therefore Coomaraswamy proceeded to study from a new point of view the symbolism which pervades the whole early Vedic literature of India, trying to discover whether concepts expressed symbolically in the literature of the aniconic Vedic period may not have found their first iconographic expression in early Buddhist art.

In the second place, he noted many surprising similarities between passages in the mediaeval Christian theologians and mystics, such as St Thomas, Meister Eckhart, Ruysbroeck, and Böhme, and passages in the Vedic literature — similarities so striking that many sentences from the Christian writers might be taken as almost literal translations of Sanskrit sentences, or vice versa. The conviction developed in him that mystical theology the world over is the same, and that mediaeval Christian theology might be used as a tool to the better understanding of ancient Indian theology. This theory he proceeded to apply even to the Rig Veda, assuming, contrary to the general opinion, no complete break in thought between the Rig Veda and the Brahmanas and Upanishads. In many obscure and so-called "mystical" stanzas of the Rig Veda and Atharva Veda he finds the same concepts vaguely hinted at which are employed in a more developed form in Brahmanism and Buddhism.

The present study of the Tree of Life, the Earth-Lotus the Word-Wheel, the Lotus-Throne, and the Fiery Pillar tries to show that these symbols can be traced back beyond their first representation in Buddhist

"Symbols cannot be studied apart from the references which they symbolise."

Ogden and Richards, *The Meaning of Meaning*, p. 20

"To determine the import of names is the same as to determine the fundamental character of concepts."

Stcherbatsky, *Buddhist Logic*, I, p. 459

"I speak thus (in images) because of the frailty of the intelligence of the tender children of men." "But since thou takest thy stand upon the principles (*dharmeṣu*), how is it that thou dost not enunciate the First Principle (*tattvam*) explicitly?" "Because, although I refer to the First Principle, there is not any 'thing' in Intellect corresponding to the reference 'First Principle.'"

Laṅkâvatāra Sūtra, II, 112 and 114

"The picture is not in the colors . . . the Principle (*tattvam*) transcends the letter."

Laṅkâvatāra Sūtra, II, 118–119

Mirate la dottrina, che s'asconde, sotto il velame degli versi strani.

Dante, *Inferno*, IX, 61

iconography through the aniconic period of the Brahmanical Vedas, even into the Rig Vedic period itself, and that they represent a universal Indian symbolism and set of theological concepts.

Objective linguistics is apparently near the end of its resources in dealing with the many remaining obscurities of Rig Vedic phraseology. This new metaphysical approach is welcome even though to the matter-of-fact linguist it may seem that ideas are not being built up on the basis of words but that words are being made to fit ideas.

Walter Eugene Clark

Harvard University
June 27, 1934

PART I

TREE OF LIFE, EARTH-LOTUS, AND WORD-WHEEL

"Die Menschheit . . . versucht sie, in die greifbare oder sonstwie wahrnehmbare Form zu bringen, wir könnten sage zu materialisen, was ungreifbar, nichtwahrnehmbar ist. Sie schafft Symbol, Schriftzeichen, Kultbild aus irdischen Stoff und schaut in ihnen und hinter ihnen das sonst unschaubare, unvorstellbare geistige und göttliche Geschehen."
—Walter Andrae, *Die ionische Säule, Bauform oder Symbol?* 1933, p. 65.

THE iconography (*rūpa-bheda*) of Indian and Far Eastern art has been discussed hitherto almost exclusively with respect to the identification of the various hypostases as represented "anthropomorphically" in the later art. Here it is proposed to treat those fundamental elements of Buddhist symbolism which predominate in the earlier aniconic art, and are never dispensed with in the later imagery, though they are there subordinated to the "human" icon. In neither case is the symbol designed as though to function biologically: as symbol (*pratīka*) it expresses an idea, and is not the likeness of anything presented to the eye's intrinsic faculty.[1] Nor is the aniconic image less or more the likeness of Him, First Principle, who is no thing, but whose image it is, than is the "human" form. To conceive of Him as a living Tree, or as a Lamb or Dove, is no less sound theology than to conceive of Him as Man, who is not merely *mānuṣya-laukika* but *sarva-laukika*, not merely *mānuṣa-raupya* but *viśva-raupya*, not human merely but of Universal Form.[2] Any purely anthropomorphic theology is to that extent specifically limited; but He takes on vegetative, theriomorphic, and geometrical forms and sounds just as much and just as little as he dons flesh.[3] So the Bodhisattva vows that he will not be Utterly Extinguished until the last blade of grass shall have reached its goal.

What has been said above is to dispel the notion that in discussing symbolism we are leaving life behind us; on the contrary, it is precisely by means of symbols that *ars imitatur naturam in sua operatione*, all other "imitation" being idolatry. Before proceeding, it only remains to be said that if any particular stress seems to be laid on Buddhism, this is strictly speaking an accident. Buddhism in India represents a heterodox development, all that is metaphysically "correct" (*pramiti*) in its ontology and symbolism being derived from the primordial tradition; with the slight necessary transpositions, indeed, the greater part of what is said could be directly applied to the understanding of Christian art. In the following discussion, no ideas or opinions of my own are expressed, everything being taken directly, and often verbally, from Vedic or Buddhist sources.

It has often been remarked that in Pali texts there is no express tradition prohibiting the making of anthropomorphic images of the Tathāgata, originally "So-come" or "So-gone," later "Who has entered into the Suchness," which might account for the designation of the Buddha only by aniconic symbols in the early art.[4] And this is essentially true; the representation by aniconic symbols is not in kind a Buddhist invention, but represents the survival of an older tradition,[5] the anthropomorphic image becoming a psychological necessity only in *bhakti-vāda* offices. However, the *Kāliṅga-bodhi Jātaka* (J., IV, 228), in the Introduction, enunciates what amounts to such a prohibition, and may well have been the point of view current in Buddhist circles at a much earlier date than can be positively asserted for the Jātaka text. Here Ānanda desires to set up in the Jetavana a substitute for the Buddha, so that people may be able to make their offerings of wreaths and garlands at the door of the Gandhakuṭi, as *pūjanīyaṭṭhāna,* not only when the Buddha is in residence, but also when he is away preaching the Dharma elsewhere. The Buddha asks how many kinds of hallows (*cetiya*)[6] there are. "Three," says Ānanda, with implied reference to contemporary non-Buddhist usage, "viz., those of the body (*sārīraka*), those of association (*pāribhogaka*),[7] and those prescribed (*uddesika*)." The Buddha rejects the use of bodily relics on the obvious ground that such relics can only be venerated after the Parinibbāṇa. He rejects the "prescribed" symbols also because such are "groundless and merely fanciful" (*avatthukaṁ manamattakaṁ*), that is to say only artificially and by convention referable to the absent being for whom a substitute is desired; the terms as employed here in a derogatory sense can only mean "arbitrary." So "Only a Mahā-bodhi-rukkha, Great-Wisdom-tree, that has been associated with a Buddha is fit to be a *cetiya,* whether the Buddha be still living, or Absolutely Extinguished." This occurs also in the *Mahābodhivaṁsa,* PTS. ed. p. 59.

In the absence of specific definition, it may be assumed that the class of "associated" symbols included also such other aniconic representations as the wheel (*cakra*), feet (*pāduka*), *triśūla* ("*nandi-pada*"), and/or other geometrical, vegetative, or even theriomorphic forms actually met with in early Buddhist art. It is true that, like the tree, these symbols had older than Buddhist application, and one could imagine objections made accordingly — had not Sujātā indeed mistaken the Bodhisattva for a *rukkha-devatā*? But where no objection had been made to the tree, none could have been logically raised in connection with the other symbols. These in fact came into use in connection with the setting up of local *cetiyas* as objects of reverence, as substitutes for pilgrimage to the original sites, the different symbols serving, as is well known, to differentiate between the several Events. The wheel, for example, had special reference to the first preaching in Benares. At the same time, the use of such symbols, with their inherent metaphysical implications, must have contributed to the early definition of the mythical Buddhology. It is perhaps because the Jātaka passages do not yet take account of Four Events, but only of the most important, the Great Awakening — a recent event from the Hīnayāna point of view — that the Buddha is made to say that a Buddha can *only* be represented rightly by a Great-Wisdom-tree.

By *uddesika*, "prescribed," corresponding to *vyakta*, "manifest," in the Brahmanical classifications of icons, we should expect that anthropomorphic images were indicated, and this is confirmed in the *Khuddakapāṭha-Atthakathā* (PTS. ed., 1915, p. 222), where *uddissaka-cetiyaṁ* is explained by *buddha-paṭimā*, "an image of the Buddha." Notwithstanding that a use of anthropomorphic images of any kind must have been rare in the Buddha's lifetime, it is clear that the Commentators understood that the Buddha's own position was definitely iconoclastic. It is true that the Buddha image, with its non-human *lakkhaṇas*, can no more than other Indian images be thought of as the likeness of a man, nevertheless the objection made must have depended on the generally human appearance of such images, this appearance being inappropriate to him who was "not a man." We ought perhaps rather to say that it was in this way that the ancient custom of using predominantly aniconic imagery was thus explained and justified. The attitude of those who actually made use of anthropomorphic images is defined in the *Divyâvadāna*, Ch. XXVI, where it is explained that those who look at earthen images (*mṛnmaya-pratikṛti*) "do not honor the clay as such, but without regard thereof, honor the deathless principles referred to (*amara-saṁjñā*) in the earthen images." The rendering of *uddesika* as "prescribed" is supported by the expressed *yathāsaṁdiṣṭam* in the *Divyâvadāna* passage cited below.

The Buddha is represented as dealing again with the same problem in later life, and now (*Mahāparinibbāṇa Sutta*, V, 8 and 12 = *Dīgha Nikāya* II, 140–143), in view of his approaching death, he declares that after the Total Extinction there are four places proper to be visited by the community, and these "places which should stir deep feeling" (*saṁvejanīyāni ṭhānāni*, cf. *pūjanīyaṭṭhāna* cited above) are those at which the four crises of the Buddha's life had been passed. With respect to the edification resulting from such visits, we are told that at the sight of the *thūpa* of the Rāja Cakkavatti "the hearts of many shall be made calm and glad."

Later traditions represent the Buddha himself as having not merely sanctioned but actually instituted the use of anthropomorphic images. Thus, according to the *Divyâvadāna*, p. 547, Rudrâyaṇa (sc. Udâyana) desires a means of making offerings to the Buddha when he is absent; the Blessed One said "Have an image of the Tathāgata drawn on canvas, and make your offering thereto" (*tathāgata-pratimām paṭe likhāpayitvā*, etc.). Rudrâyaṇa calls his painters (*cittakarā*). They say that they cannot grasp the Blessed One's exemplum (*na śaknuvanti bhagavato nimittam udgrahītum*). The Blessed One says that is because they are affected by lassitude (*kheda*, equivalent to *śithilasamādhi* in *Mālavikâgnimitra*, II, 2), but "bring me a piece of canvas" (*api tu paṭakaṃ ānaya*). Then the Blessed One projected his similitude upon it (*tatra . . chāyā utsṛṣṭā*), and said "complete it with colors" (*raṅgaiḥ pūrayata*), adding that certain texts are to be written (*likhitavyāni*) below. And so "everything was by them depicted according to prescription" (*yathāsaṁdiṣṭaṁ sarvam abhilikhitam*).

According to the version of this legend preserved by Hsüan-tsang (Beal, *Life*, p. 91) it was an image of sandal-wood rather than a painting that was made for Udâyana; a skilled imager was transported to the Trayastriṁśas heaven by Maudgalyâyana, and after contemplating there the appearance and features of the Buddha, who was preaching the Law to his mother, the artist was brought back to earth and carved the figure in his likeness. This image, which Hsüan-tsang identified with one that he saw at Kauśambī, was nevertheless as he mentions elsewhere (*Si-yu-ki*, Beal, *Records . . .*, II, p. 322) borne through the air (we may interpret, "transferred as a mental image in the mind of a sculptor") to Khotān, and there became the archetype of innumerable later copies, which are regarded as possessing a similitude of univocation, so that we find at Long Men a statue called "Udâyana's" (Chavannes, *Mission archéologique* . . ., pp. 391–2). There is also the tradition of still another image, made in gold after the Buddha's final departure, and it is with reference to an image in this "succession" that an inscription of about 665 at Long Men (Chavannes, *loc. cit.*, p. 362), remarks "Si l'influence et le modèle ne disparurent pas, c'est grace à celà" where the thought expressed is tantamount to this, that the image is still his whose image it is. With respect to such traditional representations it is also said in an inscription of 641 (Chavannes, *loc. cit.*, p. 340–1) "Le K'i-chö est devant nos yeux; Na-kie peut être représentée," that is, "when we look at these statues, it is just as if we saw the Buddha himself on Vulture Peak, or his likeness in the cave at Nāgarahāra" (where he left his "shadow" (cf. *chāyā utsṛṣṭā* in the *Divyâvadāna* passage cited above). As the Long Men inscription of 543 (Chavannes, *loc. cit.*) reminds us, "they cut the stone of price in imitation of his supernatural person." In the absence of the past manifestation in a human body (as Śākyamuni) and before the future manifestation (of Maitreya) the Wayfarer resorts to a means of access to the transcendental principles from which all manifestations proceed. The image merely as such is of no value; all depends on what he does who looks at it; what is expected of him is an act of contemplation such that when he sees before him the characteristic lineaments, it is for him as though the whole person of the Buddha were present; he journeys in the spirit to the transcendent gathering on Vulture Peak (*Saddharma Puṇḍarīka,* Ch. XV). Aesthetic and religious experience are here indivisible; rising to the level of reference intended, "his heart is broadened with a mighty understanding" (inscription of 641, Chavannes, p. 340). Cf. Mus, *Le Buddha paré* . . ., BÉFEO., 1928, pp. 248–9. The experience of those who beheld the likeness of Buddha is further described at length in the *Divyâvadāna*, Ch. XXVI, in connection with Māra's exhibition of the Buddha's similitude.

Our present concern is, however, primarily with the aniconic representations, and first of all with the symbolic representation by means of the Tree. That the ancient symbol of the Tree of Life, *vṛkṣa* (= *rukkha*), *vanaspati, akṣaya-vaṭa,* or *eka aśvattha* of the Vedas and Upaniṣads, should thus have been chosen to represent the Buddha is highly significant; for as we have already indicated, every traditional symbol necessarily carries with it its original values, even when used or intended to be used in a more restricted sense. In order to appreciate the full content of Buddhist symbolism we must accordingly take into account the fundamental implications of the symbols employed; in fact only a knowledge of the symbols in their total significance will suffice for an understanding of their values as they are employed in connection with the developed Buddhology. To sum up, then, the pre-Buddhist and some possibly later references: [8] the Tree of Life, synonymous with all existence, all the worlds, all life, springs up, out, or down into space [9] from its root in the navel centre of the Supreme Being, Varuṇa, Mahāyakṣa, Asura, Brahman, as he lies extended on the back of the Waters, the possibilities of existence and the source of his abundance. That Tree is his procession (*utkrama, prasaraṇa, pravṛtti*) in a likeness (*mūrta*), the emanation of his fiery-energy (*tejas*) as light, the spiration of his breath (*prâṇa*); he is its wise, indestructible mover (*rerivā*).[10]

The "Lord of the Forest" (*vanaspati*) is already in the Vedas a familiar symbol of the supreme deity in his manifested aspect. There may be cited, for example, *Ṛg Veda*, I, 24, 7, "King Varuṇa as pure act lifted up in the Unground the summit (*stūpam*) of the Tree"; I, 164, 20–21, "Two Fairwings (*suparṇāḥ*, birds, angels) in conjoint amity rest in the one same Tree; one eats the tasty fig (*pippalam*), the other looketh on and does not eat . . . there those Fairwings sing incessantly their part of lasting-life"; Varuṇa, Prajāpati, or Brahman manifesting as the moving spirit in the cosmic Tree is called a Yakṣa, cf. *Atharva Veda*, X, 7, 38, "A great Yakṣa proceeding in a seething on the back of the waters, in whom abide whatever Angels be, as branches of the Tree that are round about its trunk," and *Kena Up.*, 15–26, "What Yakṣa is this? . . . Brahman."

The description of the World-tree in the *Maitri Up.*, VI, 1–4, VII, 11, and VI, 35, may be quoted at length:

"There are verily two forms of Brahman, with and without likeness (*mūrta, amūrta*). Now the That which is in a likeness is contingent (*asatya*); the That which is imageless is essential (*satya*) Brahman, light. That Light is the light of the Supernal-Sun. He verily becomes with OṀ as Self. He assumed a Trinity, for the OṀ has three factors, and it is by these that 'the whole world is woven, warp and woof, on Him.' As it has been said, 'beholding that the Supernal-Sun is OṀ, unify therewith thyself.' . . .

The threefold Brahman has his root above, His branches are space, air, fire, water, earth, and the rest. This is called the Single Fig-tree (*eka aśvattha*); and therein inheres the fiery-energy (*tejas*) that is the Supernal-Sun . . . the One Awakener (*eka sambodhayitṛ*). . . . This, verily, is the intrinsic form of space in the vacuity of the inward man (*antarbhūtasya khe*); that is the supreme fiery-energy (*tejas*), determined as the Trinity of Fire, Supernal-Sun, and Spirit . . . the Imperishable-Word, OM. And by that Imperishable-Word, the fiery-energy awakens (*udbudhyati*), springs up, and expands; that is verily an everlasting basis (*ālamba*) for the vision of Brahman. In the spiration it has its place in the dark-heat that emanates light, proceeding upwards as is the way of smoke when the wind blows, as a branching forth in the firmament, stem after stem . . . all-pervading as contemplative vision. . . . He who is yonder, yonder Person in the Supernal-Sun, I my-Self am He."

Here the World-tree becomes a "Burning Bush," in an imagery closely related to that by which in several Vedic texts Agni is spoken of as a cosmic pillar, supporting all existences. Almost all of this is valid Buddhology, if only we substitute "Buddha" for "Brahman," remember the large part played by the concept of the Fiery-Energy (*tejas*) even in canonical texts, and take account of the early iconography as well as of the literature. Especially noteworthy is the designation of the "Single Fig-tree" as the World-form of the "One Awakener" (*eka sambodhayitṛ*) and "enduring basis of the vision of Brahman" (*brahma-dhīyâlamba*); for just so also is the Buddha's Fig-tree (*aśvattha*) constantly spoken of as the "Great Awakening" (*mahā-sambodhi*); being the chosen symbol of the Buddha's unseen essence, it is an enduring basis for the vision of Buddha; it might have been called in Pali *Tathāgata-jhānâlamba*, cf. the terms *ārambaṇa, āvaraṇa, upadarśana,* used of the Tathāgata's various manifestations, *Saddharma Puṇḍarīka*, text, p. 318, and *ālamba* = *viṣaya-grahaṇa,* Vasubandhu, *Abhidharmakośa,* I, 34, and II, 34, b–d. The *Mahā Sukhāvatī-Vyūha,* 32, in fact, merely paraphrases the words of the *Maitri Up.* cited above, when it is said that "All those beings that are constant in never turning away from the vision of that Bodhi-tree are by the same token constant in never losing sight of the supreme and perfect Awakening" (*tasya bodhi-vṛkṣasya . . . yad uta anuttarāyāḥ saṁyak-sambodheḥ*). In the *Maitri Up.* text the expression *udbudhyati*, "awakens," applied to the Tree, is significant, and like the designation *uṣarbudh,* "awakened at dawn," which in the *Ṛg Veda* is commonly applied to Agni, recalls him who is typically *buddha,* the "Wake."[11] As for the Fiery-Energy (*tejas*), this is the element of fire present as an unseen energy in all existences, but preëminently manifested by Arhats or the Buddha, e. g. in the case of the "Double Miracle," the "Conversion of Kassapa," or when (*Saṁyutta Nikāya,* I, 144) the Buddha takes his seat in the firmament immediately above Brahmā. In *Theragāthā,* 1095, where *arahatta* is clearly synonymous with Buddhahood, the *uggetejo,* "sharp fiery-energy," is the flaming sword of Understanding (*paññā* = *prajñā*) whereby Māra is defeated. In *Dhammapada,* 387, the Buddha "glows with fiery-energy," *tapati tejasā.*[12]

Amongst the late Āndhra reliefs from Amarāvatī may be seen numerous remarkable representations of the Buddha as a fiery pillar, with wheel-marked feet, supported by a lotus, and with a *triśūla* "head" (Figs. 4–10);[13] these have been almost completely ignored by students of Buddhist iconography.[14] Remembering, however, (1) that Agni is born of the Waters, or more directly from the Earth as it rests upon the Waters, hence specifically from a lotus (*puṣkara*), *Ṛg Veda,* VI, 16, 13, and (2) is frequently spoken of as the pillar that supports all existences, e. g. *Ṛg Veda,* I, 59, 1–2, and IV, 13, 5, it is clear that the Buddhist fiery pillars represent the survival of a purely Vedic formula in which Agni is represented as the axis of the Universe, extending as a pillar between Earth and Heaven.[15]

No less remarkable than the fiery pillars of Amarāvatī is the unique representation of a Buddha in the form of a *kalpa-vṛkṣa* or "wishing-tree" at Sāñcī (Fig. 1).[16] This Tree of Life is like the fiery pillars at Amarāvatī as to its head and wheel-marked feet, but its trunk is built up of superimposed lotus palmettes,[17] and bears laterally by way of fruits pearl garlands and other jewels suspended from pegs such as are elsewhere spoken of as *nāgadanta.* It may be remarked that only perhaps a century later (*Mahā Sukhāvatī-vyūha,* 16, and again, *Saddharma Puṇḍarīka,* V, 29–33) the seekers after Buddhahood are compared to small and great herbs, and small and great trees, and that Sukhāvatī is said to be crowded with jewelled trees made of precious metals and gems, presumably representing various degrees of enlightenment. The jewel-tree of Sāñcī corresponds directly to the Bodhi-tree of Amitâyus, Tathāgata, described in the *Mahā Sukhāvatī-vyūha,* 31: "A thousand *yojanas* in height . . . it is always in leaf, always in flower, always in fruit, of a thousand hues and various foliage, flower, and fruit . . . it is hung with golden strings, adorned with hundreds of golden chains . . . strings of rose pearls and strings of black pearls . . . adorned with symbols of the *makara, svastika, nandyāvarta,* and moon . . . according to the desires of living beings, whatever their desire may be." Such a symbol as this, though assuredly of Buddhist import, is not of Buddhist origin; even the words "fulfilling the desires of living beings, whatever they may be" ring strangely in the ambient of early Buddhist monasticism. All this implies in relatively early Buddhism already existing Mahāyānist tendencies, which are really a prolongation of Vedic tradition. Amitâyus, "Immeasurable Life," corresponds to innumerable Vedic designations of Agni, often also invoked as Vanaspati, "Lord of the Forest," or "King of Trees," as Viśvâyus, "Life Universal," or Ekâyus, "The One Life"; Amitâbha to Vedic notions of the all-seeing Sun, or Agni whose beams dispel all darknesses, cf. I, 65, 5 *dūrebhā,* "shining from afar," and VI, 10, 4, *paprau . . . urvī dūredṛśā bhāsā,* "filled heaven and earth with a far-seen light." It is certainly not impossible that the notions "Amitâyus" and "Amitâbha" had received a Buddhist interpretation in or before the first century B.C.: this need not have prevented a connection of the jewelled tree with Śākyamuni, who is in fact the earthly counterpart of Amitâbha.

The World-tree then, equally in and apart from its Buddhist application, is the procession of incessant life. Standing erect and midmost in the garden of life, extending from Earth to Heaven, branching throughout Space (we shall see later that "space" is "within you"), that is the one Wishing-tree (*kappa-rukkha, kalpa-vṛkṣa*) that yields the fruits of life, all that every creature calls "good." Buddhism interprets this, as it interprets the corresponding symbol of the Dharmacakra, from an edifying point of view: that Wisdom-tree (*jñāna-druma*) "whose roots strike deep into stability . . . whose flowers are moral acts . . . which bears righteousness (*dharma*) as its fruit . . . ought not to be felled," *Buddhacarita,* XIII, 65. But amongst the accidents of being, the fruits of life, are also the wages of desire, that is our mortality, *jarā-maraṇa,* all that every existence, each embodied will to life, calls "evil." So the World-tree, as an exteriorization of the Will to Life, *kāma,* and corresponding Craving, *taṇha, tṛṣṇa,* from the point of view of all those who would be naughted is a tree to be felled at the root: in Buddhism, a "vine of coveting (*taṇhā-latā*), who shall cut (*chind*) it off?" (*Theragāthā,* 761 and 1094). For in a modeless mode there is a Principle "higher and other than the World-tree . . . the Bringer of Truth (*dharma*) and Remover of Evil (*pāpa*)," *Śvetâśvatara Up.*, VI, 6; note the "Buddhist" ring of these Aupaniṣada expressions. He who Understands, or who is become a Comprehensor, *ya evaṁ vidvān,* a Buddha, who beholds the tree with seeing and undesirous eyes, sees in it the One Awakener, *eka sambodhayitṛ*, the Great Awakening, *mahāsambodhi*. By that very Understanding, *paññā, prajñā,* he fells it at the root, *aśvattham . . . chittvā, Bhagavad Gītā,* XV, 3, he is quit of Brahmā, quit of Māra at one stroke;[18] for him the Garden of Life, *prâṇârāma,* becomes the Circle of Wisdom, Bodhimaṇḍa (-la); for him the world is voided of any personal content, of any self or Self, and as *anātmya, anatta,* he is emancipated from mortality, Totally Extinguished, *parinirvāta*. But he who desires and eats the fruits or shoots (*viṣaya-pravālāḥ, Bhagavad Gītā,* XV, 2), be he man or angel, and thereby comes into operation or existence, thereby also perishes at last, for, as is repeatedly enunciated in the Pali Buddhist canon, "Whatsoever has an origin, in that is inherent the necessity of dissolution." He only whose desires are all liberated (*pramucyante*), who does not desire, becomes immortal (*amṛta*), being very Brahman goes to Brahman (*Bṛhadāraṇyaka Up.*, IV, 4, 6, and 7): that is, in Buddhist terms is *parinibbuta, parinirvāta,* in Christian terms is dead and buried in the Godhead, having died to God and all his works.[19] Inasmuch as works of any kind are necessarily purposeful, being undertaken with an end in view, it is a perfectly correct theology which represents Brahmā, Buddha, or God, *qua* Creator or *qua* Saviour, as a mortal being, uttering a Word which as it is in itself cannot be thought or spoken. *Dharmacakra-pravartana,* then, has an essential content wider than that of merely "Preaching the Gospel"; it implies the creation of the world, and in this capacity as Lokapitā, and equivalent to Brahmā, the Buddha can only be thought of as *prajā-kāmya,* philoprogenitive; even in early Buddhism, that the Buddha teaches (and at first he hesitates to do so) is because he is moved by compassion. "Philoprogenitive" and "compassionate" are to be understood, of course, in a metaphysical, not in a sentimental, sense.

The distinction between Nirvāṇa and Parinirvāṇa is no less fundamental and necessary than that of God from Godhead in Christianity.[20] Those who maintain the "rationalism" of early Buddhism may deny the value of its theological development, yet the fact remains that without this development and such distinctions Buddhist and Christian iconography would be devoid of intelligible meaning; the only Buddhist or Christian art which could have existed must have been an art of realistic portraiture, "in memory" of the Founders and their Saints. For example, the representation of the Parinirvāṇa by the *stūpa*, essentially a tomb, or alternatively by the actual scene of death, is altogether appropriate, whether we regard the Great Decease from a human or a transcendental point of view. In the same way the *Bṛhadāraṇyaka Up.*, I, 2, speaks of That which is logically antecedent to the Self, and whereto the Self returns un-Selfed, as "Death" and "Privation." Again the double negative, privation being here privation of a limiting affirmation.[21]

To think of these as "pessimistic" expressions is to confuse Existence with Being and Non-being, destiny with liberty. Beside the Buddha's death-bed only Brahmā and those Arhats who were "the same" in singleness and wisdom shed no tears; Angels such as Indra wept and wailed, being still attached to their and to his existent Personality. At the same time, it was taken for granted that the possibilities of existence amply provided for those who clung to individual immortalities throughout immeasurable aeons; this would be in familiar Christian terms until the "Last Judgment"; the individual could not be liberated from limiting conditions, from himself, unless by his own effort, much less against his will. A majority of Buddhists, like the majority of Christians, looked forward to a resurrection in "Heaven," Sukhāvatī, beholding God or Buddha face to face. The Buddha by no means denied such possibilities; but he taught a Way leading to an End beyond Heaven, though he would not, because he could not, God himself could not, explain or define that End in any language, save only in terms of negation.

Although their history and significance can hardly yet be fully explained, some consideration of the symbolic forms representing the head and feet of the jewelled Tree of Life at Sāñcī and the Fiery Pillars at Amarāvatī is necessary. The *triśūla*, in Buddhism (Figs. 1, 4, 23, etc.), commonly understood to denote the jewel-trinity (*ratna-traya*) of Buddha, Dharma, and Saṅgha, is certainly not exclusively of Buddhist nor even wholly of Buddhist and Jaina (Fig. 17) significance; Buddhism, as usual, is adapting an older symbolism to its immediate purposes. Sénart (*La légende du*

Bouddha, p. 484) already regarded the Buddhist *triśūla* as a Fire symbol; we could think of it as naturally representing either the three aspects of Agni Vaiśvānara, or the primordial Agni as the triunity of the Several Angels. This would not in any way conflict with the Śaiva association suggested by Marshall, *Mohenjodaro*, p. 55, cf. our Figs. 21, 22, and indicated also by the use of the symbol in connection with Śiva at a later time, e. g. on the Śaiva coins of Kadphises II and on the Śaiva seal from Sirkap, A.S.I., A.R., 1914–15, p. 51 and Pl. XXIV.[22] That the form corresponds to that of Siva's trident in the later iconography is indeed evident enough. It has not been so much observed that if the symbol is doubled, so as to consist of two addorsed tridents connected by a common stem, there is obtained the usual form of the *vajra*, or if quadrupled that of the fourfold *vajra*. In our representations (Figs. 1, 4, 6, etc.), the *triśūla* forms the termination of a stem or trunk which we have been able to identify with the pillar (*skambha*) that supports-apart Heaven and Earth, and with the axle-tree (*akṣa*) of the Solar chariot, i. e. with the axis of the Universe.[23] Recalling now the kenning *akṣa-ja* = *vajra*, it is not implausible to assume that our *triśūla* may also be thought of as a "single *vajra*."

What we know of the form of the Vedic *vajra* suggests in fact that it was of the single type; *Ṛg Veda*, I, 52, 15, tells us that it was pronged (*bhṛṣṭimat*), I, 121, 4, that it was three-pointed (*trikakubh*).[24] In *Ṛg Veda*, IV, 22, 2, the *vajra* is said to be a four-angled rain-producer (*vṛśaṁdhiṁ caturaśrim*), and in *Aitareya Brāhmaṇa*, X, 1, to be eight-angled. In *Ṛg Veda*, VIII, 7, 22, the Maruts are said to have "put it together joint by joint" (*parvaśo saṁ dadhuḥ*); in I, 80, 6, and VI, 17, 10, it is spoken of as hundred-jointed (*śataparvan*), and in the latter text also as thousand-pointed (for joints or nodes cf. Figs. 2, 3, 41, 42). It may be noted that in *Ṛg Veda*, VI, 22, 6, Indra's weapon is called *parvata*; Sāyaṇa is probably right in saying that this refers not to the "mountain," but to the many-jointed *vajra* (*bahuparvaṇā vajreṇa*). In the *Ṛg Veda* generally the *vajra* is said to have been made by the Divine Craftsman, Tvaṣṭṛ, who is "most skilled in handiworks" (*apasām apastamaḥ*, X, 53, 9), and hence the *vajra* itself is called "most well-made" (*svapastamam*, I, 61, 6, where also it is said to be "of the nature of light," *svaryam*, as in V, 31, 4, where it is "glittering," *dyumantam*). The *vajra* is wielded typically by Indra, who represents the temporal power (*kṣatra*) in relation to Agni as spiritual power (*brahma*);

and after the weapon, Indra is styled *vajrin, vajra-bāhu,* etc. With the *vajra* he slays the dragon, Vṛtra, Śuṣṇa, or Ahi, and thus brings about the whole cosmic manifestation. In the Buddha legend, the Vedic defeat of Ahi-Vṛtra is represented (1) in the Māra-dharṣaṇa, and (2) in the Buddha's defeat of the serpent on the occasion of the conversion of the Jaṭilas. It may be observed that in the Māra-dharṣaṇa, Māra makes use of the characteristic weapons of Vṛtra (cf. *Ṛg Veda,* I, 32, 13), and that the affrighted Angels desert the Bodhisattva, as they do Indra in the battle with Vṛtra (*Ṛg Veda,* IV, 8, 11; VIII, 93, 14–15; VIII, 96, 7; *Aitareya Brāhmaṇa,*

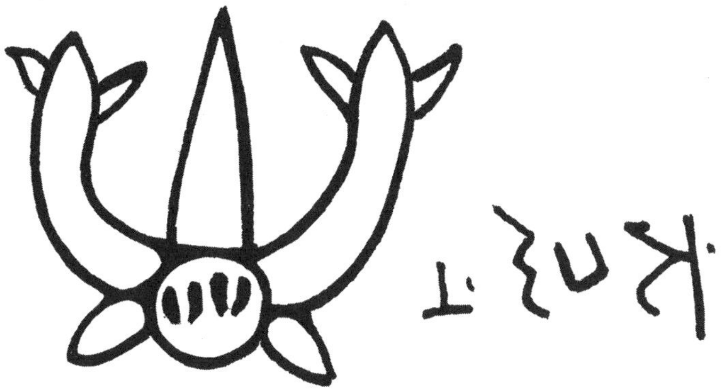

FIG. A. *Nandipaam*: from Paḍana.

IV, 5); while in the Conversion of the Jaṭilas, the serpent is referred to as *ahi-nāga* (*Mahāvagga,* I, 15, 7). In northern Buddhism Māra is sometimes identified with Namuci.

Further as to the shape of the *vajra, Aitareya Brāhmaṇa,* II, 35, tells us that it was narrow at the beginning, and divided above like a club or axe, comparison being made with the bifurcation of human legs (cf. Foucher, *Beginnings of Buddhist Art,* Pl. I, Fig. 6); this, indeed, implies a two-pronged rather than a three-pronged termination, and it may be remarked that in actual iconography (cf. Foucher, *ibid.,* Fig. 7) the two lateral tines are often much more conspicuous than the central tine, which is in fact a prolongation of the stem. Types with from one to eight tines are found in Shingon usage. In Śaiva usage, the three-pronged *triśūla* is borne by the Father (Śiva), the one-pronged *śūla* by the Son (Kārttikeya, Kumāra). In the *Kauṣītaki Brāhmaṇa,* VI, 9, "Vajra" is one of the eight names of Śiva.

The question of terminology offers still another problem. In European literature, the term *nandi-pada* (lit. "Nandi-foot" or "-trace") has been applied to the *triśūla* symbol in Buddhist or presumed Buddhist usage, this name deriving from the form *nandi-paaṁ* inscribed beside the symbol as found on the Padaṇa hill near Bombay,[25] where hoofmarks are clearly indicated (Fig. A). I have argued against the general applicability of this term,[26] and it is far from clear that the label applies to the symbol, and not exclusively to the hoofmarks. Yet in fact the designation "Nandi's track" and the actual representation of hoofprints at Padaṇa accord well enough with the Śaiva associations, the notion of hoofprints equally well also with an original connection with Agni; that Śiva and Agni can be assimilated and in certain aspects identified needs no demonstration here. The designation "taurine," employed by some authors, is probably the best available for our symbol, being appropriate equally to Agni, Śiva, or Buddha. In *Ṛg Veda,* I, 65, 1 (*padaiḥ*), and IV, 5, 3 (where Agni is a "mighty bull," and the Sāman chant "naught other than the hidden track of an ox," *padaṁ na gor apagūḷhaṁ*), the metaphor is employed of tracing the lost Agni by his footprints; cf. X, 71, 3, where the tracks (*padavīya*) of Wisdom (*vāc*) are followed by means of the ritual sacrifice, and *ibid.*, III, 39, 6, where Indra finds "by foot and hoof" (*patvat . . . śaphavat*) the wine of life and makes himself master of all the possibilities of existence "hidden" or "hoarded" in the Waters; cf. again *Bṛhadāraṇyaka Up.*, IV, 4, 23, "He should be a knower of the tracks of Brahman" (*tasyaiva syāt padavittaṁ*), and *ibid.*, I, 4, 7, "As though by a footprint (*pada*), indeed, one should find the Angel" — his trace or footprint "set down in the secret place" (*guhā, guhā nihitam, passim*) being found "by the Sacrifice in the Seers" (*Ṛg Veda,* X, 71, 3), "in the heart" (*ibid.*, X, 177, 1), "in the Sea, the Heart, in living things" (*antaḥ samudre hṛdy antar āyuṣi, ibid.*, IV, 58, 11). "Footprint" or "track" is thus tantamount to "vestige" as understood in Scholastic phraseology: *Dhammapada* should perhaps be translated in this sense as "Vestige of the Law," *dhamma-padāni* as "traces of the Law," cf. *Ṛg Veda,* X, 71, 3 *vācaḥ padavīyam . . . ṛṣiṣu praviṣṭām,* "footprint of the Word vested in the Seers," and *pada* as "statement," "dictum," in *Laṅkâvatāra Sūtra* II, 98 (see Suzuki's discussion in his translation, p. 31, note 2). One can hardly doubt that a reminiscence of these ideas underlies the Ch'an-Zen allegory of searching for the lost ox, cf. Suzuki, *Essays in Zen Buddhism,* pp. 357 ff.

The "tracks" by which He is to be found are primarily the symbolic expressions of the ritual sacrifice and hymns, "seen" and "warded" by the poetic genius (*Ṛg Veda*, IX, 73, 9, X, 71, 3, etc.); and in just the same way any symbol such as our *triśūla*, or any other "motif" of a canonical iconography, constitutes a "track" by means of which He may be "followed after," the symbol (*pratīka*) being employed, not for its own sake, but as a call to action. It is evident enough that "tracks" of this kind neither are nor need be represented literally in the form of a spoor, the indication of actual hoofprints at Padaṇa being quite exceptional. If, on the other hand, the notion be interpreted more literally and in connection with a more an-

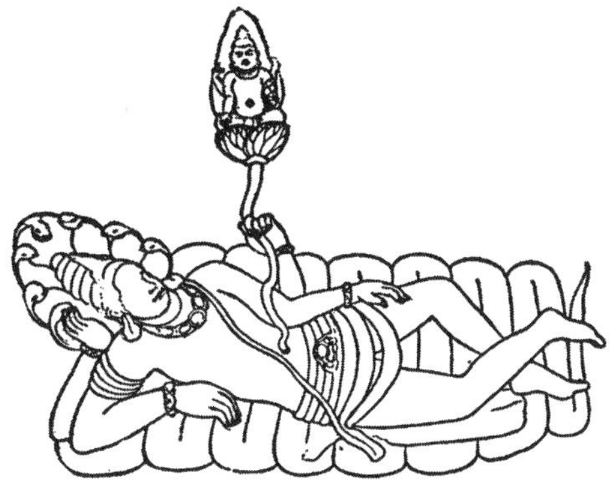

FIG. B. Birth of Brahmā; Elūrā.

thropomorphic concept, then all the passages cited above can be quoted in sanction and explanation of the cult of the "feet of the Lord" (*pādukā*, Buddha-pada, Viṣṇu-pada, etc.) in Buddhist, Jaina, and Vaiṣṇava practice alike. And if the Tree and Fiery Pillar are supported by such feet, it is because He is firmly established (*pratiṣṭha*) on solid ground (*pṛthivī*, represented by a lotus in the case of the Fiery Pillars), in the Waters, in the Depths, existent (*sthita*) in the world, that is in the last analysis "within you," in the lotus of the heart.

From the Tree of Life we turn to consider the Earth-Lotus. In Vedic formulation, the Tree of Life rises into Space from the navel-centre of deity recumbent on the back of the Waters, its trunk representing the axis of the Universe, its branches all extension and differentiation on whatever plane of being. By the time that Nārâyaṇa takes the place of Varuṇa reclining on the Waters at the dawn of a creative cycle, it is not a forest tree (*vanaspati*, often also a designation of Agni) that rises thus from the navel-centre of immortality, but a lotus. This lotus bears on its expanded flower the Father of the World, Lokapitā, Brahmā-Prajāpati, whose epithets are "navel-born" (*nābhija*), "lotus-born" (*abjaja, abja-yoni*), and "lotus-seated" (*kamalâsana, padmâsana*), while the recumbent Nārâyaṇa is "lotus-navelled" (*padmanābha, puṣkaranābha*) (Fig. B). Corresponding descriptions of this "Birth of Brahmā" appear only in "late" books of the Epic, and corresponding representations in art not before the fifth or sixth century A.D.,[27] the archaeological data thus indicating a formulation not much before the Gupta period, though, as will presently appear, the motif is really Vedic. In some remarkable Burmese representations (Fig. 16), the one stem rising from the navel of the recumbent Nārâyaṇa bears on three flowers the Trinity of Brahmā, Viṣṇu, and Śiva.[28] It would seem at first sight as though the tree of the earlier texts had later been interpreted or misinterpreted to be a lotus. The concept of the Lotus-birth of manifested creative deity is, however, coeval with that of the Tree of Life: and furthermore, a clear distinction of significance is made as between the Tree and the Lotus, the former being, as we have seen, "all existences," viz. "that which" is manifest, the latter "that wherein" or "that whereon" there is and can be manifestation. For "this lotus (of the heart, *hṛt-puṣkara*) is verily the same as Space (*ākāśa*); these four quarters and four interquarters are its surrounding petals,"[29] *Maitri Up.*, VI, 2, cf. *Chāndogya Up.*, VIII, 1–3; and it rises appropriately from the navel-centre since "the navel (*nābhi*) of Prājapati's world-form is the Firmament," *Maitri Up.*, VI, 6. Again the Lotus is explained to be the Earth, any one plane of being, that whereon and whereby existence is supported, *Taittirīya Saṁhitā*, IV, 1, 3, and IV, 2, 8, and *Śatapatha Brāhmaṇa*, VII, 4, 1, 8. Or considered as a receptacle as implied in the expressions *padma-garbha, padma-kośa*, then "in this Space (*ākāśa*), coextensive (*yāvān . . . tāvān*) with Space-in-the-Heart (*antar-hṛdayâkāśa*), are contained both Heaven and Earth . . . all is contained therein," *Chāndogya Up.*, VIII, 1, 3.

Before proceeding to a discussion of the subjectivity of Space, and therefore of Existence, implied in the expression "Lotus of the Heart," the primary connotation of the lotus symbolism must be further clarified. The earliest references to a lotus-birth, seat, or support occur in *śruti* in connection with Vasiṣṭha and Agni, in their capacity as the positive existence of all things.[30] In *Ṛg Veda*, VII, 33, 11, we have "O Vasiṣṭha, thou art the son of Mitra-Varuṇa, Brahman, born of (the Apsaras) Urvaśī and of Intellect (*manas*), thou the drop (*drapsa* = *retas*, "seed") that fell by angelic efflux (*daivyena brahmaṇā*); the Several Angels waited upon thee in the Lotus (*puṣkare*)." That is, Mitra-Varuṇa in Intellect (*manas*) beheld and were beguiled by the Fascination (Apsaras) of the possibilities-of-existence (Waters), their seed fell into the Waters, and thence arose the lotus-ground supporting Vasiṣṭha, surrounded by the Several Angels.[31] In *Ṛg Veda*, VI, 16, 13, Agni is similarly born of or (re-)produced (*niramanthata*, lit. "rubbed" or "churned," cf. "*samudra-manthana*") from a lotus, *puṣkarāt*, cf. *Taittirīya Saṁhitā*, IV, 1, 3g, and *Kauṣītaki Brāhmaṇa*, VIII, 1, "Thee, O Agni, from the Lotus"; and that he is thus mothered by the Lotus

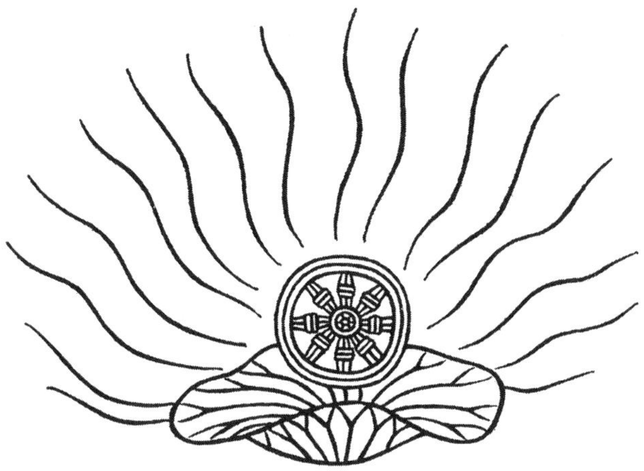

FIG. C. Rimbō (Dharmacakra) supported by a lotus leaf. After Ōmura Seigai, *Sanbon Ryōbu Mandara*. Cf. Fig. F.

flower (or leaf, as in *Taittirīya Saṁhitā*, V, 1, 3) merely enunciates in other terms the epithets constantly applied to him as "born from the lap or navel of the Earth" and "kinsman of the Waters."[32] All birth, all coming into existence, is in fact a "being established in the Waters," and to be "established" is to stand on any ground (*pṛthivī*) or platform of existence; he who stands or sits upon the Lotus "lives."[33] The Vedic passages cited above are thus valid prototypes of the "late" Epic legend of the Birth of Brahmā; the birth of Vasiṣṭha or of Agni is virtually the birth of Brahmā-Prajāpati or of Buddha.[34]

Other ritual and exegetical texts can be cited in which the meaning of the Lotus is explained in the sense already deduced. *Nirukta*, V, 14, explains the Lotus (*puṣkara*) as ~~Firmament or~~ Middle Space (*antarikṣa*), which maintains (*poṣati*) existences (*bhūtāni*), cf. *Maitri Up.*, VI, 2, cited above. *Taittirīya Saṁhitā*, IV, 1, 3 c, and IV, 2, 8 c, = *Vājasaneyi Saṁ-*

hitā, XIII, 2, identifies the Lotus (*puṣkara*) with the Earth, extended on the back of the Waters, as the birthplace (*yoni*) of Agni. Sāyaṇa, commenting on *Ṛg Veda*, VI, 16, 13, *puṣkarāt*, substitutes for *puṣkara*, *puṣkara-parṇa*, "lotus-leaf," but explains in the traditional manner that "the property of the lotus-leaf is that of upholding all the worlds," *puṣkara-parṇasya sarvajagad-dhārakatva.*[35] In *Śatapatha Brāhmaṇa*, VII, 3, 2, 14 Prajāpati finds the lost Agni on a lotus-leaf. In the construction of the Fire Altar (*Śatapatha Brāhmaṇa*, VII, 4, 1, 7–13, VIII, 3, 1, 11, and X, 5, 2, 8 and 12) a lotus-leaf is laid down centrally (that is in the centre of the Universe, as represented by the whole altar) as the "birthplace of Agni" (*agni-yonitvam*), the "symbol of his womb" (*yoni-rūpatvam*), and as a chthonic basis (*pratiṣṭhā . . . pṛthivyām*): "the lotus means the Waters, and this earth is a leaf thereof . . . and this same earth is Agni's womb." On the lotus-leaf is laid a round gold disk representing the Sun; and thus the lotus-leaf becomes in effect the Sun-boat, though this is not specifically mentioned. Over the Sun-disk is laid the figure of a golden man (*puruṣa*), representing Agni-Prajāpati, the Person in the Sun; the golden Puruṣa and the Sun-disk, lying back to back, form a Janus-type, as explained *ibid.*, VII, 4, 1, 18.

Thus it is abundantly clear that the lotus, flower or leaf (see the alternative representations, Figs. C, F), but in actual iconography usually "flower," [36] arising from or resting on the Waters, represents the ground (*pṛthivī*) or substance of existence, both that whereon and that wherein existence is established firmly amidst the sea of possibility. And just as it is said of the Cosmic Horse (Varuṇa) that he, whose birthplace is the Waters (*samudre yoniḥ*), stands firm in the Waters, and that he who understands himself stands firm wherever he may be, so we may say that he who realizes the meaning of the Lotus stands firm wherever he may be.[37]

The world-lotus naturally blooms in response to the rising of the Sun "in the beginning"; in answer to and as a reflection of the Light of Heaven mirrored on the surface of the Waters. Earth as a reflection of Heaven is stretched out in like measure (*Taittirīya Saṁhitā*, IV, 1, 3, and IV, 2, 8), this world is the counterpart (*anurūpam*) of yonder world (*Aitareya Brāhmaṇa*, VIII, 2); hence, no doubt, the two lotuses held by the Sun in iconography, corresponding to Upper and Nether Waters, *para* and *apara* Prakṛti.[38] However, the light of Heaven may be thought of not merely as the Sun, but collectively as the Lights of Heaven, and so we find in *Pañcaviṁśa Brāhmaṇa*, XVIII, 8, 6, and *Maitrayanī Saṁhitā*, IV, 4, 7, and 58, 16, a more general statement as follows: "Through the down-shining (*avakāśe*) of the Lights of Heaven (*nakṣatrāṇām*) [39] the Lotus (*puṇḍarīka*) is brought to birth (*jāyate*)," the text further making it clear that the Lotus implies Earth, the lights Heaven. It is further explained, *Pañcaviṁśa Br.*, XVIII, 8, 2, and 9, 6, that the wreath of lotuses put on by the Brahman officiating in the Rājasūya ceremony represents sensible operation, virility, and temporal power (*indriyam, vīryam, kṣatram*).

Some more familiar, but less essential, aspects of the lotus symbolism may be alluded to in passing. Amongst these is the lotus as a metaphor of purity: growing in the mud, it betrays no trace of its origin, nor is the flower or leaf wetted by the water it rests upon, and such also is the truly wise man, who lives in the world, but is not of it. For example, *Saṁyutta Nikāya*, III, 140, "Just as, Brethren, a lotus, born in the water, full-grown in the water, rises to the surface and is not wetted by the water, even so, Brethren, the Tathāgata, born in the world, full-grown in the world, surpasses the world, and is unaffected by the world"; or the metaphor may be reversed, as in *Chāndogya Up.*, IV, 14, 3, and *Maitri Up.*, III, 2, where the Self, Ātman, is compared to the drop of water that rests on a lotus leaf, but does not cling to it. It may be inferred from what was previously explained, on the other hand, that when the image of a supreme deity is represented with a lotus in hand as *līlā-kamala*, "lotus of play," it stands for the Universe, his toy, just as an actual lotus, *līlā-kamala* or *līlâbja*, held by a human being, is actually his, or more often her, toy. But when the lotus is offered by the worshipper to a deity, that would imply a rendering up of one's own existence to its source, a resignation of one's own nature and ground of separate existence; cf. *Nirukta*, V, 14, where a hermeneutic derivation of *puṣkara* from *puj* + *kar*, with the sense "to perform an office," is proposed.[40] Furthermore the lotus is a thing loved and admired by all, and is used as a means of adornment, or lends itself to laudatory similes, as when we speak of lotus-eyes or lotus-feet.

In actually surviving works of art we do not find representations of the Buddha supported by a lotus-throne before the second century A.D., viz. in the art of Gandhāra, and in late Āndhra works from Amarāvatī, nor, as we have already seen, of Brahmā *kamalâsana* before the Gupta period. A second century Kuṣāna example from Mathurā is reproduced by Foucher, *L'art gréco-bouddhique du Gandhāra,* Fig. 552. Long before this, however, at the very beginning of artistic history so far as it is recorded in permanent materials, we meet with the lotus-flower employed as a support in various ways, nor is it at all likely that these examples had not been preceded by others in evanescent material, or painted. The lotus is most conspicuously connected in this way with Śrī-Lakṣmī, viz. in representations dating from the second century B.C. onwards; I have shown elsewhere that these compositions are comprehensible only with reference to Vedic notions, and that early Indian art is essentially the continuation of a mainly aniconic "Vedic" style.[41]

Śrī-Lakṣmī is essentially Aditi, Prakṛti, Māyā, Apsaras, Urvaśī, the Waters, all the possibilities of existence substantially and maternally personified. The Lotus is preëminently hers, because she *is* the Lotus and the Earth, at once the source and support of all existences, Vasudhā or Vasudharā; that is, with respect to their substance, as the Supernal-Sun is with respect to their form. So she is represented either aniconically by the Lotus, as Padmā, springing from the brimming vessel (*pūrṇa-ghaṭa*) of the Waters (Fig. 23), or in human form upon the Lotus, as Padma-vāsinī, and then typically as receiving a lustral bath of *soma*-bearing rains downpoured from the skies by the elephants of the Quarters (Fig. 23). These early representations occur for the most part in a Buddhist association, though this need not be assumed for all the coins and terracottas.[42] It has been argued by some scholars, Foucher particularly,[43] that the representations in a Buddhist environment, as at Bhārhat, Bodhgayā, and Sāñcī, are actually of Buddha nativities, a theme which would otherwise be lacking in the series of Four Great Events, so far as the early art is concerned. Others, myself included, have opposed this view, and not without justification inasmuch as the formula is certainly of pre-Buddhist origin, and because what is represented is certainly not the birth of Siddhârtha, but rather Śrī-Lakṣmī herself, at once Earth-Lotus and Mother-Earth personified, Universal Mother, Mother Nature, Aditi, Māyā,[44] the magical ground or substance of existence, fertilized by heavenly showers.[45] It must not be overlooked, too, that *Jātaka,* I, p. 53, affirms that when the Bodhisattva was born, "two streams of water came down from the sky (*ākāsato dve udakadhārā nikkhamitvā*) and refreshed the bodies of the Bodhisattva and his mother;"[46] in this sense it may be legitimate to say that these are *virtually* Buddha nativities, inasmuch as they represent Her who is the Mother of all Existence, and so preëminently of the Buddha, when he is considered not as the man Siddhârtha, but as Universal Man, in whom all things are lively imaged, Ādityabandhu and Sūryavaṁśin, "Kinsman of the Supernal-Sun" and "Of the Solar Race," and as Māyā-maya, "magically-natured."[47] It can scarcely have been an accident that Siddhârtha's mortal mother's name was Māyā-devī, "Lady Māyā."[48] Siddhârtha's birth from his mother's side is anticipated in *Ṛg Veda,* IV, 18, 1–2, where in connection with Indra's birth from Aditi we find . . . *tiraścatā pārśvān nir gamāṇi,* "I will go forth traversely, from the side"; a lateral procession is mentioned in several other passages, e. g. VI, 10, 4, X, 129, 5, and *Jaiminīya Upaniṣad Brāhmaṇa,* I, 29, where the life-ray (*raśmi asumaya*) is *tiryaṅ pratiṣṭhitaḥ.*[49] Siddhârtha's visibility while yet unborn (*Jātaka,* I, 52, *antokucchigataṁ . . . passati*) may be compared to *Ṛg Veda,* VI, 16, 35, with reference to Agni, *garbhe mātuḥ . . . akṣare vididyutānaḥ,* "shining in the Mother's eternal womb." If we suppose that Śuddhôdana means "cloud" (as stated in the *Nighaṇṭu,* rather than "pure rice" as generally assumed), we have a striking parallel in the *Dīpaṅkara Jātaka,* where the Bodhisattva's name is Megha,[50] "Cloud," and his wife's either Bhadrā, "Abundance," or Prakṛti, "Nature"; but as designating the Father, it more likely corresponds to *pakvam odanam* and *kṣīrapākam odanam* in *Ṛg Veda,* VIII, 77, 6 and 10, *odanam pacyamānam* in VIII, 69, 14, *pacatam* in I, 61, 7, the cooking of rice with milk being thought of as an essential element of the Interior Operation; in *Jātaka,* I, 66, the Bodhisattva is represented as remembering the good food that was served in his father's house, where food and drink abounded ("fleshpots of Egypt"). The Bodhisattva's three palaces[51] may be regarded as the three seasons of the Year, Prajāpati; it is noteworthy that until the Bodhisattva leaves his palaces he knows nothing of old age, decline, or death. The Buddha himself is Āditya-bandhu, and Sūryavaṁśin, Mahāpurisa and *amanussa,* recalling Agni as the *amānava puruṣa* who leads the Comprehensor through the gateway of the worlds, *Chāndogya Upaniṣad,* V, 10, 2; that the Buddha is an Āṅgirasa, "a descendant of the Gleed," is equally significant, Agni in the *Ṛg Veda* being a son of Aṅgiras and himself *angirastama,* "the best of Gleeds." The Buddha's given name Siddhârtha, denoting the "attainment of the goal," corresponds to *artha*, the "end" or "goal" envisaged by Agni, *Ṛg Veda*, X, 51, 4.

It is clear then that the genealogy of the Buddha, as we have it, is mythical, and it may be that he had been thought of very early in, or before, the rise of "Buddhism," as "a descent of the Sun" or aspect of Agni. If the representations of Māyā-Lakṣmī with the elephants were really regarded as Buddha-Conceptions, that too implies a Buddhology far advanced in centuries B.C. The later Nativity type, in which the Buddha comes to birth from the side of Māyā-devī as she stands like a Yakṣī beneath a tree, has equally mythical implications, though more anthropomorphic in expression, and corresponds in this respect to the coming in of the "anthropomorphic" image. It would seem indeed as if the Buddha had not so much been "deified" in later times, as humanized; assuming that there had been a veridically historical figure, it would seem that this figure had been clothed with a mantle of Fire almost from the beginning, and that, just as in the case of Jesus, the Great Events of the life must be thought of as "stages crowded together as though to present, in a single lifetime, the whole Epic of the Transcending of Mortal Destiny." [52] In the development of a crowned and regal Buddha image and in the doctrinal development represented by the *Saddharma Puṇḍarīka* we seem to sense a renewed stressing of the Buddha's divinity, in conscious opposition to the rationalistic interpretations.[53]

That a very advanced Buddhology already existed in the Pali texts, if not from the beginning of "Buddhism," is also very apparent from the terminology and epithets made use of. When the Buddha is represented as saying, "I am neither Deva, Gandhabba, Yakkha, nor Man," *Anguttara Nikāya*, II, 38, it is evidently to be understood that what he *is* is a principle, *the* Principle, Dharma, Logos, Word, cf. *Dīgha Nikāya*, III, 84, and *Saṁyutta Nikāya*, III, 120, cited below, p. 33. Amongst his epithets, mostly of Vedic or Aupaniṣada origin, or taken from these sources with only very slight modification, are Mahāpurisa, "Great Person," Appati-puggala, "Ineffable Man" (*aprati-pudgala* in SP., III, 33), Ādicca-bandhu, "Kinsman of the Supernal-Sun," Rājā cakkavattī, "Sovereign Mover of the Wheel," Devâtideva, "Angel of the Angels" (cf. Agni, *devo devānām*, *Ṛg Veda*, I, 94, 13). As Mahāpurisa he is endowed with all the lineaments (*lakkhaṇa*) proper to the Superman. The conception of the Buddhas as "the Eye in the World" (*cakkhuṁ loke*, *Dīgha Nikāya*, II, 158, and *Sutta Nipāta*, III, 9, 6) corresponds to Vedic notions of Mitra ("Agni when enkindled," *Ṛg Veda*, V, 3, 1), who "seeth with unclosing eyes," *animiṣā abhicaṣṭe*, *ibid.*, III, 59, 1, or of the Sun, who "sees all things," *viśvam abhicaṣṭe*, *ibid.*, I, 164, 44, and is the "Eye of Varuṇa," *passim*. With "Lion of the Śākyas" cf. Agni as "lion," *Ṛg Veda*, I, 90, 5 and III, 2, 11, cf. I, 115, 5. The so-called deification of the Buddha, the recognition of the universality of his essence and operation, cannot be denied to the Hīnayāna.

We must now consider the representation of the Buddhas as Dharmacakra, Word-wheel (and World-wheel), or Wheel of the Law or Norm, of which early Buddhist art affords so many examples, amongst which the most famous is that wheel which was set up by Aśoka in the Deer Park at Benares on the site of the *prathamadeśanā*, "First Preaching," which was also the *dharmacakra pravartana*, "First turning of the Wheel of the Word."[54] The pre- and non-Buddhist meanings of the symbol must be studied. What the Wheel stands for in Indian symbolism is primarily the Revolution of the Year, as Father Time (Prajāpati, Kāla), the flowing tide of all begotten things (*Aitareya Brāhmaṇa*, II, 17), dependent on the Sun (*Maitri Up.*, VI, 14–16). In *Ṛg Veda*, I, 164, 2, 11, 13, 14, and 48, the one wheel of the Sun's chariot has twelve or five spokes (months or seasons), or 360 spokes (days), axle (*akṣa*), and triple nave (*nābhi*); it is a revolving wheel of life (*amṛta*) undecaying (*ajara*), therein insist (*tasthuḥ*) the several worlds (*viśvā bhuvanāni*): *ibid.*, I, 155, 6, "He (Viṣṇu) by the names of the four (seasons) has set in motion the rounded wheel that is furnished with ninety steeds" (the ninety days in each quarter of the solar Year); similarly, *Atharva Veda*, X, 8, 4–7, and *Śvetâśvatara Up.*, I, 4 (*brahma-cakra* in I, 6, and VI, 1); in the *Kauṣītaki Brāhmaṇa*, XX, 1, "the Year (elsewhere identified with Prajāpati) is a revolving Wheel of the Angels, that is undying; therein is the sixfold proper food (i. e. means of existence) . . . thereon the Angels move round all the worlds."[55] In the sense that Time is the Sun, a circle is its centre, the Wheel represents the Sun, but more exactly the movement of the Sun, in his heavenly car, with one or two correlated wheels. The Sun or Solar Wheel is constantly spoken of as "revolving" or as being revolved, with use of root *vṛt* as in the Buddhist *pavattana*, *pravartana*: e. g. I, 35, 2, where Savitṛ is *vartamānaḥ*; I, 155, 6, *cakram . . . avīvi-*

pat; II, 11, 20, *avartayat sūryo na cakram*; V, 30, 8, *aśmānaṁ cit svaryaṁ vartamānam*; VII, 63, 2, *samānaṁ cakraṁ pary āvivṛtsan*.

Actually to represent all possible states of being, the Wheel would have to be conceived in the manner of a gyroscope, revolving simultaneously in an indefinite number of planes, though still with a motionless centre: just as the Cross must be thought of from this point of view as constituted of three arms, mutually at right angles, intersecting at the one common point which is also the centre of the sphere in which the Cross stands. Actually, however, this would be to introduce a needless complication, and in fact the symbol as employed is essentially an ordinary chariot-wheel,[56] just as also in common usage the two-armed cross stands for a cross extended in three directions. Although, then, the Wheel, as the "round of the world" and "earth plain," strictly speaking corresponds only to a given ensemble of conditions, it represents analogically the indefinite totality of all possible conditions, the entire *saṁsāra*. As thus representing the Universe in its entirety, the Wheel symbol remains in use unchanged from *Ṛg Veda*, I, 164, through *Śvetâśvatara Up.*, I, 4, and *Anugītā*, XXX, to Kabīr and the present day.[57]

The content of the wheel symbolism is extraordinarily rich, and can only be outlined here. Its dimensions are indefinite, its radius the variable distance between an undimensioned (*amātra*) point and an immeasurable (*asaṅkhya*) circumference; there in the "middle space" (*antarikṣa, ākāśa*), between the "I" and the "not-I," essence and nature, lie procession and recession (*pravṛtti, nivṛtti*), there are good and evil (*dharmâdharmau*), joy and sorrow (*sukha, duḥkha*), light and shade (*chāyâtapa*), birth and death, all local movement and affection; and that motion and passibility are greater the greater the distance from the centre. Beyond the felly lies only the inexistence of the irrational, an impossibility of existence, as of square circles or the horns of a hare; within the nave, the non-existence of the supra-rational.[58]

The cycle of ego-consciousness implies an outward movement from the nave to the ever-receding felly, and a return from the however distant felly to the unchanging centre. A progressive enlightenment (*krama-mukti*) can then be expressed as a gradual contraction of the radius, bringing the circumference ever closer to the centre, until that which seemed to enclose the point is seen to be contained within it, knowledge being thus con-centrated into a single form, which is the form of very different things.[59] That is *Nirvāṇa*, unitary being, "with residual existential elements," and by a vanishment of the point becomes also Parinirvāṇa, without residuum of existence.

He whose seat is on the lotiform nave or navel of the wheel,[60] and himself unmoving sets and keeps it spinning, is the ruler of the world, of all that is natured and extended in the middle region, between the essential nave and the natural felly; "On whom the parts stand fast, as it were spokes on the nave of the wheel, Him I deem the Person to be known," *Praśna Up.*, VI, 6. In Pali Buddhist and later Sanskrit texts this Royal Person is designated Cakkavattī, Cakravartin, "He who turns the Wheel," and the same designation is applied analogically to any terrestrial "Universal Ruler" or Emperor (Figs. 19, 20). As we have seen, the term Cakravartin, as an essential name of the Buddha, and the corresponding expression Dharmacakra-pravartana denoting the setting in motion of the Word or Law, are constantly met with in early and later Buddhism. These terms do not occur as such in Vedic texts, where *cakri*, "doer," and other forms of the verb *kṛ*, to "do," "make," "cause," "instigate," etc.,[61] must be distinguished etymologically from *cakra*, "wheel"; it may be surmised, however, that the "popular" etymology of Indian hermeneutists might have seen a significance in the assonance of *cakri* and *cakra*. And if the word *cakravartin* is absent in the Vedas, the meaning is nevertheless to be found there; the notion of a supreme Power, Lord of *ṛta* = *dharma*, whose sovereignty (*kṣatra*) is over all the worlds (*viśvā bhuvanāni*) and is also the axial mover of the twin world wheel of the car of Time and Life is so constantly presented that we can hardly speak of the notion of the King of the World as something new in Buddhist times. Varuṇa alone or with Mitra is often called *samrāj*, mention is often made of the Premier Angel's autonomy (*svarājya*), and in III, 55.4, Agni is universal King, *samāno rājā*.[62] In X, 5, 3 and 4, the notions *viśvasya nābhiṁ carato dhruvasya*, "navel of all that is proceeding or concrete," and *ṛtasya vartanayaḥ*, "propulsions of the Law"; in X, 168, 2, and 174, 1, and 5, the notions *viśvasya bhuvanasya rājā*, "King of the Universe," *abhīvartaḥ*, "victorious," and *asapatnaḥ*," "without a rival," imply a sovereign power. In X, 51, 6, *rathī'va adhvānam anvâvarīvuḥ*, "as one who drives a car upon its way," tantamount to "Cosmic Charioteer," [63] X, 92, 1, *yajñasya vo rathyam viśpatim*, "your charioteer of the sacrifice and lord of the folk," and I, 143, 7, *dhūrṣadam agnim mitram na*, "Agni as Mitra seated on the pole," i. e. as driver,[63] necessarily imply the setting in motion of the principial Wheel or Wheels. No distinction of meaning can be drawn as between the driver of the solar chariot and him who makes the solar wheel revolve. "Seven treasures" (*sapta ratna*), ~~apparently the same as those of a Cakravartin~~, are mentioned in *Ṛg Veda*, V, 1, 5, and VI, 74, 1.

We considered above mainly the case in which the cosmic wheel is thought of as single. Perhaps more often the chariot of the Sun is thought of as running on twin wheels connected by a common axle-tree (*akṣa*), and this involves a consideration of the world from two distinct but inseparable points of view (cf. *Aitareya Brāhmaṇa*, VIII, 2, cited above, p. 20). As the Sun shines equally for angels and for men (*Ṛg Veda*, I, 50, 5, etc.), so of the twin wheels of his chariot one touches Heaven, the other Earth (*Ṛg Veda*, I, 30, 19, and X, 85, 18); and their common axle-tree is identified with the axis of the universe that holds apart (*vitaram, viṣvak*) Heaven and Earth (*Ṛg Veda*, V, 29, 4, and X, 89, 4). Or again, when the chariot of the Sun is thought of as three-wheeled (*tricakra*), *Ṛg Veda*, X, 85, two of the wheels are identified as aforesaid with Heaven and Earth ("one looks down upon the several worlds, the other ordains the seasons and is born again," cf. I, 164, 44 and 32), and these "proceed by magic," *māyayā caranti*; but the third is hidden (*guhā* = *guhāyāṁ nihitam*, sc. "in the heart"), and only the adepts (*addhātayaḥ*) are Comprehensors (*viduḥ*) thereof. This third wheel evidently corresponds to the "secret name," *nāma guhyam*, of X, 55, 1, and the "third light" of X, 56, 1. These doctrines of three wheels, three lights, etc., are tantamount to the *trikāya* doctrine in Buddhism.[64]

The axle-tree of the twin wheels (which axle must be thought of analogically also as penetrating the third wheel) is the primary source of moving power (as noted incidentally in *Ṛg Veda*, I, 166, 9): not itself revolving, it is the unmoved mover in relation to the wheels. But to complete our understanding of the *pratīka* it must be realized that the revolution of the wheel requires the operation of an opposing force operative at the felly, where in actual experience contact with the ground supplies a fulcrum. In other words, revolution depends on the interaction of conjoint principles, which may be called Heaven and Earth, Puruṣa and Prakṛti, *sattva* and *tamas*, I and not-I, subject and object, etc. This is recognized in several passages in which the infixation of the axle, or the movement of the wheels, is effected by the deity by means of his abilities (*śacībhiḥ*, *Ṛg Veda*, I, 30, 15, and X, 89, 4), powers (*śaktibhiḥ*, X, 88, 10), or magic (*māyayā*, X, 85, 18), *śaci*, *śakti*, and *māyā* being synonymous feminine designations of his "means whereby," the "ground" of manifestation, coöperating with his "essence," who is Śacīpati, Māyin, etc.

The axle-tree is also the axis of the universe, as most clearly stated in *Ṛg Veda*, X, 89, 4, *yo akṣeṇêva cakriyā śacībhiḥ viṣvak tastambha pṛthivīṁ uta dyām*, "by the axle of his wheeled-car indeed, by his abilities, he pillars-apart Heaven and Earth," cf. V, 29, 4, *rodasī vitaraṁ viṣkabhāyat*, and other passages cited above, p. 10, notes 15 and 139.

In *Ṛg Veda*, X, 85, 12, "the chariot is in the mode of Intellect (*ano manasmayam*), the Breath of Life (*vyāna*) was the axle (*akṣa*) fastened there." It will be understood that the axle-point (*āṇi*) that penetrates the hollow (*kha*) in the nave (*nābhi*) is central in each wheel;[65] so in *Ṛg Veda*, I, 35, 6, the Undying Angels (sc. the Several Angels, *viśve devāḥ*, Ādityas) are said to depend upon Savitṛ (the Supernal-Sun as prime mover) "as on the chariot's axle-point (*āṇi*)," and in *Aitareya Āraṇyaka*, II, 7, the Self (*ātman*) is compared to the "twin axle-points (*āṇī*)" of the Veda. We have thus dwelt at some length on the Vedic implications of the wheel or wheels, because it is important to realize the wider content and consequent power of this symbol which was so extensively employed in Buddhism, though with a more restricted application.

The continuity of the ideology is often very striking; compare for example *Ṛg Veda*, I, 164, 13, "its axle is never heated (*na tapyate*), its heavy-laden nave (*nābhi*) is never worn away," with the edifying application of the same notion in *Saṁyutta Nikāya*, I, 33 (I, 5, 7), where the chariot which with its twin Word-wheels (*dhamma-cakkehi saṁyutto*) conducts the rider to *nibbāṇa* is by name "Frictionless" (Akujana).

In actual Buddhism, the Wheel, like the Tree, is regarded from two points of view, that is to say as a pair of wheels, principial (Dharmacakra) and phenomenal (Saṁsāracakra, Bhavacakra); hence from the standpoint of the Wayfarer, broken on the wheel, as either to be turned or stayed,[66] but from that of the Omniscient Comprehensor as one and the same uninterrupted Form, his own intrinsic form. For from any point of view within it, the movement of a wheel can be regarded as having two directions, as it were right and left; or again, the movement being continuous, any point on the circumference may be regarded either as beginning or as end. It can be understood from either point of view that when Buddha "hesitates" to set going the Principial Wheel, which is also the Existential Wheel, the Angels are in despair, that Brahmā exclaims, "Alas, the world is altogether lost," *vinassati vata bho loko,* and prays that the Word may be spoken, *desetu bhante bhagavā dhammaṁ,* J., I, 81. Taking *dharmacakra-pravartana* and *prathama-deśanā* in their universal sense, that is with respect to the creation of the world, the Angels are naturally dismayed at the "hesitation," for their very existence depends on the operation of the Wheel, the revolution of the Year; as in *Ṛg Veda,* X, 51, where Agni has "fled in fear from the high priestly office (*hotrāt*) lest the Angels should thus engage (*yunajan*) me . . . which as my goal (*artha*) I foresaw," the Angels answering "Come forth, for Man is fain to serve us, he waits prepared . . . make easy paths, create the Angelic Way (*devayāna,* cf. *hīnayāna, mahāyāna, brahmayāna, dhammayāna,* etc.) . . . let the Four Quarters bow (*namantām*) before thee." [67] Or taking the words in their specifically Buddhist application, with respect not to the procession of life, but its recession, and as the preaching of a Gospel to that end, the Angels must be thought of as equally despaired at the "hesitation," for all things moving seek their rest. [68]

In monastic Buddhism and from an edifying point of view, stress is naturally laid upon the Dharmacakra only as a Word-wheel to be set in motion to the end that men may find their Way (*magga, mārga*), and here the cosmic significance of the Dharmacakra as an embodiment of the Year, "Eniautos Daimon," is thus obscured; it is only gradually brought out again that the revolution of the Principial and Existential Wheels is interdependent and indivisible, in the last analysis one and the same revolution.[69] That is developed in the *Saddharma Puṇḍarīka,* III, 33, where he who preached the Word at Sārnāth *and* on Mt Gṛdhrakūṭa is addressed as having "set in motion the Principial Wheel which is the origin *and* passing away of the factors of existence," *dharmacakraṁ pravartesi . . . skandhānām udayaṁ vyayam.*[70] That identity of Word-wheel and World-wheel — Vajra-dhātu and Garbha-kośa-dhātu in Shingon formulation — is equally implied in the well-known formula, *Yaḥ kleśaḥ so bodhi, yaḥ saṁsāras tan nirvāṇam,* "Error and Awakening, World-flux and Extinction, are the Same," cf. Maitreya-Asaṅga, *Sūtrâlaṁkāra,* XIII, 12 (Commentary),

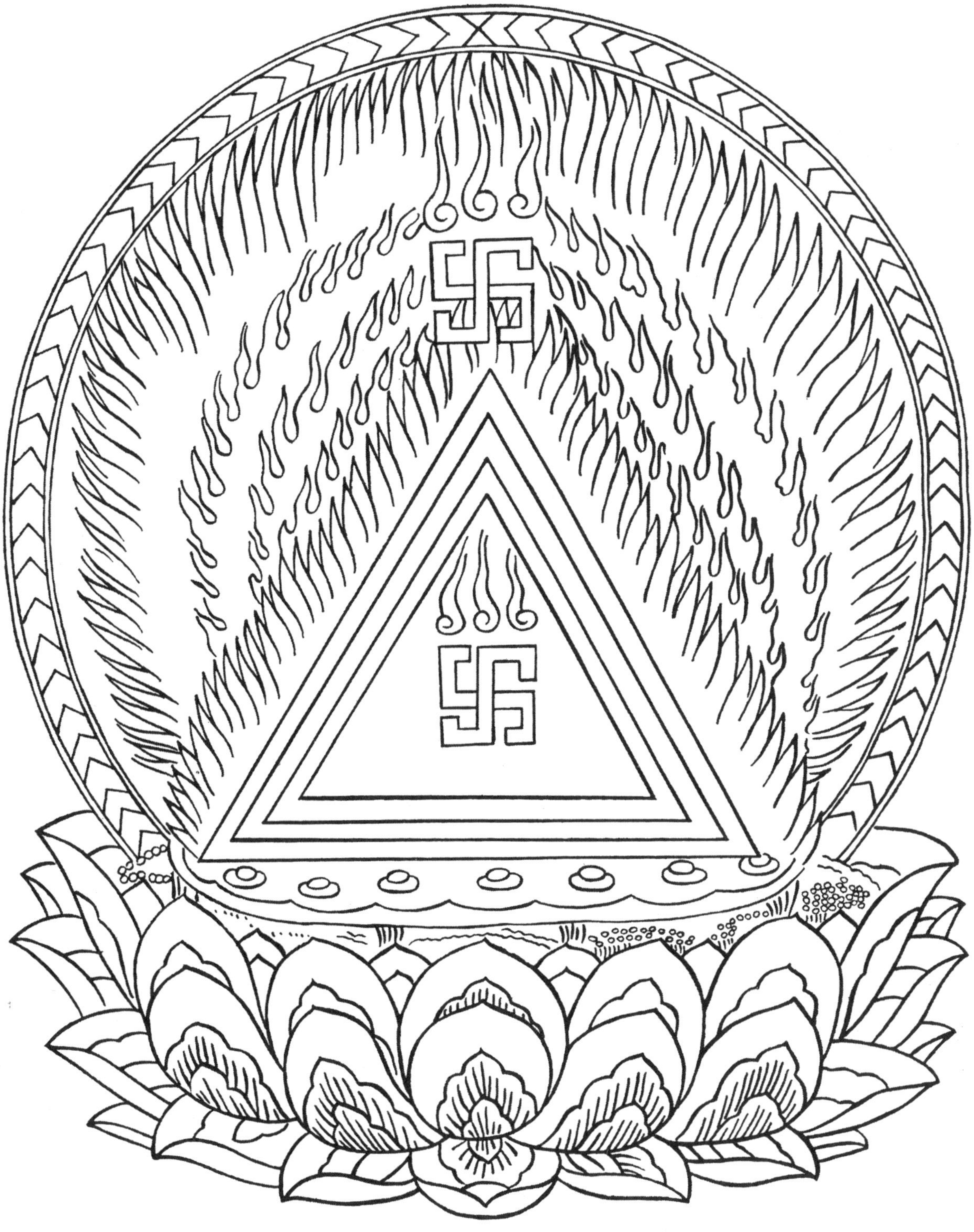

FIG. D. Issai Nyoraichi-in, "Signature of the Possible Intellect of all the Buddhas." Detail from a Shingon Garbhakośa-dhātu maṇḍala, see description of Fig. 31. After Ōmura Seigai, *Sanbon Ryōbu Mandara*.

avidyā ca bodhiś caikam, "Experience and gnosis are one," [71] and in the doctrine that Omniscience, *sine qua non* of Nirvāṇa, is the realization of the sameness of all principles, SPt., p. 133 — the same, *sama,* but differently seen by the eye of flesh (*māṁsa-cakṣus,* viz. the eye's intrinsic faculty in the sensible world), the angelic eye (*divya-cakṣus,* viz. the mind's eye in the intelligible world), and the eye of wisdom (*prajñā-, dhamma-, ananta,* or *buddha-cakṣus,* viz. the Comprehensor's eye in the world of gnosis).

In another way the correspondence of manifested and transcendental being, here viewed as a correspondence of the twin Wheels and their depend-

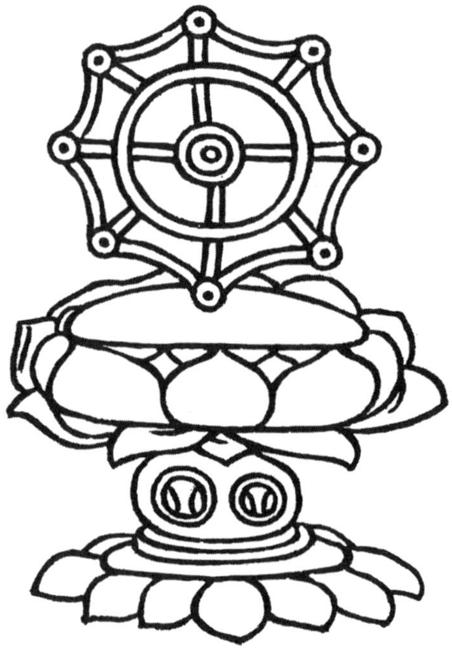

FIG. E. Dharmacakra, detail from a banner, from Tun Huang. After Stein, *Serindia,* Pl. LXXV.

ence on a common axis, is developed in Shingon Buddhism as the identity of (1) the "Germ-calyx-plane" or "Germ-womb-plane" (*taizō-kai* = *garbha-kośa-dhātu* or *garbha-kukṣi-dhātu*) and (2) the "Adamantine plane" (*kongo-kai* = *vajra-dhātu*).[72] Here the premier powers or principles of the two rationally but not really distinguished planes are represented respectively by the "seed-words" A and VAṀ (OṀ), according to the significance attached to these sounds in the Upaniṣads. In the Shingon *mandaras* these sounds are represented by diagrams or letters supported by lotus thrones (Figs. D, 32, 33, 40).

In any case, the Dharmacakra as Buddha symbol implies a conception of the Buddha as Dharmakāya, "Embodiment of the Word"; he is at once the Sovereign Mover of the Wheel, *rājā cakkavattī*, and the Wheel itself, the Word as set in motion, *pravartita*. From the fact that the words Sambhogakāya and Nirmāṇakāya do not occur in canonical Pali texts it may be inferred that the Trikāya doctrine was not originally developed; nevertheless, the Pali texts already reveal a very conscious Buddhology, as already observed above, p. 24. Here we need only indicate that the Dharmakāya concept of the Buddha is certainly presented, e. g. *Dīgha Nikāya*, III, 84, "The Tathāgata may be spoken of as Dhammakāya, or Brahmakāya,"[73] and *Saṁyutta Nikāya*, III, 120, "Who sees the Dhamma sees Me, who sees

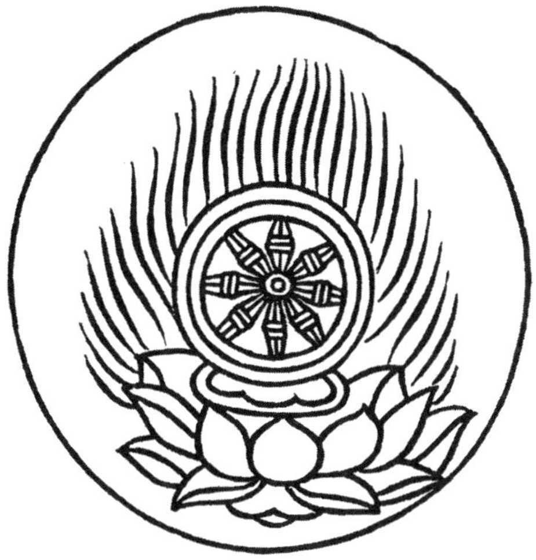

FIG. F. *Rimbō* (Dharmacakra) supported by the lotus.
After Ōmura Seigai, *Sanbon Ryōbu Mandara*. Cf. Fig. C.

Me sees the Dhamma." So then, in the abundant early Dharmacakra representations, the Buddha is already ideally iconified as a Principial Wheel supported by a universal ground; the Word is embodied (*-kāya*).

This prepares us to understand that the Dharmacakra, like any other Buddha symbol, can properly be represented as supported by a lotus, of which very clear examples can be cited from Shingon *mandaras* (Figs. C, E, F).[74] That the Wheel of Life was actually so thought of in a certainly pre-Buddhist time is clearly shown by *Atharva Veda*, X, 8, 34, a prayer for fullness of life, "I ask thee concerning that Flower of the Waters (*apām puṣpa*) wherein insist (*śrita*) Angels and Men, as it were spokes in the nave (*nābhi*) (of a wheel), the which was there infixed (*hita*) by Magic (*māyā*)," where the "flower of the waters" is of course the lotus.

In early Buddhist art the Dharmacakra is represented as supported by a pillar with a bulbous capital, upon which are four lions, on which in turn the Dharmacakra directly rests.[75] The capital and lions I take to be the lotus and lion thrones which are so often combined in the later anthropomorphic iconography. I have discussed elsewhere [76] the morphology of the lotus capital, and now take it for granted that the pillar itself corresponds to the stem, cable moulding to stamens, and abacus to pericarp. The capital, then, represents the heavenly ground on which the Word is manifested, while the actual earth in which the pillar stands is that terrestrial ground on which the Word is actually preached; the pillar extends from Earth to Heaven, it is the Axis of the Universe; the whole represents the Universe.

Allusion may also be made to one other way in which the Word may be shown as explicitly supported by a lotus; that is when the Word is embodied in a given text, any given *sūtra* or "alternative formulation," *dharma-paryāya*. Inasmuch as "he who makes a manuscript of the *dharma-paryāya* and cherishes it, thereby cherishes the Tathāgata" (SPt., p. 338), it is a perfectly correct iconography which represents Prajñāpāramitā or Mañjusrī supporting the "Lotus of Transcendent Wisdom" upon a lotus, the holding of the stem of this lotus being a formulation equivalent in significance to the support of the pillar of the Dharmacakra by its ground.

We have seen that the lotus represents that wherein existence comes to be and passes away, the seat of *pravṛtti* and *nivṛtti*, of Him who starts and stays the revolution of the Wheels of Time, but have alluded only in passing to what is ultimately the most significant aspect of the lotus symbolism, i. e. the identification of the lotus with the "heart" or "mind" of man. Again and again in the Upaniṣads that elemental Space (*ākāśa, kha, nabha, antarikṣa*, etc.[77]) in which the Principial Being is manifested as all the forms of natured being is located in the cave or secret chamber (*guhā*), dwelling (*veśma*), hollow (*kha*),[78] temple (*āyatana*), abode (*ālaya*), coffer or calyx (*kośa*), or nesting-place (*nīḍa*)[79] in the Lotus of the Heart (*hṛt-puṣkara*) or inward man (*antar-bhūta*), i. e. "in the innermost." There in a universal mode abides the Self (*ātman*), the Lord (*īśa*), Person (*puruṣa*), indefinitely dimensioned, "smaller than an atom and surpassing magnitude," *aṇor aṇīyān mahato mahīyān, Śvetāśvatara Up.*, III, 20, etc. "This space-within-the-heart (*antarhṛdaya ākāśa*), therein is the Person (*puruṣa*) in the mode of Intellect (*mano-maya*) . . . there he becomes as Brahman in a spatial embodiment, as very Self, as the playground of the Spirit (*prâṇârāma*), as Intellect and Bliss, Peace uttermost and everlasting," *Taittirīya Up.*, I, 6, 1, "who is the Logos (*dharma*)," *Bṛhadāraṇyaka Up.*, II, 5, 11. Are we not reminded that "The Kingdom of Heaven is within you"? Or again, "That golden Person in the Supernal-Sun who from that golden station looks down upon this earth, it is even He that dwells in the Lotus of the Heart and functions there. He who dwells in the Lotus of the Heart is that same numinous solar Fire that is spoken of as Time, unseen and all-devouring," *Maitri Up.*, VI, 1–2, cf. *Jaiminīya Upaniṣad Brāhmaṇa*, I, 27. So "what is within that should be searched out, that assuredly is what one should desire to understand . . . (for) everything is contained therein, both what is ours (now) and what is not (yet) ours," *Chāndogya Up.*, VIII, 1–3, i. e. not merely those possibilities that can be realized within the circle of a particular ensemble of conditions such as "ours," but all that can be realized in the indefinite totality of all states of being, all that God can "be." Thus Time and Space, manifested Deity in other words, are not external facts, but all contained at the core of our own being; there lies that "nothing" out of which the world was made; there can be realized the Kingdom of Heaven, in a degree proportionate to the measure of our Understanding.[80]

These considerations carry us far beyond the iconography of Brahmanical or Buddhist art to its ultimate content. This content is no less essential in the visual than in the literary art; to use only the eye in looking at a sculpture is no better than to use the ear alone in listening to the recitation of a text or the chanting of a hymn, however "artistic" these performances may be. The visual and literary formulations have precisely the same "uses," their references are the same; for some purposes the one, for others the other, may be more efficacious; cf. Kōbō Daishi, speaking with reference to the propagation of the doctrine, "The reverend Divine informed me that the secrets of the Shingon sect could not be conveyed without the aid of pictorial representations" (cf. Figs. C, D, E, 32, 33, 40).[81] In any case, it is the content that gives rise to the iconography, whether this be visual or verbal, just as the soul is said to be the form of the body ("form" is the principle that determines a thing in its species). To regard only the symbols, and not their form, is nothing but sensationalism, if not fetishism:[82] *Docti rationem artis intelligent, indocti voluptatem*, where *ratio* is *raison d'être*. The humane point of view, that the symbols are merely indications or stimuli, not to be judged as ends in themselves, but as means or supports of realization, has been strongly emphasized in the East, nowhere more explicitly than in the *Laṅkâvatāra Sūtra*, ed. Nanjio, p. 48: "As a master painter seated before some picture applies his colors for the purpose of making a picture, so do I preach (*deśayāmi*); the (real) picture is not in the color nor in the surface nor in the environment (*bhājana*), (but in the mind of the painter). The picture is devised in colors as a means of attracting living beings; and (just as the picture may be defective, so) the preaching may err, but the principle (*tattvaṁ*, cf. *tattvârtha* in *Bṛhad Devatā*, VII, 110; Dante's "*vera sentenzia*") transcends the letter" (*akṣara-varjitam*). As Dante expresses it, "Behold the teaching, that escapes beneath the veil of its strange verses." [83] The vocabulary of art, sensible in itself, is necessarily built up from the elements of sensible experience, the source of all rational knowledge; but what is thus constructed is not intended to resemble any natural species, and cannot be judged by verisimilitude or by the ear's or eye's sensation alone; it is intended to convey an intelligible meaning, and beyond that to point the way to the realization in consciousness of a condition of being transcending even the images of thought, and only a self-identification with the content of the work, achieved by the spectator's own effort, can be regarded as perfect experience, without distinction of "religious" and "aesthetic," logic and feeling.

PART II

THE PLACE OF THE LOTUS-THRONE

PART II

THE PLACE OF THE LOTUS-THRONE

"Where is the navel of the world?" — *Ṛg Veda*, I, 164, 34.
"Quivi è la Rosa, in che il Verbo divino carne se fece; quivi son li Gigli, al cui odor si prese il buon Cammino." — Dante, *Paradiso*, XXIII.[84]

In early Buddhist art, as is well known, the Buddha is constantly represented by a simple seat or throne (*pallaṅka*) situated at the foot of a Mahābodhi-tree, the Prince of Trees, *duminda*. After the second century A.D., in the case of *māra-dharṣaṇa* images (recognizable by the *bhūmi-sparśa-mudrā*), the manifested form of the Buddha himself, seated on a lotus-throne, or combined lotus- and lion-throne, has become the most prominent feature of the whole, the Wisdom-tree being now reduced from its original supremacy to a function merely indicative of place and event; or if some other of the *aṣṭasthāna* is in question, or indeed any scene from the Life, the Buddha is seated on a lotus-throne, or stands on a lotus-pedestal, the representation including at the same time the necessary indications of place and event. In just the same way the anthropomorphic figure displaces the Wheel, which is relegated to the pedestal as an indication of the event of the First Preaching; though it appears also as *lakṣaṇa* on the soles of the feet and palms of the hands, for the Buddha even in human form *is* essentially the Wheel, his Existence *is* its revolution.

In other words, anthropomorphic elements have now been combined with the earlier and more abstract symbolism; that was an inevitable result of the emergence of Buddhism as a popular religion, its extension as an emotional (*bhakti-vāda*) persuasion. That may have been just what the Buddha is said to have prophesied with regret on the occasion of the admission of women to the monastic order; and as we have seen a use of anthropomorphic images had been condemned as "groundless and fanciful." Even if this is not original, as it may well be, at least it represents an iconoclastic tendency, subsequent to the development of the anthropomorphic imagery. Not that monastic orthodoxy could really have feared "idolatry" in the fetishistic sense, but that he who had denied that he was either Gandhabba, Yakkha, or Man, asserting thereby his Principial essence, might have sensed, or been thought of as sensing, a psychological danger in the use of a cult image in the form of a man, danger in fact in any sort of cult susceptible of an "animistic" interpretation. Nothing, however, is really changed in principle; the "anthropomorphic" image in India remains "abstract,"[85] and rightly understood is merely a means to the realization of a given station of consciousness. Actually, in the theological development, the Principial Essence of the Tathāgata is more and more strongly emphasized, the content of the iconography, anthropomorphic or otherwise, becomes more and more ontological, less and less historical. It is just this emancipation from the historical point of view which determines the character and permits the expansion of Mahāyāna art, preoccupied as it is with the concept of the Buddha's transcendental Perfection: when it is realized that the Buddha's Comprehension (Sambodhi) dates from the beginning of time, and was merely "displayed" at Bodhgayā, and that he "has never left his seat on Mt Gṛdhrakūṭa," a mistaken attachment to his human personality is precluded. The mediaeval development of Christianity and of Christian art after the decline of Iconoclasm presents an exact analogy; here likewise it was realized that "Christ's birth is eternal," and so there came into being an art that emphasizes the Perfection of his being in Glory, far more than the course of his earthly ministry.[86]

Beneath the Bodhi-tree, within the Bodhimaṇḍa, Gautama is said to have accomplished the Great Awakening, Mahāsambodhi, becoming Buddha, "Comprehensor"; that was an attainment of Nirvāṇa, though other terms for this condition attainable by a still existent being, particularly the term Arahatta, "Perfection," are more frequently employed in the canonical Pali texts. What was then this "Full Attainment" (*samāpatti*)? Nirvāṇa is literally "despiration," but in Buddhist usage more specifically "Extinction," viz. extinction of the flame of Will. Most significant for us is the distinction of Nibbāṇa as *sa-upādi-sesa*, "having a residual existential ground," from Parinibbāṇa as *an-* or *nir-upādi-sesa*, "without any residual ground of existence";[87] for these interpretations coincide with the doctrine of the *Saddharma Puṇḍarīka* that the Buddha, though omniscient, though "extinguished," is not yet "absolutely extinguished" (*aparinirvāyamāṇa*, see p. 47). The Mahāsambodhi, Great Awakening, displayed at Bodhgayā was not then a "Drowning" in the utterly Unknowing and Unknown,[88] but the realization of a paradisiac, super-individual state of pure Being, realization of sovereign personality as Cakravartin and Dharmarājā. A transformation (Pali *vikubbana,* Skr. *parāvṛtti, abhisambhava*) is necessarily involved, which can only be described in terms of Paradise and Vision, Buddha-saukhya-vihāra (*Mahāyāna Sūtrâlaṁkāra,* IX, 46). So according to the *Nidānakathā,* J., I, 75–76, "... throughout the universe flowering trees put forth their blossoms, and fruit-bearing trees were loaded with clusters of fruit ... hells, whose gloom the rays of the seven suns had never dispelled, were filled with light [89] ... the blind from birth received their sight...." But this experience was not an effected miracle (*pāṭihāriya, inda-jāla*) made visible to any spectator: "the Great Person (*mahāpurisa*) sat there alone," J., I, 72, and if he beheld the ten thousand world-systems, the "World-picture" (*jagac-citra, Svâtmanirūpaṇa,* 96),[90] none therein beheld *him,* unless it were in a likeness, *pratibimbavat.* Paradise is ever present to the transcendental Buddha, but naturally it was not supposed that the vision remained or could have remained present to the empirical Buddha in subsequent daily life, and indeed he is made to say that were he to repeat elsewhere the Full Attainment reached in the Bodhimaṇḍa, "Wisdom-circle," earth could not sustain him (J., IV, 229).[91]

Now to consider the position of the Bodhimaṇḍa, and continuing with the *Kāliṅga-bodhi Jātaka*: with the Buddha's approval, as already explained above, p. 4, Mogallāna fares through the sky [92] to the Bodhimaṇḍa, and there procures a seed of the Wisdom-tree, and brings it back. Anāthapiṇḍika plants it in the place prepared for it at the gateway of the Jetavana, and there it springs up immediately, a full-grown "Forest-Lord," Vanaspati.[93] A Wisdom-festival (*bodhi-maha*) is held, and a railing (*vedikā*) and enclosing walls (*pākāra*) are built, clearly in imitation of those on the original site. Ānanda then prays the Buddha to repeat "at the foot of this Bodhi (-tree) that Full Attainment (*samāpatti*) to which you attained at the root of the Mahābodhi (-tree)." The Buddha replies that this is impossible, "for should I accomplish here what I accomplished in the Mahābodhimaṇḍa, the earth will not be able to sustain it"; he consents, however, to achieve during one night such a measure of Attainment as the site can support.

It is thus apparent that a particular significance attached to the (Mahā-) Bodhimaṇḍa with respect to its position in the Universe. We have already understood that the Wisdom-circle is an extent ideally equivalent to that of the whole Universe, and in gnosis realized as such. Now the meaning of a circle is with respect to its centre, which is a mathematical, and undimensioned, point, not with respect to its actual extension in physical space. It is in fact precisely at the centre of the Bodhimaṇḍa that the Bodhisattva took his seat. As related in the *Nidānakathā*, he first essays to find a seat on the north, south, and west of the Tree, but in each case the Great Earth (*mahā-paṭhavī*) fails to maintain its level, it seems to move up and down, like a great cartwheel lying on its hub (*nābhi*, "navel," "nave") when the circumference is trodden on; only when he takes his stand to the east of the Tree, that is evidently *on* the hub of the "wheel," is the level maintained.[94] Here there rises up a seat (*pallaṅka*) called "Unconquerable" (*aparājita*), and "of impartite, or adamantine, form" (*abhejja-rūpa*), and the Bodhisattva takes his seat with his back to the Tree. Māra, embodying the Will to Life, *libido, lubet*, claims the throne;[95] he assaults the Bodhisattva with every weapon known to him, but every weapon is transformed and reaches the Great Person in the form of a flower. Māra's daughters present seduction in all its most attractive forms; the Bodhisattva is equally unmoved, he does not "look," for he has passed beyond "affection" to "perfection."[96]

The location of the Buddha-seat at the navel of the World-wheel is emphasized again in the *Buddhacarita*, XIII, 68: "This is the navel of the earth-plain (*nābhir vasudhā-tala*); it is possessed of transcendent entirety (*parama-kṛtsna*[97]); no other place on earth but this is the realm of At-one-ment or Consummation (*samādhi*), the situation of the Goal (*hita*)." By the same token, this "unmoving site" (*acalaṭṭhāna*) has been occupied by all previous Buddhas (J., I, 71), by every Bodhisattva "on the day of his Great Awakening" (*abhisambujjhana*, J., I, 74, cf. *Buddhacarita*, XIII, 67).

The seat itself (*pallaṅka, patta-pallaṅka*) is spoken of as unconquerable (*aparājita*), impartite or adamantine (*abhejja*), and as a Waking-seat (*bodhi-*) and Victory-seat (*jaya-*), J., I, 73–77. It is fourteen cubits in length, and makes its appearance, "is" (*ahosi*), spontaneously; but its form is not emphasized, *pallaṅka* and *patta-pallaṅka* simply denoting a slab of stone, and as such, supported by a plain rectangular base, the seat is represented in the early art. In *Theragāthā*, 1095, however, we find it spoken of as a "lion-throne," *sīhâsana* (glossed *thirâsane aparājita-pal-*

laṅke, "unconquerable seat of firm séance"); this lion-throne is the form actually favored in the case of the oldest representations of the Buddha in human form at Mathurā, and it long survives in literature and art, often in combination with the lotus. Other royal types of seat or throne are met with at Amarāvatī. It is here also, as well as in the art of Gandhāra, mostly of the second century A.D., that the characteristic lotus seat (*padmâsana*) or lotus pedestal (*padma-pīṭha*) first appears.

We also find the term *vajrâsana,* "adamantine throne," applied to the Buddha's seat. This term does not occur in the Pali texts, but is common in

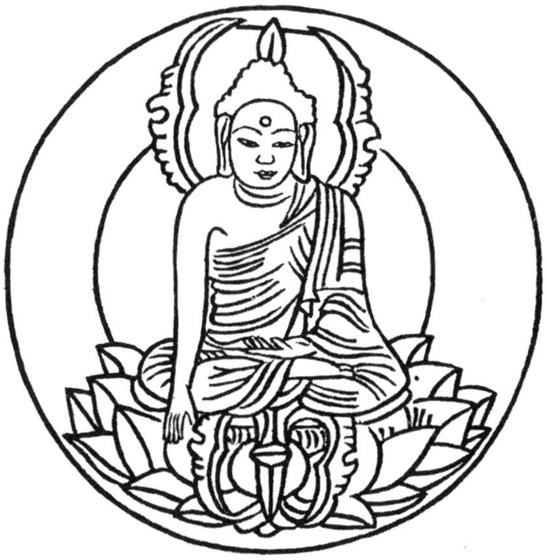

Fig. G. Vajra-dhātu form of the Dhyāni-Buddha.
After Ōmura Seigai, *Sanbon Ryōbu Mandara.*

the Mahāyāna sūtras. The word and notion led no doubt to the occasional representation of actual *vajras* on the pedestal of the Buddha throne, as at the Gal-vihāre, Poḷonnāruva, in the twelfth century; such representations are rare. In certain Shingon Buddhist representations (Fig. G) the *vajra* is combined rather with the body of the Buddha than with the throne, and this is probably to be connected with the late Tantrik form of Buddhism known as Vajrayāna, the designation of the Principial plane as Vajra-dhātu, Dharmakāya as Vajrakāya, and the personification of Vajrasattva = Vairocana, Ādi-Buddha. It will be remembered also that long before this (*Dīgha Nikāya,* I, 95, *Majjhima Nikāya,* I, 231, and in the *Lalita Vistara*) a Yakṣa Vajrapāṇi, a guardian angel and not to be confused with Indra, is closely associated with the Buddha during his ministry; and that this Vajrapāṇi, "who bears a *vajra* in his hand," soon becomes the Bodhisattva of the same name.[98] From the standpoint of Vedic angelology such a figure must be regarded simply as an externalization of the Buddha's own adamantine power, personified as an angel attendant upon him.[99]

Although the term *vajrâsana* is not directly represented in Pali texts, the idea is clearly present by implication. The throne is in fact spoken of as *abhejja-rūpa,* i. e. as of impartite or adamantine form, *abhejja* being equivalent to Skr. *abhedya,* "indivisible," and also a kenning for *vajra,* "diamond," "adamant." We have also already seen that the Buddha's seat is at the centre, on the navel of the World-wheel, i. e. also centred on the axle-tree (*akṣa*), which is also the World-axis; and it may be noted that *akṣa-ja,* "axle-born" or "axis-born," is again a kenning for "*vajra,*" while Kṛṣṇa's *cakra* is said to be *vajra-nābha.*[100]

The *vajra* (Jap. *kongō*) plays a large part in Shingon symbolism and ritual (Figs. G, H). A detailed study of the symbolism of Shingon ritual and implements is much to be desired.[101] However, it is evident from the representations and objects themselves, in the light of what has been shown above with respect to *akṣa, vajra,* and *cakra,* that the point or end of the *vajra* corresponds to *āṇi,* the "point" of the axle-tree that penetrates the nave of the Wheel, Dante's *punto dello stelo a cui la prima rota va dintorno.* In the ordinary double *vajra, kongō-sho* (Figs. 26, 27), then, the stem or handle corresponds to the vertical axis of the Universe, extending between Heaven and Earth, which are represented by the two ends, one- or three-pointed as the case may be, each in the image of (*anurūpam*) the other. That is as pure Being, *Ding an sich, in principio,* and motionless, *pūrṇa apravartin, acala, abhedya.* On the other hand the fourfold (crossed) *karma-vajra, katsuma-kongō* (Fig. 28), corresponding to Dharmacakra, *rimbō,* represents the movement or operation of this exemplary Principle either universally or on any given plane of being, as already explained in connection with the symbolism of the Wheel. Hence we find the spokes of the World-wheel not infrequently and quite naturally represented as *vajras,* extending from centre to felly; in the *rimbō* (Fig. 25), for example, the "earth-points" of the eight *vajra*-spokes are seen in contact with the felly, but it must be understood that the unseen "heaven-points" meet at the common centre, within the lotus-nave. From the point of view of anyone "on earth" the corresponding *vajra*-spoke extends as before from Earth (the felly) to Heaven (centre). From this point of view it will also be apparent why in

Shingon symbolism the *vajra, kongō,* is always represented as "supported" by a lotus, that is, by a universal "ground," the relation of *vajra* to lotus being that of "impartible essence" to "universal substance"; and it is in the "middle region," i. e. "round about" the axis of the *vajra*, between the centre and the felly of any Wheel, that all existence is extended. It should not be overlooked that *kongō-sho* and *katsuma-kongō*, the former vertical, the latter in a horizontal plane, considered together represent the poles of the Universe in the form of a three-armed cross: and as we have seen, the Buddha's throne is situated in the centre, at the intersection of the arms.

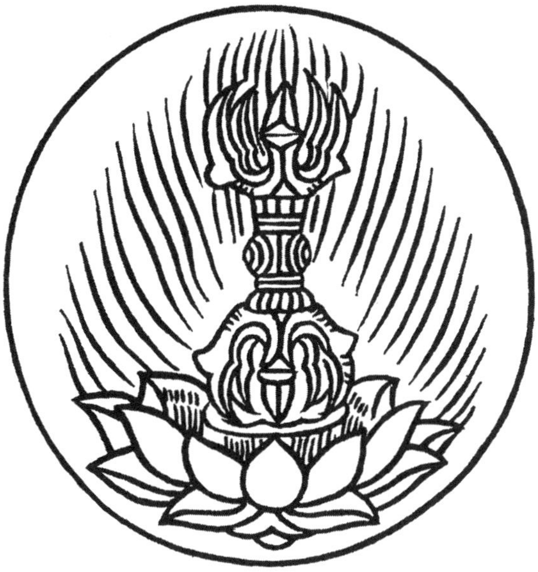

FIG. H. Vajra-Dhātu symbol of the Five Dhyāni Buddhas.
After Ōmura Seigai, *Sanbon Ryōbu Mandara.*

Furthermore, the origin of the term *vajrâsana* can also be explained psychologically, with reference to the mentality of him who sits thereon: [102] in the *Anguttara Nikāya*, I, 124, the highest type of consciousness is termed *vajirūpama citta*, "heart like adamant," [103] he having such a heart or mind "who by the destruction of the foul-issues [104] and the vision of Dhamma (Principle) has verified the gnosis of issue-free heart-and-mind-release (*vimutti* = *nibbāṇa*), and having won it abides therein. Just as, Brethren, there is nothing, whether gem or rock, which a diamond cannot cut (*vajirassa . . . abhejjam*) . . . such is one of the three types of man (*puggala*) to be found in the world." In Hinduism such a one is styled Jīvan-mukta, Freed in Life, or Vidvān, Gnostic, in Buddhism Jina, Conqueror, or Nirvāta, Extinguished, in Christianity Comprehensor. Such undoubtedly was the Mahāpurisa, Tathāgata, Buddha, Devâtideva; appropriate to him whose heart is like a diamond, adamantine, or as we should now perhaps express it, "of steel," is an adamantine throne, immovable as himself.

In the *Saddharma Puṇḍarīka,*[105] not later than A.D. 250, the Buddha doctrine is completely emancipated from its historical setting, which is preserved only with respect to the "traces" (*dhātu*) of Gautama on earth, and in the iconography in so far as the monastic type is still adhered to. The Buddha himself becomes a transcendental principle, Dharma, Logos, awakened (*abhisambuddha*) from the beginning of time (SP., XV, 1). Not merely is his throne (*āsana*), upon which he is never weary of sitting (SP., V, 23),[106] the same as that which all former Munis have occupied (SP., XIII, 67), as was also taught in the Pali texts, but he is from the beginning one and the same who has occupied throne after throne in time and time again: "again and again I take my stand on the ground of the living world" (SP., XV, 7), "showing myself as such and such forasmuch as men have fallen into sin and sorrow" (SP., XV, 22, 23, cf. *Bhagavad Gītā,* IV, 7 and 8); being thus not merely the Buddhas and Bodhisattvas of the past, but those yet to come (SP., XIV, 38, XVI, 59–62, etc.).[107] As Dharmarājā, "King of the Word" (SP., V, 1), Puruṣôttama, "Most High Person" (SP., II, 41), *Svayambhū,* "Self-subsistent" (SP., II, 48, XV, 21), Lokapitā, "Father of the World" (SP., XV, 21), and Sarvaprajāna Nātha, "Lord of begotten existences" (SP., XV, 21, cf. "Prajāpati"), "I display return (*nirvṛta*) who am not myself returned (*anirvṛtaḥ*)" (SP., XV, 21).[108] "I reveal the Ground of Extinction (*nirvāṇa-bhūmi*), speaking by accommodation for the edification of living beings, though I was not Extinguished (*na . . . nirvāmy ahu*) at that time, but am ever revealing the Dharma here. . . . Believing that my Self-nature (*ātma-bhāva*) was Wholly Returned (*parinirvṛta*), they worship variously the traces (*dhātu*), but see not Me. . . . I have not left this Gṛdhrakūṭa . . . the duration of my life is an interminable aeon" (SP., XV, 3, 5, 10, and 17). Again, "The Threefold World is seen by the Tathāgata,[109] not as childish worldlings see it, but immediately as Principles (*dharmā*); verily the Principles are not remote from the Tathāgata in the station where he is. . . . The Tathāgata who was Awakened (*abhisambuddha*) so long ago, and the measure of whose life is incalculable, is continuously (*sadā*) existent (*sthita*). . . . My ancient Bodhisattva course is not yet run, the measure of my life is not fulfilled. . . . I announce an Absolute-Extinction (*parinirvāṇa*) who-am-not-by-way-of-being-Totally-Extinguished (*aparinirvāyamāṇa*) . . . lest those whose virtuosity (*kuśala*) is insecurely rooted, thinking 'the Tathāgata is alive' (*tiṣṭhati*), should fail to exert their manhood (*vīrya*) towards a Negation-of-the-flux (*niḥsaraṇa*) of the Threefold World" (SPt., pp. 318, 319).[110] And as for those Comprehensors who may in future take their place at the foot of the Wisdom-tree, "there have I taken my seat, where that Son of Buddha is, there am I" (SP., XVI, 59–62); "moved by compassion, like a father's for his dear and only son, he appears (*avatīrya*, i. e. as *avatāra*) in the Threefold World, seeing with the eye of wisdom that living beings are revolving (*paribhramataḥ*, cf. *paribhramati* in *Maitri Up.*, III, 2) there in the Wheel of the World-flux (*saṁsāracakre*) and laboring without discovering a Negation of the Flux (*niḥsaraṇam*) . . . the Tathāgata who thus beholds the deep principles (*gambhīrān dharmān*) sees without seeing (*paśyaty apaśyanayā*) [111] the Threefold World that is the crowded home of multifarious living beings" (SPt., pp. 135–137).

The Buddha as Supreme Person (Puruṣôttama, etc.) of incalculable but not infinite age, whose enlightenment dates from the beginning of the world, is thus from the standpoints of ontology and psychology, as well as by verbal correspondences (Lokapitā, Svayambhū, Prajānanātha, etc.), virtually identified with Brahmā-Prajāpati, who is the Father of the World.[112] This virtual identification of Buddha and Brahmā appears already in certain passages of the Pali books, for example in the equation of Dhammakāya and Brahmakāya (*Dīgha Nikāya*, III, 84), or again in the Tevijja Sutta,[113] where it is affirmed that the enlightened Bhikkhu may well attain to union with Brahmā, "who is the same." As we shall presently see, this virtual identification of Buddha with Brahmā has also its equivalents in iconographic representation.

It will be understood, of course, that in the *Saddharma Puṇḍarīka* the Buddha is speaking (Fig. 30) throughout not as the Word, for the Word (Dharma) is without origin (*anutpattika*), and non-existent, not like the Sambhogakāya Buddha manifested as it is in itself, which would be impossible. The Word does not speak, it is moved or taught (*pravartita, deśita*); [114] Buddha as Cakravartin is not the permissive, but the immediate, cause of the Turning of the Word-wheel. As Crowned King of the Word, *dharmarājā paṭṭabaddha* (SPt., p. 417), [115] and Universal Sovereign, *cakravartin* (Maitreya-Asaṅga, *Uttaratantra*, I, 150), he displays to the assembled congregation of his spiritual sons the likeness of a Nature (*svabhāva*), Suchness (*tathatā*), Quiddity (*tattva*), Void (*śūnyatā*), Sameness (*samatā*), and Logosity (*dharmatā*) that are ineffable. That is, his manifestation in the station (*sthāna*) where he is, on Mt Gṛdhrakūṭa where he is always, is not of the Dharmakāya as such, but of the Dharma in a likeness, in the likeness of a Wheel, or the likeness of Gautama. What he reveals to his children, the Bodhisattvas, who alone are competent to the vision, is his Person in Majesty, the Sambhogakāya. That reflection (*pratibimba*) is in fact all that can be revealed to the angelic eye, for the attachment of *-kāya* to *dharma* is purely analogical, and must not be understood to mean that the Dharma has a form. At the same time his appearance in a designated body, Nirmāṇakāya, displaying the drama of Awakening eventfully, is for the sake of those living in the flesh in that day, or who may after the "Parinirvāṇa" (here the temporal and analogical equivalent of a Return at the End of Time) find their way to Awakening by means of the "traces" of the apparition.[116] Such temporal manifestations by way of *avataraṇa* are rare and precious, but he will "come again" as Maitreya.

The foregoing evidences of the virtual identification of the Buddha in Majesty with Brahmā-Prajāpati enthroned in the supra-mundane Empyrean heavens are paralleled by the iconographic prescription of the *Bṛhat Saṁhitā*, LVIII, 44, "The Buddha is to be shown seated on a lotus, like the Father of the World" (*padmâsanôpaviṣṭhaḥ piteva jagato bhaved buddhaḥ*).[117] The Buddha is in fact represented *padmâsana*, *kamalâsana*, from late Āndhra times onwards, that is almost from the beginning of the anthropomorphic iconography. In the common representations of a Buddha triad, the Buddha being seated or standing between a pair of Bodhisattvas, the latter are supported by paired lotuses springing from the same stem, and such triads may be compared from more than one point of view with the Several Angels (*viśve devāḥ*) of the Upaniṣads and Vedas, where the Unity of the primordial Agni is represented in a trinity of aspects; the Buddha triads, for example, corresponding iconographically to such representations of the Trinity as appear in the Burmese relief, Fig. 16. The ontology is the same, whether the stem of the Buddha-lotus be prolonged downwards and there supported by paired Nāgas representative of the Waters (as at Kārlī), or the stem of the Brahmā-lotus rises from the navel of Nārâyaṇa, originally Varuṇa, recumbent on the Waters.

An equivalence can be demonstrated also from many points of view between the Buddha paradises (Sukhāvatī, etc.) and the Brahmalokas,[118] and more specifically between the thrones of Buddha and of Brahmā when the throne is thought of as *pallaṅka*, Skr. *paryaṅka*, rather than as *padmâsana*. Thus, access to the Brahmaloka is by a crossing of the river Vijarā, "casting off of change-and-decay," which crossing must be effected "only by the Intellect" and involves a shaking off of all the pairs of opposites, including good and evil; the city of Brahmā is called Sālajya, his abode (*saṁsthāna*) Aparājita ("Unconquerable"), the throne-room (*pramita*) Vibhu ("Space"). The *Kauṣītaki Up.*, I, 3, and 5, further describes the footstool (*āsandī*) [119] and the throne (*paryaṅka*) of Brahmā: the former is called Vicakṣaṇā, "Discernment" and is explained as Prajñā, "Omniscience" or "Perfect Wisdom," the latter is called Amitaujas, "Limitless Splendor" or "Limitless Power" (the designation applies to Indra in *Ṛg Veda*, I, 11, 4), and explained as Prâṇa, "Spirit" or "Life," and it is "only by Prajñā that one ascends the throne." [120] Here the last assertion corresponds to SP., V, 75, "no Extinction without Omniscience," as cited below; and the name of the throne is equivalent to Amitâbha, a Buddha name denoting "Limitless Light," and its nature, Prâṇa, to Amitâyus, "Limitless Life," which is another epithet of the same Buddha, who represents the Sambhogakāya aspect of Gautama.

The Buddha throne, however, is usually a lotus, or lotus- and lion-throne combined; the Bodhisattvas, and all who are born again in Buddha paradises, are similarly lotus-supported, but on smaller flowers. So the predications of future enlightenment generally include such promises as "shall appear seated in the cup of a lotus on a lion-throne in Paradise" (SPt., p. 419); "there the Leader Amitâbha is seated in the lovely glistening cup of a lotus (*padmagarbhe*),[121] on a lion-throne (*siṁhâsane*) . . . there the Sons of the Conqueror come into existence (*upapāduka*) seated in the pure cups of lotuses" (SP., XXIV, 31, 32, cf. *Mahā-Sukhāvatī-vyūha*, 16, 40 and 41).[122] In these passages, *upapāduka* has generally been rendered "miraculously born," but the direct sense of *upapad* is simply "to enter into any state," "to appear," "come into a given mode of existence"; it is not miraculously but inevitably that a certain degree of enlightenment results in a future birth in a Buddha paradise. On the other hand, *upapāduka* contrasts with *anutpattika*, "unoriginated," applicable to the Dharma as being precisely that which does not come into existence, the Buddha being merely an image, *ākṛti*, of the Dharma, existent in the world, like the *mūrta* Brahman, viz. Brahmā. The primary ontological significance of the lotus is precisely with respect to this existence, *astitva, sthāyitā, sthiti*, a being "firmly grounded in the possibilities of existence," commonly called the Waters. *Padmâsana* and *vajrâsana* are equally symbols of that *sthāyitā*: both express visually *sadā sthita*, and *tiṣṭhati*, with respect to the Buddha or any Angel; both differentiate the station of Sambhogakāya from that of the Dharmakāya, which is inaccessible even to the angelic eye.

Sthāyitā in any Buddha paradise, whether with respect to the Buddha there manifested, or to his sons and disciples the Bodhisattvas and Pratyeka Buddhas, is an immortality until the end of time, viz. until the lifetime of the Buddha lord of that field or cosmos is fulfilled, not the absolute eternity of the Dharmatā, Parinirvāṇa, which never having come into existence can never pass away. The Bodhisattva in whom the Wisdom-heart (*bodhi-citta*) has opened (*utpanna*), and who is thereby born (*upapāduka, upapattika*) in the pure cup of a paradisiac lotus, whence he beholds the Buddha face to face, is indeed no longer involved in the world-flux (*saṁsāra*), but neither has he reached *nirvāṇa*, much less *parinirvāṇa*, however he may imagine: "that is a resting-place (*viśrāma*), not a Return (*nirvṛti*); it is by accommodation (*upāya*) that the Buddhas teach this doctrine (*naya*, viz. of a Paradise), actually there is no Extinction (*nirvāṇa*) without omniscience (*sarvajñatva*), strive for That" (SP., V, 74, 75).[123] Only when that Omniscience has been attained can the disciple be said to have become a Buddha, *the* Buddha; then like Prabhūtaratna he sits with the Buddha on one and the same throne, being in fact the Buddha, Tathāgata, though intelligibly and apparently to the angelic eye still "himself." As a Buddha, *the* Buddha, he is still existent, *sa-upādi-sesa*, until the end of time, *kalpânta*, in saecula saeculorum. But his appearance as a Crowned King of the Word is but the presented aspect of his being; he is *nirvāta*, and realizes the Sameness of All Principles. Not Absolutely Extinguished (*parinirvāta*), nor beyond the ken of the angelic eye, he "sees without seeing" (*paśyaty apaśyanayā*), or sees ideally, the Threefold World "as is" (*yathābhūta*); he is not merely Mover of the Wheel (*dharmacakravartin*), but also "has the Word as his intrinsic nature," *svabhāva-dharma-samanvāgata* (SPt., p. 481). He sees that Nirvāṇa and Saṁsāra are the same, he knows, he is the Sameness of all Principles (*dharmā*); [124] he is omniscient of the identity of the world and the abyss, actuality and possibility, active and passive aspects of the infinite, though he has still a "residual existential element." He has become the Universal *jīvanmukta*, super-individually existent as the One Great Person.[125]

From the one point of view he sees only the "patient-stillness of the unoriginated Word" (*anutpattika-dharma-kṣānti*), from the other and same point of view he sees the same Word in rotation (*pravartana*) or procession (*prasaraṇa*) as the causal world of birth and death, the wandering-place of living beings ignorant of a reversion (*nivṛtti*) or recession (*niḥsaraṇa*).[126] So feeling a great tenderness (*karuṇā*) towards his world, his "Buddha-field," he reveals the Word by means of various alternative-formulations (*dharma-paryāya*), either directly, or by means of other teachers; for he is infinitely skilful (*kuśala*) in the use of convenient means (*upāya*) adapted to the capacity (*bala*) of every auditor.[127]

The *Saddharma Puṇḍarīka*, summarized above, may be described as the most important of the Mahāyāna *dharma-paryāyas*, equally from ontological and iconographic points of view. But that is not all. An understanding of the ontology is essential also for the student of "art," who must realize that a work of art cannot be "understood" or rightly "valued" or "criticized" apart from the form which is its *raison d'être*. Content is not *post factum*, but *causa faciendi*; the significance of things well and truly made is with respect to the end for which they are made.[128] As religious art is never an end in itself, but always a means of communication, it can only be called "good" or "bad" in so far as it actually expresses and conveys a given "idea"; rational judgment of a given work can only be based on a comparison of the substance with its determining form. How then can one who ignores the idea or form embodied in a work of art be qualified to "criticize" it? All that such an one can do is to say that he knows nothing of art, but knows what he likes.

Let us admit the possibility of "aesthetic experience," and that this possibility is independent of the theme, whatever it may have been. This experience will be realized in an assimilation of the perceiving consciousness to the form of the thing considered. Inasmuch as "Buddhism" is the "form" of Buddhist art, it follows that an understanding of Buddhism is indispensable, not only for a rational interpretation of the iconography, in which the logic of the work is expressed, but also as prerequisite to "aesthetic experience." To assert that "aesthetic experience" of Buddhist art is possible without an *a priori* knowledge of Buddhism embodies this element of truth, that the content of Buddhism is not merely specific, but also universal, and that in so far as our experience is not, for example, merely specifically Christian, but Christian universally, we do already possess an *a priori* knowledge of Buddhism; one does not know who, however, can lay claim to so profound an understanding of any religious art as to enable him to say that he knows so much of the form of religious art that he need know no more.

Returning now to the iconography or symbolism of our art: we read in Hsüan-tsang, *Life*, Ch. III (Beal, p. 103), that the adamantine throne (*vajrâsana*) which is in the centre of the Bodhimaṇḍa was perfected at the beginning of the Bhadra Kalpa, the present aeon, and rose up when the world was brought into existence. It is at the very centre of the Universe, and extends downwards to the "golden wheel"; it is about a hundred paces round. That it is called adamant means that it is pure and indestructible. Without its support the Earth could not endure; were the seat not adamantine, there would be no place in the world that could support the Adamantine At-one-ment (*vajra-samādhi*). Here whoever desires to conquer Māra and to attain to perfect wisdom must take his seat; were it essayed elsewhere, the Earth would be overturned. The thousand Buddhas of the present aeon have all attained their emancipation here. If the world were shaken to its foundations, the Bodhimaṇḍa would not be moved.[129]

Here the only important point added to what we already knew from texts previously cited is the explanation that the Bodhimaṇḍa represents a section on the terrestrial plane of the axis of the universe, which axis extends downwards to the "golden wheel," and on which the stability of the Earth depends. What is meant by that "golden wheel" may be learnt from Vasubandhu's *Abhidharmakośa*, III, 45 ff., Poussin, II, 138 ff., where the "world-receptacle" (*bhājanaloka*) is described.[130] The Universe is conceived of as consisting of so many superimposed "circles" (*maṇḍala*): nethermost is the circle of Space (*ākāśa-maṇḍala*), "solid" and of "immeasurable" circumference, and 1,600,000 *yojanas* in thickness; over and on this rests the circle of the Waters, 1,120,000 *yojanas* in thickness and 1,203,450 in circumference.[131] The surface of these Waters, just as in the Brahmanical cosmology and in Genesis, is stirred by the dawn wind of creation, which is impelled by the latent causality of past events. The foam of the Waters solidifies to form the golden circle (*kañcana-maṇḍala*) or "Land of Gold" (*kañcana-bhūmi*),[132] the same as Hsüan-tsang's "golden wheel" and representing the "foundations of the earth" firmly established amidst the possibilities of existence. The Land of Gold has a diameter equal to that of the Waters, and displaces 120,000 *yojanas* of their depth. The surface of the Land of Gold is the Round of the World, with its mountains (Meru, etc.), continents (the four *dvīpas*), seas, and outwall (*cakra-vāḍa*). Of these continents, or rather "islands," our terrestrial world Jambudvīpa lies to the south of Meru, which rises in the centre of the whole Universe, and extends from the Waters below to Heaven above, as world-pillar and world-axis. "Midmost in Jambudvīpa, and resting on the Land of Gold, is the *vajrâsana* on which the Bodhisattva takes his seat to realize the *vajrôpama samādhi* [133] and so become an Arhat or Buddha: no other place, no other person, could support the Bodhisattva's *samādhi*."

It is clear that Hsüan-tsang merely repeats the ancient tradition of the Buddha-throne as it had been told him, or as he might have read it in the texts from which we have quoted above. It is true that the centre of Jambudvīpa cannot be regarded, unless analogically, as the actual (local) centre of the entire Universe, for that centre is on the axis of Mt Meru. In the same way with respect to this world, which is the particular Buddha-field of the Tathāgata *qua* Śākyamuni, it will be remarked that the Bodhimaṇḍa at Bodhgayā, and the summit of Mt Gṛdhrakūṭa where the Sambhogakāya is "always" revealed, are not locally on one and the same axis or meridian. That should serve to remind us that the "centre of the Universe" is not a spot fixed in space, but (as will be further shown below) a psychological centre, the focal point of consciousness, not *bahir-* but *antar-bhūtasya*.[134]

In actual iconography, the axial extension of the Buddha's throne or footstool may be clearly shown. In the case of a *padmâsana* or *padma-pīṭha* the supporting axis, viz. the stem, extends downwards through the Earth into the depths of the Waters, where it is upheld by paired Nāgas, as representative genii of the nether Waters.[135] Of this we have an excellent example in the Sambhogakāya relief of Gupta age at Kārlī (Fig. 29, also Bachhofer, *Early Indian Sculpture*, Pl. 68, central panel). Here, within a pillared structure which may be compared to Brahmā's throne-room Vibhu, the Buddha is seated on a lion-throne, with his feet supported by a lotus. To left and right are the Bodhisattvas Avalokiteśvara and Maitreya, representative of the congregation assembled on Mt Gṛdhrakūṭa; they are standing upon lotus supports. Immediately below the Buddha's lotus is a Dharmacakra, flanked by paired deer, indicative of place and event, viz. the Deer Park at Sārnāth and the First Sermon, *prathamadeśanā.* At this level is represented the earth-plane (*vasudhā-tala*), extending horizontally to left and right, but interrupted centrally where the descending axis penetrates it. The "lotus-capital" of the descending axis has now a more bulbous form, but taking wheel and pillar together, we recognize without difficulty an original formula constantly met with in the earliest Buddhist art. The rounded masses under the earth-plane correspond in position to the "foundations of the earth," the Land of Gold. All below this represents the Waters, the support given by the paired Nāgas indicating the firm establishment of the cosmic pillar in the nether sea of possibility. Above the Buddha's head, supported by angels commonly spoken of as Vidyādharas (Cherubim), is a *stūpa,*[136] symbol of the Parinirvāṇa, and that it is thus above and removed from him corresponds to the fact that he is not yet transcendentally *parinirvāta,* for as we have seen, the temporal decease represented not the realization, but only the analogy, of the final Parinirvāṇa. There is a similar relief at Kondivle.

When the throne is alternatively a *paryaṅka* and thought of as the *vajrâsana,* a condition corresponding to Hsüan-tsang's conception, the supporting axis is shown as extended downwards into the Land of Gold, and there supported by a Guhyaka Yakṣa.[137] An admirable illustration of this can be cited in the case of the pedestal (Fig. 40) of the Yakushi Buddha of the Kondo, a Japanese work of the eighth century (*Japanese Temples and Their Treasures,* Pl. 206: *Yakushiji Okagami,* II, Tokyo, 1922). Here the flat surface of the rectangular throne is an earth-plane (*vasudhā-tala*), the solid body of the pedestal corresponding to the Land of Gold. On the front side of the pedestal is represented a vertical axis extending downwards to the lower margin of the block, where it is supported by a crouching Yakṣa Atlant.[138] This representation is exactly analogous to that of the Guḍimallam liṅgam (Fig. 42 and my *History,* Fig. 66), nor need the point be labored here that the Śiva liṅgam, established in the Land of Gold (Hāṭaka) and extending thence to Heaven above, represents another aspect of the one axis of the Universe. The ornamental form of the Yakushi axis recalls that of the Dharmacakra pillars represented at Amarāvatī (e. g. my *History*, Fig. 136, right and left), and shows clearly the jointed structure of the axis. On the side of the Yakushi pedestal (Fig. 41), right and left of the axis, and as though to emphasize the character of the central supporting Atlant Yakṣa, are other figures of the same type, crouching within and peering out of caverns, which are their chambers in the bowels of the earth; similar representations are to be seen on the other faces of the pedestal. Below the level representing the base of the Land of Gold are four strata representing the Waters; on the uppermost of these, centrally on each side, are theriomorphic emblems of the Four Quarters, those on the front side being a tortoise and a snake, representing the North (the Buddha therefore "is" in the North and faces South); the lowest stratum consists of a lotus-petal moulding, which may here be understood to mean the nethermost Waters as the ultimate "ground" of all that is above them and established in them.

A part of what has been independently deduced and demonstrated above has also been stated by M. Mus in his admirable monograph, *Le Buddha paré*, etc., previously cited. For example, "The throne of the Law is the symbol par excellence of the teaching, and even of the state of Buddahood" (p. 243); "It cannot be conceived that the Body of Beatitude (Sambhogakāya) could have been seated anywhere else than on the angelic lotus, far above the throne to be seen in the holy place (Bodhgayā)" (p. 204); "The holy throne combines in itself three appearances, corresponding to those of the Three Bodies" (p. 272); "The prolongation of the stem, which is the axis of the sensible world, bears at the summit of the universe the spiritual lotus-throne of the Sambhogakāya" (p. 243).[139] M. Mus points out further that the lotus-throne which supports the Word as it is in itself can be imagined only analogically; that transcendental throne could no more than the Word itself be conceived of as visible even to the angelic eye, for the being of the Word is strictly noumenal, *un être verbal* (*nāmavat*), not contained by, only indicated by, the thought and spoken words.

We have thus discovered in the texts a sufficient explanation of the most characteristic formulae of the iconography. We now return to and conclude with the problem of the place of the Buddha's throne; i. e., of course, a special case of the general problem of the meaning of "immanence." We have already surmised that by the centre of the Universe, the navel of immortality, and similar expressions there is to be understood not a determinable spot, but a psychological centre and point of consciousness "where every where and every when is focussed"; that the traditional cosmology is in fact far more a psychology than a cosmic geography. That is explicitly enunciated in the pre-Buddhist doctrine of the Lotus of the Heart, as ground whereon and space wherein all existence is unfolded. It seems that no use of this significant image was actually made in Buddhist texts, but it can easily be shown, and has indeed already been shown in other ways, that Buddhahood, Nirvāṇa, is not in any place, but represents a state of being, viz. being universally; the Buddha-throne can only be established "within you," *antarbhūtasya*. The adamantine throne is the stability of the adamantine intellect. Knowledge of the Buddha is not the knowledge of any "thing," but a consummation of the process of de-mentation of discriminative perception, *viññānassa nirodha* = *ceto-vimutti*, *Dīgha Nikāya*, I, 223, and *Anguttara Nikāya*, I, 124, cf. *mano niroddhavyaṁ hṛdi*, *Maitri Up.*, VI, 34. So in his "Song of Victory" (*Nidānakathā*, I, 76 = *Dhammapada*, 154) the Buddha exclaims, "The key-plate of the roof has been shattered, intellect has reached the dissolution of its composite formulations." [140] That is to say that the Comprehensor, emancipated from all dialectic understanding, knows and is the Only Principle; in the Act-of-Identity (*samādhi*) he is the Sameness of All Principles.[141] He is *nibbuta*, *nirvāta*, the Supreme Identity has been touched, the Buddha essence is liberated from duration; yet speaking *qua* the Great Person, he cannot say that he is Absolutely Extinguished, he must say that he is not "yet" Absolutely Extinguished, *quâ parinirvāta*, he would not be a Person. The unity of Being and Non-being can *speak* only as Being, only as Being can he be *spoken of* or represented in a likeness.

One further word on Buddhahood and the concepts of Nirvāṇa and Parinirvāṇa. Negative expressions are inevitable, merely because all affirmation is the enunciation of a limiting condition; denial is a double negative, affirming absence of conditions, whereof the In-finite, *qua* in-finite, is necessarily indigent. That has been recognized again and again also in Europe; cf. Maimonides, *Guide for the Perplexed*, I, Ch. 59, "Superficial thinkers . . . ask 'Is that thing existing in the Creator, or not?' . . . by each additional negative attribute you advance toward the knowledge of

God"; Eckhart, I, 87, "Nothing true can be spoken of God"; Dante, *Convivio*, III, 15, ". . . certain things which our intellect cannot behold . . . we cannot understand what they are except by denying things of them." There is nothing here that the adamantine mind can fear; in the words of the *Taittirīya Upaniṣad*, II, 7, "Truly, when one finds a fearless foundation (*pratiṣṭhā*) in that which is invisible (*adṛśya*), not-selfed (*anātmya*, = Buddhist *anatta*), ineffable (*anirukta*), homeless (*anilayana*), then has he attained to fearlessness (*abhayaṁ gata*)."

Eckhart and Blake alone should have sufficed to demonstrate the naïveté of the view that Buddhism is proven "atheistic" by its negative phraseology. According to Eckhart, "It is more necessary to perfection that the soul lose God than that she lose creatures . . . the soul honors God most in being quit of God (I, 274) . . . the fastidious soul (cf. Buddhist *ariya*) can rest her understanding on nothing that has name. She escapes from every name into the nameless nothingness (I, 373) . . . this is the death of the spirit . . . the spirit puts its own self to death . . . and remains in the unity of the divine nature. . . . These are the blessed dead. . . . No one can be buried and beatified in the Godhead who has not died to God (I, 411) . . . the Godhead is as void as though it were not. . . . In this state we are as free as when we were not: free as the Godhead in its non-existence (I, 381–382). . . . She (the soul) sinks for evermore in the depths of this naught. She sinks and drowns: she drowns to her own aught. But the naught that sinks can never comprehend the naught it sinks in (I, 373)." So also Blake, "I would go down unto Annihilation and Eternal Death, lest the Last Judgment come and find me Unannihilate, and I be seiz'd and giv'n into the hands of my own Selfhood." Those who cannot bear with such thought as this can never bear with Buddhism, nor understand the ultimate significance of Buddhist art.

Any change of state is a death. Christian tradition alludes to "three deaths of the soul," namely (1) the death to self-will, which death implies the attainment of angelic being, a state of grace, (2) the death of the soul to its own separate form, implying a conscious conformity to the Principial Being, and (3) a death, called a Drowning, in Waters where God is unknown to himself, unknown as oneself; there as Eckhart expresses it the soul is "free as the Godhead in its non-existence." In corresponding Buddhist formulation we have a lower mortification, (1) that of the man who adopts the homeless life, and attains to so much Awakening as to ensure his birth in a Buddha paradise, (2) the attainment of Buddhahood, Nirvāṇa, extinction of self, but with residual existential elements, and (3) Extinction Absolute, Parinirvāṇa without residual factors of existence. To any of these deaths can be applied the thought of Chuang Tzŭ, "How do I know that he who dreads to die is not as a child who has lost the way and cannot find his home?" He who shrinks from the Drowning, from Death, Privation, Extinction, Night, may reflect, *Mors janua vitae.* Unitary Being, that is only One, both His and ours, even a stone has being, is at the same time fontal and inflowing, *saṁsaraṇa, niḥsaraṇa;*[142] "He who is Death is likewise the Year, the Father of his children," [143] "Pillar of Life, at the parting of the Ways . . . there, where Life was erst, insists our Agni, First-born of the Law," [144] "born ever and again." [145] If then we lay aside all thought of temporal succession, all considerations of mortality, viz. of eventful birth and death, we shall understand that Life and Death, Being and Non-being, Nirvāṇa and Parinirvāṇa, are incessant aspects of That which is emancipate from all possible contingency, even from such accidents of Being as the phrase "not yet Absolutely Extinguished" implies. "That" is neither "here" nor "there," but "within you," *antarbhūtasya khe,* in the Calyx of the Heart.

All this the Buddha refused to discuss. His business was to proclaim a Way (*mārga, pantha*), he would not speak of That, the Goal (*artha*) whereof nothing can be spoken truly or intelligibly. How indeed, as Confucius expresses it, should those who have not yet understood Life, aspire to comprehend Death? whilst we are on the way, we are not there. We can then only take the Buddha as he *is*, as manifested operative presence, and strive to realize ourself as Same, by following his or any alternatively formulated Way, taught by himself or any "other" Comprehensor. That Way is mapped, not only in spoken words, but equally in painted or sculptured iconographies. These "works of art" [146] are "footprints of the Law," "traces of the Buddha," which we cannot say that we have really heard or seen, otherwise than by merely animal perception, unless we have seen through them at least a shadow of the form by which they are what they are. Let us not forget that the Brahmanical or Buddhist craftsman was required to *be* that which he was commissioned to *represent,* and that only in so far as we can be again the Same, can we begin to understand his operation.

To resume: it has been shown by reference to chapter and verse of canonical texts, both Buddhist and pre-Buddhist, that the Buddha, humanly presented, is in fact connatural with the Vedic Agni, and that Buddhist symbolism, far from being an isolated language, is proper to the one great tradition which has persisted from the Vedic or a pre-Vedic period until now. The lotus denotes ontologically a firm establishment amongst the possibilities of existence, denotes a birth and manifestation primarily in the intelligible, or also and consequently in the sensible, world; while it denotes ethically, detachment, as of one who is in the world but not of it. The throne of deity is a lotus-throne from the foregoing points of view; as impartite and immovable, it is adamantine; as royal, it is a lion-throne. The Tathāgata, Buddha, seated on such a throne, standing on such a pedestal, affirms an infinite negation, a sable stillness against which his golden Person shines resplendent, unconfined by any form, but omniform. As crowned King of the Word he utters to angelic ears as much as can be spoken of the silence, that is our existence.[147] As an individual teacher with a given name, he plays a part and proclaims a Way. From any point of view his intellect is adamantine, regal, and intangible. The foundations of his manifestation are established in the depths of the upper and the nether seas: he is the Axis of the Universe, in whom it comes to be and goes to be not. By whatever name, personal or essential, the Spoken Word, the Wheel in Revolution, the Tree of Life, or Fiery Pillar, he may be called, in whatever form he may be imagined, who surely takes the forms imagined by his worshippers, for all convenient means are at his command, he, Tathāgata, Agni Vaiśvānara, Brahmā-Prajāpati, Christ, or Idea of Muḥammad, is one and the same, his throne is single. As Kabīr expresses it, echoing classic formulae in what is still the lingua franca of a hundred million speakers:

> What a wonderful lotus it is that blooms at the heart of the wheel; who are its comprehensors?
>
> There in the midst thunders the self-supported lion-throne, there the Great Person shines resplendent.[148]

NOTES

NOTES

1 (*page 3*). The likeness of any thing as such, presented to the eye's intrinsic faculty, is merely an occasion of sensation, and necessarily without meaning; recognition being an animal, not an intellectual operation.

2 (*page 3*). In one sense, though not essentially, the aniconic image may be regarded as *more* a likeness of Him, that is in so far as it reminds us of the relative unimportance of the human mode, as merely a particular case amongst the possibilities of existence.

3 (*page 3*). Cf. *Jaiminīya Upaniṣad Brāhmaṇa*, III, 32, "This the Sātyakīrtas say: 'As to the Angel whom we worship, of him we say that there is one aspect in the cow, another in beasts of burden (horses), another in the elephant, another in man (*puruṣa*), another in all existences; such is the Angel's omni-aspectuality (*sarvaṁ rūpaṁ*).' That same single aspect is the Spirit (*prâṇa*)."

"Just as little" should be noted, for this is not a pantheistic point of view, it is merely "not anthropocentric." St. Francis also preached to the birds and fishes, for "the whole creation groaneth and travailleth together."

4 (*page 4*). A prohibition of this kind is alluded to in Ch. 48 of the *Vinaya* of the Sarvastivādins. See Waley in "Mélanges chinois et bouddhiques," *Inst. Belge des Hautes Études Chinoises*, I, 1932, 352. Compare Nanda's refusal to provide biographical material for the representation of the events of the Buddha's life in a drama, related in the Kah-gyur (Schiefner, *Tibetan Tales*, no. xiii). With *tathāgata*, or *tathâgata* cf. *ā agāt*, *Ṛg Veda*, X, 53, 1, with reference to Agni.

5 (*page 4*). That of Strzygowski's "Mazdean art," but this is no more Iranian than Indian.

6 (*page 4*). A *cetiya*, as appears from the present text and elsewhere, is not primarily a building, but any object made use of as a sacred symbol or cult object. A shrine in the sense "temple" is *cetiya-ghara*. Cf. my *Yakṣas*, I and II, *passim*, and B. C. Law, "'Cetiya' in the Buddhist Literature," *Studia Indo-Iranica*, 1931, pp. 42–48.

7 (*page 4*). From *paribhoga*, objects used by or in connection with the person; thus equally in the case of the dead or absent person, traces or relics other than any part of the body itself. In the present case, for example, the Buddha's begging bowl, garments, the tree under which he attained enlightenment, the hut occupied by him; and probably, though more abstractly, such "things" as the wheel which he set in motion in Benares. The *sārīraka* and *pāribhogaka cetiyas* are then precisely those symbols which are alluded to as "traces" (*dhātu*) in the *Saddharma Puṇḍarīka*; the term *dhātu* appearing also in *dhātu-gabba* = *dāgaba* = *thūpa* = *stūpa*, "tope."

8 (*page 8*). *Ṛg Veda*, I, 24, 7; IV, 13, 5; X, 82, 5 (?); *Atharva Veda*, X, 7, 38; *Chāndogya Up.*, VI, 8, 4; VI, 11, 1; VI, 12, 2; *Śvetâśvatara Up.*, III, 9; *Taittirīya Up.*, I, 10. For the pre-Buddhist tree cults and their survival in Buddhist ritual see my *Yakṣas*, Pts. I and II, Washington, 1928 and 1931, and "Early Indian Architecture, II, Bodhi-gharas," in *Eastern Art*, III, 1931.

9 (*page 8*). Regarding the "up" or "down" of the roots and branches, it should be observed that this is not a question of local direction: if certain texts say "down" as if from Waters enclosing the *brahmâṇḍa*, and the representations are of upward

growth, as if from a given platform of being, both are equally correct, in that the Waters are no less omnipresent substance than the Self is omnipresent essence. There is no question so far of "aerial roots"; these are alluded to only in the *Aitareya Brāhmaṇa*, VII, 31, and *Bhagavad Gītā*, XV, 2, where they are explained as the "bonds of works."

10 (*page 8*). Śaṅkarâcārya interprets *rerivā* (*Taittirīya Up.*, I, 10) as either "mover" or "remover" (for the latter implication cf. *Bhagavad Gītā*, XV, 3, *aśvatthaṁ . . . chittvā*): "mover" is most appropriate in our text, but either sense would be intelligible, inasmuch as *pravṛtti* and *nivṛtti*, outflow and inflow, spiration and despiration, are simultaneous movements of the cosmic "pulse" of the Self.

Vedic "*yakṣa*," in its general application to Varuṇa, later Brahman, represents in our view an essential name of the manifested deity as mover in the Tree of Life.

11 (*page 10*). The tree itself *is* analogically the Great Awakening, not merely the sign of the place where the Awakening was accomplished, which from the standpoint of the developed Buddhology was not an event in Time. Cf. *pratyabudhyata*, "awakened," "illuminated," with reference to angelic, prophetic, or human knowledge of Brahman, whereby the one awakened is identified with That, *Bṛhadāraṇyaka Up.*, I, 4, 10; and *pratibodhaviditaṁ matam amṛtatvaṁ hi vindate, ātmanā vindate vīryam vidyayā vindate amṛtam*, "It (*brahman*) is thought of as known with Awakening, for thus one finds what is deathless; by the Self one finds the virile-strength, by knowledge one finds the Deathless," *Jaiminīya Upaniṣad Brāhmaṇa*, IV, 19.

Budh is primarily "to awaken," and metaphysically, from the sleep of potentiality to actuality of operation; in this sense we find in the *Ṛg Veda* not only *uṣarbudh*, but the verbal form *abodhi*, "awakened" (I, 157, 1; III, 5, 1; V, 1, 1; VII, 9, 1), applied to Agni, who is the Enlightener rather than the Enlightened. Hence we prefer to the familiar "Great Enlightenment" the rendering "Great Awakening" for *mahāsambodhi*; and for *bodhi-vṛkṣa*, "Tree of Awakening" to "Wisdom-tree." If it be desired to retain the notion of illumination, which is inherent in this sense that the awakening is a beginning to shine, it should be with full awareness that the Great Awakening is with reference not only to him who wakes, but also to those on whom he shines. The Mahāsambodhi is in fact the Buddha's true birth into the worlds, all that precedes properly belonging to the Interior Operation, though developed in the texts quasi-historically.

Pali Commentators explain *budh* by *avagamane*, "coming down," tantamount to *avacaraṇa*, "descent," cf. *avaś caran*, of Agni, *Ṛg Veda*, VI, 9, 3; by *bodhane* "awakening"; and as "to rise up" (*uṭṭhahati*, *Atthasālinī*, p. 217: cf. *ud asthāt*, of Agni, *Ṛg Veda*, IV, 18, 5; Sāyaṇa on V, 19, 1, *sthitaṁ padârthajātam*, "*sthā* means to be born"; and *ṭhitako . . . paṭhaviyaṁ patiṭṭhāya*, *Nidānakathā*, p. 53) from the sleep of the kindred of the slime (*kilesa-santāna-niddāya*), or to understand the Four Ariyan Truths, or to realize *Nibbāna*." Here it can be clearly seen how edifying secondary meanings have been given to the root which meant originally to "come into existence," or "be manifested." *Kilesa* (*Skr. kleśa*) has generally in fact a moral value in Pali Buddhism, but the fundamental sense of "slime," and the involved notion of "germinal heat" (*kilissati* = *upatāpe*, Dhtp., 445 and Dhtm., 686), cf. *kliś*, "to suffer," and *ciklīta* = "slime" in *Śrīsūkta*, 12, and the imagery of the lotus, born in the mud and yet unstained (p. 21), whereas in the *Śrisūkta*, 11 and 17, we have merely *kardamena prajā sraṣṭā sambhūtiṁ gamayāmasi* "we thy children emanated from the mud would go forth into existence." The force of these comparisons is to show that the language of Pali Buddhism is inherited directly from Vedic sources, though generally with an ethical in place of the originally metaphysical application. In the *Ṛg Veda*, the Awakening is to Existence, in Buddhism to Non-existence. The contrast is less than might appear at first sight, for the "Turning of the Principial Wheel" has neither beginning nor end (*dharmaṁ deśemy ahu nityakālam*, *Saddharma Puṇḍarīka*, XV, 1, or as *Ṛg Veda*, V, 58, 5 expresses it, "none of the spokes is last in order"); Dawn and Sunset, Life and Death, follow each other in unending sequence, and from the standpoint of the Understanding of Sameness (*samatājñāna*) this is not really a sequence but an act in simultaneity.

12 (*page 10*). On *tejas* in Buddhism see J. Ph. Vogel, "Het Sanskrit woord tejas (= gloed, vuur) in de beteeknis van magische kraft," *Med. K. Akad. Wet., afd. Letterkunde*, 70, B, 4, Amsterdam, 1930. An error should be corrected here, viz. p. 107 and Pl. II, for on the occasion of "Indra's visit" the Buddha's grotto is illuminated, not by his own *tejas*, but by that of the visiting angels, as expressly stated in *Dīgha Nikāya*, II, 264 and 269. *Tejas* as one of the "five elements" (e. g. in *Śvetâśvatara Upaniṣad*, VI, 2) corresponds to "phlogiston," Böhme's "ignited air."

13 (*page 10*). Also Fergusson, *Tree and Serpent Worship*, Pl. LXVII, mid-left, and LXX, top-centre and mid-right; Bachhofer, *Early Indian Sculpture*, Pl. 114, left-centre.

14 (*page 10*). The fiery pillars are mentioned by Kramrisch, *Indian Sculpture*, 1933, note 209. The importance of the fiery element in Buddhist symbolism was recognized by Maisey, *Sanchi and its Remains*, 1892, Ch. X, and later by Foucher and Vogel in connection with the representation of shoulder-flames, the double miracle, etc. I have argued elsewhere (*A New Approach to the Vedas*, 1933, p. 43) that Agni Vaiśvānara, Christ, the idea of Muḥammad, and others, are ontologically identical Persons. The historical narrative of the Buddha's "life," for example, like that of the Christ's, must be regarded as a contraction or reflection of the cosmic relations; the Buddha as Gautama is an *incarnation* of Agni. Assuming that an historical Gautama may really have taught, the mere "man" is altogether hidden by the aegis of divinity, and surely would have willed it to have been so.

15 (*page 10*). In *Ṛg Veda*, I, 59, 1 and 2, Agni is "a pillar (*sthūṇa*) supporting the kindreds" (*janān*, viz. angels and men); in IV, 13, 5, "established as an angelic pillar (*skambha*) he rules-and-wards (*pāti*) the firmament" (*nāka*, that Middle Space, *antarikṣa*, in which all existence is extended); *ibid.*, X, 5, 6, "He is a pillar (*skambha*) of life at the parting of the ways"; *ibid.*, V, 29, 4, "Heaven and Earth he pillars-apart" (*vitaraṁ viṣkabhāyat*). That axis of the Universe is also, as stated explicitly in *ibid.*, X, 89, 4, the axle-tree of the Solar Car, "by the axle of his wheeled car he indeed by his powers pillars-apart Heaven and Earth" (*akṣeṇeva cakriyā śacībhir viṣvak tastambha pṛthivīṁ uta dyām*). In *Atharva Veda*, X, 8, 2, the pillar (*skambha*) is "all that is hypostasized" (*sarvam ātmanvat*), and the entire hymn, X, 7, lauds the same pillar wherein all existence (*bhuvana*) is infixed (*ārpitā*); this axis of the Universe (which is also the axle-tree of the Solar Car and the trunk of the Tree of Life), though single in its proper form (*svarūpa*, Dante's *forma universal*, *Paradiso*, XXXIII, "one simple Light, that in its depths encloses, as in a single volume, all that is scattered on the pages of the Universe)," is also the form of very different things (*viśvarūpa*). The Scholastic notion of *exemplarism* is implied, cf. Eckhart, I, 182, "Everything is pictured in His Providence," which corresponds again to the notion of the world-picture, "painted by the Self on the canvas of the Self," Śaṅkarâcārya, *Svâtmanirūpaṇa*, 95.

NOTES

The axis of the Universe is coincident also with the fiery Śiva-liṅgam set up, according to the Devadāruvana legend, in the foundations of the Earth (*Hāṭaka*, the Land of Gold, see p. 531) and extending upwards to Heaven, see F. D. K. Bosch, "Het Linga-Heiligdom van Dinaja," *Tijdschr. K. Bat. Genootschap van Kunsten en Wetenschapen*, LXIV, 1924. The axis in its most general aspect corresponds to the vertical of the Cross, as to which, and for further details of application, see M. René Guénon's admirable treatise, *La Symbolisme de la Croix*, Paris, 1931.

16 (*page 10*). Also Fergusson, *Tree and Serpent Worship*, cut on p. 114. At the very summit of the jewelled tree, hardly visible in the reproductions, is represented a royal umbrella, comparable to those which are seen above contemporary more realistically depicted Bodhi-trees, or stood over the early anthropomorphic Buddha images, and to the more elaborate baldachins of Far Eastern art. Considering the symbol of royalty above, and the marks of the *dharmacakra* on the feet, it could not have been more clearly asserted, "This is the anointed King of the Word."

17 (*page 10*). The formula is not remote from that employed in the representations of the Tree of Life in Assyrian art, cf. for example *Propyläen Kunstgeschichte*, II, Pls. 498, 499.

18 (*page 12*). Māra, Will-spirit, Kāmadeva, angel of love and death, Vedic Gandharva (whose "daughters" are three forms of the Vedic Apsaras), is the indwelling Yakṣa of the Tree itself. It is at the foot of the tree that any Yakṣa has his seat or altar (cf. my *Yakṣas*, I, Pl. 20, lower-left), where his presence is to be inferred or may be manifested in an image made with hands. So when the Bodhisattva takes his seat at the foot of the Wisdom-tree "with his back to its trunk," *bodhikhandam piṭṭhito*, J., I, 71, he is trespassing on Māra's ground, and Māra naturally lays claim to and defends the throne as his by right, as well he may, who is the "first born of the angels," the Will to Life, Eros, *causa causans* of the world, prime mover of the Tree, autonomous in the realm of existence, inasmuch as all existences live-dependent-on (*upajīvanti*) their such-and-such desired ends (*Chāndogya Up.*, VIII, 1, 5).

It should be observed that the "Awakening" of the *Ṛg Veda* is from potentiality to act and with respect to works; while in the Upaniṣads and Buddhism, the "Awakening" is from activity to understanding, and towards a cutting off of the will to experience. These opposite points of view, though both at one and the same time inherent in the ultimate reality, correspond to those from which, on the one hand, the Tree of Life is regarded as a manifestation to be fostered, and, on the other, as one to be cut off. The conflict is precisely between those principles which are represented by Māra and Buddha; who however opposite in nature are one in essence, and therefore at one beyond experience where "all principles are same." Cf. the characteristic Mahāyāna text *saṁsāraṁ caiva nirvāṇaṁ manyante tattvadarśinaḥ*, "Those who have vision of the Quiddity do not distinguish between the Vortex of Life and the Extinction" (*Cittaviśuddhi*, attributed to Āryadeva, see H. Shastri in JASB., LXVII, p. 178).

In Christian terms, *saṁsāra* is "storm of the world-flow" (Eckhart, I, 192).

19 (*page 12*). As the *Saṁyutta Nikāya*, IV, 102, very correctly expresses it, "even the king of the Angels (*devānām inda*) is not emancipated so long as there remains in him any occasion of existence," and this must hold for the Buddha himself, "Angel of Angels" (*devâtideva*), whose *nibbāṇa* is by definition *sa-upādi-sesa*.

Will is the cause of existence (*Ṛg Veda*, X, 129, 4; *Mahābhārata*, III, 313, 98, *kāmaḥ saṁsārahetuḥ*); Buddhism makes its goal not the *saṁsāra*, but *nissaraṇa*. A

Jātaka preserved only in a Chinese text, but illustrated at Mathurā, has for its motif that "existence is the worst of all evils" (Foucher in JBORS., 1920, pp. 47–53, Vogel, *La Sculpture de Mathurā*, Pl. XVI, a).

Those who attempt to show that Buddhism does *not* teach the extinction of all desire miss the point: that Bodhisattvas and those like them are moved by what we believe are *right* desires, commendable ambitions, concerns the Way, and not the Goal. The very fact that the Buddha speaks to "others" reminds us that "whiles we are on the way to God we have not gotten him." All traditions as to the last death of the soul are in agreement that that is a total death with respect to all self-willing and self-thinking: "prudence (*adhyavasāya*), conception (*saṁkalpa*), and notion of I-and-mine (*abhimāna*)," *Maitri Up.*, VI, 30, must be destroyed, the "last way" (*parama-gati*) implying a state of "de-mentation" (*amanībhāva*) and a "self-naughting" (*nirabhimāna*), *ibid.*, VI, 30 and 34. Our resistance to these points of view, our reluctance to admit that Nirvāṇa implies a super-individual existence, Parinirvāṇa a total release from existence, is purely sentimental; actually, existence of any kind is being in a mode, therefore indigent and uninfinite, less than the *summum bonum*. On "de-mentation" see also note 128.

20 (*page 12*). On the other hand, we must not be disconcerted if these distinctions are not always rigidly maintained; they are, in fact, "logical, not real." Buddhahood is virtually, if not actually, Parinirvāṇa; God is virtually Godhead; the *jñāna-* and *svabhāva-* aspects of the Dharmakāya are not divided.

21 (*page 13*). According to the well-known Aupaniṣada aphorism, the Ultimate Reality is "Not so, not so"; cf. Böhme, "God is properly to be spoken of as No Thing," Dante, *Convivio*, III, 15, "Things which our intellect cannot behold . . . we cannot understand what they are except by denying things of them," and Maimonides, *Guide for the Perplexed*, 1, 59, "By affirming anything of God you are removed from Him." Hence the Buddha's refusal to discuss Nirvāṇa.

22 (*page 14*). Cf. also my "Notes on Indian Coins and Symbols," *Ostas. Zeitschr.*, N. F. IV, 1927/28, pp. 180, 181.

23 (*page 14*). The *vajra* of iconography represents the axis with its two three-pointed ends. Comparison of *Ṛg Veda*, I, 51, 10, and I, 121, 12, gives us the synonymy *vajra* = *sahasa*, "strength": in the former passage, it is by the "strength" found by Kāvya Uśanā ("the Poetic Will") that Indra with strength holds Heaven and Earth apart (*rodasī vi bādhate* — Sāyaṇa glosses *vibādhate* by *te bibhīte, a ity arthaḥ*, "are afraid," an interpretation to be correlated with *abībhatsata* and *te vyadravatām* in *Jaiminīya Upaniṣad Brāhmaṇa*, I, 50, and 54). Indra is here acting instead of or on behalf of Agni, whose function it is to divide or pillar-apart (*viṣkabh*, etc.) Heaven and Earth throughout the Cosmic Day, and is often called the "Son of Strength," *sahasas putraḥ* or *sūnuḥ*. Thus *sahasas pūtra* = *akṣa-ja* = *vajra*, and we have proof that the *vajra* originally represented "Fire"; and at the same time another link between Agni and the Buddha, with his "adamantine" nature.

24 (*page 14*). The sacrificial post as a *vajra* is eight-angled, "for the attainment of all desires" (*aṣṭaśrir, Kauṣītaki Brāhmaṇa*, X, 1), which form might be expected in connection with (1) the notion of eight directions meeting at a common centre, and (2) the known prevalence of eight-sided pillar forms in early Indian art, cf. *aṭṭhaṁsā sukatā thambhā, Jātaka*, VI, 173. Cf. descriptions of Figs. 3, 13.

Account should also be taken of the history of the "thunderbolt" in Western Asiatic iconography, see Jacobsthal, *Der Blitz in der orientalischen und griechischen*

Kunst, Berlin, 1906; Jacobsthal's Figs. 1, 2, 4, 5, for example, depict single, bifurcated "vajras."

25 (*page 16*). Indraji, "Antiquarian Remains at Sopārā and Padaṇa," *J. Bombay Br. R.A.S.*, XV, 320 and Pl. 3.

26 (*page 16*). "Notes on Indian Coins and Symbols," *loc. cit.*

27 (*page 18*). E. g. at Bhitargaon, Cunningham, *A.S.I. Reports*, XI, 1880, Pl. XVII; at Bādāmī, *Mem. A.S.I.*, XXV, Pls. XI and XXII*a*; also at Elūrā, in the Daśavatāra cave.

28 (*page 18*). Temple, "Notes on Antiquities from Ramannadesa," *Indian Antiquary*, 1894, also Ray, *Brahmanical Gods in Burma*, 1932, Pls. 4, 5, cf. Kak, *Ancient Monuments of Kashmir*, 1933, Fig. 39.

The Birth of Brahmā compositions (as well as older representations of lotus forms arising from a Yakṣa's navel) are very like, and may be the source of, the Tree of Jesse formula which appears in Christian art towards the close of the eleventh century; the example which forms a pulpit panel in the Church of S. Leonardo at Arcetri may be cited as showing very clearly the equivalence of western Rose and eastern Lotus, the Mother of God, who is the central flower on the stem that rises from the navel of the recumbent Jesse, corresponding to the Indian Māyā-Lakṣmī; see my "The Tree of Jesse and Indian Parallels or Sources," *Art Bulletin*, XI, 1929, and further discussion in *Parnassus*, Jan. 1935.

29 (*page 18*). Cf. Dante, *Paradiso*, XXX, 116, 117, *quant'è la larghezza di questa rosa nell' estreme foglie?*

30 (*page 18*). Vasiṣṭha: *Ṛg Veda*, VII, 33, 11, cf. *Bṛhad Devatā*, V, 154–155, *Nirukta*, V, 14, *Sarvânukramaṇī*, I, 166. Agni: *Ṛg Veda*, VI, 16, 13. *Atharva Veda*, X, 8, 34, where the Year- or World-wheel is supported by a lotus, will be discussed later. Another version of the same myths is represented in the legend of Purūravas and Urvaśī, and their son Āyus. In each case we are concerned with a primordial trinity of Father (Mitra-Varuṇa, Heaven), Mother (Urvaśī, Earth), and Son (Vasiṣṭha, Agni, Āyus, Life) of God. Identification of Agni Vaiśvānara with Vasiṣṭha and Āyus is further implied by *Atharva Veda*, X, 8, 20, where the expression "churned, or rubbed, forth" (*nirmanthate*), appropriate to Agni, is used with reference to Vasu (= Agni or Vasiṣṭha), and *Ṛg Veda*, I, 31, 5, I, 67, 5, I, 68, 3, etc., where Agni is spoken of as "Single Life" or "Universal Life" (*ekâyu, viśvâyu*). Our present concern is with the ontological equivalence of the Buddha with Agni, Āyus, etc.; we have already recognized the Buddha in the form of a fiery pillar supported by a lotus, and seen that this corresponds to a Vedic image of Agni.

Note that in *Bṛhad Devatā*, V, 154, *puṣkare sthitaḥ* need not mean "standing up in the Lotus," but rather "insistent in the Lotus," *sthitaḥ* being virtually the same as *pratiṣṭhaḥ*. Just as in *Bṛhadāraṇyaka Up.*, II, 3, 1, *sthitaḥ*, applied to the *mūrta* Brahman, i. e. Brahmā, means "existent," and as *sthitaḥ* is used in the *Saddharma Puṇḍarīka* to express that the Buddha is still living, not yet Wholly Extinguished. Similarly, *sthāyitā*, "persistence," "continued subsistence," is used of the relative immortality of the "angels with respect to works," such as Indra. *Sthitaḥ* is thus by no means contrary to *padmâsana*; in the *Bhagavad Gītā*, XI, 15, Brahmā is *kamalâsana-sthaḥ*, that is "present," "born," or "manifested"—not "standing"—on a lotus-throne. Cf. my *New Approach to the Vedas*, 1933, note 111 (*sthā* is *existare*, or as Sāyaṇa says, "to be born").

NOTES

"Earliest references" is said with respect to Indian sources. The texts cited from the *Ṛg Veda* can scarcely postdate 1000 B.C., a conservative estimate, not to mention that the Vedas represent an already late and sophisticated tradition. In Egypt, Ḥeru-pa-kharṭ (Harpocrates), the child Horus, son of Isis and Osiris, image of ever-young and self-regenerating life, is represented as lotus-born and lotus-supported throughout the Ptolemaic period, i. e. from about 900 B.C. onwards. See E. W. Budge, *The Gods of the Egyptians*, I, opp. p. 484, and *Book of the Dead, Papyrus of Ani*, Pl. 28; *Catalogue générale du Musée de Cairo*, XXIX, Pl. XI, items 38, 221 and 222; *Illustrated London News*, January 21, 1933, p. 84. A head of Tutankhemen supported by a lotus has been interpreted as representing him as "the young Sun-god emerging from a lotus flower which sprang out of the primeval waters when creation took the place of chaos" (*Illustrated London News*, May 23, 1931). See further A. Moret, "Le Lotus et la Naissance des Dieux en Egypte," *Journal Asiatique*, May, 1917. The conception of Horus goes back at least to the New Empire (nineteenth century B.C.), but there is no evidence for the representation of the child in or on a lotus until later. Lotus forms are said to appear in Mesopotamian art "only with the pressure of Egyptian influences, from the middle of the second millennium" (B.C. onwards), Andrae, *Coloured Ceramics from Ashur*, p. 5; but Indian sources would be equally conceivable. We can only assert that lotus symbolism must date back at least to the second millennium B.C., without being able to determine its precise origins.

31 (*page 19*). For they are of mutual origin, *anyonyayonitā, itarêtarajanmānā, Bṛhad Devatā*, I, 71, and *Nirukta*, VII, 4. The trinity of the Several Angels who are thus of one and the same sphere and birth (*sālokyatva, ekajātatva, Bṛhad Devatā*, I, 98) corresponds to those numerous Buddha trinities in which the Buddha stands between two Bodhisattvas, supported by three several lotuses springing from a common stem, which rises from the Waters.

32 (*page 19*). I. e. Agni as First Principle is embodied as Agni Vaiśvānara, the "Distributive Fire" "grandson of the Waters."

33 (*page 19*). By no means necessarily in the terrestrial mode; in fact, the lotus is generally employed to denote a universal, or at least angelic, existence.

That the "Earth" is not merely our terrestrial land, but any "ground" of life (cf. Böhme, "even thy own earth, that is thy body"; *puṇḍarīka* as human body, e. g. in *Atharva Veda*, X, 8, 43, *puṇḍarīkaṁ navadvāram . . . tasmin yad yakṣam ātmanvat tad vai brahmavido viduḥ*, "the lotus of nine gates, what Self-ish Genius is therein, that only the Comprehensors of the Brahman know," where *yakṣas*, as usually in the Brāhmaṇas and Upaniṣads, = Brahman; and *Chāndogya Upaniṣad*, III, 12, 3, "what this earth is, that is the same as what the body in man here is . . . the heart, whereon are established, *pratiṣṭhata*, the breaths of life"), is clearly recognized by Sāyaṇa, commenting on *Ṛg Veda*, VI, 16, 13, where he says "Earth is the support of existences in every world" (*bhūmiśca sarvajagata ādhārabhūtêti*), cf. *pṛthivī* used in the dual or plural to denote the Two Worlds or Three Worlds, *Ṛg Veda, passim*, e. g. I, 108, 9 and 10, VII, 104, 11, X, 59, 4.

34 (*page 19*). Vasiṣṭha, primarily an aspect of Agni (as was recognized by Siecke, *Liebesgeschichte des Himmels*, 1892, p. 73), is also rightly identified with Prajāpati and Dakṣa, *Śatapatha Brāhmaṇa*, II, 4, 4, 2, and called a Prajāpati, *Mānava Dharmaśāstra*, I, 34. Prajāpati is Brahmā, *padma-ja*; cf. *Bhāgavata Purāṇa*, III, 20, 15–16, "From the navel of the Lord sprang up a lotus, resplendent as a thousand suns, the

abode of all living things (*sarva-jīva-nikāya*) where the Ruling Power (*svarāj*) himself of himself came to be (*svayam abhūt*, cf. "*svayambhū*" = Brahmā)." It may be observed that *svayambhū*, characterizing Prajāpati as demiurge, corresponds to the conception of Agni as "self-lighted" (*agninā agniḥ samidhyate, Ṛg Veda*, I, 12, 6): and this idea in the *Ṛg Veda*, where Agni is typically *punar punar jayamānaḥ*, "constantly reborn," underlies the Buddhist comparisons of rebirth as the lighting of one flame by another without "individual" identity of the substance enflamed.

35 (*page 20*). Summarized more fully, "the lotus-leaf is a basis (*pratiṣṭhā*), for it is this earth (*pṛthivī*), and earth is a basis . . . this same earth is Agni's womb (*yoni*) . . . one who is not thus supported (*pratiṣṭho na bhavati*), he is as it were unsupported in a far country." Cf. the epithet *supratiṣṭhapāda*, "with firm-based feet," applied to the Sambhogakāya Buddha, Maitreya-Asaṅga, *Uttaratantra*, II, 16, where it may be taken for granted that the Buddha is understood to be lotus-seated. Cf. J., I, 53, *paṭhaviyaṁ patiṭṭhāya*, "standing on the ground," corresponding to the iconography of the Nativities, in which the infant Bodhisattva is usually represented as standing on a lotus.

In connection with the phrase "extended on the back of the Waters" it should be noted that some of the commonest designations of "Earth," e. g. *pṛthivī*, *urvī*, *uttānā*, imply precisely "extension," and further that it is expressly stated that the extent of Earth is necessarily equal to that of Heaven, for the Sun, though represented on earth by Fire, cannot be thought of as confined, "for he fills all these worlds" (*Śatapatha Brāhmaṇa*, VIII, 7, 2, 1 and X, 5, 2, 8).

36 (*page 20*). In the older texts we find simply *puṣkara*, "lotus," which may imply the whole plant or only the flower. In *Atharva Veda*, X, 8, 34, the flower is specifically mentioned (*apām puṣpam*); in *Maitri Up.*, VI, 2, cited above, the mention of petals implies "flower," as do the later terms *padma-kośa* and *padma-garbha*. In any case, the expanded flower is the immediate support, though the whole plant, consisting of stem, leaves, and flower, is often represented. In *Jaiminīya Upaniṣad Brāhmaṇa*, IV, 3, the "flowers of aeviternity" (*amṛtasya puṣpāṇi*) are no doubt lotuses.

37 (*page 20*). It is by no means intended to assert that the chthonic basis of existence can be or is *only* indicated by the Lotus. On the contrary, the Earth may be represented by the spirits of the Earth, viz. the Guhyaka Yakṣas, or Bhumma Devas, cf. my *Yakṣas*, I, 8, my *HIIA.*, Figs. 38, 66, and the Yakushi Buddha pedestal described below. Or various animals may be the supporting bases of angelic beings, their "vehicles"; or the ground may be represented simply by a plane surface or platform.

In *Ṛg Veda*, VII, 88, 3 and 4, by a closely related image, the support of Vasiṣṭha in the Waters is called a ship (*nau*), wherein he, Varuṇa's Son, appointed Prophet (*ṛṣi*), rides gladly with Varuṇa in mid-ocean "when first the heavens were spread out and dawns outstrung," that is when time began, the ship of life left port, the Flower of the Waters showed above the waves. That image of a ship wherein the Universal Man and Progenitor sails upon the Waters is clearly an aspect of the Vedic *devayāna* and *pitṛyāna*, and corresponds to Manu's voyage in an ark (*nau*) in the Indian form of the Flood Legend; and provides an archetype for all that Buddhist imagery of a voyage across the sea of life which is implied in the terms Hīnayāna and Mahāyāna, the Lesser and the Greater "Voyage" (not, as generally translated, "Vehicle"), which are at the same time one and the same voyage, Ekayāna. The Lotus is the vehicle of life: for him who understands (*vidvān*) bearing him on toward a known port, but for the foolish (*avid*) storm-driven to an unknown landfall. Cf. *Ṛg Veda,* VIII, 42, 3, and 72, 3.

38 (*page 20*). In the present monograph we have not emphasized the distinction of Upper (*para*) from Nether (*apara*) Waters, representing respectively the possibilities of existence "above" and "below," in yonder world and this world, Heaven and Earth. It may, however, be remarked that the Lotus nearly always appears in the glory or nimbus (*prabhā-maṇḍala*) of the Buddha and other celestial figures (cf. Fig. 36) of the Buddha or other angelic figures; the two flowers, one behind the "head," the other beneath the "feet," and each a reflection of the other, representing the "grounds" (*pṛthivī*) of existence *in extenso* (*rājasika, antarikṣe*) between them. Cf. *Śatapatha Brāhmaṇa,* IV,I, 5, 16, "Agni is verily the lotus of this Earth, the Sun the lotus of yonder Sky": and *ibid.*, VII, 1, 1, 24, Upper and Nether Waters.

39 (*page 21*). The version of Caland, *Pañcaviṁśa Brāhmaṇa,* 1931, p. 494, is too specific: *nakṣatra* in the plural need not mean only "stars," cf. *Ṛg Veda,* X, 55, 4, where the first of lights (*vibhānām,* glossed by Sāyaṇa as *grahanakṣatrâdīnām*) by its shining brings to birth (*ajanayaḥ*) the *puṣṭasya puṣṭam,* tantamount to the *apāṁ puṣpam* of *Atharva Veda,* X, 8, 34. Nor need *avakāśa* imply a light shining only at night; Caland himself cites *Mānava Gṛhyasūtra,* II, 1, 5, where *avakāśe* = "at daybreak."

40 (*page 21*). Apart from this hermeneutic etymology, the more strictly correct derivation of *puṣkara* is from root *puṣ,* to grow or increase, be nourished, etc., cf. *Ṛg Veda,* X, 55, 4, where *puṣṭasya puṣṭam,* "the amplitude of increase" or "growth of growth," which is brought forth by Dawn, is tantamount to *puṣkara,* the World-Lotus rising from the Waters at the dawn of creation, just as the day-lotus opens at sunrise in actual experience. Cf. Yāska, *Nirukta,* V, 14, *puṣkaram antarikṣam, poṣati bhūtāni,* "The Lotus is mid-space, it propagates beings," and *Viṣṇu Purāṇa,* I, 8, 23, *padmā svadhā śāsvatapuṣṭidā,* "The Lotus-lady is intrinsic power, the constant giver of increase."

41 (*page 22*). *Śrī,* "glory," "beauty," in the *Ṛg Veda,* is constantly an "attribute" of Agni; *lakṣmī,* "auspicious sign," is mentioned only once. In the Brāhmaṇas, Upaniṣads, and later, Śrī-Lakṣmī is usually one angel (*devī*) and corresponds to the Vedic Apsaras, and other aspects of Aditi. The description of Śrī-Lakṣmī in the *Śrī-sūkta,* of Brāhmaṇa-Upaniṣad period, corresponds in all respects with the iconographic formula as found in Early Indian art (see my "Early Indian Iconography," II, in *Eastern Art,* I, 1928); here again the close connection is with Agni (Jātavedas). The following is abbreviated and condensed from the full text as given by Scheftelowitz, *Apokryphen des Ṛgveda,* 1906, pp. 72–79: "Who is gladdened by elephants . . . bathed by elephant-kings, with golden vessels (*gajendrair . . . snāpitā hemakumbhair*) . . . Mother Śrī (cf. Sirimāta at Bharhut) . . . the lush, in the lotus lake, the pillar (*yaṣṭī*), golden . . . we, thy children, coming forth from the mire (*kardamena prajā sraṣṭā,* cf. the human body as "*puṇḍarīka*"), have proceeded to existence. . . . Lotus-faced, lotus-shouldered (*padma-ūrū*), lotus-eyed, lotus-born, darling of Viṣṇu . . . Mahālakṣmī, lotus-wonted . . . set down thy lotus-foot within my heart (*hṛdi saṁ ni dhatsva*)." The cult of Siri-devatā is referred to in *Milindapañha,* 191, her followers being spoken of as *bhaktas.*

Lakṣā (Śrī, Lakṣā, listed amongst the *brahmavādinī,* or feminine seers, in *Bṛhad Devatā,* II, 84) is evidently synonymous with *Lakṣmī.*

42 (*page 22*). See my "Early Indian Iconography, II, Śrī-Lakṣmī," *Eastern Art*, I, 1929; "Notes on Indian Coins and Symbols," *Ostas. Zeitschr.*, N.F., IV, 1927/28; and "Archaic Indian Terracottas," *Ipek*, 1928, Figs. 25, 30.

43 (*page 22*). "Images indiennes de la Fortune," *Mem. conç. l'Asie Orientale*, I, 1913; and "The Buddhist Madonna" (in *The Beginnings of Buddhist Art*, 1917).

44 (*page 22*). Lakṣmī's own "lotus-birth" is thus not exactly the same thing as Agni's or Vasiṣṭha's, for she is the Lotus as well as Sirī-mata; mother, not sister, of all those whose coming to be is from a lotus-womb, *abja-yoni*. It may be noted that Lakṣmī as Goddess of Fortune consistently preserves her fickle *āpsaras* character, reminiscent of Urvaśī; it is only as the Earth, as Bhūmi-devī, that she stands firm.

45 (*page 22*). In *Ṛg Veda*, I, 164, 8, if we accept the interpretation of Sāyaṇa, we have "the germ (*garbha*) was in the cloud" (*vṛjanī*); but it would be more natural to take *vṛjanī* as "holy site," hortus inclusus (cf. *vrajaḥ . . . sapariśrayaḥ*, *Bṛhadāraṇyaka Up.*, VI, 4, 23, where cosmic analogies are applied to human generation). In any case, the Mother (Earth) is here associated (*yukta*) with the Father (Heaven) and it is made quite clear that she is fertilized by an essence that can only have fallen from Heaven as rain; "she the shy one was penetrated by the tincture (*rasa*)," cf. *Ṛg Veda*, VII, 101, 3, "The Father's juices (*payaḥ*) grasped (*prati-gṛbhṇāti*) the Mother, thereby are increased both Father and Son," *Ṛg Veda*, I, 164, 51, "the rain-clouds (*parjanyāḥ*) animate (*jinvanti*) the Earth," and similar passages. It is the descent of the *rasa*-bearing rains that is represented in the Gaja-Lakṣmī composition, which is rather a Conception than a Nativity. But that Conception, being of Life universally, may well have been thought of as Siddhârtha's, whose name signifies "Accomplishment of Purpose." The notion of impregnation by a cloud or rain is present even in the more familiar Buddhist Conceptions, where the Bodhisattva descends in the form of a white elephant, though this is rationalized by calling it a "dream." Cf. the elephant Paccaya, of sky-faring descent, connatural rain-giving talisman of the Bodhisattva in the *Vessantara Jātaka*, which is certainly not a tale of human happenings (incidentally, *vessa* = *viśva* rather than *vaiśya*; the "*vessa*-street" is not the merchant's street, but "Everyman's Way").

The Gaja-Lakṣmī composition further corresponds (1) to Christian Annunciations, where the descent of the Spirit is indicated by rays of the Supernal Sun, and by the Dove (birds, *suparṇa*, representing also in Vedic symbolism, e. g. I, 35, 7, and I, 164, 47, rays of the Sun), and (2) to Danae's conception of Perseus, if we substitute for the Sun, Agni with his golden seed.

In Buddhist legend, the Nativity has been so far rationalized that no great stress is laid on virgin birth, though both conception and birth are in other respects miraculous. As to the virgin birth, "on n'a jamais cru que Çâkyamouni fût né des œuvres de Çuddhodana," de la Vallée Poussin, *Le Dogme et la Philosophie du Bouddhisme*, p. 57, and his notes. Indian tradition, however, knows a virginity of the Mother, Aditi, calling her *anarvā, apravitā, kumārī, mātā yuvatī, kanyā, yoṣā*, etc. An ultimate "virginity" of both parents is indeed a metaphysical necessity, for the twin poles of being, the unmoving centres of the Principial and World Wheels, act only by their presence and not by local movement: "He" is undiminished by his largesse, "She" by her parturition.

46 (*page 23*). The analogous lustration of Siddhârtha by two Nāgas, genii of the *nether* waters, is represented on the well-known stele from Sārnāth, see Foucher, *Beginnings of Buddhist Art*, Pl. XIX, Fig. 1, lower-left panel.

NOTES

47 (*page 23*). On this meaning of Māyā see my "On Translation: *māyā, deva, tapas*," in *Isis*, No. 54, 1933.

48 (*page 23*). The name Māyā-devī occurs in *Dīgha Nikāya*, II, 7; Mahā-Māyā in the *Nidānakathā* (J., I, 52 etc). That the name of Māyā-devī's sister, co-wife of Suddhodana, should have been Pajāpatī is equally significant; as remarked by de la Vallée Poussin, *Le Dogme et la Philosophie du Bouddhisme*, 1930, p. 188, "Jamais femme indienne s'est nommée Māyā . . . Mahāpajāpatī n'est pas non plus un nom."

The various accounts of the Buddha's birth are conveniently assembled in Windisch, *Buddha's Geburt*, Leipzig, 1908.

In the *Buddhacarita*, I, 16–18, Māyā is *uttama devatā*, which may be freely rendered "Queen of Heaven," and as regards her earthly being, is said to have "abandoned, in accordance with the Law (*dharma*), her subtle nature (*sūkṣmāṁ prakṛtim*)."

Māyā-devī who bears and her sister Pajāpatī who fosters the Bodhisattva correspond in fact to the Vedic sisters Night and Day, the two mothers of Agni, cf. *Ṛg Veda*, I, 95, 1, "Two of unlike aspect, each in succession cherishes the Babe," III, 55, 4 "One mother bears, another cherishes the Calf," and V, 2, 2, the *mahiṣī* and *peṣī* as mother and nurse. Māyā-devī corresponds also to Aditi, Indra's mother whose death is caused by his birth full-grown from her side, *pārśvāt tiraścatā*, *Ṛg Veda*, IV, 18, see Sieg, *Sagenstoffe des Ṛgveda*, Stuttgart, 1902, 76 f. It is noteworthy that the name of the seer of this hymn is Vāmadeva Gautama (*gautama* being patronymic, as in the Buddha's case), to whom also there is attributed a lateral birth from his mother's side, this birth taking place in a wood (*vana*, cf. Lumbinī-vana), as related in Sāyaṇa's introduction to *Ṛg Veda*, IV, 18. It may be remarked that in *Jātaka*, I, 52, Māyā-devī is already on her way to Devadaha, her ancestral home, when the child is born in the Lumbini grove, which was common ground to the people of both cities, Kapilavatthu and Devadaha. Now *devadaha* = *devahrada*, "angel-pool," and must surely be the same as the *hrada* or *śaiśava* of the Sarasvatī which is "as far from here as Heaven" (*Pañcaviṁśa Brāhmaṇa* XXV, 10, 12–18), and is the same "source" as that in which the aged Cyavāna was restored to youth by the Aśvins (*apaḥ*, *ibid.*, XIV, 6, 10, *hrada*, *Śatapatha Brāhmaṇa*, IV, 1, 5, 12, *śaiśava*, *Jaiminīya Brāhmaṇa*, III, 120 and 125 expanding *Ṛg Veda*, I, 116, 10), likewise Varuṇa's abode "at the source of the rivers of life," *sindhūnām upodaye*, *Ṛg Veda*, VIII, 41, 2, the Fountain of Life (*utsa*, *Ṛg Veda*, *passim*). That the Bodhisattva is conscious, and speaks, while yet in the womb is anticipated also in the *Ṛg Veda* with respect to Agni, Indra, Gandharva. Correspondences of this kind could be cited without end; cf. my *Ṛg Veda as Land-náma-bók*, London, 1935.

49 (*page 23*). In metaphysical formulation, lateral procession is an inevitable concept; the branches of the tree, or arms of the cross, proceeding from the vertical laterally. Cf. also the origin of Eve from Adam's side; and the Caesarian birth of Rustam.

50 (*page 23*). *Megha*, from root *migh* = *mih*, to sprinkle, micturate, emit; cf. *mīḷhuṣa*, outpouring, bountiful, applied to Varuṇa and Agni, *Ṛg Veda*, *passim* (VII, 88, 1; IV, 5, 1, etc.).

51 (*page 23*). *Anguttara Nikāya*, I, 145 (III, 38).

52 (*page 24*). Omicron, *Letters from Paulos*, 1920, p. 219.

53 (*page 24*). Just as in mediaeval Christianity it was asserted again of him who said of himself, "Before Abraham I am," that "Christ's birth is eternal."

54 (*page 25*). For the Sārnāth capital see Sahni, *Catalogue of the Museum of Archeology at Sārnāth*, 1914, Pl. IV and p. 28. This and corresponding reliefs are further discussed

below. Note that from the standpoint of a more metaphysical Buddhology the "first turning of the Wheel" must be thought of as not first eventually, but first primordially, *in principio, agre*. For the pillared wheel as a representation of the sun, see P. E. Dumont, "The Indic God Aja Ekapād, the One-legged Goat," *J.A.O.S.*, 53, 326 f.

55 (*page 25*). In more detailed exegesis: *Bṛhadāraṇyaka Up.*, I, 5, 15, "Self (*ātman*) the nave (*nābhi*), properties (*vitta*) the felly (*pradhi*)"; *Śvetāśvatara Up.*, I, 4, "we understand him as with one triple (*trivṛt*) felly (*nemi*) . . . one mystery (*moha*) dually manifested (*dvinimitta*)"; *Praśna Up.*, VI, 5 and 6, "on whom the parts (*kalā*) rest firm, like the spokes on the nave (*nābhi*) of a chariot (-wheel), Him I deem the Person to be known."

56 (*page 26*). It is not at all unlikely that the notion of the revolving well-wheel may also be present; cf. citations in my "The Persian Wheel," *J.A.O.S.*, LI, 283.

57 (*page 26*). We do not mean to exclude particular adaptations, as when the *cakra* becomes the "weapon" of a given deity, e. g. Viṣṇu, though even in this case the Wheel could be understood to mean "Time," as a destructive power. The use of the *cakra* as a divine weapon is analogous to the similar use of the *vajra*.

Nor is the symbol of the World-wheel by any means exclusively Indian. It is constantly employed, for example, by Dante. It survives even today in the semi-pagan, semi-secular form of the "Wheel of Fortuna." To be "broken on the wheel" represents a form of martyrdom which, like a death on the Cross, is not without its cosmic analogies. We cannot pursue these considerations further here, nor discuss the ultimate origin of the symbol (observe that the *svastika* antedates the wheel), but may remark that the wheel appears also in Greek symbolism, where it is probably of Oriental origin (see Cook, *Zeus*, I, p. 198 f., and Roes, *Greek Geometric Art*, 1933, especially p. 46). Here too the Olympians are "only spokes in the great wheel of nature, not the driving force that sets and keeps her going . . . India and China best help us to the understanding of Dike as the *way* of the world and also as Right and Justice," J. Harrison, *Themis*, pp. 464 and 523–527, cf. also Jackson in *J.A.O.S.*, XXI, 171, and Kaegi, *Rig Veda*, note 85. Dike = *aša* = *ṛta* = *dharma* = *tao* as "Way."

58 (*page 26*). Most of the confusion which has been introduced into discussions of Nirvāṇa and Parinirvāṇa has arisen from a failure to distinguish between the non-entity of the irrational (viz. very *impossibility* of existence) and the non-existence of the non- or supra-rational (viz. very *possibility* of existence).

59 (*page 27*). *Ekībhūtaḥ prajñāna-ghanaḥ*, *Māṇḍūkya Up.*, 5; *sarūpeṇa jyotiṣā vivratena*, *Ṛg Veda*, X, 55, 3; *viśvaṁ satyam*, II, 24, 12; *viśvam ekam*, III, 54, 8; *sarvadharma-samatā*, SPt. 133, etc.

60 (*page 27*). In many of the early Buddhist Dhammacakkas, the nave or hub (*nābhi*) of the wheel is represented either as an open lotus (petals being indicated) or as the pericarp (*kaṇṇikā*) of a lotus (the characteristic circular marks being shown on its surface). Cf. Śaṅkarâcārya's gloss *pṛthivī-padmamadhye merukarṇikâsanasthaṃ* on *kamalâsanastham* qualifying "Brahmā" in *Bhagavad Gītā*, XI, 15; *kaṇṇikā* as the key-plate of a domed roof, the sole support of its rafters, *Jātaka*, III, 317–319; and in connection with these passages, *Ṛg Veda*, I, 35, 6 "as on the chariot's axle-point depend the deathless (principles)," and VIII, 41, 6, "in whom all creative-utterances (*kāvyā*) inhere as does the nave within the wheel."

61 (*page 27*). E. g. I, 9, 2, "Let flow the soma to Indra, the instigator (*cakri*) to the operator (*cakri*) of all things (*viśvāni*)"; III, 16, 4, where Agni, "who conducts (*cakri*) the offering amidst the Angels, is the maker (*cakri*) of the several worlds (*viśvāni bhuvanā*) and has full power over them"; cf. IV, 2, 9, and VIII, 31, 9.

62 (*page 27*). Varuṇa, Indra, etc., are Kṣatriya, so too is the Buddha by birth; he does not think of himself as a "priest," but as militant. The "Buddha-field" (*buddha-kṣetra*) is at the same time in this sense a "field of battle" and also a trackless wilderness wherein he alone can point out the Way (*mārga*). In the latter connection we find again the reflection of Vedic concepts of Agni, *vidvān pathaḥ pura-etā*, *Ṛg Veda*, V, 46, 1, *kṣetravit*, *ibid.*, IX, 70, 9, and X, 32, 7 (Indra), *niyānam saṁjñānam*, X, 19, 4 (in I, 164, 47 *niyānaṁ . . . divaṁ ut* contrasts with *āvavṛtran . . . vi ut*, in V, 46, 1 *vimucaṁ* with *āvṛtaṁ*, hence *niyāna* = *devayāna*), etc. In *Ṛg Veda*, I, 45, 9, the "field" (*kṣetra*) is the extended world over which the sun passes with his seven horses; *ibid.*, X, 32, 7 those that are not way-wise therein seek to be taught by him that is the knower of the field (*akṣetravid kṣetravidam hy aprāṭ*), cf. *Majjhima Nikāya*, No. 108 "revealed a path until then unrevealed" (*asañjātassa maggasa sañjānetā*); in the Upaniṣads similarly *kṣetra* is "world," e. g. *Śvetâśvatara Up.*, VI, 16, and *Maitri Up.*, II, 5. Agni is typically *viśpati*, "Lord of the dwellers in this field."

63 (*page 28*). "The chariot is the Year," *Atharva Veda*, VIII, 8, 23.

64 (*page 28*). In making use of the symbol of two wheels, progressive enlightenment must be represented by a simultaneous contraction (con-centration) of the circumference of each (cf. *Maitri Up.*, VI, 1), and by a contraction (con-centration) of the axis, resulting as before in the inconnumerable unity of the single point, viz. Ātman *quâ* Īśvara, Cakravartin. That is the meeting point of all the spokes, and also the intersection of the arms of the two- or three-armed Cross. Cf. Chuang Tzŭ, II, 3, "When subjective and objective are both without their correlates, that is the very axis of Tao. And when that axis passes through the centre at which all indefinites converge, positive and negative alike blend into an infinite One . . . viewed from the standpoint of Tao, the (horizontal) beam and the (vertical) pillar are identical." In Giles' translation I have substituted "Indefinites" for "Infinities."

Where there is a question of three wheels, of which the third is known only to the adept, it will be evident of course that this hidden wheel, of which there is no extension, must be thought of as coincident with the one "point" (intersection of all axes) which represents principially the two manifested wheels.

65 (*page 29*). Cf. Dante, *Paradiso*, XIII, 21–22, *punto dello stelo a cui la prima rota va dintorno*, and *ibid.*, XVII, 28, and XXVIII, 16 and 41–42; and *Jaiminīya Upaniṣad Brāhmaṇa*, I, 3, where the way out of the worlds, by which one "wholly escapes" (*atimucyate*) (= *loka-dvāra* in *Chāndogya Up.*, VIII, 6, 6, "I am the Door" in John, x, 9), viz. the "hole in the sky" (*divaś chidram*), "at the place of meeting in the Sun" (*ādityam samayā*), is very correctly symbolized by the "space" (*kha*) of a cart (*anas*) or chariot (*ratha*), that is the space at the centre of the wheels, and "that is seen to be all covered over by rays" (*raśmi*). Cf. St Thomas, STh., III, Q. 91, A. 1, "things belonging to the state of glory are not *under the sun*." (My explanation of *ratha-chidra* in *J.A.O.S.*, LI, 172, should be rejected.)

66 (*page 29*). For the opposing points of view in dramatic contrast, cf. *Bhagavad Gītā*, III, 16–25, and *Anugītā*, Ch. XXX. The contrast, however, is more apparent than real: what is taught in the *Anugītā* and in early Buddhism is indeed the stoppage (*nissa-*

raṇa, nivṛtti) of the Bhavacakra, but the real meaning of abstention is better expressed in the *Bhagavad Gītā* and in later Buddhism as a transformation of action, or perfected facility in action, achieved when the action is performed willingly but not from will.

67 (*page 30*). The Angels whose existence is as yet merely potential are thought of as fearing lest being should not flow out into existence. The fear is needless, since in him potentiality and act are indivisible, he works willy nilly, doing what must be done. That the Buddha remains in seclusion during the period of hesitation corresponds to the occultation of Agni (*tamasi kṣeṣy agne, Ṛg Veda*, X, 51, 5; *sūryaṁ gūḷhaṁ tamasâpavratena, ibid.*, V, 40, 6, etc.) antecedent to the dawn of a creative cycle. That seclusion (in Christian terms "interior operation" or "eternal rest," *solus ante principium*) is the same as the "pleroma non-revolving" (*pūrṇam apravarti*) of *Kauṣītaki Up.*, IV, 8.

The hesitation corresponds in the life of Christ to the Passion in the Garden of Gethsemane, "O my Father, if it be possible, let this cup pass from me"; and when he adds, "nevertheless, not as I will, but as thou wilt," that corresponds to Agni, who performs what is required of him (*Ṛg Veda*, I, 165, 9, *kariṣyā kṛṇuhi*, VI, 9, 3, *vaktvāni vadāti*, VII, 20, 1, *cakriḥ . . . yat kariṣyan*), and the Buddha, who does what must be done (*kartavyaṁ karoti*, SPt. Ch. XV). This is, technically, "*necessitas infallibilitatis*."

In the individual, it is represented by everyman's idleness, who will not put his shoulder to the Wheel (*evaṁ pravartitaṁ cakraṁ na anuvartayati, Bhagavad Gītā*, III, 16), or speaking Christianly, will not take up his Cross.

"Let the Four Quarters bow before thee": as in fact the Four Great Kings ward the unborn Bodhisattva, and receive him when he proceeds from the Mother's side. It is often overlooked that the notion of the Four World Warders is met with already in the Vedas and Brāhmaṇas, for example *Ṛg Veda*, VIII, 28, 2–3, where the *gopāḥ* are Agni (E), Mitra (N), Varuṇa (W), and Aryaman (S); *Kauṣītaki Brāhmaṇa*, VII, 6, with Agni (E), Soma (S), Savitṛ (W), Pathya Svasti, i. e. Vāc (N), and Aditi (Zenith); and *Jaiminīya Upaniṣad Brāhmaṇa*, I, 28, with Agni (E), Manas (S), Cakṣu (W), Śrotra (N), and Prâṇa (Zenith).

That the Bodhisattva stands erect and takes seven steps as soon as he is born corresponds to numerous Vedic texts in which Agni is described as great (*bṛhat*, IV, 5, 1), erect (*ūrdhva*), and strong the moment he is born (*sadyo jātasya dadṛśānam ojaḥ*, IV, 6, 1 and IV, 7, 10).

68 (*page 30*). *Ṛg Veda*, II, 38, 6, "The seeker, having gone forth, returns; home is the desire of all things that proceed (*car*); abandoning his never-completed task, he comes back again, according to the rule of Savitṛ" — with reference primarily to the close of a cosmic day, the end of time, and analogically to the fall of night on earth. Cf. *Jaiminīya Upaniṣad Brāhmaṇa*, I, 3, "Having slain by food this and that hunger (i. e. sated by experience) . . . he is utterly-released (*atimucyate*)."

69 (*page 30*). This must follow in any case directly from the principle "as above, so below," as e. g. in *Aitareya Brāhmaṇa*, VIII, 2.

70 (*page 30*). Cf. the use of *skandha* in *Maitri Up.*, VII, 11, where the proliferation of the World-tree is *skandhāt skandham*, "branch after branch."

71 (*page 32*). See Suzuki, *Outlines of Mahayana Buddhism*, pp. 352 ff., and similar passages cited by de la Vallée Poussin, "Ā propos du Cittaviśuddhiprakaraṇa d'Āryadeva," *Bull. Sch. Or. Stud.*, VI, 1931.

72 (*page 32*). See Anesaki, *Buddhist Art . . .*, 1915, p. 39; Ōmura Seigai, *Sanbon Ryōbu-Mandara*, Tokyō, 1913; Getty, *Gods of Northern Buddhism* (2nd ed.), pp. 28 ff.

73 (*page 33*). A text significant also in connection with the later virtual identification of the Buddha with Brahmā. In *Majjhima Nikāya*, I, 69, we have *brahmacakkaṁ pavatteti*, synonymous with *dhammacakkaṁ pavatteti* (cf. *yenedaṁ bhramyate brahmacakraṁ*, *Śvetāśvatara Up.*, VI, 1), and in *Saṁyutta Nikāyā*, V, 5–6, "This Ariyan eightfold Way may be spoken of as Brahmayāna or as Dhammayāna." Cf. also Keith, *Religion and Philosophy of the Veda*, p. 550, and de la Vallée Poussin, *Le Dogme et la Philosophie du Bouddhisme*, 1930, p. 186, "le nirvāṇa, c'est-à-dire . . . le *brahmaloka* des bouddhistes."

74 (*page 33*). Ōmura Seigai, *loc. cit.*, XV, 3, 4.

75 (*page 33*). In addition to the Sārnāth pillar are the various representations at Bhārhat, Bodhgayā, Sāñcī, and Amarāvatī, and the large and elaborate Dharmacakras from Siam; see Cunningham, *Stupa of Bharhut*, 1879, Pl. XXXIV, 4 (cf. Pl. VII, showing a Dharmacakra supported by a lotus palmette); Bachhofer, *Early Indian Sculpture*, Pls. 44, 46, 55, 66, 104, 110, 152; my *History*, Figs. 45, 136, 144, 318, also the sun-wheel pillar on an early coin, Fig. 112; Salmony, *Sculpture in Siam*, Pls. 3a and 5a.

For the fundamental symbolism see Mus, "Barabuḍur . . .," Ch. iii (Le Pilier de Sārnāth et le Problème des Cinq Orients), in *BÉFEO.*, 1932, pp. 413 f.

76 (*page 34*). See my "Origin of the Lotus (so-called Bell) Capital," *Ind. Hist. Qtly.*, VI, 1930, 373–375, and "Origin of the Lotus Capital," *ibid.*, VII, 1931, 747–750 (827–830). A. K. Mitra, "Origin of the Bell Capital," *ibid.*, pp. 213 f., and "A further note on the Origin of the Bell Capital," *ibid.*, X, 1934, 125 f., and G. L. Fabri, in *Études d'Orientalisme*, 1932, p. 249, disagree. (Although Mitra argues as if against my interpretations, I cannot see any difference between his explanation of the lotus as being primarily a symbol of divine or "miraculous" birth, and of fertility, and my own of the lotus as representing the universal Ground — *pṛthivī, bhūmi* — of existence and as at once the birthplace — *yoni* — and indispensable support — *pratiṣṭhā* — of Life in the Worlds. Dr Mitra seems scarcely to understand the use of the expression "Ground" in metaphysics and theology, where it corresponds to "Substance" as opposed to "Essence." As to the derivative application of the lotus symbol in architecture and ornament, I see no reason to modify views already expressed; and as to the supposed "mystery" will only remark that an established symbol can easily become a *cliché*, and may be used as such without conscious reference to its ultimate significance; the Greek "Egg and Dart," really a lotus-petal moulding, affords a good instance of such usage.) J. Przyluski, "Le symbolisme du pilier de Sarnath," in *Études d'Orientalisme*, pp. 481 f., and Dumont, *loc. cit.* note 54, deal with other symbolic aspects of the Sārnāth capital.

We have deduced elsewhere (*New Approach to the Vedas*, note 67) that conch (*śaṅkha*) and lotus (*padma*), as a formulation alternative to that of paired lotuses (one in the nimbus, the other beneath the feet, or both in the hands of the Sun, *padmahastau*), stand for the powers derived respectively from the Upper and the Nether Waters. As the Nether Lotus is the Earth, the substance of things, so the Conch or Upper Lotus is their form; in other words, while the lower symbols stand for means or ground of utterance, the upper symbols stand for the power of utterance, all that is uttered (*vyāhṛti, deśita*) coming into existence between them. And although I cannot cite a text, it will not be rash to regard the conch as a symbol of the Spoken Word. On these lines the symbol of a conch supported by a lotus which occurs at Ajaṇṭā (Yazdani, *Ajaṇṭā*, Pt. II, p. 53 and Pls. XLVIIa, XLIXd), but is not to my knowledge represented elsewhere, can be explained as an alternative formula equivalent to that of the *sūtra* supported by a lotus, discussed above.

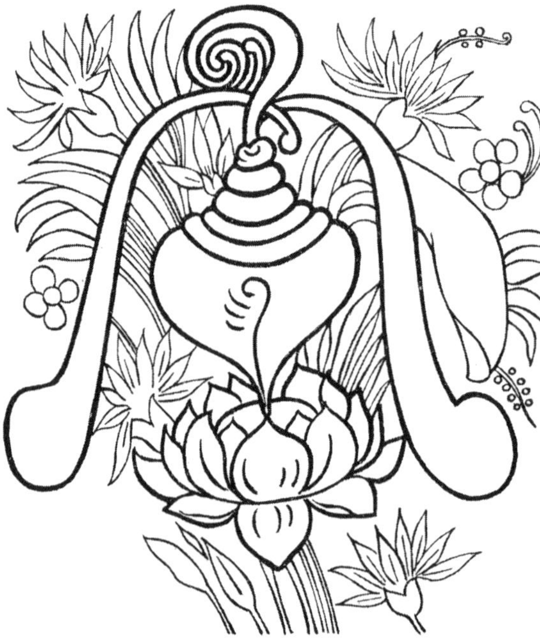

FIG. I. Conch and Lotus, as represented at Ajaṇṭā. After Yazdani, as cited in note 76.

77 (*page 34*). The connection of *nābhi,* nave and navel, with *nabha,* space or firmament, is anything but accidental, cf. *Maitri Up.*, VI, 6, with respect to Prajāpati's world-form, "the firmament (*bhuvas*) is his navel." Observe that from the Vedic-Aupaniṣada point of view "Space" (*ākāśa*) is an elemental substance, cf. our "ether": "Space (*ākāśa*) is the permissive cause or necessary medium (*nirvahitṛ*) of name-and-aspect (*nāma-rūpa*, i. e. individuation)," *Chāndogya Up.*, VIII, 14. This Space should not be confused with the Void, *śūnya,* although in Buddhism, which is an atomistic system, a confusion is unavoidable; actually, it is correct to speak of the Space-body (*ākāśa-śārīra*) of Brahman, where it would not be correct to speak of a "Void-body."

78 (*page 34*). Note that *kha* is used both with respect to space in the inner man, and to denote the space within the nave of a wheel, into which space fits the point (*āṇi*) of the operating axle (*akṣa*), see above, note 65. *Kha* is at once "void" and "plenum."

79 (*page 34*). For this use of *nīḍa* as "place of being," cf. Dante, *Paradiso*, XVIII, 110, *virtù ch'è forma per li nidi,* "power that is form unto the nests," cf. *nīḷa* and *kulāya* in the *Ṛg Veda* and Brāhmaṇas, *passim,* e. g. *Ṛg Veda*, VI, 15, 16, and X, 5, 6, *Atharva Veda*, IX, 3, 19–20, *Pañcaviṁśa Brāhmaṇa*, XI, 15, 1, and *Maitrāyanīya Up.*, III, 12.

80 (*page 35*). The Buddhist doctrine of the heart (*cit, bodhi-citta*) is already developed not only in the Upaniṣads, but also in the *Ṛg Veda,* where *hṛt, hṛdaya,* correspond to *bodhi-citta*. For example, in *Ṛg Veda*, IV, 58, 11, Agni *antaḥ samudre hṛdy antar āyuṣi*; X, 177, 1, the Sun-bird, *hṛdā paśyanti manasā vipaścitaḥ*; I, 65, 1, and 67, 2, Agni, *guhā catantam, niṣīdan*; VII, 76, 4, *gūḷhaṁ jyotiḥ*; VI, 9, 6, *jyotir hṛdaya āhitam.*

81 (*page 35*). Cited in the *Kokka*, No. 198, and Sirén, *History of Early Chinese Painting*, p. 101.

82 (*page 35*). Cf. *Divyâvadāna*, XXVI, ed. Cowell and Neill, p. 363, where it is taken for granted that "those who venerate earthen images of the Angels do not revere the clay, but the Immortals thereby represented." A great part of the modern "love of art" is a veneration of the clay, and this preoccupation with sensible shapes and materials, to the neglect of *raison d'être*, is tantamount to idolatry in the religious sense, fetishism in the psychological sense (fetishism being an attachment to the sign, rather than to that of which it is the sign). The shapes of images are not His shapes, but imagined; He is their form, not they his. Before a Buddhist icon, it is pertinent to ask, "Whose image and superscription is this?" We cannot know whether a Buddhist "work of art" is "good" or "bad," that is to say well and truly made with regard to the end in view, so long as we remain in ignorance of that end; cf. my *Transformation of Nature in Art*, 1934, and "Understanding the Art of India," in *Parnassus*, April, 1934.

83 (*page 36*). *Inferno*, IX, 61, *Mirate la dottrina, che s'asconde, sotto il velame degli versi strani*; cf. *Paradiso*, XXXIII, 142, *all'alta fantasia qui mancò possa*, and *Taittirīya Up*., II, 4, "Before Whom words and intellect turn back,, not reaching Him." In accordance with the Indian theory of aesthetic experience, the accomplishment of the aesthetic act depends not on the accidents of the representation, but on the spectator's or hearer's own effort or energy. In other words, iconography can be regarded only as a curious and sterile science, a cataloguer's art, until we proceed from the denotation to a realization of, and assimilation to, the ultimate significance (*paramârtha*) of the symbols (*pratīka*) employed. But, as the *Tao Teh Ching* expresses it, "There are but few in the world who attain to the teaching without words."

84 (*page 39*). "There is the rose wherein the divine Word was made flesh; there are the lilies by whose fragrance the Right Way is found"; or to venture a Sanskrit version, replacing "rose" by "lotus," *Tatrâsty apāṁ puṣpaṁ yasmin saddharmo 'nnamayaḥ samabhavat, tatra puṣkarāṇi yeṣāṁ gandhenâryo mārgo labhyate.*

85 (*page 40*). It is taken for granted that "those who venerate earthen images of the Immortals do not revere the clay, but the Immortals thereby designated," *Divyâvadāna*, XXVI (ed. Cowell and Neill, p. 363).

Cf. Zimmer, *Kunstform und Yoga im indischen Kultbild*, 1926, p. 31, "Das Kultbild ist ein *yantra* und nur ein *yantra*." A *yantra* is a "device" of any kind, here a "piece of psychological apparatus."

86 (*page 40*). Cf. "his manhood is a hindrance so long as they cling to it with mortal pleasure; they ought to follow God in all his ways and not keep solely to his way of manhood who reveals to us the way of Godhood," Eckhart, I, 187.

87 (*page 40*). For the textual references see the P.T.S. Pali Dictionary, s. v. *upādi*.

88 (*page 40*). "Where God gives up the ghost, darkness reigns in the unknown known unity. This is hidden from us. . . . Plunge in: this is the drowning," Eckhart, I, 368.

89 (*page 41*). The "Harrowing of Hell," cf. St Thomas, *Sum. Th.*, III, Q. LII. It must be assumed from the Buddha's point of view that Māra himself was not merely defeated, but transfigured and restored, just as the weapons with which he had assaulted the throne-sitter had been transformed. For angels are fallen, not in nature (*svabhāva*) but in grace, their divine prototypes cannot be affected; and what the Buddha sees is things in their perfection: he who attains Perfection sees only perfection, neither good nor evil having any place in the perfectly simple understanding (*samatā-jñāna*).

Just as in Islam, the curse laid upon Iblīs (Satan) lasts only until the Day of Judgment, and at the End of Time he will be restored to his place with Allāh. It cannot be supposed that the Great Person "now" sees things differently from the manner in which he "will" see them at the End of Time, for to him all time is simultaneously present; so Māra, who plays the part of Satan in relation to the man Gautama, by the omniscient Buddha could have been seen only in his eternal perfection.

90 (*page 41*). The World-picture is the "Eternal Mirror," cf. Augustine, *De Civ. Dei*, lib. xii, c. 29, *speculum eternum mentes se videntium ducit in cognitionem omnium creatorum* (here "mens" = *manas* = *daiva cakṣu*, "the angelic eye," as in *Chāndogya Up.*, VIII, 12, 5), and Chuang Tzŭ, "The mind of the sage, being at rest, becomes the Mirror of the Universe."

91 (*page 41*). "The moment of supreme illumination is short-lived, and passes like a flash of lightning," Eckhart, I, 255, cf. *svaprakāśa, camatkāra*, in *Sāhitya Darpaṇa*, III, 2.

92 (*page 41*). *Ākāśena . . . gantvā*, which some might well have understood to mean *hṛdayâkāśe*. For "Sky" (*ākāśa*) is also "space in the lotus of the heart"; and the "place prepared" may be regarded as the ripened consciousness of the individual being, in which the planted seed of the Wisdom (-tree) springs up full-grown.

93 (*page 41*). "Vanaspati," in the Vedas, commonly designates Agni as the Tree of Life.

The "springing up immediately," as is also outwardly symbolized in the mango trick, cf. *Dhammapada Atthakathā*, III, 207, and in *Jātaka*, No. 489, "Vessavaṇa's Mango" (the same is attributed to Manannan mac Lir, God of the Sea, in Irish myth, see O'Grady, *Silva Gadelica*, 1892, p. 321), is characteristic for any manifested deity or "Hero."

94 (*page 42*). The (Mahā-) Bodhimaṇḍa is *paṭhavī-nābhī* also in *Mahābodhivaṁsa*, 79. The notion of the navel of the earth, which is also a point on the axis of the universe, is found again and again in the Vedas: for example, *Ṛg Veda*, I, 59, 1–2, where "Agni, navel of the earth (*nābhir āgniḥ pṛthivyāḥ*)," is compared to a "column (*sthūṇa*) supporting the kindreds," *i. e.* all the hierarchies of existence; X, 1, 6, where Agni is again *nābhā pṛthivyāḥ*; X, 5, 3–6, where Agni is the navel (*nābhi*) of all that proceeds or is concrete, a pillar (*skambha*) at the parting of the ways (*pathāṁ visarge*); X, 82, 5–6, where "the Waters held that same Germ (*garbha*) in which the Several Angels appeared together (*samapaśyanta*, cf. *paryapaśyata* in *Pañcaviṁśa Brāhmaṇa*, VII, 8, 1), on the Navel (*nābhāv adhi*) of the Unborn, and wherein stood (*tasthuḥ*, from *sthā*, to exist) inherent (*arpitam*) the Several Worlds (*viśvā bhuvanāni*)"; IX, 72, 7, where Soma, *nābhā pṛthivyāḥ*, sustains the Mighty Heaven; X, 13, 3, "At the centre (*nābhau*) of the Law (*ṛta*) I make all things clean (*sampunāmi*)"; X, 64, 13, "Where we are met together at the navel (*nābhā*, here the place of Sacrifice), there Aditi confirms our uterine relationship (*jāmitva*)"; *Maitri Up.*, VI, 6, where Svar is the head, Bhur the feet, and most significant, Bhuvas (Space) the navel, of Prajāpati.

For the navel of the earth in universal tradition cf. O. Rank, *Art and Artist*, New York, 1932, pp. 138 f. and 189 f., and references there cited, especially W. Roscher, *Der Omphalosgedanke* . . ., 1918 ("The whole of antiquity seems to have thought . . . that the navel of the earth was also the starting point of the world's creation").

As to the primordial importance attached to the East, which at first sight seems to contradict the notion of "centre," a careful comparison of Vedic texts (see my *New Approach to the Vedas*, note 65, and Appendix) shows that by successive analogical transpositions the "East" implies "North," "Zenith," and "Within," i. e. ultimately the "centre of consciousness," centre of life, *amṛtasya nābhi*.

95 (*page 42*). As well he may, who is the "wise, indestructible, undying Mover" of the Tree, *Taittirīya Up.*, I, 10 (*rerivā*), one with the Buddha himself as Pravartin of the Bhava-cakra. Dhamma-cakka and Bhava-cakka are sharply distinguished in Pali texts from the standpoint of edification (especially in the phrase *dhamma-cakka-pavattana*, where *dhamma* has the restricted sense of "Gospel"), but in reality the Principial and Existential wheels revolve on a common axis, the omniscient eye perceives their identity, he who moves and he who stays the Wheel are one. The Māra-dharṣaṇa is thus not an external conflict, but simply the involution (*nivattana*, *nivṛtti*) of the Buddha's own Will. All redemption is God's redemption of himself, every Passion a sacrifice unto the Sacrifice.

96 (*page 42*). Exegesis ordered to edification has missed the point here. "Evil" is that by which existence is diminished or denied: "Good," that by which existence is enhanced or affirmed. Evil is what a given being would naturally avoid, good that which a given being would naturally possess. That is all a matter of the affections, and relative. The point here is not that the Great Person is "good" as other than "bad," viz. morally, but that he is transcendent equally with respect to evil and to good. Māra assaults the Bodhisattva with every weapon in the category "evil"; Māra's daughters present the category "good" in all its most attractive forms. Māra's weapons are transformed into offerings of flowers; the Bodhisattva does not look at Māra's daughters, he remains un-affected. Cf. *Saddharma-Puṇḍarīka*, V, 22–27, like *Bhagavad Gītā*, V, 15, and XII, 17; also the discussion in my *Buddha and the Gospel of Buddhism*, II, 5, and Eckhart, I, 272, "God is neither good nor true." In the Christian "Temptation," Jesus is equally immune to "good" (the kingdoms of the earth) and to "evil" (the being cast down from the mountain); this temptation corresponding to Māra's of the Bodhisattva when he offers him the lordship of the world, J., I, 63. It may be noted that in all Messianic concepts, the possibility of an exercise of either the temporal (*brahma*) or spiritual power (*kṣatra*) is presented, and that in the type of the priest-king these are united. In the *Ṛg Veda* the dual powers are represented in the dual Indrâgnī or Indrâbrahmaṇaspatī. The spiritual power having precedence (*Aitareya Brāhmaṇa*, VIII, 1, 5, and *Śatapatha Brāhmaṇa*, IV, 1, 4, cf. *Ṛg Veda*, IV, 50, 9), Agni is said to choose Indra for himself, and to have given the *vajra* to his hands (*Ṛg Veda*, X, 124, 4 and X, 52, 5); Indra's are the sins (*kilbiṣāni*) involved in the establishment of the temporal power, Agni the Redeemer (*kilbiṣas-pṛt*). The Buddha plays the part of, and strictly speaking "is," Agni.

97 (*page 42*). *Kṛtsna* is the term employed in the *Bṛhadāraṇyaka Up.*, I, 4, 17, to denote the entirety and plenitude of the Self, Ātman, in contrast to the privation (*akṛtsna*) out of which it proceeds. Despite the dialectical antithesis, this "Pleroma" is not other than, but is the affirmation of, the "Void" of the Śūnya-vādin. Just as in Christian theology the omnipotence of God springs from the unground (= *abudhna*) of the Godhead, "which is as though it were not," so also in our own experience, the source of our highest powers is "unconscious."

98 (*page 44*). See my *Yakṣas*, I, 30–31.

99 (*page 44*). See *Bṛhad Devatā*, I, 73, and IV, 143: the weapon of any Angel is his Fiery Energy (*tejas*), and conversely, the Angel is the Self (*ātman*) of the weapon. The Buddha employs his own *tejas* directly as a weapon when he overcomes the Nāga on the occasion of the Conversion of the Jaṭilas, and perhaps also in his conflict with

Māra, cf. description of Figs. 8–9; the *vajra* only indirectly, through Vajrapāṇi, cf. *Ṛg Veda*, X, 52, 5, where Agni entrusts the *vajra* to Indra. In Buddhism, the "Angel with the flaming sword" is specifically Mañjuśrī, cf. Fig. 39.

100 (*page 44*). Axle-tree and axis are the same, of course, as the trunk of the Tree of Life, the stem of the Lotus of Space, the vertical of the Cross, and with the Liṅgam based in the "Land of Gold"; also with the Fiery Pillar, and with the Sacrificial Post when universally considered. Cf. R. Guénon, *Le symbolisme de la croix*, Paris, 1931; E. Rouselle, "Die Achse des Lebens," *Chinesische-Deutsche Almanach*, 1933; J. Strzygowski, *Asiatische Miniaturmalerei*, 1933, pp. 102, 170.

Islamic theology has also its exactly equivalent expression in the doctrine of the Quṭb, the axis and pole or centre of the Universe. This pole, primarily the Divine Idea (*ḥaqīqa*), Word (*amr* = Logos, Fiat), and Spirit (*rūḥ*), is an aspect (*wajh*) of Allāh, and called the Premier Angel, on him "turns the mill-stone of created things" (= Skr. *bhavacakra*), he has dominion over heaven, earth, and hell. To that same Idea also the Saint and Comprehensor attains, "he become the Pole on which the Universe revolves." Furthermore, the throne (*'arsh*) of Allāh is supported by eight Angels (presumably guardians of the quarters and inter-quarters) who are the "powers" of this axis or pole. See R. A. Nicholson, *Studies in Islamic Mysticism*, 1921, pp. 105–114, 194, 195, and D. B. Macdonald, "Development of the Idea of Spirit in Islam," *Acta Orientalia*, IX, 1931, 346, 347.

101 (*page 44*). Amongst the Japanese sources may be mentioned Ōmura Seigai, *Sanbon Ryōbu Mandara*, Tokyō, 1913; Mossaku Ishida, *A Study on the Excavation of Buddhistic Remains at Nachi*, Tokyō Imperial Household Museum Investigation Series, No. 5, Tokyō, 1927; and Takakusu and Ono, *Taisho Shinshu Daizōkyō Zuzō* (the Tripitika in Chinese, picture section), Tokyō, 1934. See also Anesaki, *Buddhist Art* (1st ed., 1915), pp. 38 f. and Pl. XVI, and Getty, *Gods of Northern Buddhism* (2nd ed., 1928), pp. 28 ff., and s. v. *tri-koṇa* and *vajra* in Index. (In Anesaki, Pl. XVI, the places of the illustrations A and B are reversed.)

102 (*page 45*). "In material seats is displayed strength, forasmuch as a person sits firmly thereon. But here the reverse is the case; for the Angels themselves are made firm by God," St Thomas, *Sum. Th.*, I, Q. 108, A. 5.

103 (*page 45*). *Citta* corresponds to Brahmanical *hṛdaya*, Islamic *qalb*, Christian "soul," the "heart" psychologically. Cf. Bodhi-citta, "heart of awakening," or "wisdom mind," the virtual Buddhahood in every consciousness.

104 (*page 45*). The four *āsavas*: generally will (*kāma*), contingency (*bhava*), opinion (*diṭṭhi*), and empiricism (*avijjā*).

105 (*page 46*). Translation in *S.B.E.*, XXI; text, *Bibliotheca Buddhica*, X. References given here as SP. are to the verses, and those given as SPt. to the prose text of the edition. By far the best interpretation of this fundamental Mahāyāna Sūtra, both from the theological and the iconographic standpoint, appears in A. Mus, "Le Buddha paré . . .," in *BÉFEO.*, 1929. For the Prabhūtaratna section, in which the identity of present and past Buddhas is demonstrated, see H. E. Fernald, "An Early Chinese Sculptured Stele," *Eastern Art*, III, 1931.

106 (*page 46*). "It is an unthinkable number of myriads of aeons (*kalpa*), whereof there is no measure, since I was first awakened (*prâptā mayā eṣa tadāgrabodhiḥ*, cf. Vedic *uṣarbudh*), and I proclaim the Dharma eternally (*dharmaṁ deśemy ahu nityakalam*) . . . My standing-place (*adhiṣṭhāna*; also in *Ṛg Veda*, X, 81, 2, and *Chāndogya Up.*, VII, 12, 1, in the same way, as ground or platform of the Self) endures for

inconceivable myriads of aeons, such is my quality (*etad īdṛśam*), nor do I move from this Gṛdhrakūṭa downward to any other seat (*śayyâsana*) during myriad ages," SP., XV, 1 and 10. Maitreya's bewilderment at the Buddha's assertion, voiced in SP., XIV, 44–54, exactly parallels Arjuna's in the *Bhagavad Gītā*, IV, 4, "Later was thy birth, how then am I to understand that thou sayest 'in the beginning'?" In the Christian Gospels, cf. "Before Abraham I am."

107 (*page 46*). This point of view seems to be reflected iconographically in the Buddha-Maitreya types of Mathurā, which are called "Bodhisattva" in the inscriptions.

The statements as to the Buddha's repeated messianic "descents" are to be reconciled with his perpetual and real presence on Mt Gṛdhrakūṭa (SP., XV, 10) by the doctrine of Nirmāṇakaya, the earthly likeness being merely a shadow or reflex of his being in majesty.

108 (*page 46*). Note that *nivṛtti*, "return" (to unconditioned being), cf. *nirvṛtatva* in *Maitri Up.*, VI, 22, is here equivalent to Parinirvāṇa; elsewhere also in the SP., Nirvāṇa is often used where Parinirvāṇa is to be understood. Actually, the Great Person stands "where void looks into void, equally spirated, despirated"; what he reveals, even to the Bodhisattvas on Mt Gṛdhrakūṭa, is necessarily his face, his light directed towards the world, not that aspect which faces the unknown darkness of the altogether inexpressible, with respect to which he is from the beginning silent, for "this Brahman is silence." Hence the necessary frontality of the worshipped icon, for no man worshipping objectively can see the back of the deity (that Moses is said to have seen God's "back," Exodus, xxxiii, 23, implies that Moses was more than a man, *amānava*, like Agni and Buddha). Cf. *Ṛg Veda*, IV, 1, 2, where Agni is besought to "turn hitherward thy brother Varuṇa" (*ā vavṛtsva*, and Sāyaṇa's gloss, *abhimukhī kuru*, "make him to face towards us"), which is effectively a prayer to Agni to reveal himself, who is in fact Varuṇa's "face" (*anīka*, VII, 88, 2).

The contrary of *nivṛtti*, "return," is *āvṛtti*, "hither-turn," or *pravṛtti*, "out-turn," towards existence and embodiment (cf. *āvavṛtran* contrasted with *niyāna* in *Ṛg Veda*, I, 164, 7, *vimucam* with *āvṛtaṁ punah* in V, 46, 1). *Niḥsaraṇa* and *prasaraṇa* = *pravartana* are similarly contrasted; though *pravartana* is often used with respect to Dharma in the restricted sense of "Gospel," and is then an operation undertaken solely to the end that *niḥsaraṇa* may be accomplished.

109 (*page 46*). In Hīnayāna and Mahāyāna Buddhism, "Tathāgata" or "-âgata" is the most usual designation of the Buddha. Presumably compounded of *tathā* + *āgata*, the meaning is either "He who has reached Suchness," or "He who has thus attained," i. e. has reached the goal. The Commentary on *Dīgha Nikāya*, III, 84, very well explains *tathāgata* as *dhamma-sabhāva*, "having the Word as his intrinsic nature," cf. *svabhāva-dharma-samanvāgata*, "having gotten to the Word as his intrinsic-nature," SPt., p. 481, and *dharmatā*, the "Wordness," SP., II, 34. Dharmakāya and Svabhāvakāya are interchangeable terms (*Bodhicaryāvatāra*, III, 16), essence and nature being indivisible in pure Being. For this identity see also Maitreya-Asaṅga, *Uttaratantra*, I, 149. Synonyms of *dharmatā* are *tathatā*, "suchness," and *bhūtatā*, "is-ness." On *dharma* and *dharmatā* as essence and nature see also Maitreya-Asaṅga, *Dharma-dharmatā-vibhaṅga*, as analyzed by E. Obermiller, "The Sublime Science of Maitreya," *Acta Orientalia*, IX, 1931, 87, 88.

Svabhāva in Mahāyāna texts has been well and more fully discussed by St. Schayer, "Die mahāyānistische Kritik des hīnayānistischen Pluralismus (im Anschluss an das Problem des svabhāva)," *Z.D.M.G.*, N.F. IX, 1930, 105. Cf. note 117.

Svabhāva is generally "intrinsic nature" as distinguished from *svarūpa*, "intrinsic form," *nirguṇa* as distinguished from *saguṇa* Brahman, Godhead (which "is as though it were not") from God. Equally correct, though perhaps not stated quite from this point of view, is the comparison of the Absolutely Extinguished (*parinibbuta* = *parinirvāta*) Buddha with the Deep Sea (*gambhīra samudda*), *Saṁyutta Nikāya*, IV, 376: for the Deep Sea is the Waters, the Abyss, cf. *Ṛg Veda*, X, 129, 1–3, *gahanaṁ gambhīram* . . . *ānīd avātam* . . . *apraketaṁ salilam*; V, 85, 6 and X, 5, 1, Agni as "single sea" (*ekaḥ samudraḥ*); and Eckhart, I, 176, "the sea of his own unfathomable nature."

Some Buddhist scholars use these terms very loosely: Mrs Rhys Davids for example (*Manual of Buddhism*, 1932, pp. 144–146) treats *svabhāva* as "essence," "own-being," and speaks of the body as "giving 'more being' to what we judge we really are," as though a "more" could be added to "being." What is meant is that *the body is that whereby being is manifested in a given mode*; but that neither adds to nor detracts from "being," cf. *Bṛhadāraṇyaka Up.*, IV, 4, 23, "This everlasting omnipotence of the knower of Brahman is neither increased nor diminished by action."

110 (*page 47*). Compare the case of the angel Baka, *Saṁyutta Nikāya*, I, 142 (VI, 1, 4, 2), who labors under the delusion that there is no "further recession" (*uttariṁ nissaraṇam*) beyond the Brahmā-world; and "the light beyond Heaven," *Chāndogya Up.*, III, 13, 7.

111 (*page 47*). Cf. *Ṛg Veda*, X, 129, 2, *ānīd avātam*, "breathes without breathing," *Atharva Veda*, VIII, 9, 9, *aprâṇaiti prâṇena prâṇatīnām*, "moves breathless in the breath of those that breathe," *Maitri Up.*, II, 7, *acala* . . . *carati*, "moves without moving," *Bṛhadāraṇyaka Up.*, IV, 3, 23, *paśyan vai tan na paśyati*, "sees but does not see," *Śvetâśvatara Up.*, III, 19, *paśyaty acakṣuḥ*, "sees without looking," etc.

112 (*page 47*). Verbal and ideological correspondences between the SP. and the Upaniṣads and *Bhagavad Gītā* abound. We do not, however, by any means intend by what is said above to imply that an identification of the Buddha with Brahmā was ever accepted by Buddhists literally; Brahmā by name is never from the Buddhist point of view, whether Hīnayāna or Mahāyāna, more than the wisest and best of the Brahmanical Angels.

Cunningham, *A.S.R.*, III, Pl. 18, illustrates a Buddha image having the inscription *bhagavato pitāmahasya*, "of the Bhagavata Grandfather."

113 (*page 47*). *Dīgha Nikāya*, I, 252, "There is agreement and likeness between the Bhikkhu and Brahmā . . . it is in every way possible that the Bhikkhu should be united to Brahmā, who is the same," i. e. in purity and wisdom. The adjective *brahma* is freely used in Hīnayāna texts (e. g. *brahma-vihāra*, with reference to the four stages of Jhāna which lead to rebirth in the Brahma-worlds), but generally in a specifically ethical rather than theological sense, so that "*brahma*" is made to mean "sublime," rather than "of or belonging to Brahmā." With Buddhist usage cf. *brāhmaṇa* in *Bṛhadāraṇyaka Up.*, III, 5, and the special use of Brahman to mean not any priest but that priest who "voices the lore of Genesis," *vadati jātavidyām*, *Ṛg Veda*, X, 71, 11.

114 (*page 47*). The "utterance" of the Word may be understood (1) with reference to the manifestation and exposition on Mt Gṛdhrakūṭa, and (2) with reference to the manifestation and preaching on earth, the one being heard by the angelic, the other by

the sensible, ear. In either case the teaching is not the Word itself, but merely an echo of the Word; not that anything is deliberately withheld, but that words or other symbols are inadequate. Cf. pp. 35–36.

115 (*page 47*). The Cakravartin and later Sambhogakāya concepts explain the iconographic type of the "Crowned Buddha," see A. Mus, "Le Buddha paré . . .," *BÉFEO.*, 1929.

Observe further with respect to the revelation on Mt Gṛdhrakūṭa that this was a place exactly appropriate to the manifestation of the Buddha in his capacity as Cakravartin and Dharmarājā; for according to Hsüan-tsang it was on Mt Gṛdhrakūṭa that kings were accustomed to announce their accession with great ceremony.

116 (*page 48*). On the "Three bodies of a Buddha," viz. Dharmakāya, Sambhogakāya, and Nirmāṇakāya, see de la Vallée Poussin, "Studies in Buddhist Dogma: the Three Bodies of a Buddha (*trikāya*)," *J.R.A.S.*, 1906, pp. 943 ff.; Masson-Oursel, "Les trois corps du Bouddha," *Journal Asiatique*, May–June, 1913, pp. 581–618; de la Vallée Poussin, "Note sur les trois corps du Bouddha," *Muséon*, 1913, pp. 261, 262; Demiéville, "Les versions chinoises du Milindapañha," *BÉFEO.*, 1924, esp. pp. 52–70; E. Obermiller, "The Sublime Science of Maitreya," *Acta Orientalia*, IX, 1931; "The Doctrine of Prajñā-pāramitā as exposed in the *Abhisamayālaṁkāra* of Maitreya," *ibid.*, XI, 1933, and Mus, *loc. cit.* In the expositions of Maitreya there is posited a fourth "body," the *svabhāvakāya* or "intrinsic-nature body," as being in potentiality transcendental with respect to the actual (*saṁskṛta*) *dharmakāya*, the "relation" being that of non-being to being, essence to nature, Godhead to God; it is inasmuch as these are one and the same in the Tathāgata that the two aspects of the Dharmakāya (viz. *svabhāva-* and *jñāna-*) are not distinguished in the familiar arrangement in "three bodies" (*trikāya*). A rendering of *kāya* as "substance" rather than as "body" might be preferable. The "three bodies" (*trikāya*) may be compared to the three modalities of the Self (*ātman*) in the ontology of the Upaniṣads, viz. the *annamaya, manomaya,* and *ānandamaya* bodies (*śarīra*) and to the states of "Waking," "Dream," and "Deep Sleep"; *svabhāva-kāya* to "the Fourth." The four bodies correspond to "states" of non-being, being, being in the angelic mode, and being in the human mode; only the two latter can be said to "exist" (*existare*). The following may serve to clarify the meaning of the conception of Buddhahood on three distinct planes of being: "There is one Word both thought and spoken: angels, the soul, and all creatures. Another Word, thought but unspoken, I can conceive. And there is still another Word unthought of and unspoken which never proceeds forth but is eternally in him who speaks it," Eckhart, I, 214, cf. Plotinus, *Enneads*, I, 2, 3, "as the uttered thought is the image of the soul-thought, so the soul-thought images a thought above itself and is the interpreter of the higher sphere." Islamic *kalima* includes the Word thought and spoken, and thought but unspoken, these expressions corresponding to an interior Word, *kalām*, unthought and unspoken. The application of the *nirmāṇakāya* doctrine corresponds to that of the Docetic heresy in Christianity.

117 (*page 48*). One should not, of course, be misled by such expressions as "Father of the World," or *prajāpati*, "Lord of his children," to identify Prajāpati with "God the Father" in the Christian Trinity. Brahmā-Prajāpati, Agni, Buddha are the begotten Son, and as such the exemplary cause of the whole emanation; it is precisely their filial relation to the Father that is reflected in the iconography of the lotus-birth, cf. Fig. B, where the recumbent "Father" is Nārâyaṇa.

NOTES

118 (*page 49*). Max Müller in *S.B.E.*, XLIX, ii, xxii, rightly derived the Buddhist Sukhāvatī from the Paradise of Varuṇa, but for this the Purāṇas are by no means the oldest sources; see for example *Jaiminīya Brāhmaṇa*, I, 42–44 (*J.A.O.S.*, XV, 234–238).

119 (*page 49*). The *Kauṣītaki Up.* description of the *āsandī* corresponds to that of the Vrātya's throne in *Atharva Veda*, XV, 3, 3–9, and to that of Indra's throne in the *Aitareya Brāhmaṇa*, VIII, 12. It is moreover quite intelligible that the *throne* of Indra should be the *footstool* of Brahmā. A very near parallel to the Indian *āsandī* and *paryaṅka* can be pointed to in the Muḥammadan conceptions of the Footstool (*kursī*) and Throne (*'arsh*) of Allāh, the former representing the analytical aspect and the latter the synthetic aspect of the Divine Understanding, see Nicholson, *Studies in Islamic Mysticism*, p. 111, note 3.

120 (*page 49*). Observe that union with Brahmā, the sharing of his throne, while it corresponds ideologically to the sitting together of Gautama and Prabhūtaratna in the *Saddharma Puṇḍarīka*, is not *ati-mukti*, "Total Release" (cf. Sāyaṇa on *Aitareya Āraṇyaka*, II, 3, 7, citing also *Bṛhadāraṇyaka Up.*, IV, 1, 2; and Śaṅkarâcārya on *Brahma Sūtra*, IV, 4, 22), just as union with the Sambhogakāya Buddha, the sharing of his throne, is not Parinirvāṇa (for the Buddha enthroned is *sadā sthita* (cf. Agni, *anipadyamāna*), not *parinirvāyamāṇa*, SPt., pp. 318, 319).

121 (*page 49*). From what has already been deduced, it will be evident that *padmagarbhe* is also *garbhe mātuḥ*, e. g. in *Ṛg Veda*, VI, 16, 35.

122 (*page 49*). The famous Lamaist formula *Oṁ maṇi padme hūṁ*, which may be more or less adequately rendered "Hail, the Jewel in the Lotus," is unquestionably connected with Avalokiteśvara, and in Tibet is understood to refer to his lotus-birth in the Western Paradise of Amitâbha (Rockhill, *Land of the Lamas*, pp. 326 ff.). It is also suggested that Maṇipadme can be read as one word, vocative of Maṇipadmā, who would be the Śakti or Tārā of the Bodhisattva, cf. such other *dhāraṇīs* as *Oṁ vajrapuṣpe hūṁ*, and the discussion by F. W. Thomas, in *J.R.A.S.*, 1906, p. 464.

123 (*page 50*). With the notion of the Buddhist paradise as merely a resting place, compare Eckhart (Evans, I, 274, 276) with respect to Heaven and the vision of God, "As this is not the summit of divine union so it is not the soul's abiding place," for the soul in Heaven is "not yet dead and gone out into that which follows created existence." Cf. also Préau, in *Le Voile d'Isis*, XXXVII, 566.

124 (*page 51*). "Extinction (*nirvāṇa*) is indeed the transcendental knowledge (*avabodha*) of the sameness (*samatā*) of all principles (*dharmā*)," SPt., p. 133; "Without understanding of the World-Wheel, the Return is not understood," *saṁsāracakrasyâjñānān nirvṛtiṁ na vijñānate*, SP., V, 50. Cf. "In God all things have the same form, though that is the form of very different things," Eckhart, I, 211, and "Not till she knows all that there is to be known does she cross over to the unknown good. This crossing is obscure to many a religious," Eckhart, I, 385. Whereas "He who sees the principles separately (*dharmān pṛthak*), runs to waste after them," *Kaṭha Up.*, IV, 14. Keith, who is much concerned to show that the texts of the Vedas and Upaniṣads do not mean what they seem to mean, denies the correspondence here, *HOS.*, XXXII, 547; but already in *Ṛg Veda*, X, 90, 16, *dharmāṇi* is "principles," *dharma* in all these passages coming very near to *nāma*, "form" in relation to *rūpa*, "thing," or better "phenomenon." As for *dharmya* contrasted with *aṇu*, as "thingish" with "undimensioned," in *Kaṭha Up.*, II, 13, cf. *dharmin* and *dharma* as "thing" and

"quality" in *Sāhitya Darpaṇa*, II, 10, that which is qualified being "thingish," while the quality is "essential".

125 (*page 51*). "One and one uniting, void shines into void, equally spirated, despirated, there is the Supreme Being," Eckhart, I, 368. Buddhist scholars apparently ignore that the Upaniṣads (e. g. *Bṛhadāraṇyaka Up.*, II, 3, 1) distinguish the Brahman in a likeness (*mūrta*), mortal (*martya*), selfed (*ātmanvī*), etc., from the Brahman that is imageless (*amūrta*), not-a-self (*anātmya*), immortal (*amṛta*, to be understood absolutely, not as when applied to the Angels, relatively), etc. The Buddhist emphasis on *anatta* cannot have been a purely monastic development, for that would be to assert that the Buddha's Buddhism had been strictly and merely a theistic doctrine. Why does the Buddha teach an Absolute Extinction, who is him-Self merely Extinguished-with-residual-existential-elements (*sa-upādi-sesa*)? Why does Eckhart (Evans, I, 274, 376) assert that it is God's full intention that we should become what He is not, that the soul honors God most in being quit of God? Because there lies beyond the idea (*nāma*) of Buddha, God, Self, Person, Being, the *possibility of these assumptions*; these assumptions are not All that "is" (here "is-ness" can be predicated only analogically). The *bhakta* deliberately rejects this last death of the soul. Nevertheless, in order to attain to the Supreme Identity of that which is the Self, and that which is-not the Self, the soul (individual or super-individual consciousness) must become, be lost in, That of which the Self is the first assumption: the soul, in order to be one with the Supreme Identity, must go beyond its Selfhood to the unselfed source of Self. That is the "Drowning," "Absolute Extinction," from which every individual or even super-individual existence naturally shrinks, which only the adamantine mind (*vajirūpama citta*) dare essay.

126 (*page 51*). Hence the Tathāgata may be represented either in Samādhi, or on the other hand in one of the customary active poses, e. g. *dharmacakra-pravartana*.

127 (*page 51*). "With-due-regard-to (*vyavalokya*) their faculties and energy he reveals to living beings in each generation his name and his extinction (*nirvāṇa*) and by various alternative-formulations (*paryāya*) gladdens these beings . . . and the Word (*vāc*) that the Tathāgata utters (*vyāharati*) for their instruction (*vinaya, nirṇaya*), whether in his own aspect (*ātmôpadarśana*) or another's, whether on his own basis (*ātmârambaṇa = ātmâlambaṇa*) or under the cloak (*āvaraṇa*) of another, all that the Tathāgata declares, all those alternative-formulations are true," SPt., pp. 317, 318. The Bodhisattva Gadgadasvara, for example, is said to have preached the alternative-formulation known as the *Saddharma Puṇḍarīka* ("Lotus of the True Doctrine"), "sometimes in the shape (*rūpa*) of Brahmā, sometimes in that of Indra, sometimes in that of Śiva . . .," continuing with a list of men and women of various degree, *kinnaras, nāgas*, etc., through all of whom the True Word has been revealed, SPt., p. 433.

128 (*page 51*). We need not consider the case of things made without an end in view, because an activity of that kind can be predicated only of the insane, and enjoyed only by the insane. It is true that Deity in "making" the world "works" without an end in view, and that in so far as man becomes Godlike he too "works" without a purpose. But though there is thus an analogy between insanity and divinity (as when we say that to know Him, the mind must be de-mented), there is no likeness implying a sameness: on the one hand, insanity depends on a defect of substance, not of form, on the other the "work" and "making" of the world by Deity are merely

figurative expressions for what is not a *working*, but a *being*, not a procedure from potentiality to act, but an identity of "cause" and "effect."

129 (*page 52*). An almost identical account appears in the *Si Yu Ki* (*Records of the Western World*, Ch. VIII, Beal, pp. 115, 116).

130 (*page 52*). This cosmology, in the main of pre-Vedic antiquity, is also outlined in the Pali texts, e. g. *Dīgha Nikāya*, II, 107, and *Milindapañha*, 68. Cf. W. Kirfel, *Die Kosmographie der Inder*, 1920, and S. Beal, *Catena of Buddhist Scriptures from the Chinese*, 1871, pp. 101–116, cf. pp. 11, 12.

131 (*page 52*). Needless to say, these directions and measurements are purely analogical. In any case the Universe is thought of as a sphere or egg, the various circles referred to representing cross sections of this sphere, each such circle having its own characteristic possibilities.

132 (*page 53*). In the *Bodhicarya*, VI, 1, *kañcana-vajra-maṇḍala*. That is, of course, Hsüan Tsang's "golden wheel." This "land of gold," representing the foundations of the earth, must also be identified with the otherwise unexplained Hāṭaka of the Devadāruvana legend (see my *Yakṣas*, II, 44, 45), where it is Śiva's liṅgam which forms the axis of the Universe. That the first product of the Waters should have been golden is developed also in Vedic cosmology from another point of view, that of the origin of created things from Fire and Water, by either reflection or generation, e. g. *Śatapatha Brāhmaṇa*, II, 1, 15, "Agni at one time cast his eyes upon the Waters, 'May I pair with them,' he thought. He united with them, and what was emitted as his seed (*retas*), that became gold (*hiraṇya*). Therefore the latter shines like fire, being Agni's seed, hence it is found in water, for he poured it into the Waters." Hence the so often mentioned myth of the search of the Angels for the Sun or Fire "hidden in the Waters," which search is the *Quest of Life*; also the designation of the Person, Self, Brahman, in the mode of Fiery Energy and Life as "germinal" (*raitasa*, from *retas*, "seed"), Life being *found* in the "individual" Self (*adhyātman*) supported by an individual "Earth," *Bṛhadāraṇyaka Up.*, II, 5, 1–2, viz. the body, "lotus of nine gates."

133 (*page 53*). This phrase, "Adamantine Identity" or "Consummation" (of *dhyāna*), appears also in the *Mahāyāna Sūtrâlaṁkāra*, XIV, 45 and in the *Abhisamayâlaṁkāra* of Maitreya; it is proper to the very last stage of a Bodhisattva's course and simultaneous with the "One Instant (i. e. "Eternal Now") Total Awakening" by which he is unified with the Primordial Buddha-Essence. It is evident that for this Adamantine Consummation only the "Adamantine Heart" (*vajirūpama citta, Anguttara Nikāya*, I, 124) is apt.

134 (*page 53*). When a given location, such as the Bodhimaṇḍa at Bodhgayā, or any of the other places for which a similar claim has been advanced (e. g. the Delphic Omphalos, or even Bostonian "Hub"), is identified with the "navel of the earth," or centre of the Universe, that is merely an analogical assumption, not to be literally interpreted. The superimposed centres of the various cosmic circles constitute a common axis, but it must not be understood that they revolve about this axis locally, or that the axis is situated anywhere; the cause of all things is not any one of them.

135 (*page 53*). On the habitat and character of Nāgas, see J. Ph. Vogel, *Indian Serpent-lore*, 1926; also my "Angel and Titan: an essay in Vedic ontology" to appear in *J.A.O.S.* The Nāgas correspond to the mermen and mermaids of European folklore, as described for example in Fouquet's *Undine*.

136 (*page 54*). The Kārlī relief (Fig. 29) is not, as I once thought, a Buddha coronation (*J.R.A.S.*, 1928, p. 837); the stūpa is not a crown, though it is not altogether inappropriate that it should seem to be such. Other Indian and Chinese representations of the stūpa in its present relation can be referred to, e. g. Sirén, *Chinese Sculpture*, Pls. 242, 245, 246. It may be noted also that in the common Pāla reliefs representing the *aṣṭasthāna* the Parinirvāṇa is always placed at the top of the slab, above the central Buddha's head, e. g. my *History*, Fig. 228.

137 (*page 54*). For Yakṣas as chthonic powers, and specifically as earth-spirits, corresponding to the Germanic dwarfs, elves, and gnomes, see my *Yakṣas*, I, 8, and P.T.S. Pali Dictionary, s. v. *bhumma deva*.

138 (*page 54*). Atlas, in classical mythology, is a real equivalent.

139 (*page 55*). The introductory invocatory verse of the *Daśakumāracarita* mentions amongst the various aspects of the axis of the universe the "stalk of the lotus where Brahmā resides"; other equivalents including "the staff of the umbrella of the world-egg, the mast of the ship of the earth, the flagstaff of the banner of the river of life, the axis of the circle of light (*jyotiś-cakra*, the Zodiac), the triumphal pillar of conquest of the three worlds, the three-strider's (Viṣṇu's) walking-stick," and it is "the rod of death to the foes of the wake" (i. e. of the Angels, the allusion being to the value of the *akṣa* as the *vajra* in Indra's hands).

140 (*page 56*). Cf. Eckhart, "To find nature herself (*māyā, prakṛti svabhāva*) all her likenesses have to be shattered, and the farther in the nearer the actual thing" (I, 259); "None may attain be he not stripped of all mental matter" (I, 359); "this knowledge de-ments the mind" (I, 370).

141 (*page 56*). Cf. Eckhart, "On coming to one, where it is all one, she is the same" (I, 259).

142 (*page 58*). "Fontal and inflowing": *samānam udakam ut ca eti ava ca ahabhiḥ*, *Ṛg Veda*, I, 164, 51; *viṣvañc, sadhryañc, ibid.*, X, 177, 3; *yad vai vāyuḥ parāṅ eva paveta kṣīyeta . . . reṣmāṇaṁ janamāno niveṣṭamāno vāti, kṣayād eva bibhyat . . . yad u ha vā āpaḥ parācīr eva prasṛtās syanderan kṣīyeraṅs tāḥ, yad aṅkāṁsi kurvāṇā niveṣṭamānā āvartān sṛjamānā yanti kṣayād eva bibhyatīḥ*, *Jaiminīya Upaniṣad Brāhmaṇa*, I, 2; that is, "If the Spirit should blow only straight away, it would die away; (but) it blows from all quarters together, winding itself in so as to generate a whirlwind, that it may not die away. And if the Waters should flow streaming only straight away, they would come to an end; but in that they proceed making bends, winding themselves in, and making eddies, that is to avoid a coming to an end." (With the notion *āvarta*, "eddy," here, compare that of "auspicious curls," *nandyāvarta*, and the general value of spirals and "strapwork" in symbolism.)

Pali *uddhaṁsoto*, "Upstreamer," sometimes applied to the religious man, corresponds to the notion of "inflowing"; cf. *Taittirīya Saṁhitā*, VII, 5, 7, 4 "upstream (*pratikūla*) from here, as it were, is the world of heaven," and *Pañcaviṁśa Brāhmaṇa*, XXV, 10, 12–18, where the distance upstream (*pratīpam*) on the Sarasvatī (the River of Life) from the place where it is lost in the desert to its source is said to be equal to that of heaven from earth. It is, in other words, a matter of "inverse thinking" (*pratyakcetanā*, *Yoga Sūtra*, I, 29).

143 (*page 58*). *Eṣa vai mṛtyur yat saṁvatsaraḥ . . . Prajāpatiḥ*, *Śatapatha Brāhmaṇa*, X, 4, 3, 1 and 3; *Prajāpatir yaṁ prajāyamānaṁ viśvaṁ rūpam anuprajāyate*, *Aitareya Brāhmaṇa*, II, 17.

145 (*page 58*). *Navo navo jayamānaḥ, Ṛg Veda*, X, 85, 19.

146 (*page 58*). Viz. *nirmitāni*, things designed and fashioned, like the manifested flesh (*nirmāṇa-kāya*) of the terrestrial manifestation, insignificant as they are in themselves, and with respect to which the "lover of art" is no better than the hypothetical "heathen in his blindness" who worships stocks and stones, or those of whom the Buddha said, "They worship variously my traces (*dhātu*), but see not Me" (SP., XV, 5). The image is significant only with respect to its form, being His whose image it is, not his who fashions it.

In connection with the "traces," or "Footprints of the Law," discussed above and on p. 16, it may be remarked that an almost identical formulation is met with in Scholastic philosophy. The elements of the beautiful in nature and art are unity, order, and clarity: "*Ad pulchritudinem tria requiruntur. Primo quidem integritas, sive perfectio; quae enim diminuta sunt, hoc ipso turpia sunt. Et debita proportio, sive consonantia. Et iterum claritas: unde quae habunt colorem nitidum, pulchra esse dicuntur*," St Thomas Aquinas, *Sum. Th.*, I.Q. 39, A. 8. Now it is precisely these elements of integrity, harmony, and lucidity in things that are called the "traces" (*vestigia*) of God in the world, and as to this, the reader may conveniently consult Gilson, *Introduction à l'Étude de Saint Augustine*, 1931, Ch. III, *Les Vestiges de Dieu*. It is obviously from this point of view that St Bernard could say, what sounds so like a Zen dictum, "*Ligna et lapides docebunt te, quod a magistris audire non posse.*"

Even more remarkable, from the standpoint of comparative symbolism, is the fact that the "trace" is actually spoken of as a "footprint," *vestigium pedi*, cf. Bissen, *L'Exemplarisme divin de Saint Bonaventura*, 1929, pp. 70, 71, citing the Seraphic Doctor as follows: "*Egressus enim rerum mundarum a Deo est per modum vestigii. Unde si pes esset aeternus, et pulvis, in quo formatur vestigium, esset aeternus, nihil prohiberet intelligere, vestigium pedi esse coaeternum.*" It is very evident that to follow in these tracks will be to find their maker.

147 (*page 59*). The utterance (*vyāhṛti*) of the Three Worlds is their existence (*astitva*); the meaning of *ākhyāta* is *pradhāna*; the ground on which we stand is literally the "substance" of a "name" (*nāma*). Note the equivalence of *pradhāna*, "ground," to *pradhi*, "circumference" (of the Wheel of Life).

148 (*page 59*). Kabīr, Bolpur Edition, II, 62:

Cakra kē bichmẽ kambala ati phūliyā,
Tāsukā koi santa jānai?
Tā madha adhara siṁhâsana gājai,
Puruṣa mahā tāha adhika virājai.

SUPPLEMENTARY NOTES AND DESCRIPTIONS

p. 4, l. 27 . . . . *Manamattakam* is predicated of the anthropomorphic *cetiya* in a pejorative sense because the worshipper may fancy that the Buddha really subsisted or subsists in such a manner, that the Buddha is in some sense "like" the icon. The same danger inheres in the use of verbal symbols; the hearer goes far astray if he thinks that the words depict the principle, on the contrary they merely point to it, the principle itself is not a thing in any likeness. This is developed at length in the *Laṅkâvatāra Sūtra*, text pp. 194–196, cf. Ch. II, 114 and 118–119, and Ch. III, 74. *Saṁyutta Nikāya*, text I, p. 11, is also very pertinent: "Those who take their stand on what is literally expressed, without comprehending *what* was expressed, fall into the bondage of mortality; those who understand what was really indicated form no vain concepts of (*na maññati*) him who makes the indication."

p. 6, l. 21 . . . . Cf. *yāvan na khedo jāyate bhāvayet* in *Sādhanamālā* texts.

p. 16, l. 27 . . . . See also note 146, below.

p. 17, l. 13 . . . . Cf. Figs. 13–15.

p. 21, l. 9 . . . . Cf. Śatapatha Br., IV, 1, 5, 16 (Aśvins).

p. 22, l. 8 . . . . Cf. Fig. 23.

pp. 22–23, with notes 41–48 In a monograph *On the Iconography of the Buddha's Nativity*, Mem. Arch. Surv. India, No. 46, received as the present volume goes to press, M. Foucher reasserts the view that the Śrī-Lakṣmī representations at Bharhut and Sāñcī are Buddha nativities, and expresses the hope that I may agree with him. He will find that I do so to the extent that I admit the fact and propriety of a Buddhist application in this sense. At the same time I am very far from agreeing that Buddhism originated the formula; in my view there is nothing specifically or originally Buddhist in early Buddhist imagery, whether visual or verbal. The present case is very much to the point; for to postulate a Buddhist invention or development of the lotus-seated Mother Śrī type would be possible only by assigning a considerably post-Buddhist date to the *Śrīsūkta*, in which the lotus-seated (*padme-sthitām . . . śriyam . . . puṣkariṇīm . . . lakṣmīm*) Śrī-Lakṣmī is invoked as the mother of Agni-Jātavedas and darling of Viṣṇu (cf. Aditi as the "lady of Viṣṇu" in *Taittirīya Saṁhitā*, IV, 4, 12 and VII, 5, 14, and *Vājasaneyī Saṁhitā*, XXIX, 60) and described as "bathed by royal elephants with golden jars" (*gajendrair . . . snāpitā hema-kumbhair*). But "the *khila* texts . . . are by no means a modern product, they belong rather to the Vedic age. . . . Only a few of them can be assigned to a late Brāhmaṇa period. . . . The *Śrīsūkta* is connected with the cult of Śrī and Lakṣmī which came into prominence in the Yajurveda period" (Scheftelowitz, *Die Apokryphen des Ṛgveda*, 1906, pp. 2–4). It may be added that Śrī and Lakṣā are mentioned as *brahmavādinī* in the *Bṛhad Devatā*, II, 84.

p. 28, l. 6 .... Cf. Figs. 19, 20.

p. 34, l. 15 .... Cf. Fig. 39.

p. 36, l. 7 .... Cf. in the *Tilakamañjarī* of Dhanapāla, *Kāvyamālā*, No. 85, p. 144, the distinction of *cārutva-tattvam* from *rūpam.*

p. 48, l. 17 .... Cf. Vedic Mitra as "Agni when enkindled," *Ṛg Veda*, III, 5, 4 and V, 3, 1.

p. 48, l. 35 .... Fig. 29.

p. 48, l. 36 .... Fig. B.

p. 50, l. 30 .... In place of "he is *nirvāta*, and realizes" read: in reality he faces both ways, like Agni *pathām visarge* (*Ṛg Veda*, X, 5, 6, cf. *Dhammapada*, 282, *dvedhāpatha*) seeing at once the operation of and, etc.

p. 55, l. 3 .... Cf. Figs. 2, 3, 12.

p. 57, l. 8 .... Cf. *Śatapatha Brāhmaṇa*, VII, 2, 2, 14, "What is silent (*tūṣṇīm*, = *maunam*, the characteristic state of the *muni*) is unexpounded (*aniruktam*), and what is unexpounded is everything (*sarvam*)."

p. 66, note 15 .... See also notes 100 and 139.

p. 69, note 33 .... Cf. also *Majjhima Nikāya*, I, 421, *ajjhatikā paṭhavī-dhātu*, "the personal earth-element."

p. 70, note 37, l. 5 ...... Cf. Fig. 41.

p. 71, note 39 .... Add: *Nakṣatra* designates the Sun in *Ṛg Veda*, VII, 86, 1, X, 88, 13, and X, 156, 4.

p. 68, note 30 .... The *Gopatha Brāhmaṇa*, I, 16, has *brahma ha vai brahmāṇam puṣkare sasṛje*, rendered by Bloomfield "Brahman created Brahmā on the lotus." This is scarcely more than a paraphrase of RV., VII, 33, 11, where Vasiṣṭha, child of Mitrāvaruṇau and Urvaśī, as a sperm-drop fallen "by divine efflux" (*daivyena brahmaṇā*), is born in the lotus (*puṣkare*), and is addressed as "priest" (*brahman*). Although we have avoided a tendenzios translation, it can hardly be overlooked that the contrast of *brahman* (n.) and *brahmā* (m.) occurs in both texts, and it would have been very easy to render the RV. passage as "Brahmā born in the lotus, drop let fall by Brahman"; as remarked by Grassmann (*Wörterbuch*, s. v. *brahman*, m.), "die Keime der späteren Sonderung (i. e. of Brahmā from Brahman) finden sich schon im RV." Vasiṣṭha corresponds to Agni, *puṣkare*, in VI, 16, 13; and in any case the prototype of the Buddha iconography is unmistakable in all three passages.

p. 73, note 48, l. 5 ...... Add: though this is not quite true as regards Māyā-devī. See P. D. Shastri, *The Doctrine of Māyā*, 1911, p. 28.

p. 73, note 48, end ...... For the shining in the womb (*Jātaka* I, 52, *Buddhacarita*, I, 22) see *Ṛg Veda*, VI, 16, 35, and cf. the Pseudo-Matthew, Ch. xiii.

p. 82, note 104 .... Add: *avijjā* (*avidyā*) is "knowledge of," to be contrasted with *vijjā* (*vidyā*, *jñāna*), which is "knowledge as."

p. 84, note 113, l. 7 ..... Buddhism in fact preserves the older Ṛg Vedic meaning of *brahma* as spiritual power contrasted with *kṣatra* as temporal power.

p. 86, note 124, l. 1 ..... For "the transcendental knowledge of" read "an awakening to."

p. 87, note 127 .... Add: The monastic as distinguished from the dogmatic Buddha is but one such *upadarśana* and *ārambaṇa*. Cf. R. O. Franke in O. Z., N. F. IV, 1915–16, p. 10, "All the seven Buddhas are only paradigms of the dogmatic Buddha . . . which dogmatic Buddha is the cloudy image of a more ancient concept of the deity" — that is, as has been amply demonstrated, of the Vedic Agni-Sūrya.

p. 88, note 135 .... Add "They are, *ante principium*, what the Angels are *in principio*."

p. 89, note 139 .... See also notes 15, 100, and Mus, "Barabudur" in *BÉFEO*, 1932.

Fig. 28, description, add:

The "*vajra* in operation," tantamount to "*dharma-cakra-pravartana*." *Karma-vajra*, which is the direct equivalent of *katsuma-kongō* (*katsuma* being the regular Japanese transliteration of *karma*), occurs in *Mahābhārata*, I, 6487, where it is applied to Śūdras, "whose power is work," or "whose virtue is labor." As the designation of a symbol, *karma-vajra* is evidently equivalent to *dharma-cakra*, *brahma-cakra*, cf. *Śvetâśvatara Up.*, VI, 1–4: ". . . it is by the all-might (*mahimā*) of the Angel that this Brahma-Wheel is whirled in the world (*loke bhrāmyate*). For it is turned (*āvṛttam*) by him — who is ever omniscient of all this (*nityam idaṁ hi sarvaṁ jñaḥ*), whose knowledge is entire (*sarvavidyaḥ*) of time, untime, and factors — it is by him that that operation (*karma*) is revolved (*vivartate*), viz. all that is regarded as solid (*pṛthvya*), phlogistical (*teja*), liquid (*āpya*), gaseous (*anila*), or spacial (*kha*). Having done that work (*tatkarma kṛtvā*), he again desists (*vinirvartya bhūyaḥ*), unifying (*samêtya yogam* = *saṁgamya*, Śāyaṇa), Quiddity with Quiddity (*tattvasya tattvena*, cf. the Buddhist "sameness of all *dharmas*"). . . . Thus undertaking (*ārabhya*) all these factorial operations (*guṇânvitāni karmāṇi*), and again laying them aside (*viniyojayed yaḥ*), there being a negation of active operation (*kṛta karma-nāśaḥ*) in non-being (*abhāve*), he, in that annihilation of operation (*karma-kṣaye*), remains other than the Quiddity-nature (*tattvato'nyaḥ*)."

FIG. 30, description, add:

The appearance of the "totally extinct" (*parinirvāta*) Prabhūtaratna side by side with the "still living" (*sthita*) Śākya-muni forms the theme of innumerable Chinese sculptures (cf. Sirén, *Chinese Sculpture*, Pls. 47, 55, 121, 181). The appearance of Prabhūtaratna is a resurrection of the "body," and the whole manifestation on Mt Gṛdhrakūṭa (Jap. Ryōzen Jōdo) is a "Last Judgment," at least in this sense, that those unqualified are excluded. How can such a resurrection be understood? How can one who was "totally extinguished" (in European terms, "drowned," "dead and buried in the Godhead") in a former aeon now appear and be seen and heard by the still living Angels of the present aeon?

Without discussing in detail the whole problem of the condition of past and present Sādhyas, Munis, Jinas, Tīrthaṁkaras, etc. (which the Buddha refused to discuss), it may be pointed out that in all traditional formulations such beings are evidently thought of, not indeed as "individuals," but as distinct "Persons" in the same sense that the Persons of the Trinity (the "Several Angels" who are *anyonyayonita*, *itaretarajanmāna*, etc.) are distinct, at the same time that they are One (*ekam bhavanti*, *Aitareya Āraṇyaka*, II, 3, 8, "where all existence becometh of one nest," *Mahānārâyaṇa Up.*, II, 3 = *Vājasaneyī Saṁhitā*, XXXII, 8, *yatra viśvam bhavaty ekanīḍam*); and the condition of *sadasat*, tantamount to "simultaneously quick and dead in the Supernal" may be partially explained. Thus, allusion to an individual by name so and so, and of aspect such and such, of whom it is asserted that he attained to complete extinction in a former aeon, includes the assertion that the manifestation of such a form and aspect had been amongst the primordial possibilities of existence. Now possibility in this sense is in no way bound up with time; whatever has been a possibility of manifestation remains a possibility not merely *in saecula saeculorum*, but without regard to time, as well in one aeon as another. By the same token, any such possibility will always be visible to the *jñāna-cakṣu* (for which there is no proceeding from potentiality to act) as an actuality. Or we may express this by saying that every part of the World-picture "painted by the Self on the canvas of the Self" is necessarily ever-present to the Self. Whatever has been mirrored in the *speculum eternum* (Augustine, *De Civ. Dei*, lib. a, xii, c. 29) is now and forever imaged there, and *mentes se videntium ducit in cognitionem omnium creatorum*. Inasmuch as Prabhūtaratna, who had been totally extinguished, had seen with the Eye of Wisdom, a vision that cannot change, his own image, that is his understanding of himself, must be thought of as remaining for ever within the range of his own vision, and in this sense "he" is always virtually "present." The notion is similar to that of John x, 9, "I am the door (= *loka-dvāra*); by Me if any man enter in, he shall be saved, and *shall go in and out*, and find pasture," where "find pasture" = *annam ad*, "to exist," cf. John, 1, 3 "All things that have been created were in him as life." and Matthew xii, 29, "For he is not a God of the dead but of the living: for all live unto him." This immortality of one who has been utterly extinguished and is dead and buried in the Godhead is not indeed an immortality of the ego as commonly understood; it is rather the potential being of a "name" (*nāma*) that cannot be annihilated, and of an "aspect" (*rūpa*) which must be presented whenever this "name" is recalled.

SUPPLEMENTARY NOTES

FIG. 31, description, add:

By far the most interesting of these representations is the upper central symbol of the "Wisdom of All the Tathāgatas," corresponding to the manifested form of Prajñāpāramitā in the centre of the lower panel. Prajñāpāramitā, corresponding to Vedic Aditi and Gnostic Sophia, is also Tabhāgata-garbha, "Womb of all the Buddhas," potential and maternal: for a more detailed exposition see Obermiller, E., "The Doctrine of Prajñāpāramitā, etc.", in *Acta Orientalia,* XI. This universal potentiality of the possible intellect is represented by a flaming equilateral triangle (see illustration, p. 31) resting on its base, and supported by a lotus "ground." Of the two *svastikas,* one situated at the "point" *(bindu)* within the triangle is principial, and represents the Unmoved Mover or First Cause of Motion, the second external to the triangle implies the actual motion of the worlds. As corresponding to the rising Sun, this triangle is situated in the East; it corresponds also to Manas in the Trinity Manas, Vāc, Prâṇa. The corresponding Vajra-dhātu symbol of the operative intellect is a triangle in the image of this, but with its point downwards, situated in the West, where the Sun is reflected or "sets" in the Waters, corresponding also to Vāc in the Trinity Manas, Vāc, Prâṇa.

PLATES

PLATE I

FIGURE 1. The Buddha (Amitâyus) as the Tree of Life. Sāñcī, north *toraṇa*, left pillar, outer face, 100–50 B.C. India Office photograph.

Above, *triśūla, vajra*, or "*nandi-pada*" symbol forming a head; middle, a column of superimposed lotus palmettes (cf. *skandhāt skandham, Maitri Up.*, VII, 11) forming the trunk; below, the *pādukā*, feet, "firmly established," *supratiṣṭhā*; cf. Figs. 13, 14. Above the "head" will be observed the umbrella (*chattra, uṣṇīṣa*) of the Cakravartin; corresponding to the prescription *uṣṇīṣa-śīrṣa* proper to the Buddha's anthropomorphic likeness. The triple division may be compared to that of the cosmic (*lokavat*) aspect of Prajāpati as described in *Maitri Up.*, VI, 6, where the "Three Worlds" constituting this "body" are *svar, bhuvas*, and *bhūr*, celestial, spiritual, and chthonic.

The whole is to be regarded as a "support for contemplation" (*ārambaṇa, Aṣṭasahasrikā Prajñāpāramitā, passim; dhīyâlamba, Maitr, Up.*, VII, 11, see p. 9; *ālamba, Yoga Sūtra*, I, 10).

For a description from other points of view, see text, pp. 8–10.

FIGURE 2. The Buddha as Supernal Sun. Amarāvatī, in the Indian Museum, Calcutta, *ca.* 200 A.D. India Office photograph.

Above, the Dharmacakra or Principial Wheel, supported by four lions of which two only are visible in the frontal view.

The nave is lotiform, the eight petals representing directions; there are sixty-four spokes; the triple felly is fringed with twelve *triśūla* symbols, representing solar "months." At this level also are two dancing apsarases, supported by lotuses (of the "upper waters"). Above the wheel are "cherubim." For the solar significance of the addorsed animals cf. Roes, *Greek Geometric Art*, 1933, pp. 94–122. The wheel is supported by a column, the Axis of the Universe, corresponding to the trunk of the Tree of Life, and the "one leg" of the Sun, when alluded to as *eka-pād.* At the base level there are a throne and footstool, with wheel-marked feet (*pāduka, pada*, Buddha-pada), as in Figs. 1, 13, 14. These, his "traces" (*dhātu*) on earth, are adored by human worshippers.

FIGURE 3. The Buddha as Supernal Sun. Amarāvatī, *ca.* 200 A.D. British Museum (?). India Office photograph.

Similar to Fig. 2, but the pillar is differently treated and the paired riders are replaced by flying angelic types, except at the top, where two riders take the place of the apsarases. The pillar has three lotiform nodes. The segments (*parva*) between the three nodes are octagonal, and geometrically patterned, with human worshippers at the base level. Such arrangements, indeed, as those of Figs. 2 and 3 correspond exactly to such representations of superimposed worlds as may be seen at Sāñcī, east *toraṇa*, right pillar, front face (Bachhofer, *Early Indian Sculpture*, Pl. 59), where the Brahmaloka is sharply differentiated from the *kāmarūpa lokas* below.

Cf. the similar examples, Burgess, *Buddhist Stūpas of Amarāvatī and Jaggayyapeṭa*, Pl. XXXVIII, Figs. 1 and 7. In one of these the Dharmacakra symbol is combined with that of the Cross with equal arms.

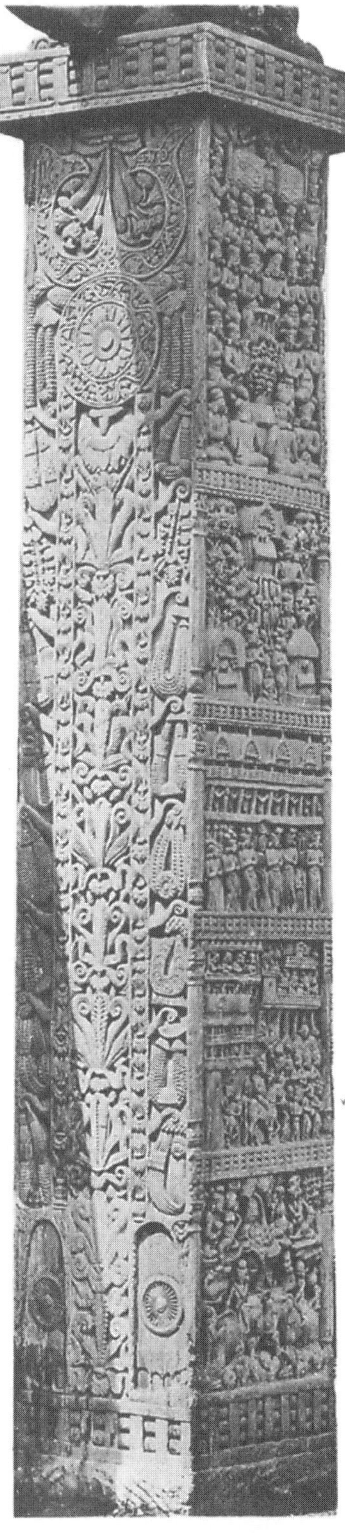

1

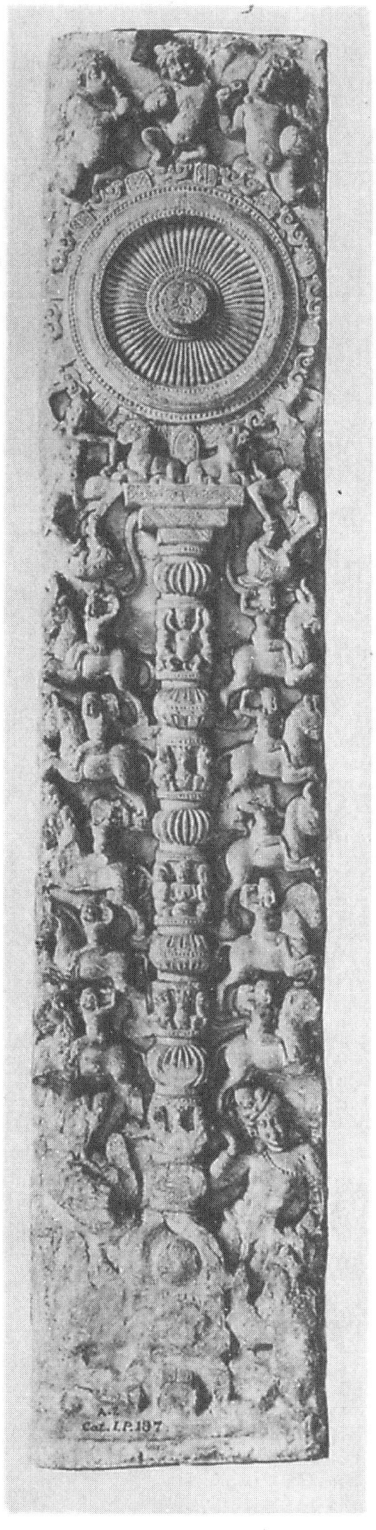

~~2~~

3

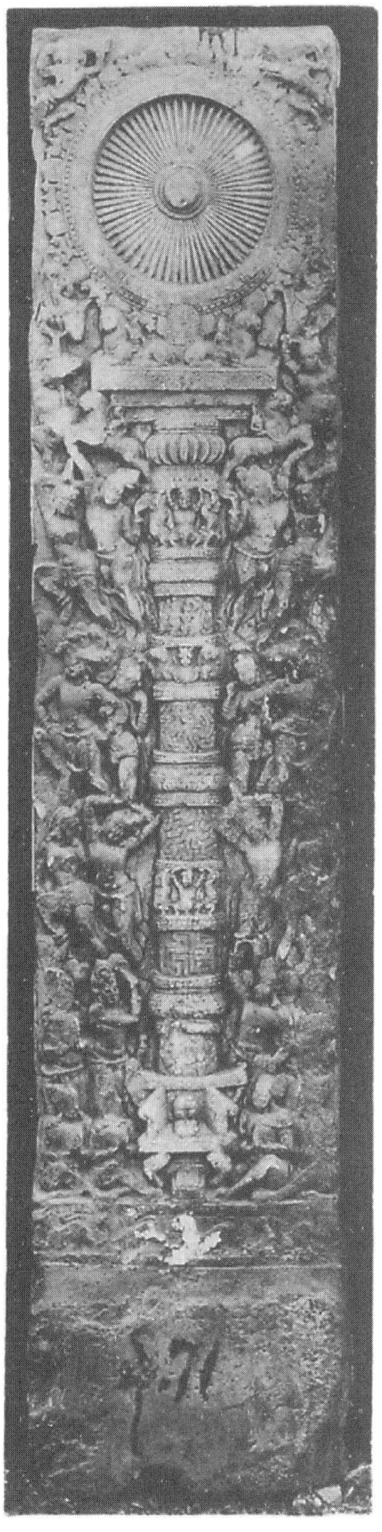

~~3~~

2

PLATE II

FIGURE 4. The Buddha as Pillar of Fire. Amarāvatī, 3rd century A.D. Madras Museum. India Office photograph.

The head and base as in Figs. 1–3, the pillar segmented and fringed with flame. See descriptions in text, p. 10.

FIGURE 5. Scene from a Jātaka (?) Amarāvatī, *ca.* 200 A.D. Madras Museum. India Office photograph.

The Buddha as Pillar of Fire, with human worshippers.

The feet are very clearly lotus-supported (*padma-pīṭha*), and are turned in the direction of movement or response.

FIGURE 6. Cult of the Buddha as a Pillar of Fire. India Office photograph.

Type as before, but the pillar is spirally marked. Amarāvatī, *ca.* 200 A.D. British or Madras Museum. Cf. Fig. 10, upper centre, where the seated Buddha is surrounded by a flaming glory.

FIGURE 7. Scene from a Jātaka (?) Amarāvatī, as Fig. 6.

The feet are *padma-pīṭha*, and seem to be turned in the direction of movement or response.

FIGURE 8. Relief from Amarāvatī, as Figs. 6 and 7.

Perhaps the Offering of Sujātā, and Assault of Māra or that of Aṅgulimāla (cf. relief from Nāgârjunikoṇḍa, reproduced by Bachhofer in OZ., NF. 10, Abb. 5, a similar scene with the Buddha in human form). In any case, the Buddha, as before, is represented by a Pillar of Fire, with *triśūla* "head" and lotus-supported (*padma-pīṭha*) feet.

For Sujātā = Apālā = Uṣas, see my "The Darker Side of Dawn" in the press (Smithsonian Miscellaneous Publications).

FIGURE 9. The same scene as Fig. 8, in an older style. Amarāvatī, *ca.* 100 B.C. Madras Museum. India Office photograph.

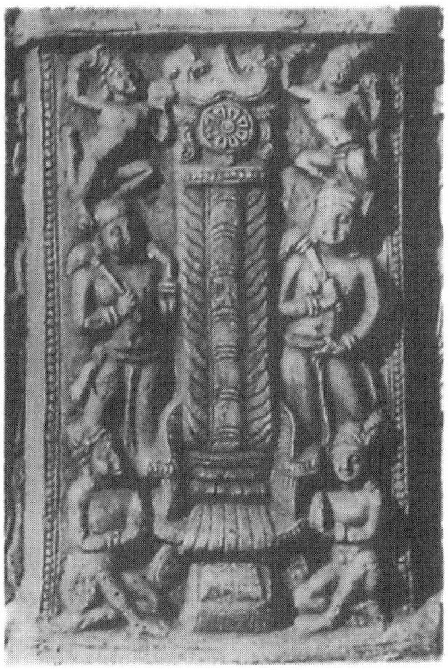
4

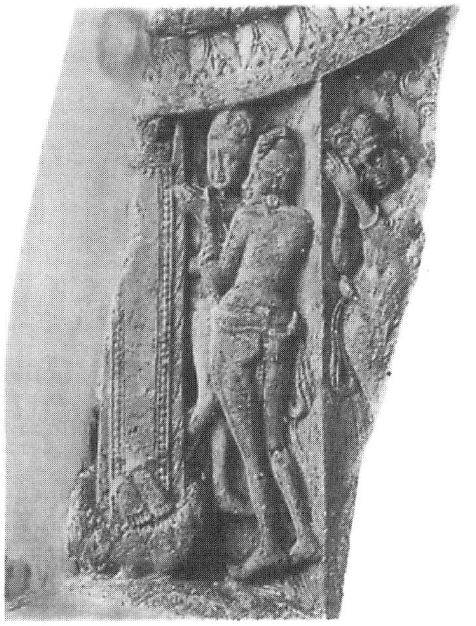
5

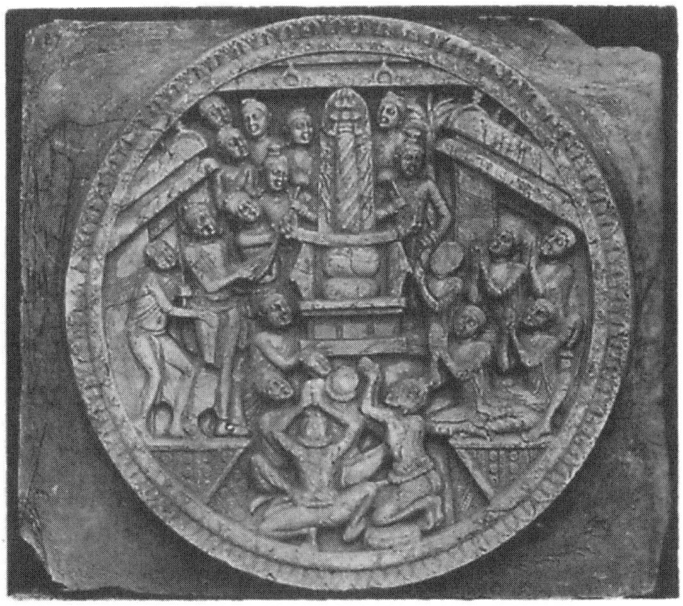
6

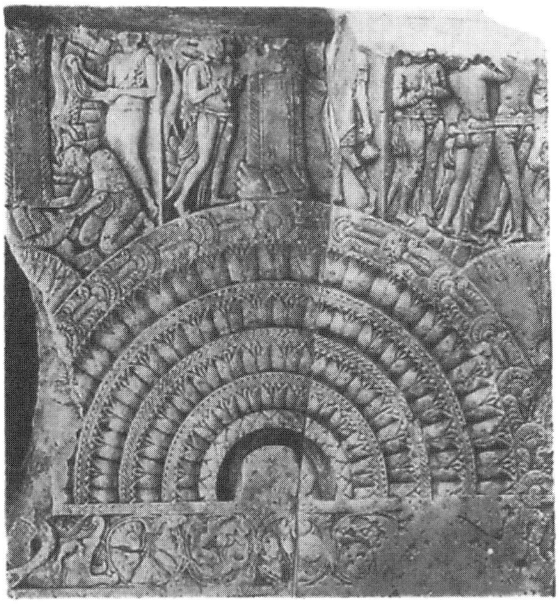
7

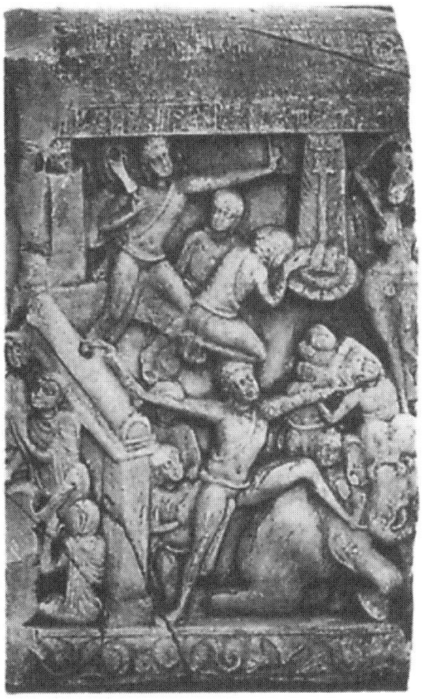
8

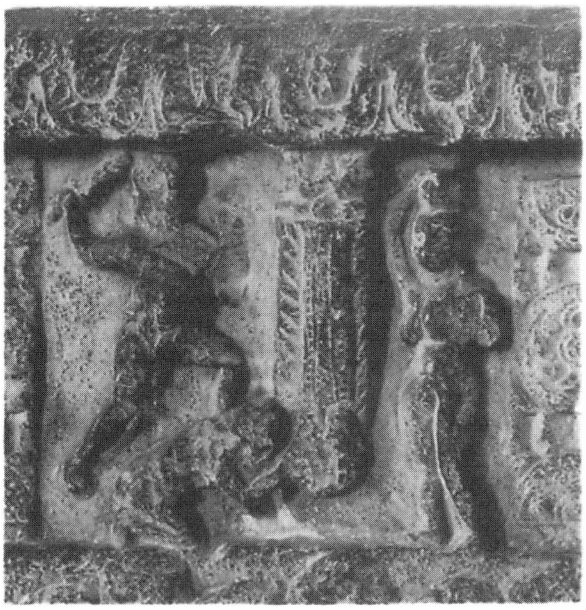
9

PLATE III

FIGURE 10. Above, possibly the same as Figs. 8 and 9; in any case, the Buddha seated with a flaming aura completely surrounding him. Below, Worship of the seated Buddha as a Pillar of Fire (as in Fig. 6), beneath the Bodhi-tree. Amarāvatī, *ca.* 200 A.D. Madras Museum. India Office photograph.

There is some reason to suppose that the Pillar of Fire type is in a special way connected with the Māra Dharṣaṇa and Mahāsambodhi, cf. Burgess, *Buddhist Stūpas of Amarāvatī and Jaggayyapeṭa*, Pl. XXI, Fig. 2, where the Assault of Māra is taking place immediately to the right of the Bodhighara, the Buddha being represented by a throne and Pillar of Fire.

For two other representations of fiery auras or pillars, see *ibid.*, Pl. XXVI, Figs. 1 and 2.

FIGURE 11. Cult of the Bodhi-tree; part of an early enclosing wall (*pākāra*) from Amarāvatī, *ca.* 100 B.C. Madras Museum. India Office photograph.

This representation may not be in fact, but could be regarded as, an illustration of the Kālinga-bodhi Jātaka.

/ FIGURE 12. Cult of the Buddha as Supernal Sun. Amarāvatī, *ca.* 200 A.D., as before.

The pillar is represented as in Fig. 3, abbreviated. Note again the octagonal form of the lower part. The worshippers may be angelic or human.

On the lower right will be seen, as part of another composition not identified, Buddha-pada supported by a lotus like that of Fig. 7.

The paired deer right and left of the throne designate the scene as a representation of the "Final Turning of the Wheel" or "First Sermon."

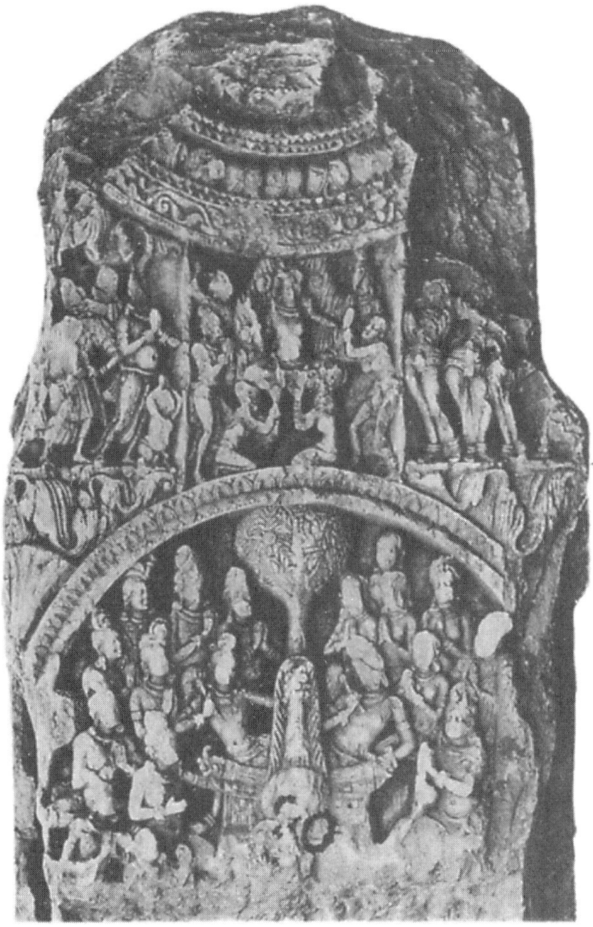

10

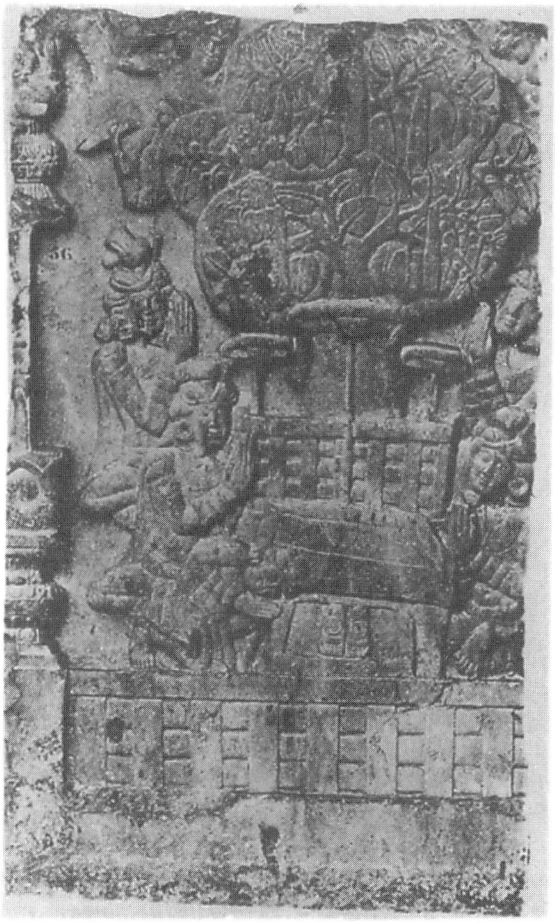

11

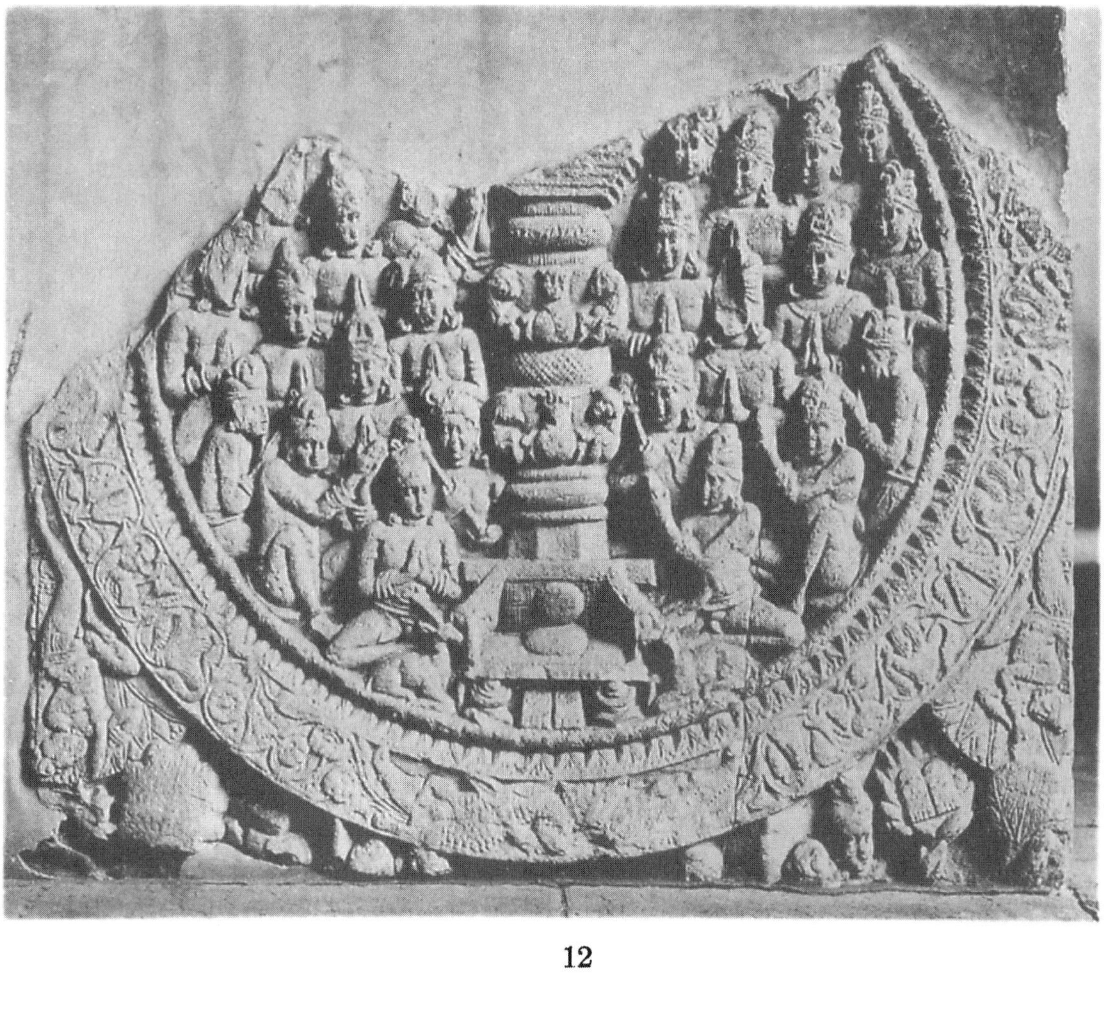

12

PLATE IV

FIGURE 13. Buddha-*pādukā*, with Dharmacakra and other symbols. Amarāvatī, *ca.* 100 B.C. Madras Museum. India Office photograph.

The Dharmacakras are as usual lotus-centred: the number of spokes is evidently intended to be sixty-four in each case. The central symbol on the heel is the same as that within the *triśūla* in Fig. 23, and which I regard as *śrīvatsa* "Notes on Indian Coins and Symbols," *O.Z.*, N.F. IV, 1927/28, p. 183), but which Mr Johnston identifies as *vardhamāna* (*J.R.A.S.*, October, 1931, April, 1932, and July, 1933); it is the "shield" or "nāga" symbol of numismatists. The position of the feet shows that the Buddha is thought of as facing the worshipper, as in Figs. 1, 5, 7, 15, etc.

FIGURE 14. An *āyāgapaṭa*, similar to Fig. 13, but fragmentary and with additional symbols. Amarāvatī, *ca.* 200 A.D. Madras Museum. India Office photograph.

The position of the feet is reversed, and should have been as in Figs. 13, 15, etc.

FIGURE 15. Worship of the Buddha-*pādukā*. Amarāvatī, *ca.* 200 A.D. Madras Museum. India Office photograph.

The *pada* are represented as usual on the footstool of the throne. Behind the throne must have stood a Tree or pillared Wheel.

FIGURE 16. Jaina *āyāgapaṭa*, from the Kankālī Ṭīlā, Mathurā, now J 55 in the Lucknow Museum. Photograph by the Archaeological Survey of India.

Figure of a Jina (Mahāvīra?) in the centre of a fourfold *triśūla*. The symbol occurs again in single form in the lower margin. The "shield" symbol discussed in the description of Fig. 13 occurs in the upper margin. To left a solar pillar supported by a lotus pedestal; to right an elephant pillar of similar type.

See discussion of the symbols in the literature cited under Fig. 13.

FIGURE 17. Lotus birth of the Brahmanical Trinity, Brahmā, Viṣṇu, Śiva. Thaton, Burma, about 8th century. Phayre Museum, Rangoon (?).

The stem of the lotus rises from the navel of the recumbent Nārâyaṇa. More often Brahmā (-Prajāpati) alone is thus represented as lotus-born. Cf. p. 17 and Fig. B. Cf. Temple, "Notes on Antiquities from Ramannadesa," *Ind. Ant.*, 1894, Pls. XIV, XIVa; Ray, *Brahmanical Gods in Burma*, Calcutta, 1932, Pls. 4, 5; my "Stem of Jesse and Indian Parallels or Sources," *Art Bulletin*, XI, 1932; "The Stem of Jesse and Oriental Parrallels," *Parnassus*, January, 1935; and my *Yakṣas*, I and II, Washington, 1928 and 1931.

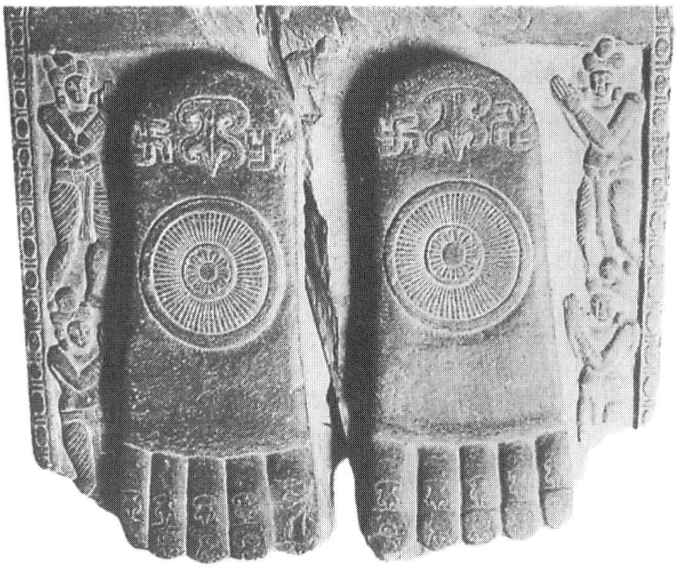

13

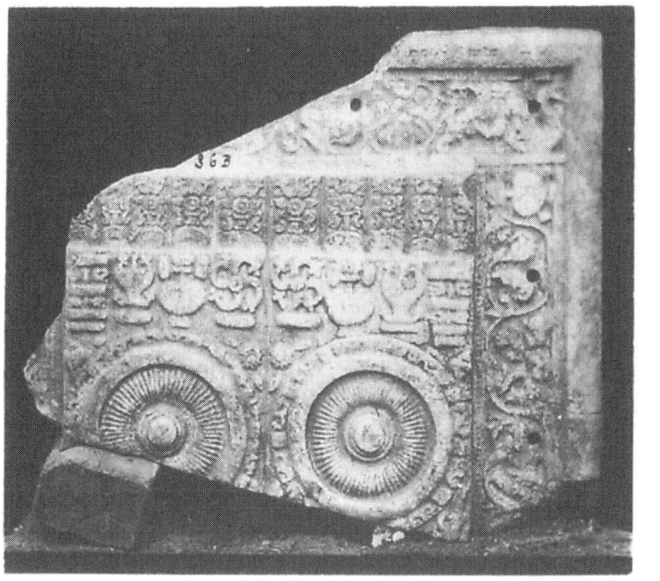

14

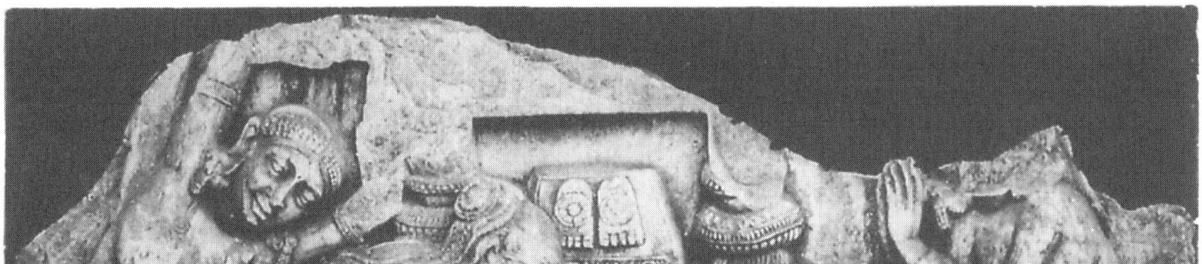

15

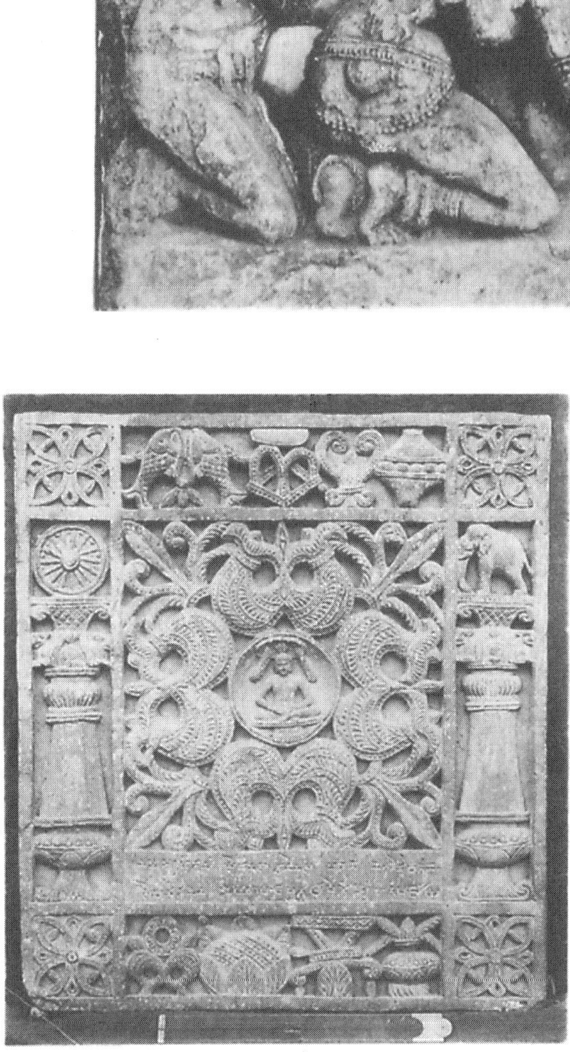

16

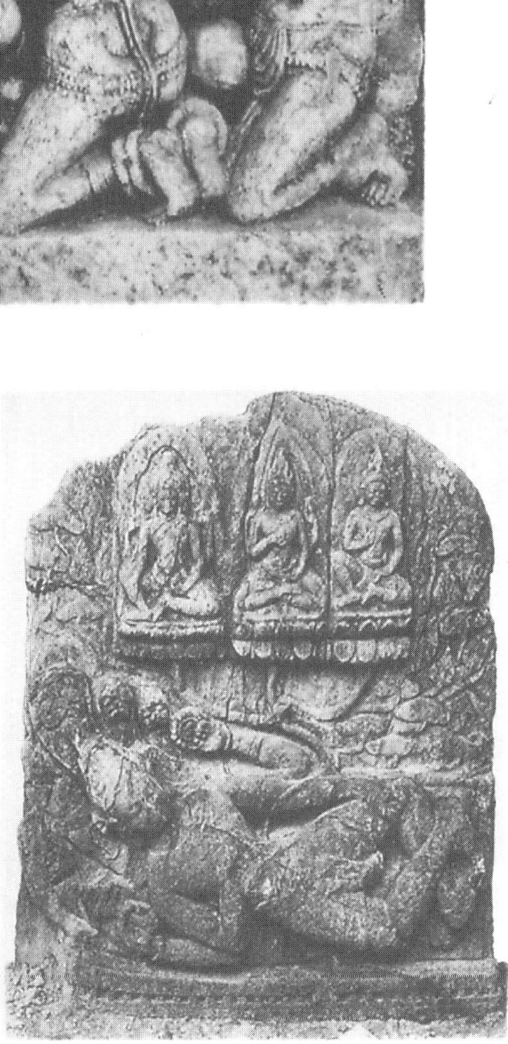

17

PLATE V

FIGURE 18. Cult of the Buddha as Dharmacakra, Principial Wheel, i. e. as Supernal Sun, cf. Figs. 2 and 3. Bharhut, *ca.* 175 B.C. Freer Gallery, Washington. Photo by same.

Above the Wheel is an umbrella of Lordship (as in Fig. 1, above the "head" of the Tree). A heavy floral garland hangs from the nave, which is of lotus form.

FIGURE 19. Cakravartin, surrounded by the Seven Treasures. Part of an early enclosing wall (*pākāra*) from Jaggayyapeṭa, 2nd century B.C. Madras Museum. India Office photograph.

According to the *Mahāsudassana Sutta* (*S.B.E.*, XI, *S.B.B.*, III) and *Lakkhaṇa Suttanta* (*S.B.B.*, IV) the treasures of a Cakravartin consist of a Wheel (*cakra*, explained by one commentator as representing the solar disk), an elephant, horse, light-giving jewel, queen, treasurer, and minister. In the present relief the latter is represented by a boy, evidently the Crown Prince; according to Buddhaghosa, the king's eldest son in fact officiated as *pariṇāyaka*, and the Jaggayyapeṭa relief shows that this was not "a mere putting back into the (Mahāsudassana) Sutta a later idea," as was surmised by Rhys Davids, *S.B.E.*, XI, 259, note 1. That the Emperor's hand is raised to the clouds, from which falls a rain of coins, corresponds to ancient conceptions of Varuṇa and others as givers of wealth; Varuṇa or Agni as *mīḷhuṣa*; Indra's designation as Maghavat; *Ṛg Veda*, X, 19, 7, *rayyā saṁ sṛjantu naḥ*, "pour down wealth upon us"; and later passages in the *Mahābhārata* where Indra is spoken of as "raining gold" on a favorite king, and where Bhīma addresses Yudhiṣṭhira with the words "Thy hand can rain gold"; and even more striking a passage of the *Prabandhacintāmaṇi* (Tawney, p. 76), "O king! when the cloud of your hand had begun its auspicious ascent in the ten quarters of the heavens, and was raining the nectar flood of gold, with the splendor of the trembling golden bracelet flickering like lightning"; cf. also *Buddhacarita*, I, 22, "Like a range of clouds she relieved the people about her from the sufferings of poverty by raining showers of gifts."

This and other representations of the Cakravartin are illustrated and discussed in my "A Royal Gesture, and Some Other Motifs," in *Feestbundel K. Bataviaasch Genootschap van Kunsten en Wetenschapen*, I, 1929. T. N. Ramachandran (in *Papers published by the Rao Sahim G. V. Ramamurthi Pantulu's 70th Birthday Celebration Committee*, which I know only in an offprint) has recently connected the Cakravartin types of Jaggayyapeṭa, Amarāvati, and Goli with the *Māndhātu Jātaka*.

FIGURE 20. Cakravartin, similar to Fig. 18, but later style. Amarāvatī, about 200 A.D. Madras Museum. India Office photograph.

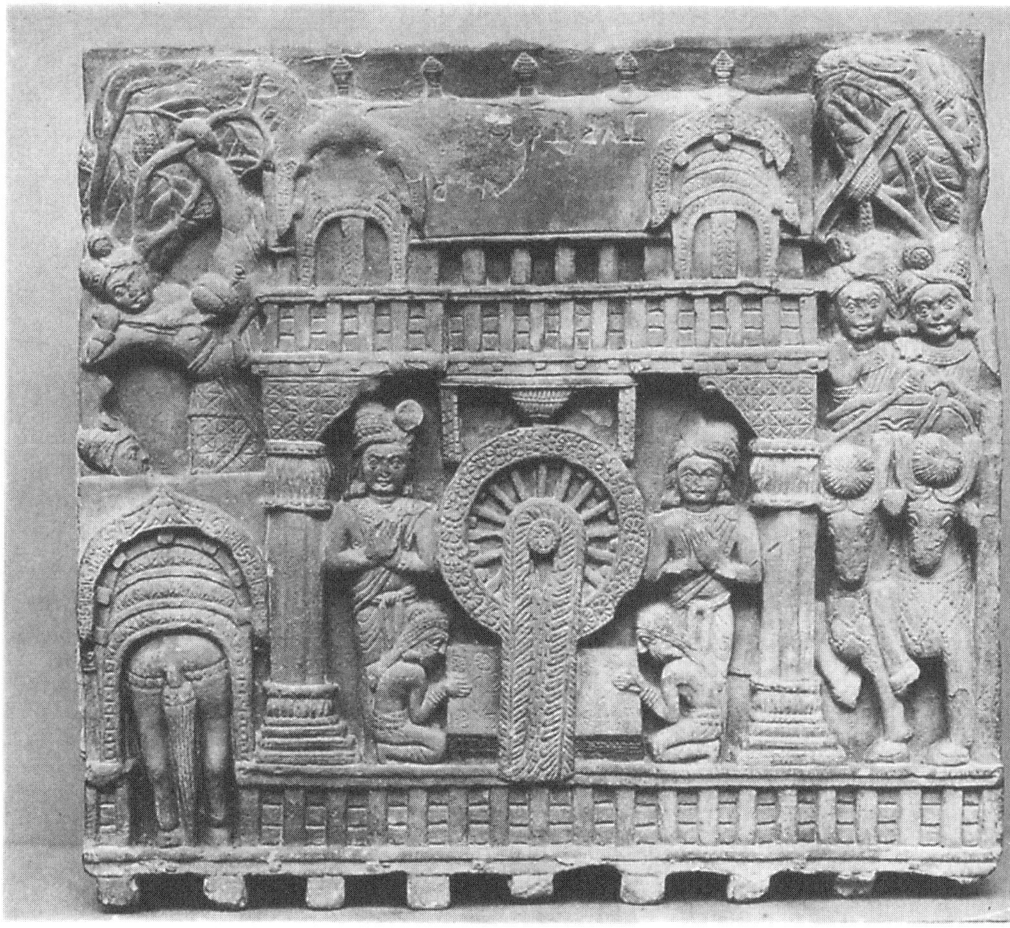

18

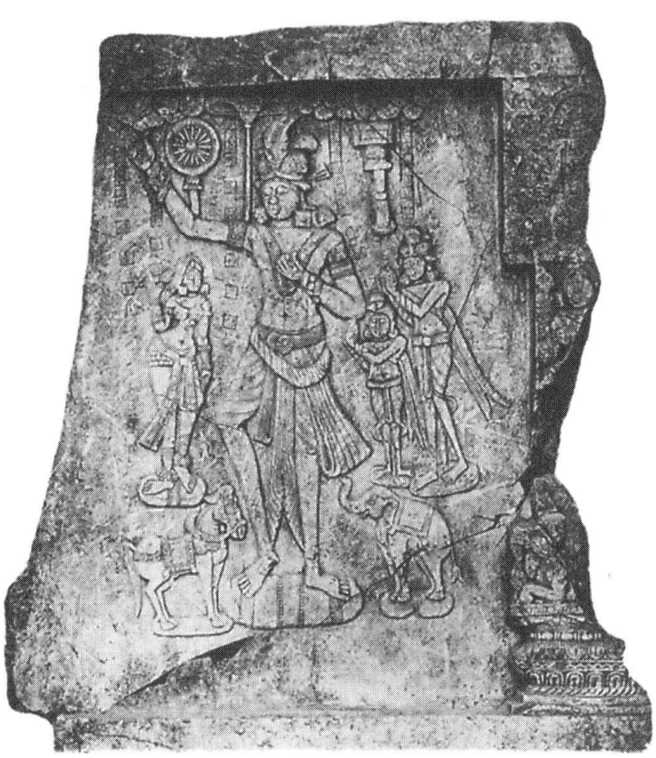

19

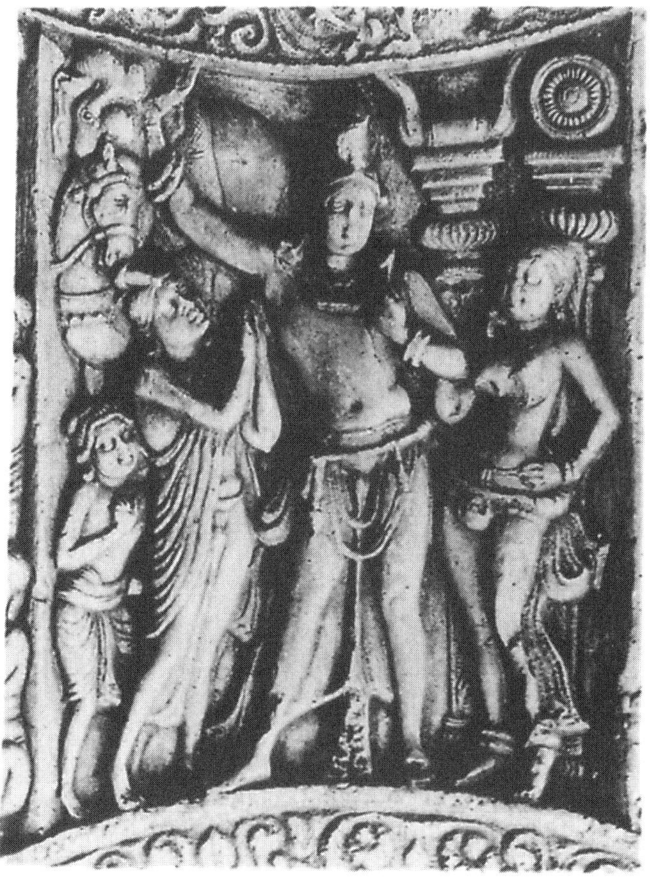

20

PLATE VI

FIGURE 21. Indus Valley seal, *ca.* 3000 B.C. Archaeological Survey of India photograph.

The cult of the deity (Yakṣa?) of the *pippala* (*Ficus religiosa*, the Bodhi-tree of Buddhism) is represented. The deity wears a three-pointed ("*triśūla*"? symbol, cf. the Vedic conception of Agni as Vanaspati, and as latent or nascent in vegetation, etc. Cf. Marshall, *Mohenjodaro*, London (Probsthain), 1931, Pl. XII, Fig. 18, and p. 65 f.

FIGURE 22. Indus Valley sealing, *ca.* 3000 B.C. India Office photograph.

The deity seated cross-legged as in the later iconography is three-faced, and has been identified, probably rightly, with Śiva. He has as before a three-pointed, *triśūla*-like headdress. Cf. Marshall, *Mohenjodaro*, London (Probsthain), 1931, Pl. XII, Fig. 17, and p. 53f.

FIGURE 23. Part of the inner face of the north *toraṇa*, Sāñcī. Early 1st century B.C. India Office photograph.

Above, the *triśūla* symbol as discussed in the text, pp. 13 f. Combined with this is the "shield" symbol discussed under Fig. 13. The supporting column is eight-sided.

Below, the *abhiṣeka* of Śrī-Lakṣmī, here perhaps regarded as Māyā-devī, the Mother of the Buddha, see text, p. 22.

Between, Śrī-Lakṣmī or Māyā-devī represented aniconically by the lotus. On the left, two *yakṣīs* with their trees.

FIGURE 24. Coping detail from Amarāvatī, *ca.* 200 A.D. Madras Museum.

In the bend of the lotus-rhizome is represented the cult of the Dharmacakra, the Buddha as Supernal Sun. Below this is a fourfold *triśūla* or *vajra*; cf. Figs. 16, 18.

FIGURE 25. *Rimbō, dharmacakra*, used in Shingon ritual. Museum of Fine Arts, Boston, No. 22.527.

Lotus centre; eight spokes of the single-*vajra* type.

FIGURE 26. *Kongō-sho, vajra*, used in Shingon ritual. Museum of Fine Arts, Boston, No. 22.509.

The "single" type, *tokkō* at each end.

FIGURE 27. *Kongō-sho, vajra*, used in Shingon ritual. Museum of Fine Arts, Boston, No. 22.510.

The usual "*triśūla*" type, *sankō* at each end.

FIGURE 28. *Katsuma-kongō, karma-vajra*, used in Shingon ritual. Museum of Fine Arts, Boston, No. 22.505.

Cf. Ishida, *A Study on the Excavation of Buddhistic Remains at Nachi*, Tokyo Imperial Household Museum Investigation Series, No. 5, Tokyo, 1927, p. 55.

See also Supplementary Notes, p. 93.

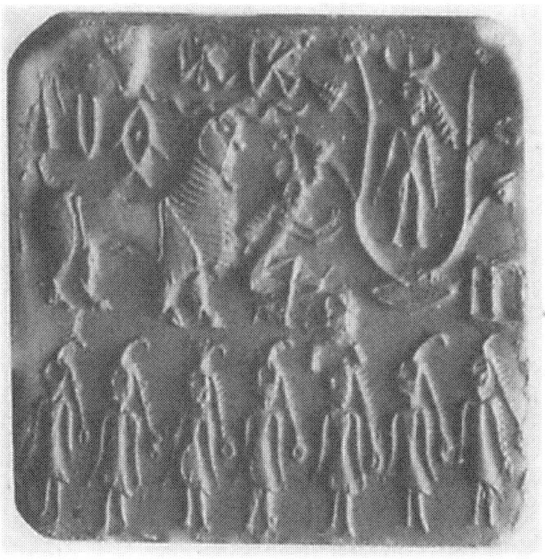

21

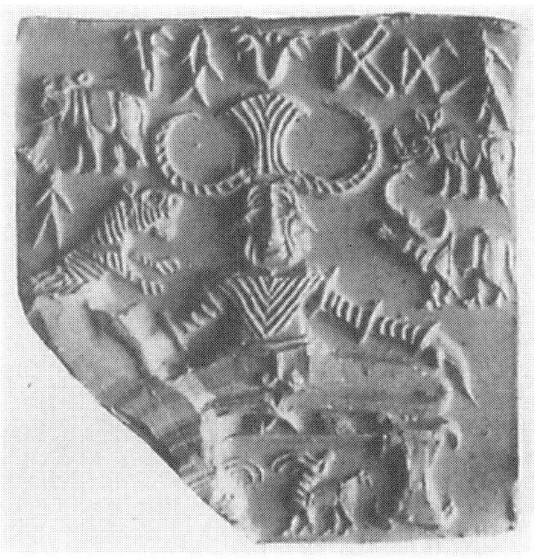

22

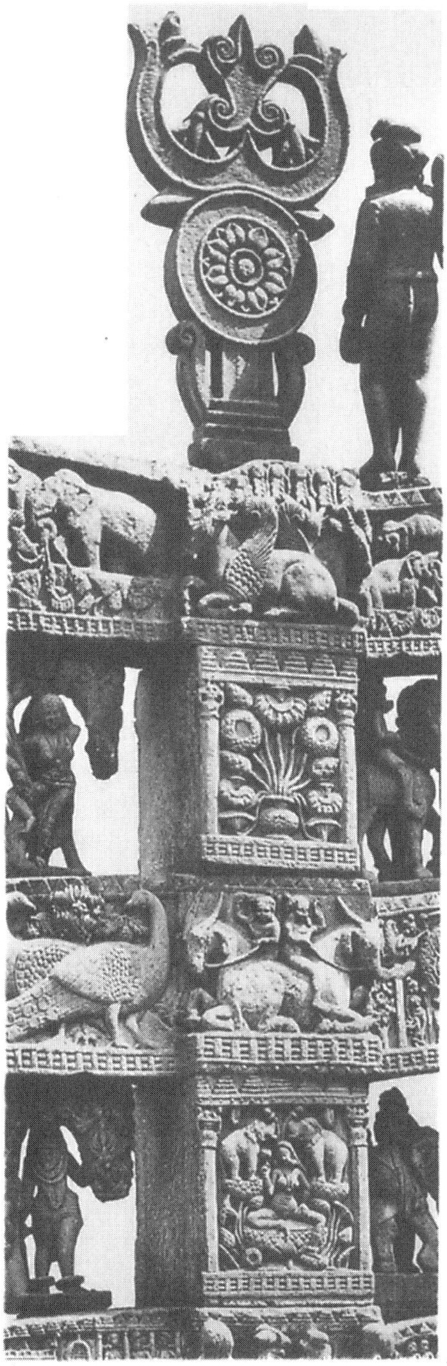

23

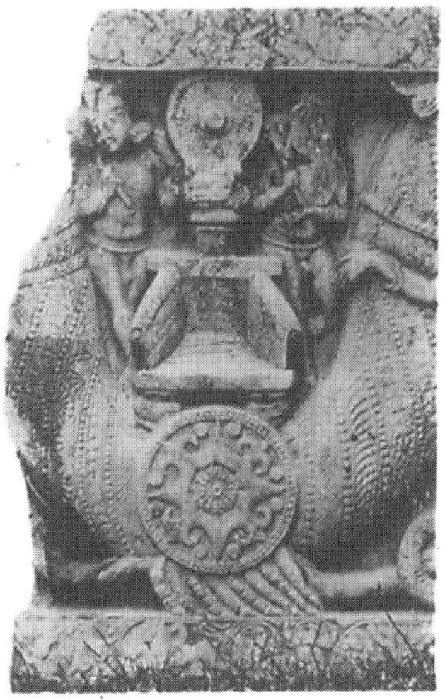

24

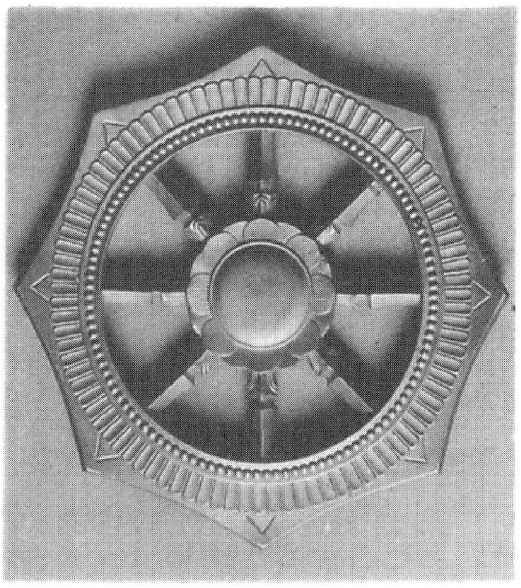

25

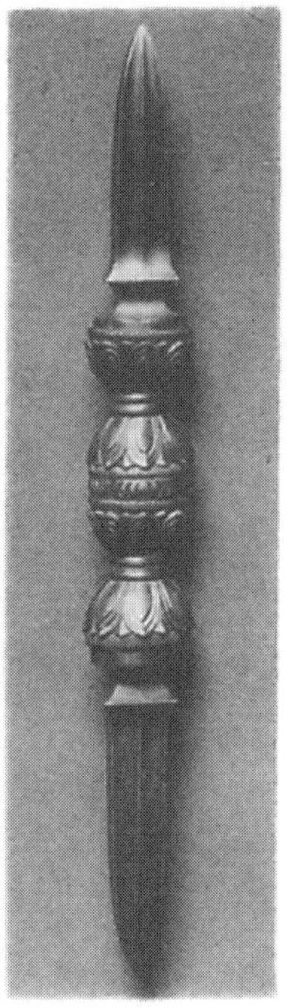

26

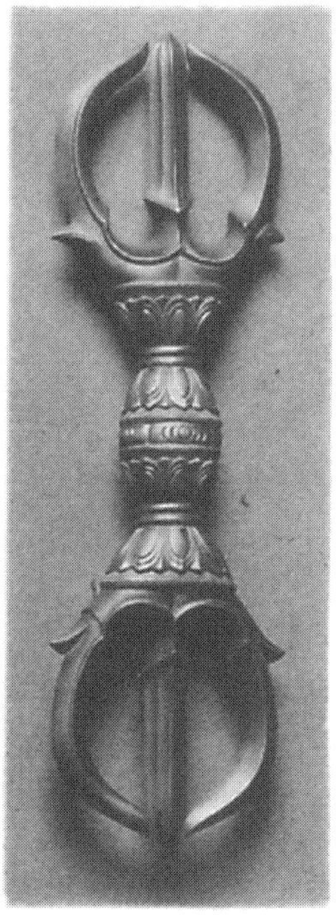

27

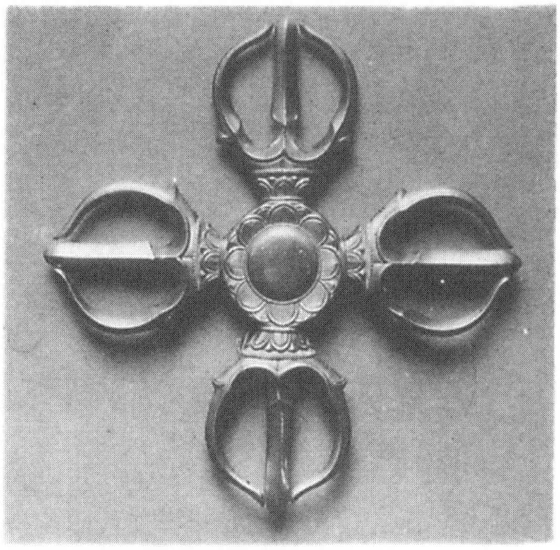

28

PLATE VII

FIGURE 29. The Buddha preaching to Bodhisattvas on Mt Gṛdhrakūṭa. Kārlī, *ca.* 500 A.D. Photograph by Johnston and Hoffman, Calcutta.

See the detailed analysis in the text, pp. 53–54.

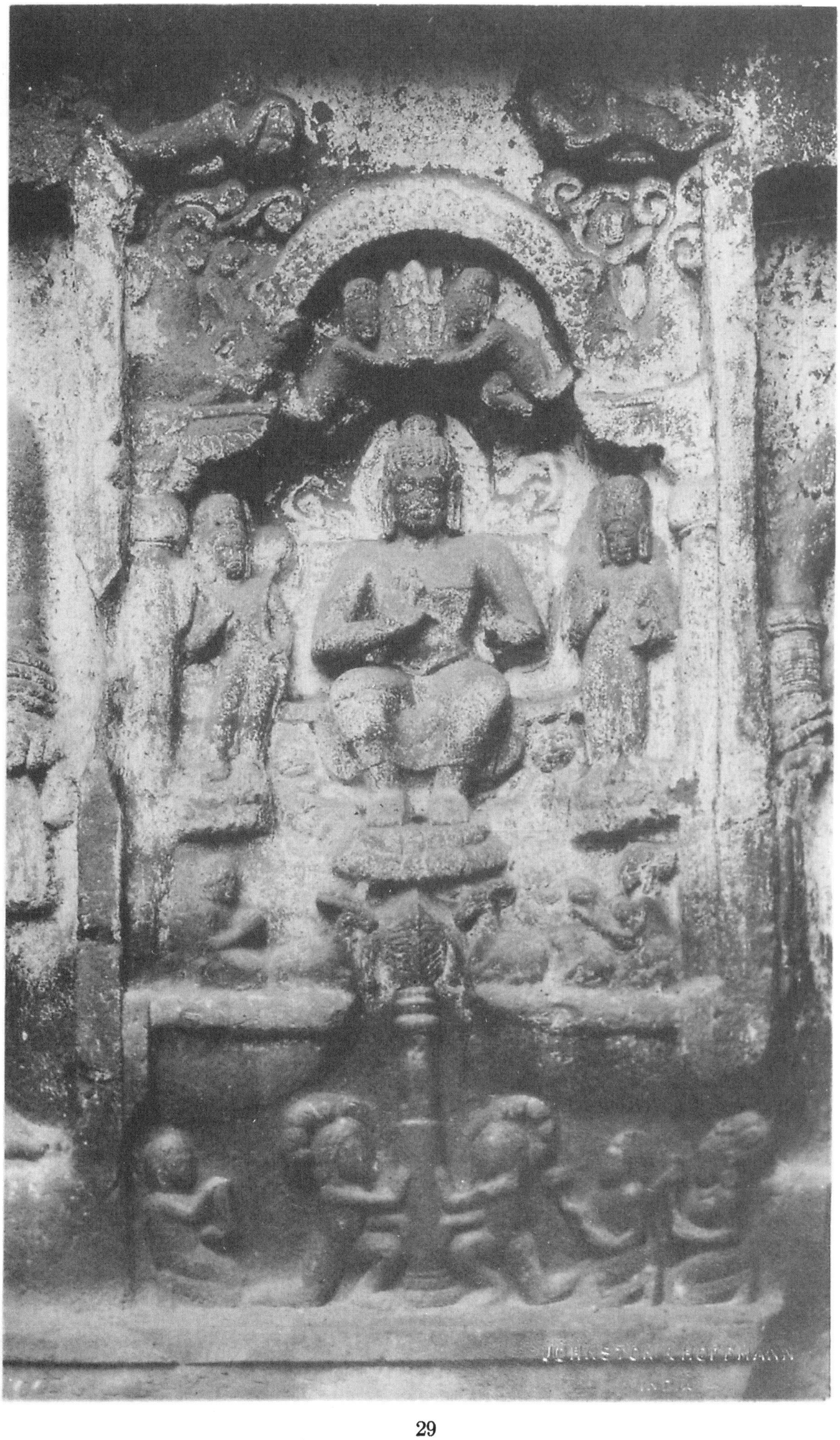

PLATE VIII

FIGURE 30. Hokke Mandara. Bronze, work of the monk Dōmyō, in the year Hakuhō 2, equivalent to A.D. 673. Owned by the Hasedara Monastery, Nara. From a photograph lent by Professor Langdon Warner.

In the middle panel, the Manifestation and Teaching on Mt Gṛdhrakūṭa, as described in the *Saddharma Puṇḍarīka*, Jap. *Hokke-kyo*, Chs. XI and XX. On the left, the Tathāgata, Śākya-muni, in teaching pose (cf. Fig. 29), attended by Ānanda and Rāhula and four Bodhisattvas. In the centre, the stūpa (Jap. *taho-tō*) of Prabhūtaratna ("Then arose a stūpa from the place of the earth (*pṛthivīpradeśāt*) . . . its *chatra*-spire rose up so high as to reach the Four Great Kings; therein exists the very-Self (*ātma-bhāva*) of the Tathāgata (the former Buddha Prabhūtaratna) . . . and according to his solemn vow, the stūpa is opened and shown . . . and there was seen sitting the Tathāgata Prabhūtaratna on his throne . . . and yielded to the Lord Śākya-muni the half of the throne . . . so that both Tathāgatas were seen sitting on the throne within the great Jewel-stūpa . . . (Ch. XI) . . . the Tathāgata, Śākya-muni, and the altogether extinguished (*parinirvṛtta*) Tathāgata Prabhūtaratna, both seated on the lion-throne within the stūpa, smiled at each other, and from their opened mouths gave tongue, so that their tongues extended to the Brahmaloka, and from those two tongues there issued countless myriads of rays, and from each ray countless myriads of Bodhisattvas, of golden body, with the thirty-two particular marks of a Mahāpuruṣa, and seated on lion-thrones in lotus-calices . . . who, stationed in every quarter, preached the Law (*dharma*) . . . so that every existence in every Buddha-field heard that voice from the sky . . . (Ch. XX)").

On the right, in all respects a replica of the Buddha Śākya-muni, except as regards the costume and throne, is seated the Bodhisattva Maitreya, who is the principal speaker on behalf of the assembled Bodhisattvas, and in response to whom the Buddha utters the all-important fifteenth Chapter of the text.

It will be seen that the stūpa, which "rises from the earth," is accordingly represented as supported by a lotus, combined with which are the four "adamantine lions" (*kongō shishi*) mentioned in the inscription.

On the lowest level, representing the terrestrial plane (and corresponding to the lower level in Fig. 29), are placed only the dedicatory inscription and the figures of the guardian Yakṣas (*niō*).

See also Supplementary Notes, p. 94.

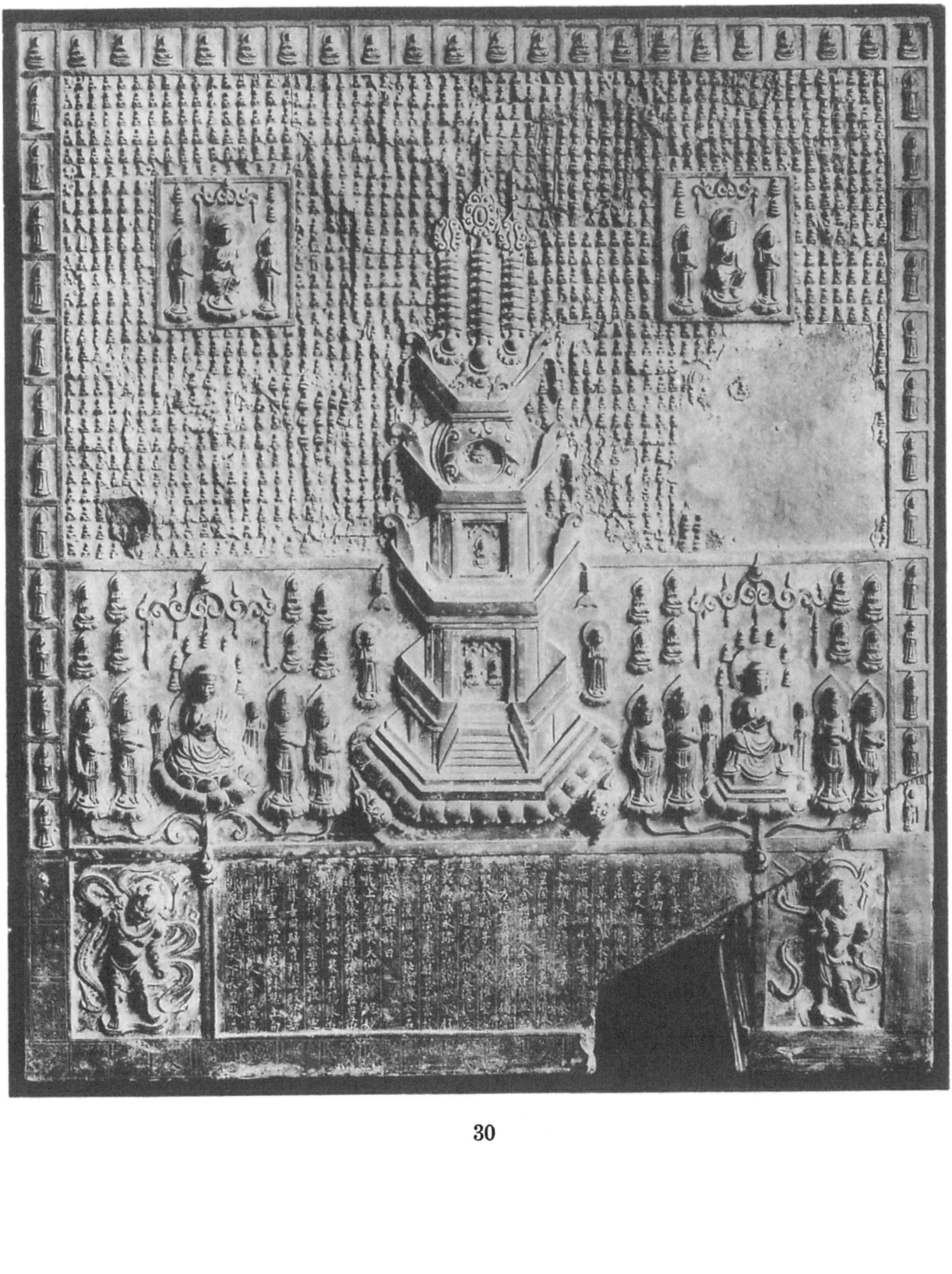

PLATE IX

FIGURE 31. Taizō-hō mandara, Garbha-kośa (-dhātu) maṇḍala, central portion. Japanese original in the Tōji Monastery, Kyotō. After Ōmura Seigai, *Sanbon Ryōbu Mandara*, Tokyō, I, 1913.

This Japanese original, painted in A.D. 1693, is the third copy of the Chinese original brought to Japan by Kōbō Daishi in A.D. 806, the first and second copies having been made in 1195 and 1292.

The Persons (Hypostases) are as follows:

	Hoshō Nyorai (Ratnaketu Tathāgata)	
Miroku Bosatsu (Maitreya Bodhisattva)		Fugen Bosatsu (Samantabhadra Bodhisattva)
Tenkoraion Nyorai (Divyaduṇḍubhimegha-nirghoṣa Tathāgata)	Birushana Nyorai (Vairocana Tathāgata)	Kaifukeō Nyorai (Saṁkusumita-rāja Tathāgata)
Kwanjizai Bosatsu (Avalokitêśvara Bodhisattva)		Monjushiri Bosatsu (Mañjuśrī Bodhisattva)
	Muryoju Nyorai (Amitâyus Tathāgata)	

The Buddhas occupy the centre and four petals of the lotus, Bodhisattvas the four remaining petals. Vairocana is the primordial (Ādi-) Buddha identified with the Supernal Sun; the four other Dhyāni Buddhas represented being those of the four quarters, the orientation in the diagram being

	East	
South		North
	West	

The exact equivalent of the *maṇḍala* as here illustrated may be seen in the Shuji (seed-letter) form in the central field of Fig. 32.

A *maṇḍala* in all respects like that of Fig. 31 is reproduced by Getty, *Gods of Northern Buddhism* (2nd ed.), Pl. XVI. A corresponding representation of Vairocana (as Ichijikinrin) in Vajra-dhātu form, No. 09.387 in the Museum of Fine Arts, Boston, is reproduced by Anesaki, *Buddhist Art* (1st ed.), Pl. XIV. Here "the fingers of the right hand clasp the forefinger of the left . . . the gesture symbolises the unity of the cosmic and the individual souls in the final spiritual enlightenment" (*ibid.*, pp. 34, 35 [1]), whereas in the Garbha-dhātu form the two hands hold the Dharmacakra, implying their distinction on the plane of operation.

In the original, panels immediately above and below the central area here reproduced contain each five representations, as follows, reading from left to right:

Above, Shishigute-butsumoson (Cuṇḍā-bhagavatī, Saptakoṭi-buddha-mātṛ), Butsugen-butsuno (Buddha-locana), Issai Nyoraichi-in (Sarvatathāgata-jñāna-mudrā), Daiyūmō Bosatsu (Mahāvīra), Daianrakufukūshinjitsu (Vajrâmogha-samayasattva, Mahāsukhâmogha-vajrasattva), also smaller figures above the central symbol, viz. on the left Kaya-kasho (Gayā Kāśyapa), and on the right Urubinra-kasho (Uruvilva Kāśyapa). Below, Shosanzeson (Trailokya-vajra), Daiitokuson (Yamântaka), Hannya-haramitsu (Prajñapāramitā), Gōsangeson (Vajra-hūṁkara), and Fudōsan (Acalanātha).

See also Supplementary Notes, p. 95.

[1] Cf. "Si-do-in-dzou, gestes de l'officiant dans les cérémonies mystiques des sectes Tendai et Shingon," *Annales du Musée Guimet*, VIII.

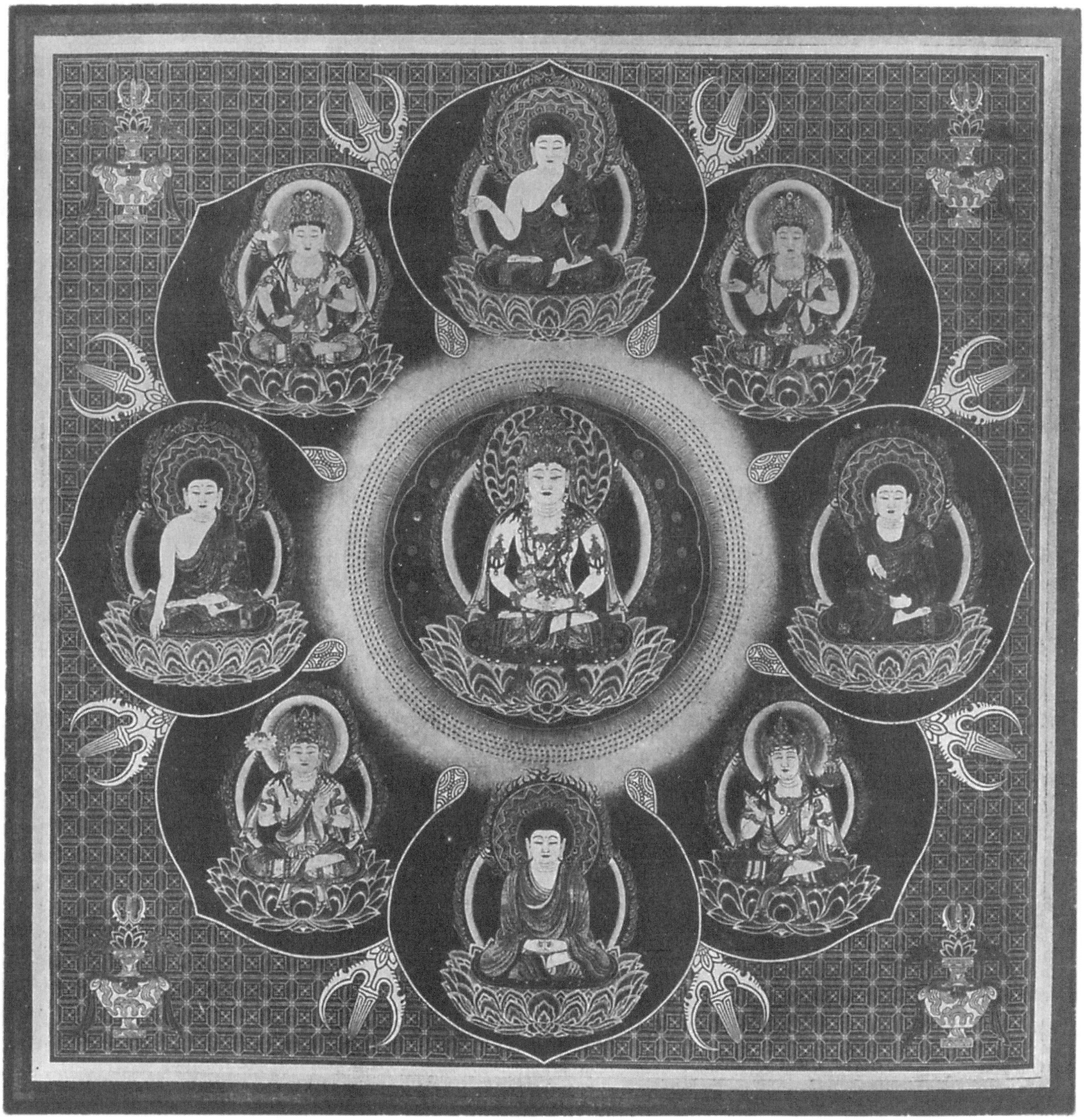

PLATE X

Ryōbu mandara, viz. the Garbha-kośa-dhātu and Vajra-dhātu maṇḍalas represented as Shuji ("seed-letter") mandaras. "Diagrammatic representations in which Sanskrit letters are substituted for figures of the deities in the two Cycles. These letters, called *Shuji* (Sanskrit, Bīja) or seed, are regarded as efficacious symbols of the *Shingon* deities" (Anesaki, *Buddhist Art*, Pl. XVI). Japanese, late 17th century. Museum of Fine Arts, Boston, Nos. 11.7114 and 7113. The latter bears the signature "Siddha (characters) written by Kwaien in his latter years," Kwaien being *alias* the Shingon monk Chōzen, who was famous for his workmanship in this kind.

FIGURE 32. Garbha-kośa-dhātu *maṇḍala,* in which the *tattvas* (Quiddities or Principles) are shown in their sensibly manifested forms. The central field corresponds to the whole area shown in Figs. 30 and 33. Vairocana is represented by the syllable (seed-letter) "AḤ:" with which may be compared a representation (Fig. 40) of Vairocana by the syllable A upon a lotus throne, supported by a *vajra* "stem," which rests in turn upon a lower lotus.

FIGURE 33. Vajra-dhātu *maṇḍala,* in which the *tattvas* (Quiddities or Principles) are shown in intellectually manifested forms. Here Vairocana is represented by the syllable (seed-letter) "VAṀ."

Compare the great density of the elements of order represented in this figure with the notion *prajñāna-ghana* in *Bṛhadāraṇyaka Up.*, IV, 5, 13, and *Māṇḍūkya Up.*, 5.

On Shingon symbolism see also Getty, *Gods of Northern Buddhism* (2nd ed.), 1928, pp. 28 ff., and under *trikoṇa* and *vajra* in Index. In Anesaki, *Buddhist Art* (1st ed.), 1915, Pl. XVI, reproducing our Figs. 32, 33, the relative positions of the *mandaras* on the Plate are reversed.

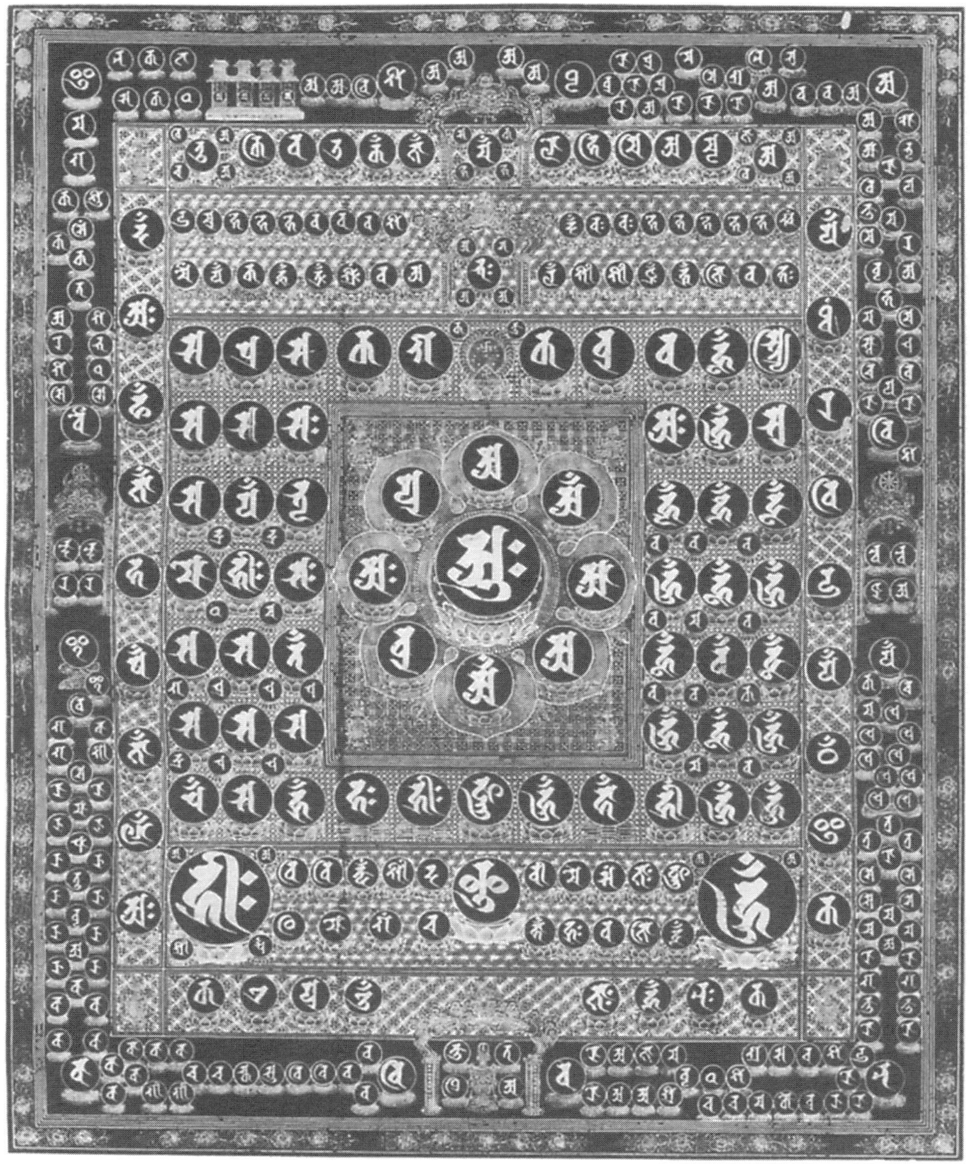

32

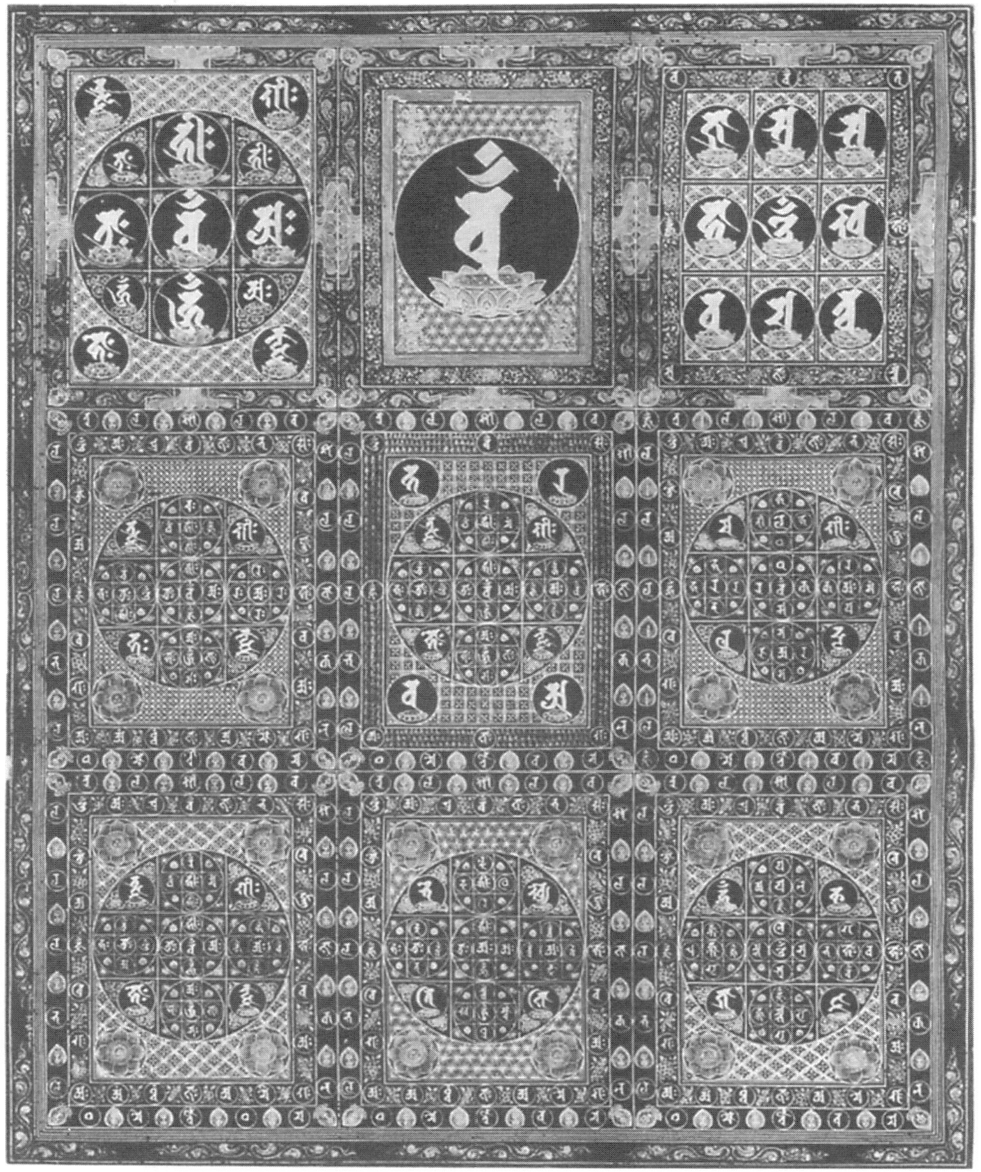

33

PLATE XI

FIGURE 34. The Buddha (Amida, Amitâbha), accompanied by the Bodhisattvas, Padmapāṇi on the proper right, Mahāsthāmaprâpta on the proper left. Amida Trinity of Tachibana Fujin. Japanese, early 8th century. Owned by the Hōryuji Monastery, Nara. From photographs lent by Professor Langdon Warner.

Each member of the Triad is supported by a lotus, the stems of the flowers rising from the rippled waters which form the horizontal base of the shrine.

FIGURE 35. The Waters, from which rise the stems of the lotus-thrones supporting the Trinity, as shown in Fig. 34.

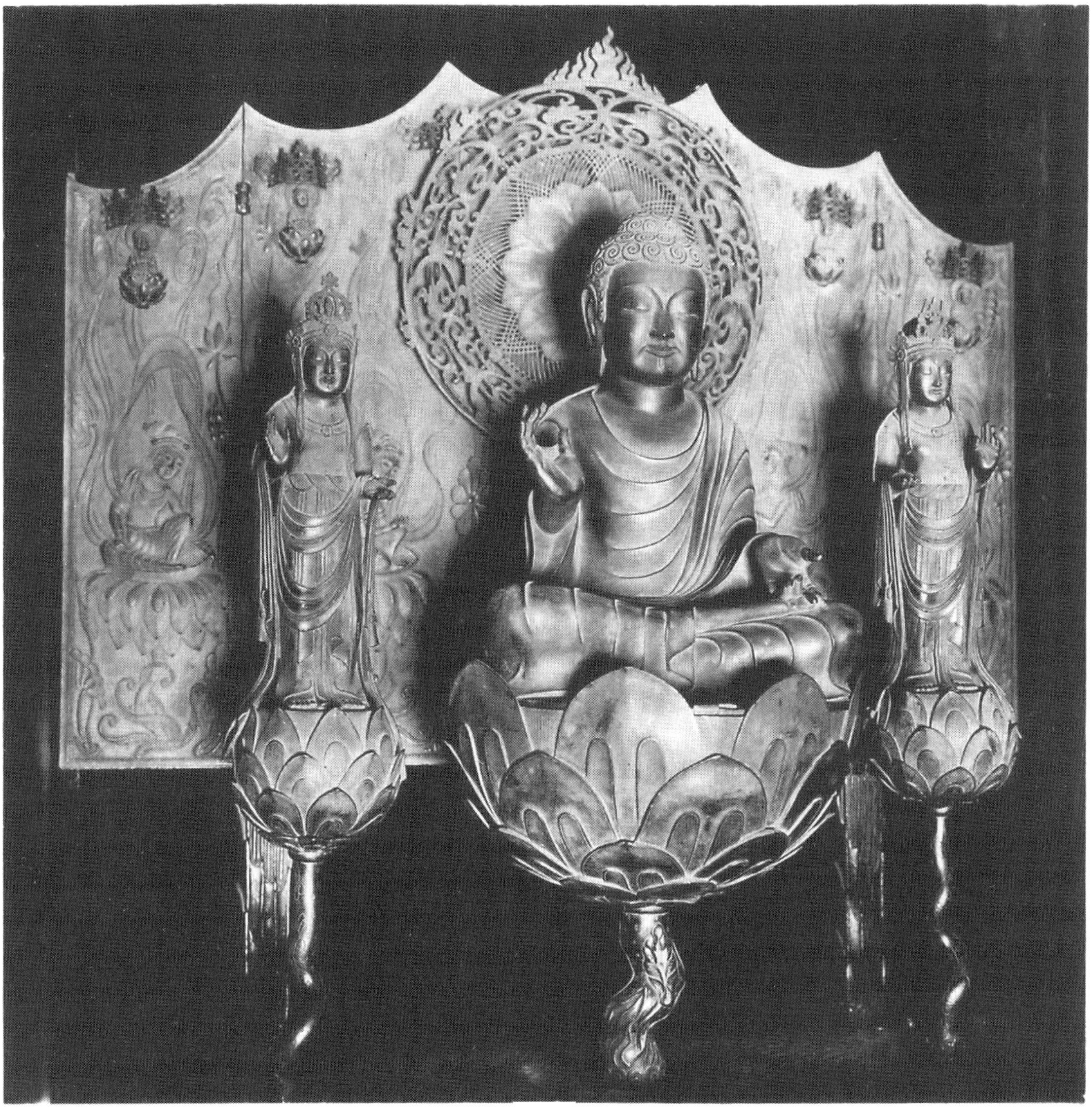

34

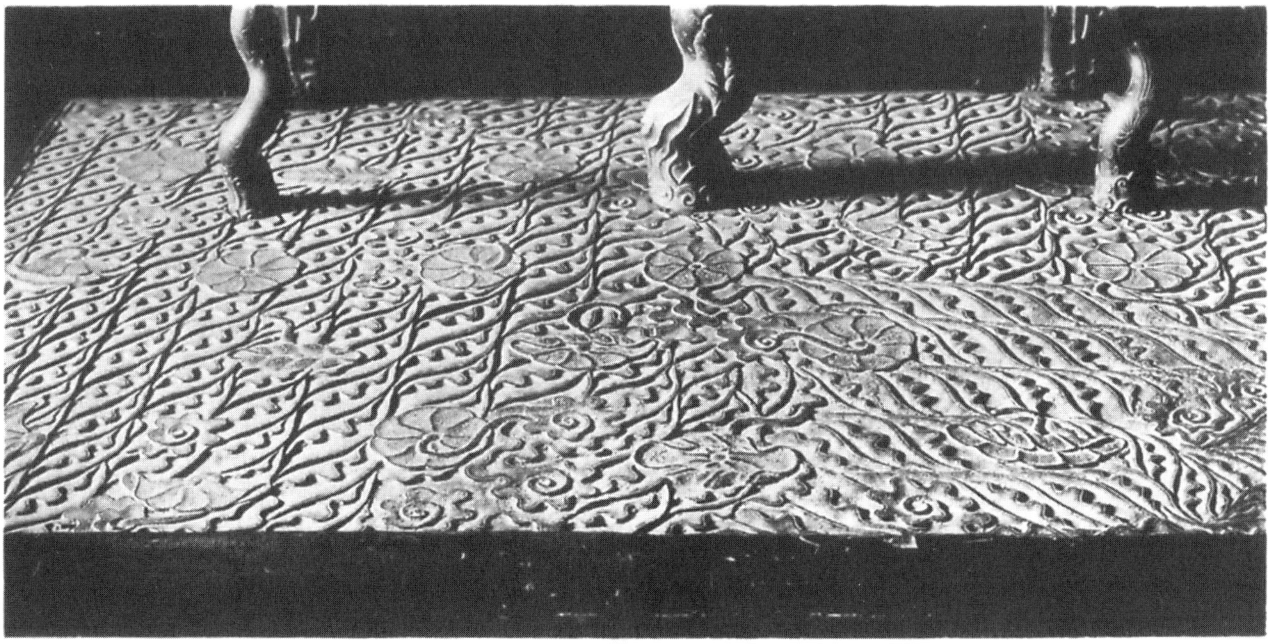

35

PLATE XII

FIGURE 36. Reredos of the Amida Trinity, Figs. 34, 35. From a photograph lent by Professor Langdon Warner.

The nimbus is represented with a central lotus, of which the supporting lotus must be regarded as a reflection in the Nether Waters.

FIGURE 37. The Buddha preaching to Bodhisattvas on Mt Gṛdhrakūṭa; or perhaps, more exactly, Amida, attended by the Bodhisattvas Padmapāṇi (?) and Maitreya. Chinese, A.D. 678. Collection of the Marquis Osokawa. After Ōmura Seigai, *Shina Bijutsushi Chosohen*, Tokyo, 1915, Pl. 777.

Double lotus-throne, the lower flower with lions, forming the usual lotus- and lion-throne.

FIGURE 38. Above, the Buddha preaching to Bodhisattvas on Mt Gṛdhrakūṭa; below, the monastic manifestation on the earth-plane.

The Buddha is represented as teaching on two "levels," cf. Fig. 29. The supporting lotus and its stem forms a kind of "Jesse Tree." The feet of the Buddha at the lower level are supported by two separate lotus flowers.

A monument in the Wu Ting Village, China, A.D. 678. After Ōmura Seigai, *ut supra*, Pl. 778.

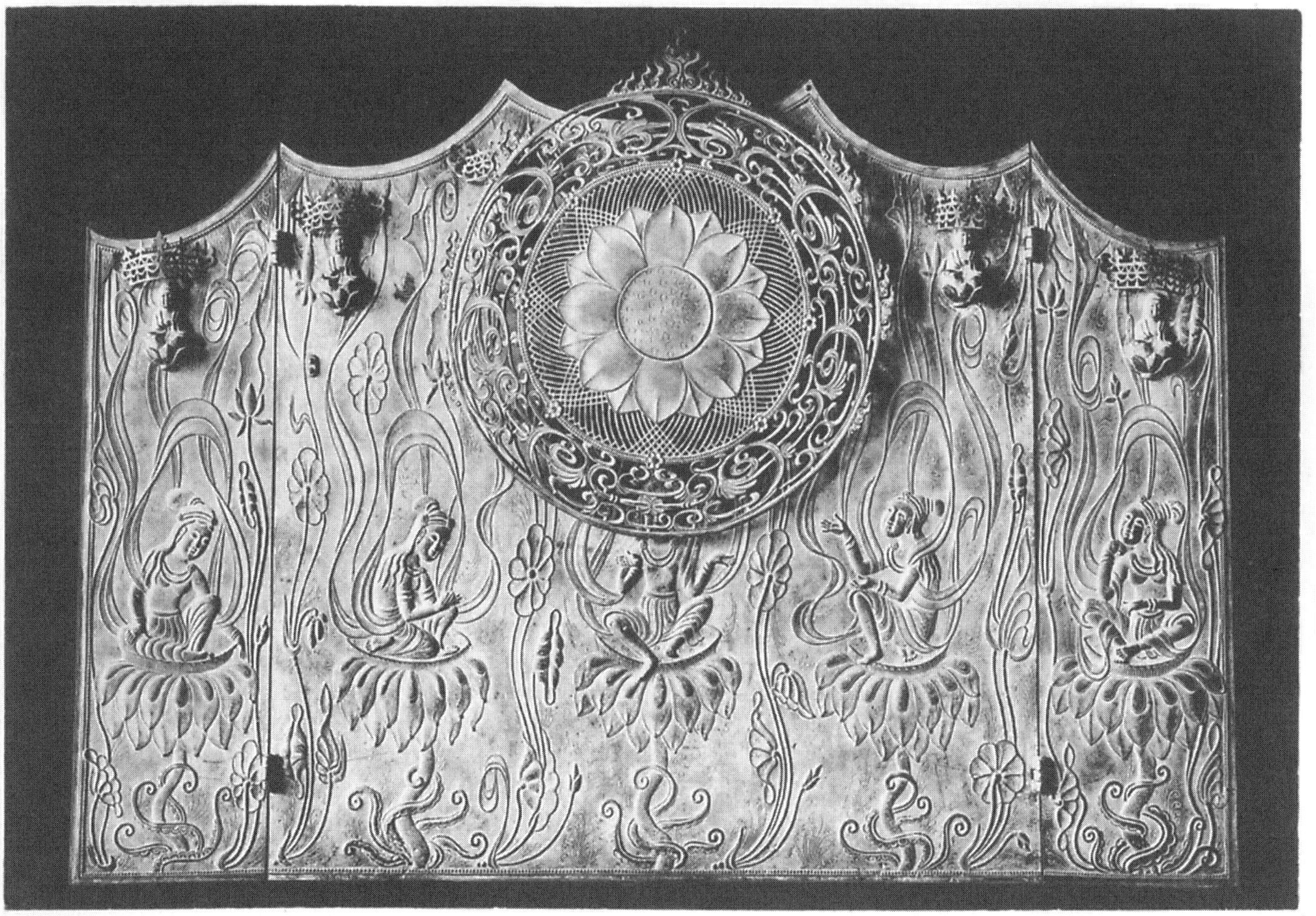

36

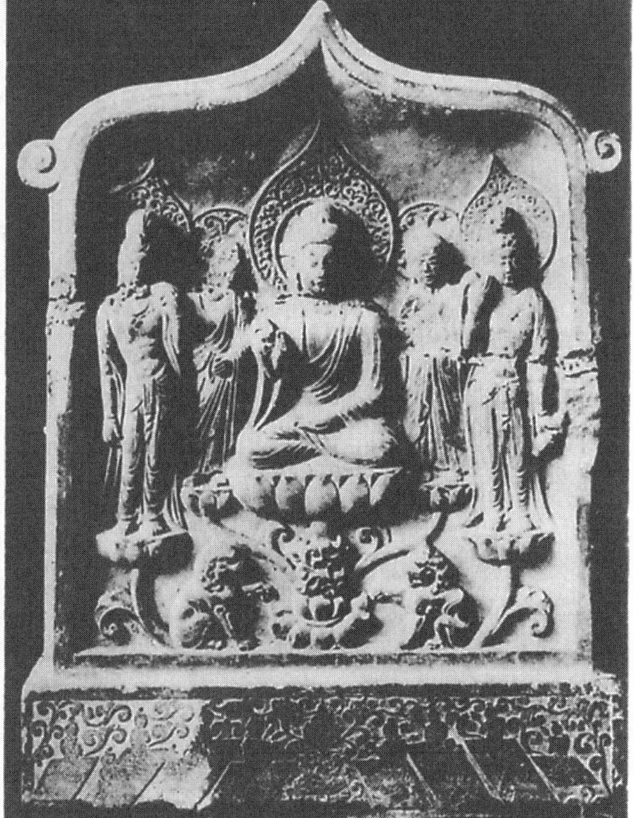

37

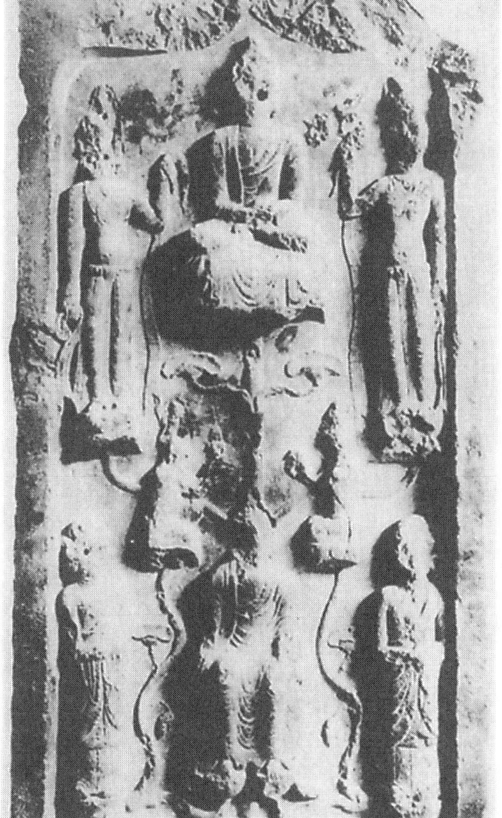

38

PLATE XIII

FIGURE 39. The Bodhisattva Mañjuśrī. Japanese, 14th century. Museum of Fine Arts, Boston, No. 17.748.

The Angel of Wisdom. He holds in his right hand the flaming sword of Understanding (with a *vajra*-handle), and in his left a lotus spray, the flower supporting a book (*Saddharma Puṇḍarīka*), upon which stands erect a flaming *vajra*, cf. Fig. H.

FIGURE 40. Garbha-dhātu form of Vairocana. Japanese, early 15th century. Museum of Fine Arts, Boston, No. 11.6296.

Vairocana is represented by the seed-letter A, supported by an encircled lotus (of the Primordial Waters), above a second lotus (of the Upper Waters), separated by an erect *vajra* (Axis of the Universe), which rests upon a third lotus (of the Nether Waters). Cf. description of Fig. 32.

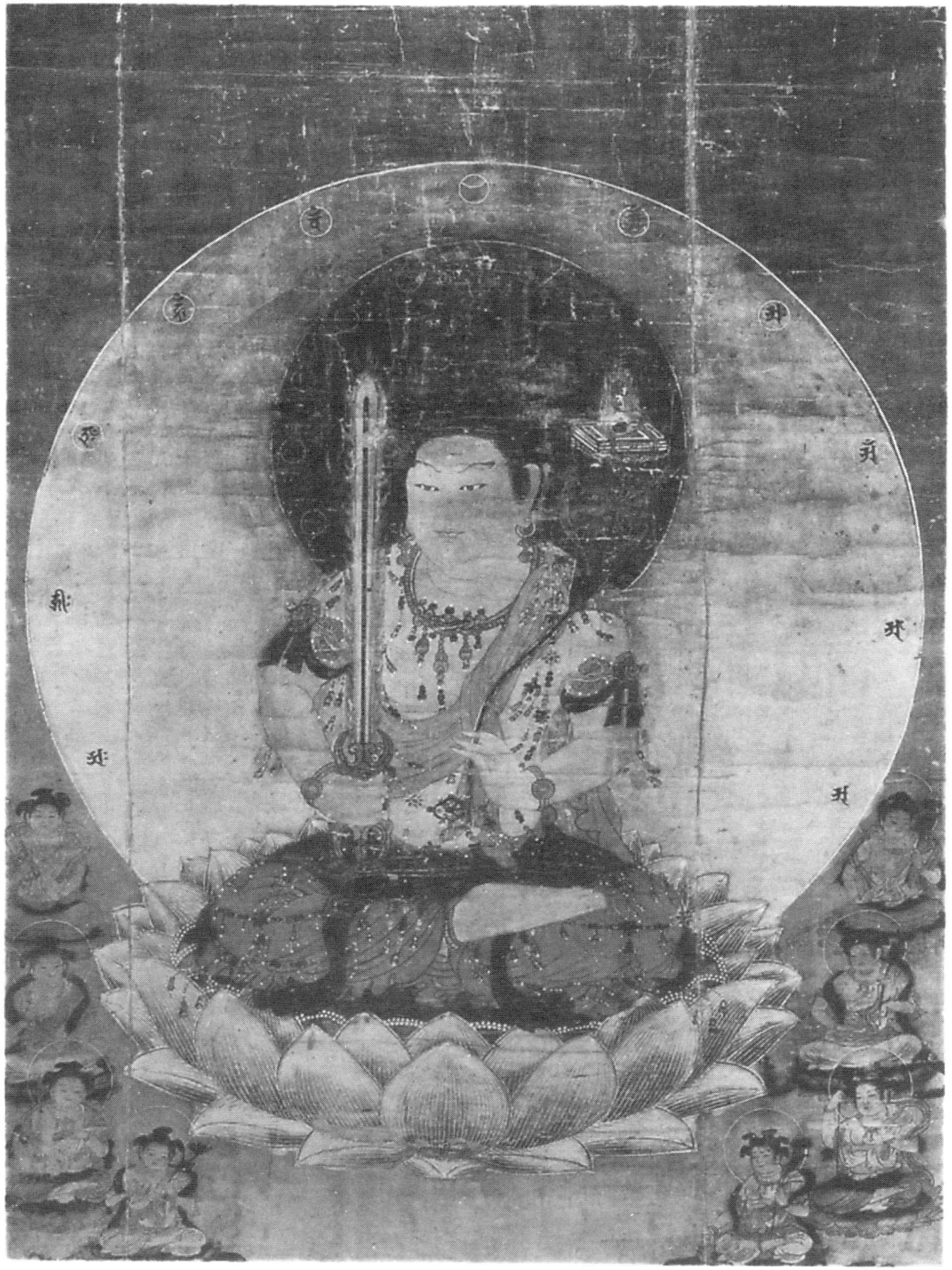

39

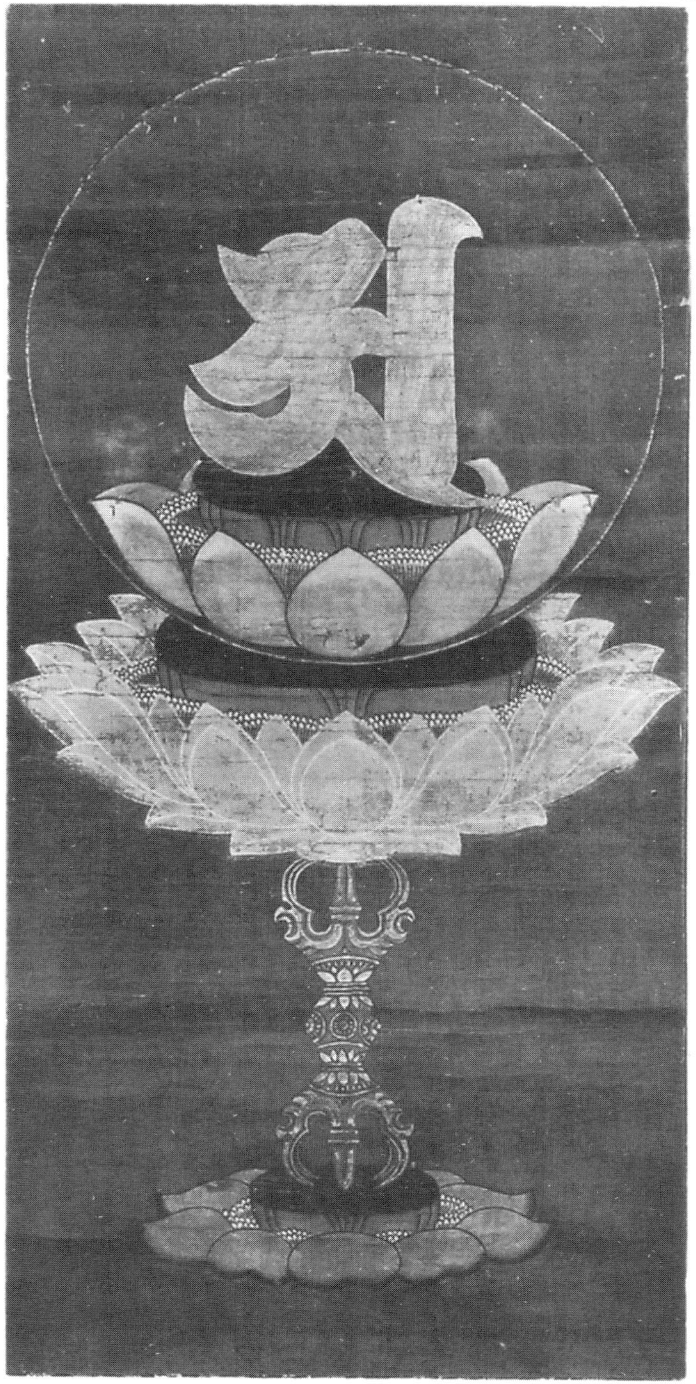

40

PLATE XIV

FIGURE 41. Front face of the pedestal of the Yakushi (Bhaiṣajyaguru Vaidūrya) Trinity. Japanese, dedicated in A.D. 697. Yakushiji ~~Monastery~~, ~~Nara; kept in the Kondo~~, Nara. See text, pp. 54–55.

FIGURE 42. Fukū-Kenjaku, Amoghapāśa, a form of Padmapāṇi (Avalokitêśvara) chiefly in Tendai usage. Japanese, probably Kamakura. Kanchi-in Temple, Kyotō. Photo by Institute of Art Research, Tokyō.

The Bodhisattva is eight-armed, the lower (normal) hands in *namaḥkāra* position, second right and left holding a rod (*daṇḍa*) and noose (*pāśa*), third right and left in *varada mudrā*, upper right holding the staff (*khakkara*, Jap. *shakujō*) with six rings. A standing Dhyāni Buddha in the crown. The central ornament of the *channavīra* is a Dharmacakra (Jap. *rimbō*) which rests immediately over the navel (cf. *Śatapatha Brāhmaṇa*, V, 7, 1, 9, and *Hiraṇyakeśin Gṛhya Sūtra*, I, 6, 24, 1, as cited in my *Yakṣas*, II, 24). The lotus-seat is supported by an eight-sided column or axis, with eight protuberances, which axis rises from a pedestal representing four earth-planes. In the Zenith hangs the Supernal Sun (Amitâbha), of which the lotus-seat is the reflection, *ābhāsa*.

The form of the shaft should be compared with that of the Axis of the Universe (*vajra*) represented in Figs. 2, 3, 12, 40, 41, E.

FIGURE 43. Śiva-liṅgam. 1st or 2nd century B.C. In *pūjā*, Guḍimallam, Indra. Photograph by the Archaeological Survey of India.

Another "Axis" type. The Atlant Yakṣa may be compared with the supporting Yakṣa of Fig. 41.

Cf. Rao, *Elements of Indian Iconography*, Pt. I, Vol. II, 65–69, and my *History*, p. 68. For the Paraśurāmêśvara temple, in which, where the liṅgam is in *pūjā*, see *Indian Antiquary*, XL, 1911, 104–114, and *Mem. A.S.I.*, No. 40, p. 24, and for the dating, my note in *I.H.Q.*, VII, 750 (830).

For other Indian examples of the Yakṣa type, see Burgess, *Stūpa of Bharhut*, Pl. XXII, Fig. 1, and Vogel, "La sculpture de Mathurā," *Ars Asiatica*, XV, Pl. XVII, Fig. b. See also above, pp. 54–55.

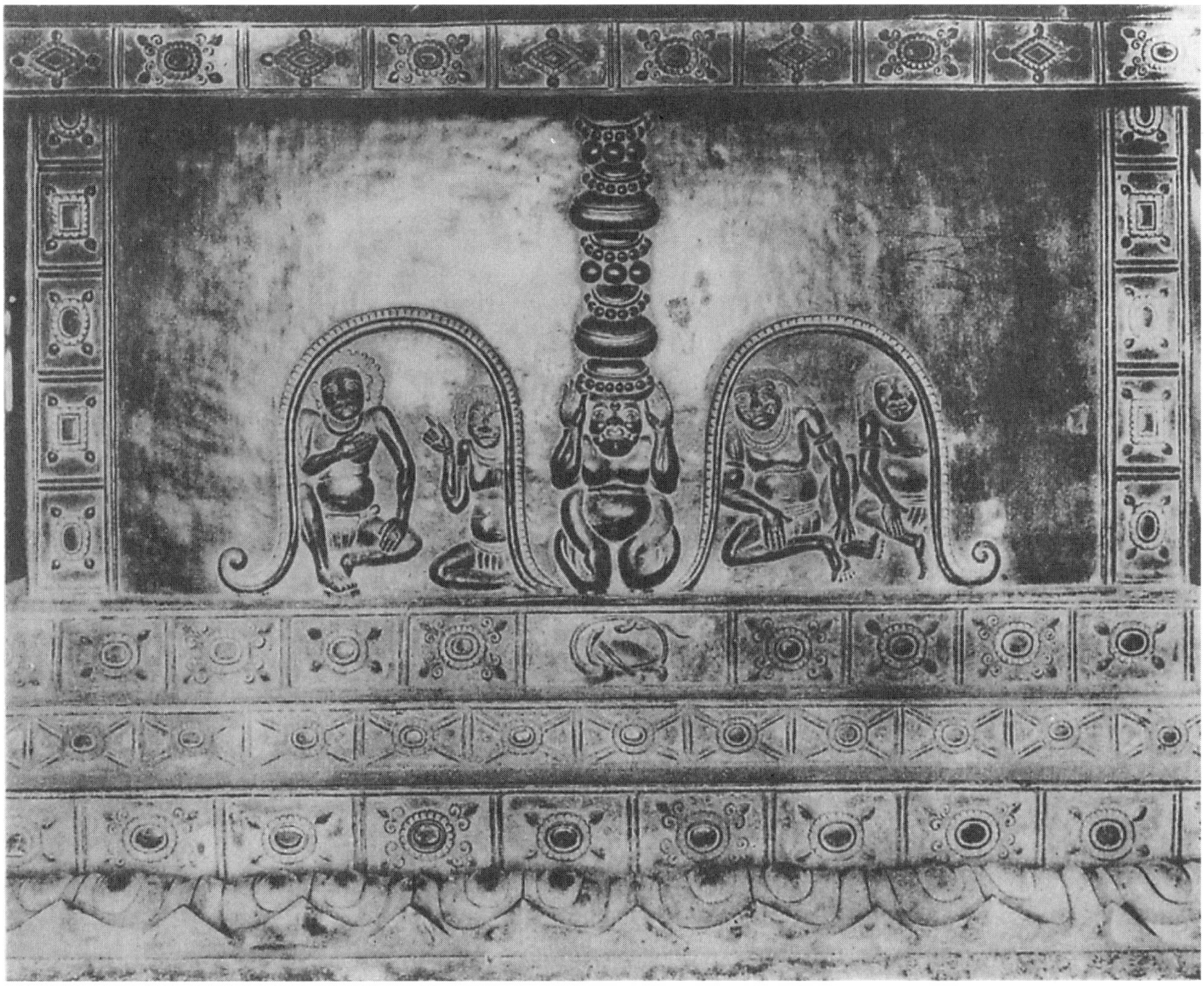

41

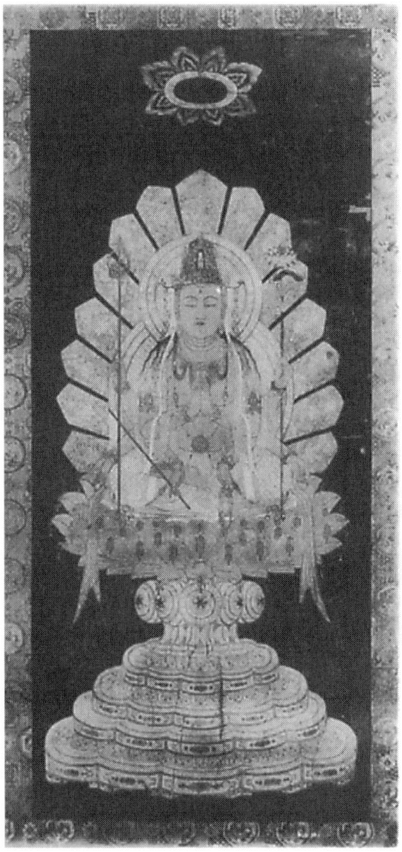

42

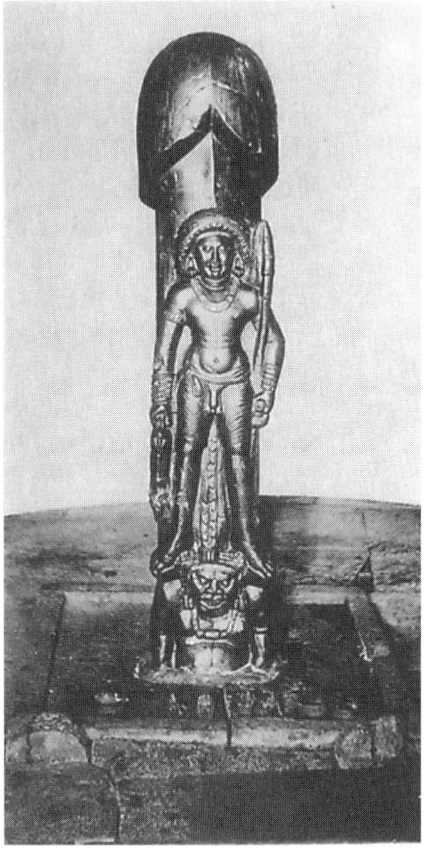

43

PLATE XV

FIGURE 44. The Bodhisattva Padmapāṇi, six-armed and supported by a lotus. From Bäzäklik, Murtuq, Turkistan, *ca.* 9th century. After Grünwedel, *Altbuddhistische Kultstätten in Chinesisch-Turkistan*, 1912, Fig. 590.

The lotus support is double. The lower stem, rising directly from the Waters, corresponds to the earthly or Nirmāṇakāya level of manifestation; its flower supporting Mt Meru, as the *skambha* or *sthauros* that pillars-apart Heaven and Earth. This sheaf-like and fasciated column is on the one hand formed like a *vajra*, and on the other corresponds in shape to such representations of Mt Meru as may be seen in Grünwedel's Figs. 243, 482. The knotted dragons or *nāgas* about the "waist" correspond to the many dragons that girdle the Meru "waist" in Grünwedel's Fig. 243, and also to the paired dragons attached to the trunk of the Tree of Life (*aśvattha*) in the well-known Indus Valley seal, Fig. 6 in my *History of Indian and Indonesian Art*. The upper lotus stem and flower, corresponding to the heavenly and Sambhogakāya level of manifestation, rest upon the plane summit of Meru. The Bodhisattva seated on the crowning flower is an aspect of the "Boundless Light" indicated by the Amitâbha of the headdress. The lateral branches of the upper lotus bear unidentified nimbate figures.

This representation, like our Fig. 17, is one of those that has been compared to the Tree of Jesse formula as it appears in Christian art from the eleventh century onwards (see Kingsley Porter, "Spain or Toulouse? and other questions," *Art Bulletin*, VII, 15 f.; Coomaraswamy, "The Tree of Jesse and Indian parallels or sources," *ibid.*, XI, 217–220; Watson, *Early Iconography of the Tree of Jesse*, 1934, pp. 58–66; Coomaraswamy, "The Tree of Jesse and Oriental Parallels," *Parnassus*, VI, Jan., 1934). Without assuming any contemporary borrowing or influence, it may be safely asserted that all these are cognate forms, having an ultimately common origin and the same fundamental significance. This common significance is most apparent in the fact that the Christian *virga* (often hermeneutically assimilated to *virgo*) is identified with the Virgin, as being the ground of the divine manifestation that flowers above (St. Bernard of Clairvaux, "The Virgin Mother of God is the stem, her Son is the flower. . . . O Virgin! stem of the highest, to what a summit thou liftest on high thy holiness! even to Him that sitteth on the throne") the Indian lotus, as "earth," being in precisely the same manner the support and ground of manifestation.

As explained in our text, the lotus can be distinguished logically from the Tree of Life and Axis of the Universe in its various other aspects, at the same time that it is coincident with these and extends from base to summit of the manifested universe, with branches proceeding to right and left like those of the Cross; which branches are the supports or "nests" of individual principles, and the means of their connection with the centre, as may be seen in most examples of the Tree of Jesse, as well as in the upper half of the present figure. When there are doves on the branches, this corresponds exactly to RV., I, 164, 21, *yatra suparṇā amṛtasya bhāgam . . . abhi svaranti*, "There the Fairwings chant their share of aeviternity," X, 91, 2 where Agni "as a bird finds a home on every tree," *Bṛhadāraṇyaka Up.*, IV, 3, 2, "The *haṁsa*, the Golden Person, by the Spirit wards His lower nest," and many analogous texts.

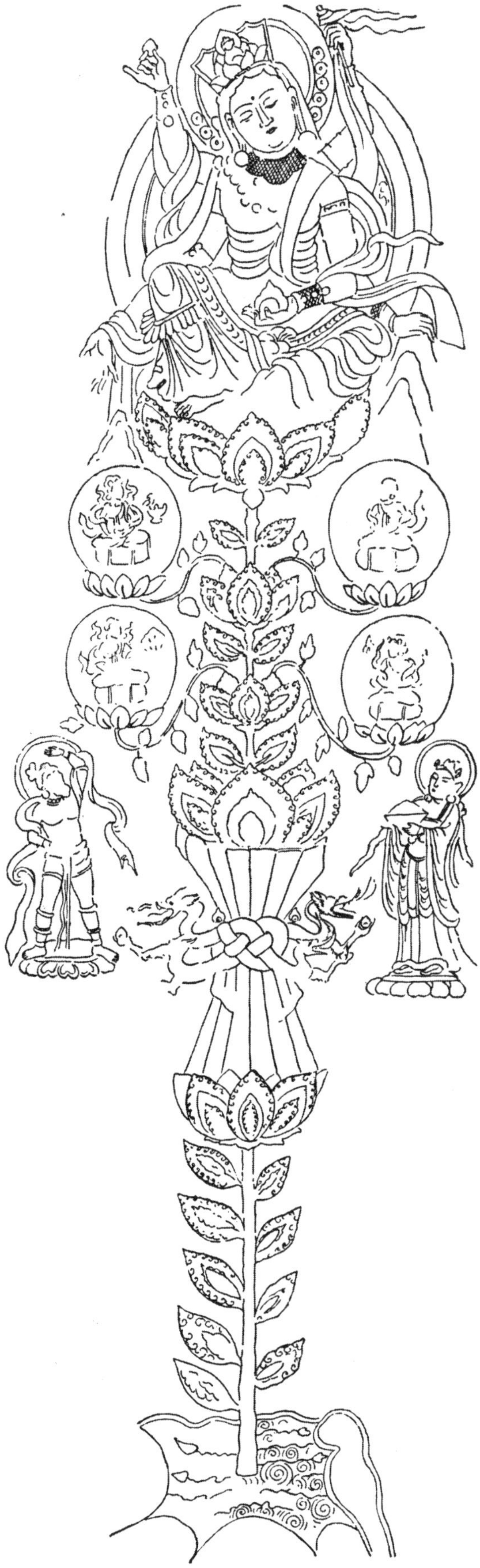